Assuring Food and Nutrition Security in Africa by 2020

Prioritizing Actions, Strengthening Actors, and Facilitating Partnerships

Kampala, Uganda • April 1–3, 2004

Proceedings of an All-Africa Conference

International Food Policy Research Institute
Washington, D.C.

Suggested citation: International Food Policy Research Institute, *Assuring Food and Nutrition Security in Africa by 2020: Proceedings of an All-Africa Conference,* April 1–3, 2004, Kampala, Uganda (Washington, DC: IFPRI, 2004).

Printed in the United States of America.

International Food Policy Research Institute
2033 K Street, NW, Washington, DC 20006-1002 USA
Telephone: +1-202-862-5600
Fax: +1-202-467-4439
Email: ifpri@cgiar.org
www.ifpri.org

Library of Congress Cataloging-in-Publication Data

Assuring food and nutrition security in Africa by 2020 : proceedings of an
all-Africa conference.
p. cm.
Includes bibliographical references.
ISBN 0-89629-650-4 (alk. paper)
1. Food supply—Africa—Congresses. 2. Nutrition—Africa—Congresses. 3. Food relief—Africa—Congresses. 4. Agricultural productivity—Africa—Congresses. 5. Sustainable development—Africa—Congresses. 6. Africa—Economic conditions—21st century—Congresses.
I. International Food Policy Research Institute.
HD9017.A2A87 2004
338.1'96—dc22

2004029480

Table of Contents

Table of Contents

Table of Contents

Table of Contents

Table of Contents

Foreword

Africa may at last be poised to make real progress on achieving food and nutrition security. Although the number of Africans who are undernourished has been on the rise for decades and now stands at about 200 million, a new commitment to change has emerged both among African leaders and in the international community.

The seeds for the 2020 Africa Conference documented in this volume were planted on September 4–6, 2001, when the International Food Policy Research Institute's (IFPRI's) 2020 Vision for Food, Agriculture, and the Environment Initiative held an international conference on "Sustainable Food Security for All by 2020" in Bonn, Germany. A wide variety of stakeholders—more than 900 from over 70 countries—came together to examine how to cope with emerging developments, assess progress in alleviating food insecurity, and forge a consensus on how best to realign local and global priorities for eliminating hunger. During and after that conference, African partners, arguing that hunger and malnutrition remain Africa's most fundamental challenges, repeatedly urged IFPRI to organize a similar multistakeholder, multisector forum focused on how to bring about change and action to assure food and nutrition security in Africa.

Recognizing that the changing policy environment provided excellent preconditions and unique opportunities for moving forward decisively on action, IFPRI facilitated an all-Africa conference on "Assuring Food and Nutrition Security in Africa by 2020: Prioritizing Actions, Strengthening Actors, and Facilitating Partnerships," in Kampala, Uganda, on April 1–3, 2004. The conference was cohosted by the Government of the Republic of Uganda and co-sponsored by more than a dozen organizations. It was organized by the 2020 Vision Initiative in close consultation with a distinguished Conference Advisory Committee chaired by John Joseph Otim, senior adviser to Uganda's President Yoweri K. Museveni.

More than 500 traditional and new actors from over 50 countries participated in the conference (see Appendix 2 for a list of participants). About 70 percent of the participants were Africans, and one-quarter were women. Participants represented a range of perspectives and experiences and came from all major sectors: 13 percent from nongovernmental or community-based organizations; 12 percent from government; 10 percent from bilateral, multilateral, or United Nations organizations; 8 percent from the media; 5 percent each from the farm community, parliament, business and industry, and regional institutions; and the remainder from research and academia.

More than 500 participants from over 50 countries gathered at the Speke Resort and Country Lodge, Munyonyo, in Kampala, Uganda, for the conference.

The conference featured three major parts, each day with its own set of plenary sessions and parallel breakout groups for more in-depth discussions. Plenary sessions

Presidents Obasanjo, Museveni, and Wade stand as the Ugandan national anthem is played during the official opening of the conference.

and selected parallel sessions were conducted with simultaneous French translation. The first part of the conference set the stage, with sessions addressing the current food and nutrition situation in Africa, the forces driving African food and nutrition security, and the long-term prospects. President Museveni of Uganda, President Wade of Senegal, and President Obasanjo of Nigeria delivered powerful keynote addresses, with frank analyses of the fundamental issues influencing Africa's well-being and with bold calls for action. Regional priorities for action were fleshed out in the breakout sessions. The second part of the conference focused on how to bring about change and implement action. Following keynote addresses on options and strategies for action, participants during the extensive breakout sessions focused on five priority areas of action—raising agricultural productivity, fostering economic growth, building human capacity, improving nutrition and health, and strengthening governance. The third part focused on how different actors can strengthen their capacities and work better together. Keynote speeches addressed the roles and responsibilities of different actors as well as ways of building political will and changing attitudes. Breakout sessions then brought stakeholder groups together in creative groupings—parliamentarians and business leaders; national policymakers and development partners; and nongovernmental organizations, farmers' organizations, and media. As the conference neared its end, President Museveni returned and was briefed on the way forward to assure a food- and nutrition-secure Africa, before he formally declared the conference closed.

The conference, which was the centerpiece of a longer-term policy consultation process on African food and nutrition security, was accompanied by several auxiliary activities. Two lead-in events, focusing on successes in African agriculture and on food and nutrition security policies for West Africa, set the stage for deliberations there (for more information see Box 2). Also in preparation for the conference, a youth writing contest drew entries from more than 200 young people across Africa, who described their vision for achieving "A Full Food Basket for Africa by 2020." The 17-year-old winner from South Africa delivered her essay at the conference (see Box 4), and a booklet containing the winning entries was widely distributed.

Throughout the three days of the conference, a digital voting system allowed participants to give instant feedback on food and nutrition security issues. The voting results, which revealed among other things that although many believe food and nutrition security *can* be achieved, far fewer believe it *will* be achieved, are presented in Box 5.

Extending the reach of the conference, about 35 journalists from influential African, European, and American media outlets actively participated in the 2020 Africa Conference. Many more attended press events and reported on the deliberations. The conference website, www.ifpri.org/2020africaconference, produced in both English and French, was extensively used before, during, and after the conference to raise awareness and share conference outputs. We invite you to visit the website to get a complete overview of the conference and its associated activities and outputs.

To contribute to more informed conference deliberations with solid, research-based knowledge on key issues influencing food and nutrition security in Africa, the 2020 Vision Initiative commissioned a number of background materials—including discussion papers, policy briefs, and CD-ROMS—from IFPRI staff and other leading experts from around the world (see Appendix 3 for the complete list of materials). These materials, primarily in draft form, were made available to participants in Kampala before being finalized for publication and widely disseminated.

The Conference Advisory Committee has developed a framework pointing toward a food- and nutrition-secure Africa. The draft of "A Way Forward from the 2020 Africa Conference" was shared with participants at the conference and subsequently finalized and distributed to stakeholders within and outside Africa (see Chapter 25).

This comprehensive proceedings volume shares the richness of the presentations and discussions that took place at the 2020 Africa Conference. Over the course of three days, the conference featured more than 110 speakers, chairs, panelists, moderators, and rapporteurs, including, among others, three heads of state, one former head of state, one current and one former First Lady, two Nobel Prize winners, and several World Food Prize laureates (see Appendix 1 for the full conference program). The speeches printed in this proceedings are largely based on transcripts of speakers' remarks, edited for publication. All speakers were invited to submit written summary notes for distribution during the conference. These are available, along with speakers' biographical information, on the CD accompanying this volume. Their slide presentations are on the conference website.

IFPRI and its 2020 Vision Initiative are proud to have facilitated the 2020 Africa Conference. We express our deep appreciation to the Government of the Republic of Uganda, and in particular to President Museveni, Chairman of the 2020 Advisory Council, for their warm and kind hospitality in hosting this all-Africa event. We sincerely thank the cosponsoring organizations for their generous support: European Commission; Canada Fund for Africa; Centre de coopération internationale en recherche agronomique pour le développement (CIRAD); Centre Technique de Coopération Agricole et Rurale (CTA); Deutsche Welthungerhilfe (German Agro Action); Development Cooperation Ireland; German Federal Ministry for Economic Co-operation and Development, with Deutsche Gesellschaft für Technische Zusammenarbeit (GTZ), and Internationale Weiterbildung und Entwicklung (InWEnt); Ministère des Affaires étrangères, France; Regional Land Management Unit (RELMA); The Rockefeller Foundation; Sasakawa Africa Association; The United States Agency for International Development; World Food Programme; and World Vision International. In addition, we thank the Swedish International Development Agency (SIDA) for providing support for African participants to attend the conference.

We are extremely grateful to the Conference Advisory Committee—composed of about 35 leading African policymakers, civil society leaders, and researchers, as well as representatives of cosponsoring organizations—for their invaluable guidance and unstinting support in the design, implementation, and follow-up of this conference (a complete list of committee members appears in Appendix 4). We offer our very warm appreciation and acknowledgment to the Chair, Dr. Otim, whose extraordinary dedication, unbounded enthusiasm, and wise counsel throughout the conference process inspired and energized all of us.

Special thanks go to the keynote speakers, panelists, chairs, moderators, and rapporteurs for sharing their knowledge and for provoking insightful, frank, and stimulating exchanges. Similarly, we thank all of the authors of the conference publications for enriching the knowledge base underlying the conference deliberations.

This conference would not have been possible without the collaboration of our many partners in Uganda. We greatly appreciate the work of the Uganda National Organizing Committee, chaired by David Obong, for their invaluable coordination of various aspects of the organization of the conference. Our warm thanks also go to Dr. Otim's staff at the Agricultural Council of Uganda for their kind assistance. The on-ground logistical support from all of our other partners in Uganda is also gratefully acknowledged. In particular, we extend our gratitude to the management and staff of the Speke Resort and Country Lodge at Munyonyo, led by Prabhat Mishra and Jonny Munro, who provided exceptional support throughout the planning and implementation of the conference.

The Conference Advisory Committee met several times before the conference to guide the process.

Joachim von Braun, Rajul Pandya-Lorch, Klaus von Grebmer, and Jenna Kryszczun of IFPRI discuss logistics during the conference.

We are indebted to our colleagues throughout IFPRI for their extraordinary support before, during, and after the conference. In particular, we would like to thank the 2020 Vision Initiative team—Jenna Kryszczun, Djhoanna Cruz, and Malgorzata Kowalska—for their outstanding efforts in every aspect of the conference's programmatic and organizational activities. We express our warm appreciation to Klaus von Grebmer for his invaluable contributions and brilliant insights. While the entire Communications Division provided exceptional support, we particularly thank Laurie Goldberg and Simone Hill-Lee for handling the complex logistical details entailed in a conference of this magnitude and scope; Evelyn Banda for providing varied design and publication services and Uday Mohan for coordinating editorial services, both under tight time constraints; Corinne de Gracia for handling the translation of conference materials; and Michael Rubinstein, Janet Hodur, and Michele Pietrowski for managing the many media-related activities, including a media tour of Uganda immediately prior to the conference. We were very fortunate to gather a committed conference support team who went above and beyond the call of duty during the days of the conference. In addition to those already listed, we are extremely grateful to Bernadette Cordero, Luisa Gaskell, Michael Go, Vickie Lee, and Amanda Segovia. Finally, we thank Heidi Fritschel for taking the lead in compiling and editing this proceedings volume, which captures the richness, enthusiasm, and intensity of the deliberations in Kampala.

With this conference, issues of food and nutrition insecurity have been placed squarely onto the African agenda. IFPRI and its partners are undertaking follow-up activities to ensure that these issues will be mainstreamed into appropriate processes and forums at the local, national, regional, and continental levels. The members of the Conference Advisory Committee, which agreed to remain active until the end of 2004, are carrying the messages of the conference to their networks and forums. Follow-up visits to heads of state and heads of key regional organizations have been undertaken to convey conference outcomes. IFPRI is honored that the Government of Uganda and Posta Uganda have issued a set of stamps to commemorate the 2020 Africa Conference. In the wake of the conference, IFPRI itself is revisiting its strategy for research, policy communications, and capacity building in Africa and is increasing its presence on the ground in Africa to support these activities.

IFPRI has been extremely pleased to facilitate the 2020 Africa Conference and thereby contribute to identifying and prioritizing the necessary solutions and strategies to bring about food and nutrition security in Africa. We at IFPRI hope that this African-owned, African-driven conference has set the stage for real action to achieve food and nutrition security for every African by 2020.

Joachim von Braun
Director General, IFPRI

Rajul Pandya-Lorch
Head, 2020 Vision Initiative, IFPRI

Acronyms and Abbreviations

AATF	African Agricultural Technology Foundation
ACBF	African Capacity Building Foundation
ACP	African, Caribbean, and Pacific Group of States
AEEB	Agricultural Economics Education Board
AERC	African Economic Research Consortium
AGOA	African Growth Opportunity Act
AHP	Anti-Hunger Programme
ART	antiretroviral therapy
ASARECA	Association for Strengthening Agricultural Research in Eastern and Central Africa
ASO	AIDS support organization
AU	African Union
CAADP	Comprehensive Africa Agriculture Development Programme
CBO	community-based organization
CGIAR	Consultative Group on International Agricultural Research
CILSS	Permanent Interstate Committee for Drought Control in the Sahel
CIRAD	Centre de coopération internationale en recherche agronomique pour le développement
CMAP	Collaborative Master's Programme
COMESA	Common Market for Eastern and Southern Africa
CPP	Collaborative Ph.D. Programme
CSO	civil society organization
CSRS	Centre Suisse de Recherche Scientifique en Côte d'Ivoire
CTA	Centre Technique de Coopération Agricole et Rurale
DRC	Democratic Republic of Congo
EBA	Everything But Arms
EC	European Commission
ECA	United Nations Economic Commission for Africa
ECAPAPA	Eastern and Central Africa Programme for Agricultural Policy Analysis
ECOWAS	Economic Community of West African States
EU	European Union
FAO	Food and Agriculture Organization of the United Nations
FARA	Forum for Agricultural Research in Africa
FFE	Food for Education
GDP	gross domestic product
GM	genetically modified
GMO	genetically modified organism
GNP	gross national product
GTZ	Deutsche Gesellschaft für Technische Zusamenarbeit
HMIS	health management information system
IARC	international agricultural research center
ICM	information and communication management
ICN	International Conference on Nutrition
ICTs	information and communication technologies
IDP	internally displaced person
IER	Institut d'économie rurale
IFAD	International Fund for Agricultural Development
IFAP	International Federation of Agricultural Producers
IFPRI	International Food Policy Research Institute
IITA	International Institute of Tropical Agriculture
ILRI	International Livestock Research Institute
IMF	International Monetary Fund
IMPACT	International Model for Policy Analysis of Agricultural Commodities and Trade
InWEnt	Internationale Weiterbildung und Entwicklung
IPM	integrated pest management
MCA	Millennium Challenge Account
MDGs	Millennium Development Goals
NARS	national agricultural research system
NEPAD	New Partnership for Africa's Development
NERICA	New Rice for Africa
NGO	nongovernmental organization
ODA	official development assistance
OECD	Organisation for Economic Co-operation and Development
OIE	World Organisation for Animal Health
OPAM	Office des Produits Agricoles du Mali
ORS	oral rehydration solution
PRMC	Cereals Market Restructuring Program
PRSP	poverty reduction strategy paper
RATES	Regional Agricultural Trade Expansion Support
RATIN	Regional Agricultural Trade Intelligence Network
SADAOC	Sécurité Alimentaire Durable en Afrique de l'Ouest Centrale
SADC	Southern African Development Community
SAP	structural adjustment program
SMS	short messaging system
SOMIEX	Société Malienne d'Importation et d'Exportation
USAID	United States Agency for International Development
WAHO	West African Health Organization
WARDA	The Africa Rice Center
WFP	World Food Programme
WFS:fyl	World Food Summit: five years later
WHO	World Health Organization

Part I | Introduction and Taking Stock

Chapter 1 Welcome and Opening Remarks

Conference Director: Rajul Pandya-Lorch
Head of the 2020 Vision Initiative, International Food Policy Research Institute (IFPRI), USA

Chair: Isher Judge Ahluwalia
Chair, Board of Trustees, International Food Policy Research Institute (IFPRI), India

We sit here in this beautiful setting with an urgent task at hand. The number of hungry people on this continent continues to rise rapidly. If freedom from hunger—the acknowledged right of every human being—is to become a reality here in Africa, we must move to action and go beyond the statements of good intentions issued at dozens of previous conferences.

Let me emphasize that the International Food Policy Research Institute (IFPRI) is here today in a facilitating role. This conference has been, from its conceptualization through all the planning, African-driven and African-owned. I remember well that almost three years ago, when IFPRI held its international conference on "Sustainable Food Security for All by 2020" in Bonn, Germany, there was considerable demand from the African participants for a meeting such as this one. IFPRI is proud that our African partners had confidence in us to serve as facilitators.

For those of you who are not familiar with IFPRI, we are one of the Future Harvest international agricultural research centers supported by the Consultative Group on International Agricultural Research (CGIAR). We spend about 50 percent of our research budget in Africa, and we collaborate closely with local partners such as the Makerere University, the National Agricultural Research Organization, and the Ministry of Agriculture, Animal Industry, and Fisheries here in Uganda.

On behalf of IFPRI, allow me to express our deep gratitude to the Government of the Republic of Uganda, with the strong support of His Excellency President Museveni, for cohosting the conference with us. We are also extremely grateful for the support of our cosponsors.

John Joseph Otim
Senior Presidential Adviser to H. E. President Museveni of the Republic of Uganda; President, Uganda Agricultural Council; and Chair, Conference Advisory Committee

This conference has been from inception owned and driven by Africans who have participated actively in the distinguished Conference Advisory Committee meetings. The superb program was developed by IFPRI under the guidance of this Committee.

As lead-in events to the conference, we held two ex-tremely successful workshops elsewhere in Africa: one on "Successes in African Agriculture," held in Pretoria, South Africa, in December 2003 and one on "Food and Nutrition Security Policies for West Africa," held in Bamako, Mali, in January 2004. These meetings focused on scaling up and replicating successes as well as implementing food and nutrition security plans, policies, and programs. We will continue to take such a focus over the next three days.

This conference is timely because Africa is a continent that is reshaping itself.

— John Joseph Otim

This conference is timely because Africa is a continent that is reshaping itself. New political and economic initiatives are gaining momentum both inside and outside Africa. Thus this conference provides an excellent opportunity to move forward decisively to combat hunger, malnutrition, and poverty and to improve on the management of HIV/AIDS. Indeed, African governments are increasingly focusing their attention on how to cope with the task of dealing simultaneously with short-term food emergencies and the long-term challenge of economic growth to enable them to feed the extra half a billion Africans expected to be born over the next 20 to 25 years.

We will devote a great deal of attention over the next three days to agriculture and how it relates to food, nutrition, economic growth, health, and poverty eradication. This is clearly appropriate because the center of gravity of poverty and food and nutrition insecurity on this continent is in the rural areas, where the majority of our people are dependent on agriculture for their livelihoods.

To underscore the importance of this conference, we are reminded that the history of governance reveals that no sustainable democracy has ever been built on empty stomachs and rampant poverty. In other words, food and nutrition security has had a far-reaching impact on democratization processes. It has been a sound road map to rural development and political stability. Therefore, the issue of assuring food and nutrition security for all in Africa is a critical concern not only for African governments, but also for the international community. We are all affected, though at different levels.

You, the distinguished participants in this conference, can and must take action when you leave the conference to add value to ongoing initiatives related to food and nutrition security in Africa and move us from mere promises to action. The challenge facing all of us is to use this process to create insight on how to bring about change and stimulate action by all key stakeholders to meet the ever-increasing and changing demands for food and nutrition on this continent.

If all the key actors are strengthened and walk forward together in new partnerships, we are convinced we can end hunger in Africa by 2020, eliminate the worst aspects of micronutrient malnutrition, and make solid progress toward achieving food and nutrition for all in this generation. The success of the conference is now in your hands.

Joachim von Braun

Director General, International Food Policy Research Institute (IFPRI), USA

The two goals of this gathering are clearly defined: first, assuring food security, with availability of and access to food; and second, assuring nutrition security, where secure access to food is coupled with adequate health. The focus of this conference is therefore on people, on poor people, and not on a particular sector of the economy.

During the past three decades, the number of food-insecure people in Sub-Saharan Africa has more than doubled. Let us be frank when looking at the causes of food and nutrition insecurity. Failures of governance in Africa are one reason for this bleak picture. The blame for Africa's plight must be also partly placed outside of Africa—for instance, on developed countries' protectionist trade policies that prevent markets from flourishing. We can, however, point to successes in food and agriculture in Africa. Farmers and researchers around the continent have undertaken impressive and varied innovative efforts to sustain soil fertility and water resource utilization in more efficient ways and efforts that reduced the degradation of the natural environment. Agricultural scientists have made a number of important breakthroughs that are relevant to resource-poor farmers in Africa and even beyond Africa.

A relatively large share of Africa's agricultural output is traded internationally. Ironically, African agriculture is among the world's most globalized at the

Joachim von Braun, director general of IFPRI, highlights five key areas of action for achieving food and nutrition security in Africa.

African agriculture is among the world's most globalized at the same time that it is the world's most subsistence-oriented.

— Joachim von Braun

same time that it is the world's most subsistence-oriented. Globalization is marginalizing Africa, mainly because the continent relies so heavily on bulk exports of unprocessed agriculture commodities such as cotton, coffee, and cocoa. Low levels of productivity in African agriculture are a sign of malfunctioning markets. Pan-African cooperation on trade in food and agricultural products, as well as in research, offers great promise, and the African Union and the New Partnership for Africa's Development (NEPAD) are key vehicles for such cooperation. But the challenge of spreading successful local and national experiences in food and agriculture is substantial, and we need to recognize that one size does not fit all, that a model appropriate in one place may not work well elsewhere. Sound concepts and strategies are needed.

We at IFPRI believe that the next three days offer a new and exciting approach to food and nutrition security in Africa because the conference is research- and knowledge-based, and the voices of the diverse audience participants and stakeholders count.

The priority actions should focus on five areas:

1. agricultural productivity;
2. fostering pro-poor economic growth through improved markets, better infrastructure, and greater trade competitiveness;
3. building institutional and human capacity;
4. improving health with new attention to HIV/AIDS; and
5. strengthening governance.

It would be good if we could focus just on one priority. But I don't see the potential to reduce a viable strategy to fewer than those five areas. All of these five priorities require added resources, but the benefits of food and nutrition security far exceed the resource needs. The investment in food and nutrition security has high returns. And this is an investment in peace as well.

We have with us today representatives of governments, parliaments, nongovernmental community-based organizations from Africa and elsewhere, farmers, business and industry leaders, research, media, and donor investor institutions. We may not arrive at consensus on the issues here at this conference. And the key is not to arrive at consensus, but to bring all issues to the table.

This conference is unique in one other respect. It takes an all-Africa approach to those issues before us. We believe that such a perspective is crucial if we are to make progress because it facilitates learning from experience across Africa.

What do we want you to take away from this conference? The main objective is to identify strategies for food and nutrition security that can be implemented. If strategies cannot be implemented, they are not sound. But if implementation without a sound strategy is attempted, that is also not satisfactory.

Successful implementation must happen at a local level. Communities are key to achieving food and nutrition security in Africa, and we need effective decentralized management for public investment. But we also need sound public administration, wise public investment, and adequate resource allocation from central government. All actors need to shoulder their responsibilities and collaborate effectively. Strengthening education and universities in Africa is central to building the capacity for sound strategies and strong implementation capacity.

Ending hunger is not just a complex technical and political matter. Cultural aspects also matter. It includes the question of motivation for action. That motivation must be addressed as well. Therefore, cultural and spiritual leaders of Africa must play key roles. I welcome the participation of Ms. Graça Machel, a leader in motivating the youth of Africa, and I welcome Professor Wole Soyinka, Nobel laureate for literature. They will help us to sharpen our focus on action.

Can we end hunger in the year 2020 in Africa? I believe we can, if we focus on change and action.

If strategies cannot be implemented, they are not sound. But if implementation without a sound strategy is attempted, that is also not satisfactory.

— Joachim von Braun

Wilberforce Kisamba-Mugerwa

Minister of Agriculture, Animal Industry, and Fisheries, Republic of Uganda

Your Excellency, President Museveni, I wish to thank you for having agreed to host this important conference and for inviting these distinguished presidents who are known for spearheading the fight against hunger.

Our country is cosponsoring this conference with IFPRI. We are collaborating not only on this conference, but also on studies pertinent to modernizing agriculture in this country. IFPRI has carried out studies on increasing agricultural productivity, which is fundamental, and together we are focusing on research to generate technologies that can help us ensure increased productivity. We are also using data from IFPRI's studies on growth and improving markets and are collaborating on studies on integrating HIV/AIDS into agricultural policies and on sustainable use of natural resources. There is talk of Uganda's being very fertile, but when we became independent we had 8 million people; now we are about 25 million. We are no longer talking about cultivation, but about intensive farming. Our studies with IFPRI on the role of women in agriculture can guide us in extension and research work and in empowering women and other vulnerable groups in agriculture. We also collaborate on studies related to policies and institutions. Finally, we are working on issues regarding nutrition and health. We emphasize nutrition issues because many of our people do not eat what they produce or know the nutritional value of what they eat.

H. E. Yoweri Museveni

President of the Republic of Uganda

I welcome you to Uganda. We are hopeful that by the end of your deliberations, the way forward to assuring food and nutrition security in Africa by 2020 will emerge.

Africa leads in hunger, malnourishment, and undernourishment. Experts assure us that unless an extraordinary effort is made by all of us, 40 million children on this continent will be malnourished by 2020. That is why a new vision is so urgent.

This conference represents a wide spectrum of stakeholders—policymakers, scientists, investors, and civil society. And if we can all work as a team, we can achieve food and nutrition security within the next 16 years. I wish to assure you, and I am confident I speak on behalf of all my colleagues, that there is the political will to revise the grim statistics of food and nutrition

In his opening address, President Yoweri Museveni of the Republic of Uganda stresses the need for all to make an extraordinary effort to combat hunger and malnutrition.

security. Through NEPAD, African leaders have committed themselves to the consolidation of democracy, the promotion of peace and security, and sound economic management, where the welfare of the people is paramount. Our development partners made a solemn pledge to provide more aid for infrastructure projects, health, and education; to reduce our debt burdens; and most important of all, to invest in our economies and allow greater access for our products in their markets. If African leaders and our development partners can each fulfill their part of the bargain, Africa can meet and even exceed the Millennium Development Goals, and indeed fulfill the 2020 Vision of IFPRI, the organizers of this conference.

I can assure you that it is not all gloom and doom on our continent. I am sure everyone here knows of a success story somewhere on this continent in agriculture, health, education, and governance. What we need is to multiply those success stories to encompass the whole continent.

Here in Uganda, the prevalence of HIV/AIDS some 15 years ago was in the region of 30 percent in some categories of the population; today it is about 6 percent. Although we shall only be satisfied with zero prevalence, we can still claim some progress in this area.

In 1997 we launched our Universal Primary Education Programme. Before the program was launched, only 2 million children were enrolled in the primary schools. Today, close to 7.4 million children are in primary schools. This is some progress.

All these advances are relevant to the assurance of food and nutrition security. As you know, HIV/AIDS and

> *Education is vital in our struggle to assure food and nutrition security.*
>
> — H. E. Yoweri Museveni

other diseases, especially malaria, reduce people's capacity to work and hence grossly affect output. This is especially the case in agriculture, where most Africans work. Mass education also makes a difference in agricultural output. Those who can neither read nor write, those who are without basic numeracy, cannot be relied upon to modernize our agriculture and to achieve the quantities and quality we need to compete globally or even regionally and continentally.

With regard to nutrition, it is not always, or even primarily, the absence of nutrients that condemns our children to malnutrition. It is mainly ignorance—mothers not knowing what is needed to feed their children properly. Education is therefore vital in our struggle to assure food and nutrition security.

For too long we have relied on the poor and the not-so-well-informed to feed us and to produce our exports. We have left agriculture to the peasants, to the people who are not educated. The idea has been that when you get education, you get out of agriculture. That was the emphasis of education in the colonial period.

The peasants have done their part in the most difficult conditions imaginable. They have often worked under exploitative landlords and governments; they have not had access to credit and markets; and they have lacked the basic information and infrastructure they need for efficient production.

Peasants will be with us for some time. The aim of our government is to transform our society so that in about 20 years' time we have a society of a middle class and a skilled working class. This will obviously take that much time. While peasants will still exist, the greatest challenge for all of us is to improve their conditions of production in order to reduce their poverty and their numbers.

The reason 3 percent of the population of the United States feeds all Americans and the rest of the world is that their farmers farm on a large scale and use the latest technologies in their production. They can produce in commercial quantities, have consistent quality, and put their products on the markets at competitive prices—although, quite often, they are also assisted by unfair subsidies. We, too, must move toward medium- and large-scale commercial agriculture to attain the goals we have set for ourselves.

The Maputo Declaration commits us, as governments, to the devotion of 10 percent of our national budgets to agriculture. We should steadily work toward the realization of this commitment. With increased public funds going into agriculture, we can support research and the infrastructure needed to modernize and increase the production and productivity of agriculture.

Investment by the private sector is crucial to the agriculture sector. Hitherto, with few exceptions, peasant agriculture, which is dominant, had only two resources on offer: land and labor. And often, even access to land was problematic. Although there's a lot of land, for instance in Uganda, policy distortions created some distribution problems. Modern agriculture requires capital and technology, and for these inputs we need both local and foreign investors to produce food and other products in sufficient quantities and the right quality for both domestic consumption and for the export market.

However, the main motivation for investors is the market. We need a level playing field in the global market. And I appeal to our development partners in Europe, the United States, and Japan to level the playing field. Market access is the main stimulus for us to produce sustainably. There are only three reasons to engage in agriculture: (1) subsistence agriculture, when you produce for the stomach; (2) commercial agriculture, when you produce for the market; and (3) to engage in agriculture as a hobby.

Now, how shall we achieve food security? By subsistence farming? So our farmers have food in their stomachs, but how about money to build a better house? How about money to send the children to school? How about money for health care? Where would they get it? Can you have food security when you do not have income security?

It is a fact that agriculture in developed countries is protected through heavy subsidies. Their agriculture is subsidized at the rate of 1 billion dollars a day at both ends—production and exports. At this rate, there is no

> *We need a level playing field in the global market.*
>
> — H. E. Yoweri Museveni

way we can develop our agriculture because we are outcompeted in our own markets and cannot sell competitively in their markets. The developed countries introduced to us the magic of free markets. But you cannot preach free market and practice protectionism.

We appreciate the markets the developed countries are opening up for us through efforts such as the Everything But Arms (EBA) program of Europe and the African Growth Opportunity Act (AGOA) of the United States. This is a good beginning, provided it is consolidated. AGOA III is not yet addressed. This is very serious. I have written to President Bush and Congressman Thomas to get the U.S. Congress to address the outstanding issues in AGOA III, such as the extension of third-party fabrics for some years.

We have been using third-party fabrics from some places, and we make them into garments and export them to the United States. And we are really warming up—we are getting excited. But this agreement is ending in November. If it is not renewed, then all these factories that have been attracted here will collapse. All of us need to speak with one voice on this, and now. Otherwise the AGOA-generated jobs and increased export earnings, which we are beginning to realize, will evaporate.

I have described AGOA and the EBA as the greatest acts of solidarity extended by the West to black Africa in the last 500 years, and I am repeating that statement here. Otherwise, much of our interaction in the last 500 years has been either parasitic or mere tokenism. AGOA and EBA are the first acts of real mutually beneficial solidarity. Now, it is wobbling, so we better wake up.

The previous interactions between black Africa and the West have obviously failed. In the 47 years since independence, not a single black African country has transitioned from the Third World to the First World category, as Singapore, Malaysia, or South Korea did. Those African countries that were with the capitalist West have not transitioned. Those that were with the communist East have not transitioned. What is the problem?

AGOA and EBA are only modest beginnings. We need to broaden trade partnerships and to eliminate the trade-distorting subsidies for agriculture; we must work harder to export our products to developed countries and some of the more developed Third World countries such as India, China, and Brazil, because those also lock us out. How can we have South-South cooperation across a very high wall of tariffs? Here in Uganda, we have tariffs of only 15 percent; this was our maximum, partly due to pressure from the World Bank. But why do you put pressure only on us; why don't you put it on others?

The other factor that has stunted the growth of agriculture in Africa is the curse of exporting only raw materials without adding value.

— H. E. Yoweri Museveni

Of course, we need to organize regional and continental markets better. Sometimes it is not the lack of food, but the lack of logistics for moving the food that leads to famine within our countries and regions. There is also a tendency, when there are food crises, to look beyond the country, region, and continent to sources in Europe and America. I appeal to organizations that handle these crises to exhaust resources here before they look elsewhere. That way they will be making a great contribution to the development of our agriculture.

The other factor that has stunted the growth of agriculture in Africa is the curse of exporting only raw materials without adding value, without producing final goods out of these raw materials. This is why I have described the African countries as the real donor countries.

I will show you how Uganda is a donor. Until recently, Uganda has been donating to the world about US$20 for every kilogram of coffee sold. When we sell unprocessed coffee, we are donating US$20 for every kilogram, and Uganda is the fourth-largest exporter in the world, after Brazil and Colombia and Viet Nam.

Likewise, for the last 100 years, Uganda has been donating US$12 for every kilogram of cotton because we have been selling the cotton at lint level. Lint cotton means you remove seeds from the cotton and then sell it. Then somebody else does the spinning, the weaving, the finishing, and the tailoring. So you get US$1, and somebody else gets US$15 from the same kilogram.

We not only donate money, we also donate jobs. If you export lint cotton, that means you export all the spinning jobs, all the weaving jobs, all the finishing jobs, and all the tailoring jobs to others. Your sisters and your brothers are just sitting at home; they have no jobs. And since they have no jobs, they have no money in their pockets. Their purchasing power is very low.

I'm very happy that most of the stakeholders who can cause a revolution in our agriculture and in our policies and therefore lead us to food and nutrition security are gathered here to deliberate on food security.

Sustainable food and nutritional security is only achievable in a sustainable way through social transformation.

— H. E. Yoweri Museveni

I urge you to make realistic propositions and to dedicate yourselves to their implementation. All of you here are leaders in your various fields and are in a position to influence events at the highest policymaking levels. I urge you to use your influence to effect a change in our agriculture so that Africans can attain security of food and nutrition in the timeframe we have set ourselves.

I am tempted to add that sustainable food and nutritional security is only achievable in a sustainable way through social transformation. I cannot remember a society in history that sustainably guaranteed food security and nutrition but also remained backward. Food security and nutrition came to Europe after those societies were transformed, and on account of social transformation, food insecurity in Europe is now history.

Let me end by thanking IFPRI for organizing this conference, and all the sponsors for the material support that has enabled all of us to be here today. We are very happy to host this conference. I wish you fruitful deliberations and declare the conference on "Assuring Food and Nutrition Security in Africa by 2020" open.

H. E. Maître Abdoulaye Wade*

President of the Republic of Senegal

President Joachim Alberto Chissano of Mozambique, president of the African Union, asked me to represent him here and to convey his greetings and congratulations, as well as his encouragement, to his brother, President Museveni. He believes that the problems that you are going to deal with here are important economic and human problems, and he congratulates you and all those who had the idea for this conference, which brings together personalities from the world of politics and science to help Africa reach the objectives of food and nutrition security by 2020.

For my part, I would like first of all to give a recap of NEPAD and the place of agriculture in NEPAD, then to make a diagnosis of the situation, and then to try to make a contribution to the definition of an African strategy for food and nutrition security.

NEPAD is unfortunately not always well understood. NEPAD is a new vision of Africa that was established by several heads of state. Hence, it has the special feature of having been applied immediately, contrary to preceding plans made by experts that never got implemented.

In NEPAD there are a number of long-term parameters, i.e., factors that are essential for development. First of all is the new appeal to the private sector. Before, we thought the public sector could do it all. This time, we thought it was necessary to appeal to the private sector and that foreign capital must play an important role in our development, as happened for Europe, the United States, Canada, and Japan. We do not know of one country in the world that has been developed solely by the public sector. The Russians tried it, and it was a failure. The international development strategy based on aid and credit also failed. In the 1970s it was a question of transferring 0.7 percent of the gross national product of the developed countries to the developing countries. After more than 30 years, we have not reached even half that. As for public and private credits, they led us to a state of indebtedness that has become a brake on our development. We are now in the process of setting up a conference of heads of state and government on African "disindebtedness – debt reduction."

The second parameter is good governance, public and private. Good public governance involves having long-term stability, free and democratic elections, and respect for human rights; and good private governance involves creating the conditions for the investment of private capital, so that the national private sector, African or foreign, can play its role. This assumes good justice, for example.

We know what must be grown to eat well. We know the problems of agriculture. The big problem is financing agriculture, including people, equipment, and scientific knowledge.

— H. E. Maître Abdoulaye Wade

* This presentation was originally delivered in French and has been edited for this volume.

But there is another very important long-term factor—the region. NEPAD's special feature is its emphasis on the region. Africa is divided into five regions: Central Africa, East Africa, Southern Africa, West Africa, and North Africa. We must not think, as some people have, that NEPAD is in conflict with the national economies. NEPAD is a plus. It deals with questions that the national economies cannot handle. Take the interconnections between the roads in the different countries; no one is dealing with them. You can't go from Senegal to Mali, or Senegal to Guinea, if the road stops a few kilometers from each border. Thus, there are problems in infrastructure, in agriculture, in water, etc., that are regional.

We in West Africa defined NEPAD in terms of our community, the Economic Community of West African States, and drew up programs in all countries and sectors of West Africa. We met recently, and we are going to move toward implementing these programs. To perfect good governance, we have developed a "peer review" mechanism that allows the heads of state to help one another to create good governance. The "peer review" is voluntary; it is not forced on anyone. We have set up a forum of a dozen African personalities whose role is just to be in touch with the countries that are volunteers, to make inquiries, and to present a report to the meeting of heads of state that will let us see how we can help each other make progress in good governance.

Within these parameters, NEPAD has set some priority sectors: infrastructure, education, health, agriculture, the environment, the new information and communication technologies, energy, and access to the markets of the developed countries. Recall that NEPAD was adopted by the heads of state and of government in Lusaka. It has therefore become a standard document that must guide us in our choices and policies. In any case, my policy in Senegal rests on the NEPAD sectors as they have been defined in other documents. Once NEPAD was developed, the Board, presided over by President Obasanjo, had discussions with the G8 at its summits in Genoa, Italy, in Canada, and in Evian, France. There have been discussions between our experts and the experts from the developed countries, and all this has resulted in the announcement of an action plan for Africa by the developed countries. It must be understood that NEPAD is based on partnership with the developed countries, not on unilateral assistance, as before.

That being true, some developed countries have announced their participation in the financing of NEPAD. Canada decided to supply Can$500 million in development assistance and set up a fund of some Can$6 billion in additional funds for five years. The United Kingdom announced £360 million in funds earmarked for Africa. The United States is not participating in NEPAD as such, to my knowledge, but decided, for example, on US$15 billion for their contribution to AIDS, and we can say that that is for the health sector of NEPAD. We are also in the process of setting up the Millennium Challenge Account, which will allow the United States to help certain countries that meet a number of criteria for five years. The European Union has announced aid of US$1 billion for the health funds, but neither the United States nor the European Union has announced funds, for example, to participate in the infrastructure of Africa. India has proposed US$200 million, and we are in the process of holding discussions with that country to find out what the conditions for that aid are. Japan has confirmed a very large investment of US$1.06 million for infrastructure, US$300 million for health, US$3 billion for debt reduction to the African countries, and US$400 million for aid to Japanese businesses that want to invest in the African countries.

President Maître Abdoulaye Wade of the Republic of Senegal emphasizes the potential of NEPAD to stimulate action.

NEPAD today is in the African Union; it is not a separate organization. We are now in the process of considering the transfer of NEPAD to the African Union. The question is under discussion.

Now I would like to make a diagnosis of African agriculture. For a long time, colonization required cash crops from us; that is to say, the economic theory was

A farmer must be able to read documents and use them. And it is for that reason that we are exhorting the youth to go and receive at least a minimum of training.

— H. E. Maître Abdoulaye Wade

that the Africans had to produce agricultural products and raw materials to export so as to have income for our development. But a farmer cannot grow both food crops and export crops. In my own country, which I will cite often, food crops were sacrificed for peanuts, which have gone through a big expansion. The result is that today we import 600,000 tons of rice to live. That makes US$150 million that a small country like Senegal must spend to live and eat. This poses a problem in terms of food security. We are trying to bring about a reconversion—to develop a rice crop in the interior of the country—and we are in the process of starting a large perimeter of irrigation. Some African countries produce rice or have the capacity to produce rice, but unfortunately, there is no trade network between us. Mali has large areas that were intended for rice before and that can produce a lot of rice, so it is possible for two rice-producing African countries to trade. The economic problem is that African rice is more expensive than imported rice. But I think we can solve it. The price differential can be financed by a fund, which we could set up rather easily. This would allow us to consume "African" and at the same time develop intra-African trade, which today accounts for only 2 percent of our volume of international trade.

Consequently, food security and nutrition programs for children must be seen through the lens of internal development, or "endogenous" development. We have the land area. We have the water, even in some savanna and semi-desert countries like Senegal. We can create water reservoirs; some countries have a lot of experience in this field. What is lacking is financing. We know what must be grown to eat well. We know the problems of agriculture. The big problem is financing agriculture, including people, equipment, and scientific knowledge.

Here is my definition of the African strategy for food and nutritional security. I will deal with the national level, the African level, and then the international level.

At the country level, the first challenge is the problem of soil. There are rich soils and poor soils, but we now know that the soil is no longer a decisive factor in agricultural production, since we can add what it lacks. I just was in Egypt, where I saw ultramodern farms planted on the desert sand. No soil can be as bad as the desert from the standpoint of crops and nutritive elements. So it is merely a question of investment. In Senegal we have created a Soil Institute, which will be decentralized at the department level. Every farmer will be able to go and say: "I would like to grow such and such a plant on this soil. What do I have to do?" And the Soil Institute will describe what nutritive elements must be added so that the soil can support the crops that the farmer has chosen.

The second challenge is the relationship between man and the land—it is the problem of ownership and exploitation. We have land laws going back to the colonial era that make land ownership indisputable but at the time of independence in Africa, there was a law that gave the state all the land held by the former tribal chiefs.

Today, for a farmer or investor to develop a piece of land, he must have the possibility of transferring it to his children. We have a commission that is studying this question to define the cities' domain, the communities' domain, the villages' domain, and the inter-village domain, as well as the state's domain. Agrarian reform is essential for many countries so that a national or foreign investor can hold a title of ownership, or in any case a title for long-term use.

Our specific problem is, who should issue these legal titles? The state or the local communities? We have been using the rural communities, but as they have no training, are nearly illiterate, and have no idea of the value of the land, they started selling off the land at dirt cheap prices, and that is why this is a problem today.

Another challenge of African agriculture is productivity. African yields are way below Asian yields, although the Asian countries were in the same situation

If we want to modernize agriculture, we must define the role of women and make sure that they can own land.

— H. E. Maître Abdoulaye Wade

we were in 20 or 30 years ago. These differences certainly stem from equipment, but also from the training of farmers. We have long said that in Japan the farmer has a high school diploma, but our peasants are illiterate. A farmer must be able to read documents and use them. And it is for that reason that we are exhorting the youth to go and receive at least a minimum of training. Productivity is also a commercial problem. If we cannot increase productivity, our products will not be competitive. And high productivity is achieved through people and land.

In some countries, women play a very important role. If we want to modernize agriculture, we must define the role of women and make sure that they can own land. This is what we did in Senegal. In the constitution adopted in Senegal after I came to power, we wrote that rural women have property rights exactly like men. If we had not done so and the distribution of land were left up to the traditional authorities, women would not have any land.

Another challenge is the problem of transportation. The farmers do the farming, and then they either have to take the harvests to the factory or export them. Now, when you talk about the international price, there are taxes, profits for the middlemen, profits for the factory, and profits for the carrier. Ultimately there is very little left over for the farmer.

There are two theories: Some say the price must be set when it gets to the factory, and the factory pays the farmer and the carrier. The other theory is that the products must be paid for in the farmer's own field.

The other challenge is marketing agricultural products. Last year we launched a program to market corn. I asked the minister of agriculture if we could produce a million tons of corn. He threw up his arms and told me it was not possible; he had tried already. Then we mobilized everyone—the farmers and all those who are in the corn chain of production—and we were able to produce 500,000 tons of corn.

When I came to power four years ago, there was a famine in the north. I did not want to appeal to the international community, so I took US$20 million out of the budget to feed the people who were starving. And then I said to the minister of agriculture, we have to grow what the people are lacking on site. And that is what we did. Today we can produce, and the people are eating corn.

Here are the results that we obtained this year. Simply through volunteerism, peanut production went from 261,000 tons in 2002 to 440,000 tons in 2003. We doubled it. Cotton went from 30,900 tons in 2002 to 55,000 tons in 2003. Millet went from 415,000 tons to 620,000 tons. Rice went from 112,000 tons to 230,000 tons. And corn, which was 80,000 tons, went to 491,000 tons. It was a question of political determination. Of course, you have to have the means, but then you have to dedicate those means.

> *Development does not necessarily occur by chance; people have to be fed, and fed well.*
>
> — H. E. Maître Abdoulaye Wade

In terms of means, I would like to emphasize the factor of human resources. Earlier someone referred to Singapore. What did they do? They copied Japan, which devotes nearly 80 percent of its budget to education. There are no secrets. It's a question of human resources. Of course, to have human resources, you have to have money. But development does not necessarily occur by chance; people have to be fed, and fed well.

Of course, there are political problems, for example, with marketing abroad given the subsidies in the developed countries. In Cancun we had a challenge because the developed countries devoted a billion dollars a day in subsidies to their agriculture. How can an underequipped African, who is not very well trained, compete with the agricultural industry over there, where they are employed, educated, established, and can even write? Then they are also given subsidies. It is not possible. If we do not find a solution and we cannot sell in their markets, then we can no longer sell their products in Africa; it is necessary to close the doors. That is the time bomb. All parts of Africa have said that we cannot remain eternally trapped in a system that is not fair. We want trade, but fair trade. "Free trade but fair trade." That's what the Africans love about Latin America and Asia. The Cancun conference failed, but now parallel discussions are under way, and next May the African countries must meet in Dakar to continue the discussions.

Before closing I would like to analyze the water problem. There is no agriculture without water. We have launched a project for a reservoir to collect rainwater before it flows from the countryside to the sea below. This approach was known, but it had not been done. We are also going to make hill dams as they do in Morocco, Burkina Faso, and other countries.

There is no progress in agriculture without research.

— H. E. Maître Abdoulaye Wade

Above all, we are going to experiment with artificial rain. Moroccan science and technology have succeeded in producing artificial rain. Burkina Faso bought this technology, used it, and had excellent results. Last year when there was a drought in our region, Burkina Faso succeeded in having rain and producing very large quantities, particularly of corn. Through a regional project with other African countries, we have acquired all the equipment through the Islamic Bank for Development, and we have interim plans. Generous God has given us an abundance of rain, so we have not needed to use it, but the equipment is ready for use if a problem ever occurs.

The other question is research. There is no progress in agriculture without research. It is necessary to devote a lot of resources on species, on means of reproduction, etc. We in Senegal expect to do so. But Africa is not spending on research in proportion to its needs. It may be a problem of insufficient means. At the regional level, we are going to ECOWAS to try to create complementarity of resources. Some countries have surpluses and others have deficits, and it is possible to organize all that.

I would like to conclude by reporting that there will be an international scientific and political meeting in Dakar called "Dakar Agricole," whose purpose will be to see that all this scientific knowledge is put to use for the benefit of Africa.

H. E. Olusegun Obasanjo

President of the Federal Republic of Nigeria

For us as developing nations, food and nutrition security should be one of the most important goals of our national development. It is generally estimated that some 800 million people in developing countries, constituting about 20 percent of their total population, are undernourished. This situation will worsen unless drastic and well-targeted actions are taken to stem the tide. And that is why we are here.

The real question is: How did the situation arise in Africa? With our very hard-working population, fertile soil, and over 70 percent of our people involved in agriculture, how come we still suffer deficits in the area of food and nutrition? We must admit that the reasons are internal and external. The truth is that, no matter how we stretch the statistics, Africa since independence has not done well in agriculture, food production, and food security.

I am not oblivious of the historical experiences of Africa that distorted our agriculture, complicated relations between the rural and urban sectors, imposed monoculture production systems, marginalized the local farmers, and instituted a regime of internal colonization and exploitation through all sorts of bureaucratic structures such as the marketing board. What is amazing is that in most of Africa this situation inherited from the colonial governments, which were mainly interested in feeding European factories with raw materials, has not changed much even today. Whom do we blame for that after so many years of independence?

At the external level, the international regimes of trade and tariffs have never favored Africa. Why should they? Those who designed macroeconomics and capitalism didn't design them for Africa. They designed them for their own use and their own needs.

True, there have been a few positive epochs, but these have been few and far between. Let me illustrate the almost perpetual unfavorable conditions of global economic arrangements to Africa's agriculture. First is the regime of subsidies put in place by the developed world that makes their agricultural products much cheaper, thus dampening the market for our exports. In the Organisation for Economic Co-operation and Development (OECD) countries, the subsidies stand at about US$1 billion per day. We are all familiar with the cliché about Africans living on less than US$1 per day; yet a cow in Europe is subsidized at over US$2 per day. With this sort of subsidy, African agriculture cannot attain the competitive edge required to make it buoyant, either in earning foreign exchange or in precipitating necessary incentives to increase production. Through disincentives and inability to compete, Africans are directly and indirectly shut out of Western markets.

Through disincentives and inability to compete, Africans are directly and indirectly shut out of Western markets.

— H. E. Olusegun Obasanjo

Second are the very high tariffs put in place by the developed nations as barriers to our agricultural products. Where the barriers are not formal, they have been placed as nontariff barriers with exactly the same effects. Let me illustrate with a story told to me many times by our late, respected brother, President Houphouet Boigny of Côte d'Ivoire. He took loans from the West to establish two sugar complexes. His grand idea of satisfying national need was subverted by European countries that decided to produce sugar from sugar beets rather than from sugar cane, which is more economical and more efficient. The European sugar—cheaper, though not better—was then dumped in the Ivorian market. Within a few years, the two complexes had to shut down. The painful part of the story can be found in the implications: First, the debt remained—at high interest rates of course—and that debt is being paid by Côte d'Ivoire. Second, farmers in Côte d'Ivoire lost revenues. Third, the internal market became depressed. Fourth, people began to develop a taste for imported, or dumped, sugar, over the products of local factories. And finally, poverty was intensified owing to general loss of revenue to local producers and the government. You can find similar examples in almost any country at which you look.

After political independence, Africa's trade relations with the outside world actually took a turn for the worse. As the prices of our agricultural products decreased, the prices of goods from the industrialized world increased. They invested heavily in stockpiling and synthetic alternatives, while actually manipulating the prices of our exports. Their technological policies equally ensured that we had no capacity to engage in limited processing of our products, thus further complicating our ability to access their markets. This is what African nations are experiencing at the hands of developed nations, and it is not providing a foundation for sustainable agricultural development and fair competition in the marketplace.

The third external factor that I would like to mention is the strategy of the developed world to introduce and nurture by every means possible a craving in Africa for what we do not produce or need. This struggle to cultivate a taste for foreign products and imports has far-reaching detrimental effects on our agricultural and food production strategy.

A famous case is that of wheat. Through the PL-480 strategy, a wheat trap was set, and Africa fell into it. Today the continent is heavily reliant on bread produced largely from imported wheat, to the advantage of Western, especially American, farmers and to the detriment of our local substitutes, such as potato, yam, cassava, rice, plantain, sorghum, and maize. All you need from bread is energy, carbohydrates. And all these other items of food, which we produce locally everywhere in Africa, will also give you energy.

President Olusegun Obasanjo of the Federal Republic of Nigeria points to external and internal factors when acknowledging Africa's lack of progress.

Some of us have abandoned research into the use of these products in bread making, and we have developed a taste for wheat-based bread, with all its negative health implications. Any research that may lead to less dependence on importation of wheat or soya beans will not be supported—indeed, will be positively discouraged by our development partners who are major exporters of these commodities into our countries.

The internal constraints to agricultural production and food and nutrition security in Africa are legion. We have failed to restructure what we inherited from the colonialists in a fundamental way. We have neglected the rural areas and the small farmers. We have focused on producing, in the same way in most instances, exactly the same products that were imposed on us by the colonial authorities. We have not been very creative in introducing new technologies, just as we have generally mismanaged cooperatives and policies that will boost output, increase income, and promote better nutritional practices. Perhaps more important, we have dampened creativity and confidence in our people and decreased investment in agriculture through wrong policies, inconsistency, and political conflict. Hence, farms and farmers have been ruined by war, women and children have been displaced, and water systems have been destroyed, while the young and healthy are either

We have dampened creativity and confidence in our people and decreased investment in agriculture through wrong policies, inconsistency, and political conflict.

— H. E. Olusegun Obasanjo

forced into war or forced to emigrate to foreign lands to the detriment of our nations.

These factors all come together to put a negative stamp on our agricultural and food systems, deprive us of foreign exchange to promote growth and development, discourage investors, close foreign markets to our products, cast aspersions on the quality of our products, and strengthen the hands of the West in imposing nontariff barriers to our products.

Finally, until very recently—and we are still working hard on this front—the suffocation of civil society, the closure of democratic spaces, and the preponderance of bad governance did not generally augur well for agriculture and food production.

Let me come home to Nigeria. In Nigeria we have come to recognize our weaknesses, strengths, and opportunities. We have no illusions about the challenges posed by policies initiated and operated by the developed nations and their impacts on our agricultural and food production systems. Our approach has been to adopt a multipronged approach to reversing the situation we met in 1999. Hence, agriculture—which contributes 39 percent of GDP and about 3 percent of total foreign exchange earnings and accounts for over 80 percent of the non-oil exports, employing about 70 percent of the nation's active labor force—is today a priority sector.

From a food deficit situation of the late 1970s and early 1980s, the country's agriculture has recorded significant improvements in production in the last four years. Today we have attained substantial self-sufficiency in the production of major staples such as maize, sorghum, cassava, and millet. Nigeria is currently the largest producer of cassava, yams, and cocoyams in the world.

Substantial growth has also occurred in the output of some other major cereals, roots, and tubers. We are near self-sufficiency in beef and poultry products. Last year, our success in agriculture was recognized with a gold medal from the Food and Agriculture Organization of the United Nations (FAO). These achievements in domestic availability of food have increased the average national daily supply of calories above minimum per capita energy requirements.

We are not resting on our oars. Nigeria continues to intensify measures aimed at redressing the adverse conditions that militate against availability of quality food on a sustainable basis through building physical, social, and economic infrastructure in the rural areas; improving marketing infrastructure and access to markets for agricultural products; enhancing coordination and collaboration between various actors in the downstream agricultural sector; and closing the gaps between food production and nutrition issues.

Nigeria's holistic agricultural and food self-sufficiency strategy is anchored on the Presidential Initiatives on increased production, processing, marketing, and export of major agricultural commodities. Presidential Initiatives are product-specific stakeholders' consultative meetings under my chairmanship, where all stakeholders—researchers, investors, farmers, bankers, everybody—in a participatory and parliament-like atmosphere, discuss the opportunities and constraints of self-sufficiency in a particular food item or commodity. They set targets, strategies, and time frames for the achievement of national self-sufficiency, to be followed by export programs and promotion. It has become an important and successful policy formulation and implementation strategy of our nascent democracy. Then there is the periodic progress report and assessment of each commodity program. The approach has ensured broad participation of the citizenry in issues that are critical to their everyday life, making them part and parcel of the implementation process and sensitizing them to the importance of the citizens' role in nation building.

Of course, the support of the president, both at the level of policy formulation and at each stage of implementation, not only emphasizes the importance of the issue being addressed, but it also ensures that immediate corrective measures are taken within the implementation process and substantially guarantees success. I undertake

We must commit to giving agriculture priority of place in our planning processes.

— H. E. Olusegun Obasanjo

field visits to see things on the ground throughout the country, and follow-up actions are carried out.

I must hasten to add that our national food security program, jointly carried out with the FAO and our Global 2000 program, is subsumed under the Presidential Initiative, and it is part of our success story. To this must be added a South-South partnership program with China. This particular program develops small dams for irrigation and for aquaculture. To sustain production without discouraging farmers, the government remains a buyer of last resort. With a sense of humility, allow me to recommend this strategy where it is considered applicable.

The solutions to our agricultural and food crises are within our reach. However, we must get a few things right.

First, we must put our own house in order. We must commit to giving agriculture priority of place in our planning processes. We must be consistent and be predictable. We must exploit our comparative advantage and develop those products that will help our populations achieve the highest points of their creative and productive abilities, while at the same time improving their conditions of living. In line with this, we must adopt the strategy of going commodity by commodity. This has enabled us in Nigeria to achieve a 7 percent growth rate in agriculture in 2003, and we hope to maintain that.

Second, we must develop and sustain a strategy for managing soil and water. For most of Africa, this is still in a haphazard stage. The truth is that relying on rain-fed agriculture alone will simply not do for the continent.

Third, we must bring in appropriate technology, including biotechnology, improved seeds, chemicals, and mechanical, even electronic, inputs to the management of farms, especially on weather prediction, pest control, flood control, processing, preservation, packaging, storage, and marketing.

We are still weak in these areas, and through cooperation, exchange of ideas, and research, we can all do much better. We must insist on market access for our agricultural products in the industrialized nations, just as they have market access in our countries for their highly industrial products. Paralyzing subsidies must be discouraged.

In the past we have been the architects of our own misfortunes. Now, let us be the architects of our own fortunes. To be sure, we live in a largely interdependent world and must seek support and rely on others for help. But we must stand up and put the pad on our head and bend to carry our load. Then we will get assistance from others to help us in carrying it.

In the past we have been the architects of our own misfortunes. Now, let us be the architects of our own fortunes.

— H. E. Olusegun Obasanjo

There must, however, be some division of labor. Let us concentrate and produce for the world those products that we are good at and for which we have comparative advantage. Let us restructure and reposition our economies for growth, stability, development, and democracy. Let us treat the small-, medium-, and large-scale farmers with dignity and encourage them to reach higher levels of innovation and productivity. We need commercial farmers, but before we get them we have to make do with what we have. We cannot just throw away the peasant farmers.

In Africa, let us cooperate and integrate and learn from each other's best practices for sustained success. This is what NEPAD is all about. Let us adapt and adopt new ideas, new technologies, and new practices for land and water management, postharvest processing, and storage, as well as marketing.

Let no one put restrictions in our way as we produce for ourselves and the rest of the world. Let others produce what they have comparative advantage in. For instance, no matter how attractive the production of caviar is, we must leave it for the Caspian Sea, which has comparative advantage. But greenhouses in Europe to produce banana, plantain, and cassava cannot be regarded as the most efficient way of producing these commodities. It is even against the plan of nature and certainly not cost-effective.

Finally, we must reduce waste, take economic and political reform seriously, provide the required leadership for our people, and encourage the youth to return to the land to develop into new and modern farmers as well as improve the living conditions in the rural areas.

We must begin to work and speak together, adopt common positions in engaging the restrictions and obstacles prevalent in the global system, and create an enabling environment that will enhance the efficacy of policies and programs in agriculture and food production.

With commitment, unity, focus, and dedication to improving the lot of our people, we can overcome all our current problems and move toward a glorious future, even before 2020.

Box 1: A Message from Ugandan Schoolchildren

At the opening session of the conference, the participants heard a moving message of hope from several dozen schoolchildren from the nearby Buganda Road Primary School, who came to the conference hall to recite three poems on the themes of food and agriculture. Their entertaining performance offered participants much inspiration and a sense of common purpose as they embarked upon the three days of deliberation.

Poem I

By Waiswa Kibedi
Music, Dance, and Drama Head

1. Food, the life giver
To plants and animals,
God provides food to all
Through the soils he made
To bear food to all
Living organisms.

2. Good weather he provides
To let plants flourish,
Suitable environments given
To meet animal requirements
Different species, they are.

3. Man ensures food security.
Control environmental hazards,
Deforestation, bush burning
Swamp drainage, overgrazing
And other activities; they cause environmental degradation.

4. Unproductively leads to malnutrition.
The young generation needs
Nutritious food.
The young ones need it badly,
Animal species do the same.
Together let's preserve
And conserve the environment.

5. Instability in states!
Political turmoil!
Insurgencies globally!
Uncertainty for the future!
They hinder steady food production.

6. Together let's fight hunger!
Sensitize masses over food security!
Let us make peace not war,
Make proper use of the environment
By practicing:
Afforestation, no swamp reclamation,
Proper farming methods, no bush burning,
control overgrazing.
All, we shall wipe drought and famine in Africa.

Poem II

By Ssenoga Rebecca
Music, Dance, and Drama

Lift your hands we shall all join.
To promote agriculture for development.
Better health, nutrition, and family life
Is all what we need in our nation wide.

Lift your hands, we shall join, we the young generation.

Uphold and maintain to create
National wealth
To enhance better quality life and self-reliance.
We need human resource for exploitation,
Our natural resources of Uganda.

Poem: Agriculture

Music, Dance, and Drama

You are so wonderful. You are so motherly
Precious, what suitable name can we give you?
You are life itself. What would we do without you?
The ice cream, yoghurt, butter, and cheese
All are daughters of Agriculture.
What would we do without you?
Mangos, guavas, paw paws and pineapples, oranges, jackfruit, and watermelon
keep us healthy all the time.
All from Agriculture.
What would we do without you?
No Agriculture, no development
No Agriculture, no life.

Chapter 2 Taking Stock

Chair: Mamadou Kone*
Minister of Scientific Research, Côte d'Ivoire

Today we have an opportunity to share our experiences and to discuss a problem that affects all of Africa—food and nutrition insecurity. Some of you may think this is just another conference. But this conference is special. To my knowledge, it is the first time that such an important conference has been held on African territory. And better still, we have the participation of three heads of state, who are indeed great African visionaries, which Africa certainly needs in order to face the challenge ahead of us.

We Africans are dying of hunger. We are dying of lack of access to water. We are dying of AIDS. Africa's advantage is the youth of its population, and yet AIDS is wiping out this comparative advantage. In the face of all that, I would like to call upon the scientists. I am convinced that science is the only discipline that can change the destiny of our continent.

I would also like to remind this assembly, the continent, and the world that Africa cannot remain under such conditions and at the same time be prosperous. The destiny of Africa is linked to the other continents.

How did we get here? What must be done? Earlier President Wade and President Obasanjo were kind enough to share with us their vision for the New Partnership for Africa's Development. Today we need to ask ourselves: Do internationalization and democracy act as constraints or opportunities for our continent? Do the African Union and NEPAD serve as a first step toward the solution?

* This presentation was originally given in French.

Keynote Address: Africa's Food and Nutrition Security Situation: Where Are We and How Did We Get Here?

Isatou Jallow
Executive Director, National Nutrition Agency, The Gambia

Where are we, and how did we get here? That's a huge question. Years ago I read a book entitled *How Europe Underdeveloped Africa*. Today, however, I want us to focus on how the lack of adequate food, the lack of adequate health services, inadequate caring practices, and an unsanitary environment, which combine to make up nutrition insecurity, are underdeveloping Africa.

Most of us know what food security is all about. And when we say "nutrition security," most of us tend to equate it with food security. I want to emphasize that nutrition security goes beyond food security and calories. When we talk about agriculture, when we talk about food production—which is extremely important—we should also have in mind nutrition security: adequate food, adequate health services, adequate caring practices, and a sanitary environment.

Where are we? One-third of the African countries are below the recommended calorie intake level of 2,100. Two hundred million people are undernourished—that is, their access to the minimum amount of calories recommended is inadequate—and that is an increase of 20 percent since 1990. This number represents 27 percent of the African population and almost 33 percent of Sub-Saharan Africa. For countries in conflict situations, the share of undernourished people is over 50 percent.

Let's look at the prevalence and numbers of stunted children under five years of age in Africa (see Table 1). Stunting refers to low height-for-age. This is not to say that all short people are malnourished; they are not. But stunting in the sense of low height-for-age measures chronic malnutrition and is an outcome of nutrition insecurity. It is the best measure for nutrition insecurity, because a child that is stunted has had inadequate access to food, health care, and a sanitary environment. It is also a good indicator of a nation's level of socioeconomic development. This is why stunting is used as an outcome indicator in poverty reduction strategy papers.

In East Africa the prevalence of stunting remains the same from 1990 to 2000. But look at absolute numbers: estimates of stunted children rise from 12 million in 1990 to 19.4 million in 2000. In Central Africa there is a slight decline in prevalence. Southern Africa and West Africa stay the same or decline slightly in prevalence. But as the population increases, even when the prevalence rate of stunting does not increase, the absolute numbers of malnourished children rise. Northern Africa is the only subregion where the prevalence rate and the absolute numbers have decreased.

The maps show the prevalence of underweight—that is, low weight-for-height—among African children, illustrating the hunger spots throughout the continent (Figure 1).

In 1990, 32.8 million children were malnourished. Where are these children? How many of them are still alive? How many of them survived with the consequences of malnutrition for their mental development?

Isatou Jallow explains the causes and consequences of nutrition insecurity.

TABLE 1—Prevalence and numbers of stunted children (0–5 years) in Africa, 1990 and 2000

	%		Millions	
Region	1990	2000	1990	2000
Africa	37	35	32.8	45.1
Eastern	44	44	12.0	19.4
Central	42	38	4.5	6.8
Northern	27	22	6.2	4.6
Southern	25	25	1.3	1.5
Western	35	33	8.8	12.7

Source: M. De Onis, M. Blössner, E. Borghi, R. Morris, and E. A. Frongilla, "Methodology for Estimating Regional and Global Trends of Child Malnutrition," *International Journal of Epidemiology* (submitted).

FIGURE 1—Underweight children in Africa

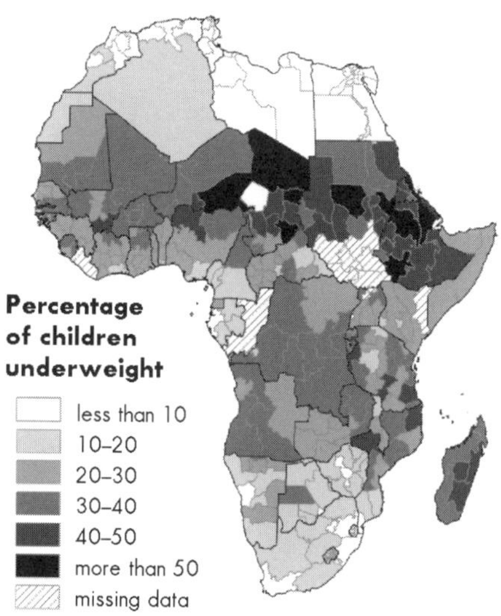

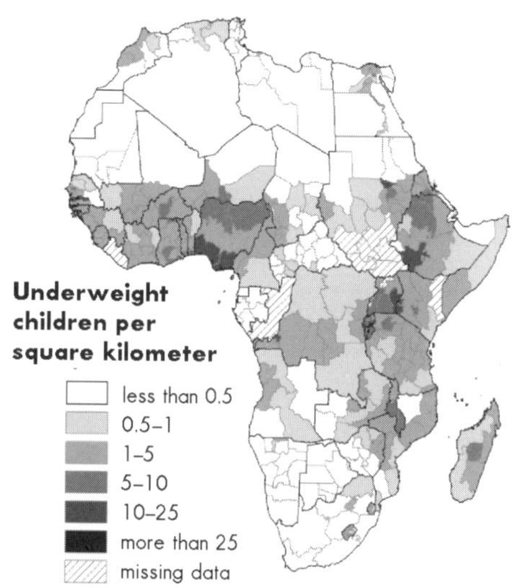

Source: Hunger Task Force, *Halving Hunger by 2015: A Framework for Action*, Interim Report of the Millennium Project (New York: United Nations Development Programme, 2003).

How many of them are adolescents now with poor intellectual performance? How many of them are going to grow into adults with less productive capacity? How many of them are going to continue living in the web of poverty that was formed long before they were born?

Then in 2000 there were 45 million children malnourished, and the number is expected to increase by about 1.5 million by 2005—next year. When we see these figures, they are just figures. Sometimes it is difficult to even conceptualize 45 million children malnourished in Africa. After all, who are these children? What are their names? Where do they live? How does this affect me? How does this affect you? Let's see how these huge numbers of malnourished children link to the development and prosperity of our continent.

Figure 2 is complicated, but it illustrates the vicious cycle of malnutrition. It is a burden that gets heavier and heavier, until finally those carrying the burden collapse.

Let's look at this vicious cycle: I am a woman. I am malnourished. I get pregnant. I have low weight gain during my pregnancy because I am still malnourished. I work too hard in the fields. I have too little food. My environment is unsanitary. I have infections. I give birth to a low-birth-weight baby.

That baby has a disadvantage right from the start. Because of my poverty and the conditions I live in, my baby does not stand a chance. So that low-birth-weight baby grows into a stunted child with frequent infections, inadequate care, and inadequate health services.

That child has reduced mental capacity. When that child goes to school, the learning capacity is not what it should be. That child grows into a stunted adolescent with reduced physical labor capacity and low educational attainment. What chance does this child stand?

And if that adolescent is a girl, because of the high teenage pregnancy rate in Africa, she probably gets pregnant and has low weight gain. She gives birth to a low-birth-weight baby, and the vicious cycle continues.

FIGURE 2—The burden of malnutrition

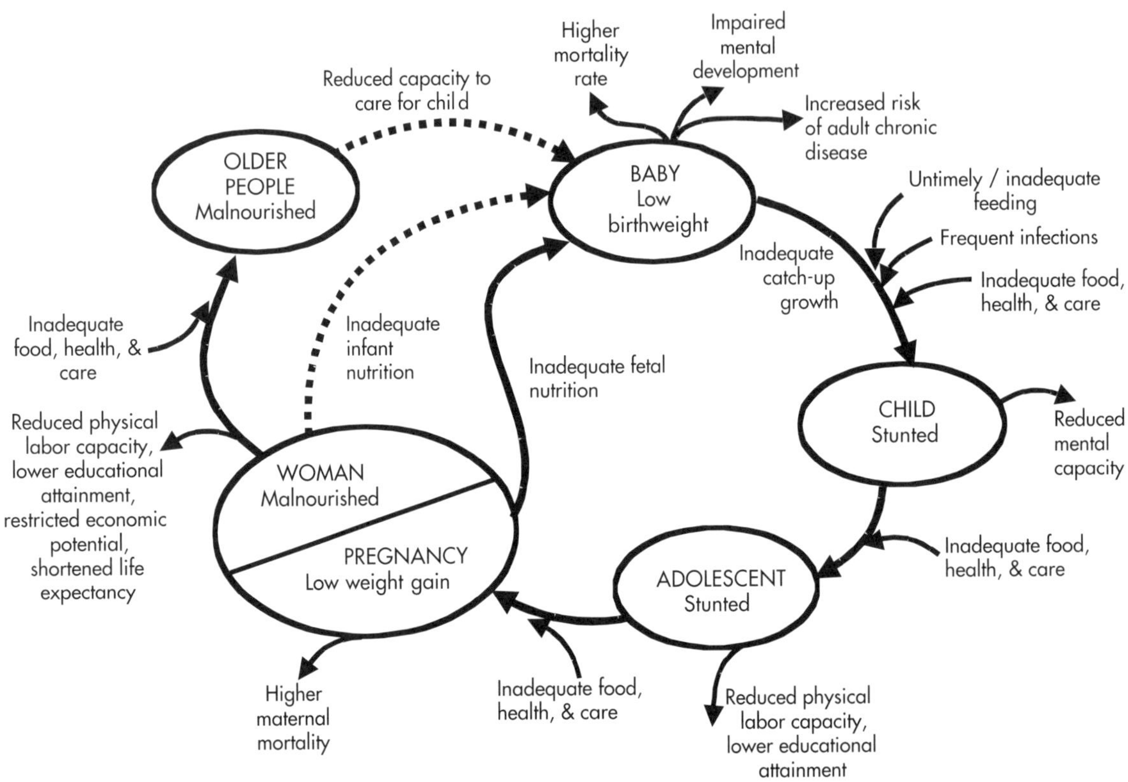

Source: Todd Benson, *Africa's Food and Nutrition Security Situation: Where Are We and How Did We Get Here?* 2020 Discussion Paper 37 (Washington, DC: IFPRI, 2004).

The malnourished woman grows into an elderly woman who is still malnourished. In our culture it is the elderly who take care of our children. She has reduced capacity to help me take care of my child. So that is the vicious cycle of malnutrition. It haunts you throughout your life, and it impacts the next generation, on and on and on.

But there is hope. Because it is a cycle, we have the chance to intervene. Let's look at the relationship between the burden of malnutrition and our investments. Right now our governments all want to attain the Millennium Development Goals, we all want to increase agricultural productivity, and we all want to reduce poverty, so we are investing in these areas. Yet we are investing less in attaining nutrition security.

If we invest in education but the children go to school malnourished, what chance do they have? If we try to increase agricultural productivity but the farmers are malnourished and have lowered productive capacity, what chance do they have? If we want to reduce poverty but we do not address the vicious cycle of malnutrition and poverty, what chance do we have? Investments in these areas will pay off and be sustainable only if we break the cycle of malnutrition.

Now, why are we where we are today? North Africa shows positive trends. Agricultural productivity is low, with minor gains, but North Africans have more access to food through markets. They have provision of health care services and a hygienic environment. The female adult literacy rate is uneven but high.

Sub-Saharan Africa, however, faces challenges: lack of access to food, care, health care, and a sanitary environment. But what are the real issues? They are conflicts and/or absence of effective central governments, environmental factors like droughts and floods, economic factors, the burden of disease, and the lack of political will and commitment.

Most countries in Africa have no institution that has authority in nutrition, that has responsibility for nutrition, and that is accountable for nutrition.

— Isatou Jallow

What is the way forward? The title of this conference refers to "prioritizing actions, strengthening actors, facilitating partnerships." When we talk about taking actions, let's think about direct nutrition interventions, access to nutrition services, and women's education.

How do we strengthen actors? Create an institution with authority, responsibility, and accountability. Most countries in Africa have no institution that has authority in nutrition, that has responsibility for nutrition, and that is accountable for nutrition. These functions are scattered all over the place.

How do you facilitate partnerships within countries, between countries, and between regions? Assess and profile the interests of potential partners. Develop a process to get their collaboration.

There is a momentum going forward now, because we have African initiatives like NEPAD. If we show commitment, we can unleash our greatest resource, which is the intellectual power of our people.

We are talking about the African continent. That is me, mine, you, yours, us, ours. So we have to do what needs to be done. In the spirit of African women, whenever we are going to do heavy work, whether in Uganda, Ethiopia, or The Gambia, we do this: We tie our waist to get ready for heavy work. And that is what we are doing now.

If we invest in education but the children go to school malnourished, what chance do they have? If we try to increase agricultural productivity but the farmers are malnourished and have lowered productive capacity, what chance do they have?

— Isatou Jallow

Excerpt 1: Assessing Africa's Food and Nutrition Security Situation

Todd Benson

Food security and nutrition security are not necessarily the same thing. A household is food secure if it can reliably gain access to food of a sufficient quality in quantities that allow all its members to enjoy a healthy and active life. But individuals in food-secure households may still have deficient or unbalanced diets. Nutrition security is only achieved when secure access to food is coupled with a sanitary environment, adequate health services, and the knowledge and care needed to ensure the good health of all individuals in a household. Whether or not an individual attains his or her full personal and economic potential, however defined, depends to a large degree on the level of his or her nutrition security. The availability of nutrition resources and the degree to which an individual has access to such resources are a function of how a society is organized economically, politically, ideologically, and administratively. Consequently, nutrition security must be a subject for political debate and of immediate concern to any national development strategies.

Though nutrition insecurity is generally being reduced worldwide, the problem is actually growing worse in Africa, where child stunting rates (an indicator of undernutrition) declined by less than 4 percentage points between 1980 and 2000. Consequently, as a result of population growth, the number of stunted children actually increased by more than 12 million, to 31 million.

When considering the status of children on the continent as a whole, North Africa stands out as an area in which child malnutrition is being addressed quite effectively. In Sub-Saharan Africa, however, the pattern is less encouraging and somewhat more complex. Countries in coastal West and Central Africa and Southern Africa have lower rates of child malnutrition than the countries of East and Central Africa and those with a large proportion of their population in the interior of the continent. Thus, the picture painted of poorly nourished populations in the Sahel and Ethiopia in the 1980s remains relatively accurate today. However, the highest prevalence of stunting occurs in countries in East and Central Africa, reflecting the civil conflicts, droughts and floods, and economic downturns (resulting from macroeconomic mismanagement or commodity price shocks) that have affected those areas. Finally, any effort to reduce the level of malnutrition in Africa must target Ethiopia, Nigeria, and the Democratic Republic of the Congo, home to 40 percent of all the stunted preschoolers on the continent.

Deficiencies of vitamin A, iron, zinc, and iodine are the four main micronutrient deficiencies affecting public health in Africa. Many Africans still consume insufficient amounts of these nutrients, even though they are only required in relatively small quantities. As a result, between 15,000 and 20,000 African women die each year of severe iron-deficiency anemia, while hundreds of thousands of children suffer a lowered intellectual capacity as a result of iodine deficiency. Vitamin A deficiencies in children are also common, reducing their ability to resist infection and contributing to the deaths of more than half a million African children annually.

Globally, progress has been made in reducing undernourishment. However, Africa is lagging behind. Estimates of the overall numbers of undernourished people in Africa have actually been rising over the past few decades—from 111 million in the period 1969–71, to 171 million in 1990–92, to 204 million in 1999–2001. Moreover, food shortages so severe that they require an international response continue to occur regularly.

This has been excerpted from 2020 Africa Conference Brief 1, published by IFPRI, Washington, DC, 2004. See also 2020 Discussion Paper 37, *Africa's Food and Nutrition Security Situation: Where Are We and How Did We Get Here?* published by IFPRI, Washington, DC, 2004.

Keynote Address: Looking Ahead: Long-Term Prospects for Africa's Food and Nutrition Security

Mark Rosegrant
Director, Environment and Production Technology Division,
International Food Policy Research Institute, USA

What is the future for food production, demand, prices, and trade in Africa under alternative sets of policies and investments? And more important, will current policies and current plans for investment provide for acceptable progress on child malnutrition and health? If not, can we in fact devise a plausible and feasible set of policies and investments by which we really can achieve food security?

As I go through my presentation, a number of key messages are going to emerge. First, a continuation of current policies and current investments will not do the job. They will in fact lead to increasing child malnutrition and a growing number of households without access to clean water and proper sanitation. On the positive side, however, the evidence will show that key Millennium Development Goals can be met through increased investments and policy reform and that we can go a long way toward assuring food security and nutrition security by 2020.

The foundations for success lie in two major areas. One is investment in agricultural productivity growth, and the second is investment in human resource development.

Success will depend mainly on actions by Africans for Africans. But developed countries also have an important role to play. They need to provide direct investments, but even more important, they need to reform trade and agricultural subsidy policies that are currently constraining African development.

We assess future prospects using the scenario approach. The models we use to implement these scenarios are IFPRI's International Model for Policy Analysis of Agricultural Commodities and Trade (IMPACT) and IMPACT-water. The first scenario I will describe is the "business as usual" scenario, which is our best estimate of what outcomes will be, given recent past trends plus current plans for investments, agriculture and economic policy, and agricultural growth. I will then describe a "pessimistic" scenario, which postulates a slowdown in each of those investments and policy reform factors. Then, perhaps the most important scenario I will describe is a "vision" scenario, which looks at how improved policies and sharp increases in investments in agricultural research, rural infrastructure, irrigation, education, and clean water can achieve much better outcomes. I am also going to highlight the issue of developed-country policies in a "trade liberalization" scenario that postulates the removal of those trade restrictions over the next couple of years.

Let's turn to some results. Figure 1 shows effective cereal demand in North Africa and Sub-Saharan Africa in 1997 and 2020. Even under "business as usual," we project more than a doubling of demand in Sub-Saharan Africa and about a 70 percent increase in North Africa. There are some increases in per capita demand and per capita calorie consumption, but unfortunately this large increase in cereal demand is primarily due to population growth rather than improvements in per capita income.

For meat, we see an even more dramatic increase in demand, with both North Africa and Sub-Saharan Africa experiencing significantly more than a doubling in demand for meats and livestock products (Figure 2).

But Figure 3 shows net cereal trade with negative numbers, meaning net imports for both Sub-Saharan Africa and North Africa. Production will not keep pace with the increase in demand. Projected imports of

FIGURE 1—Cereal demand in Africa under "business as usual" scenario, 1977 and 2020

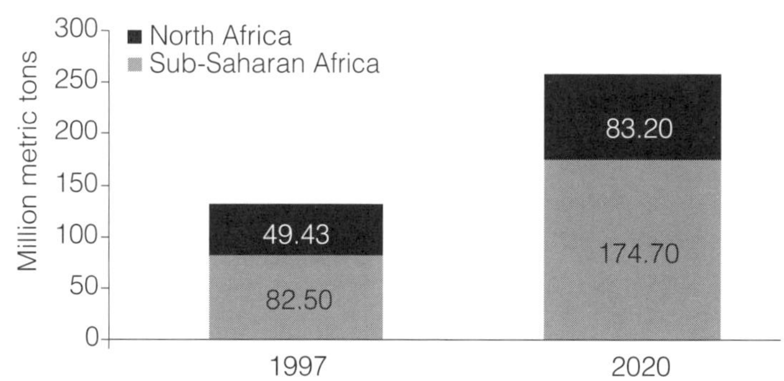

Source: IFPRI IMPACT simulations.

FIGURE 2—Meat demand in Africa under "business as usual" scenario, 1997 and 2020

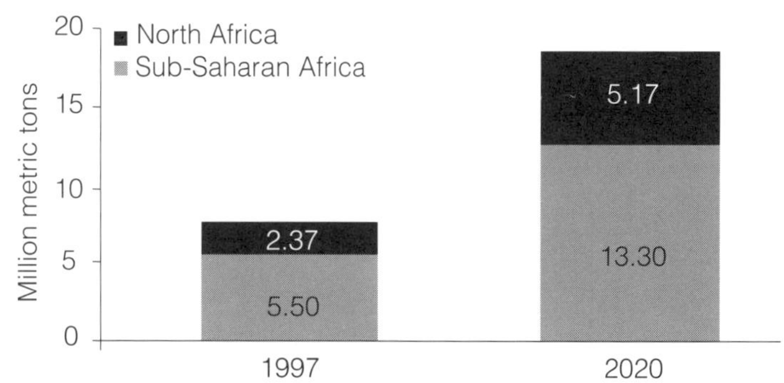

Source: IFPRI IMPACT simulations.

FIGURE 3—Net cereal trade for Africa under "business as usual" scenario, 1997 and 2020

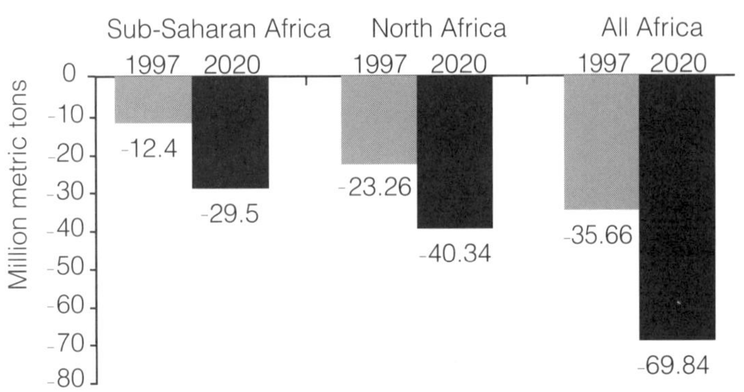

Source: IFPRI IMPACT simulations.

FIGURE 4—Annual benefit for Africa of global trade liberalization for IMPACT commodities, 2020

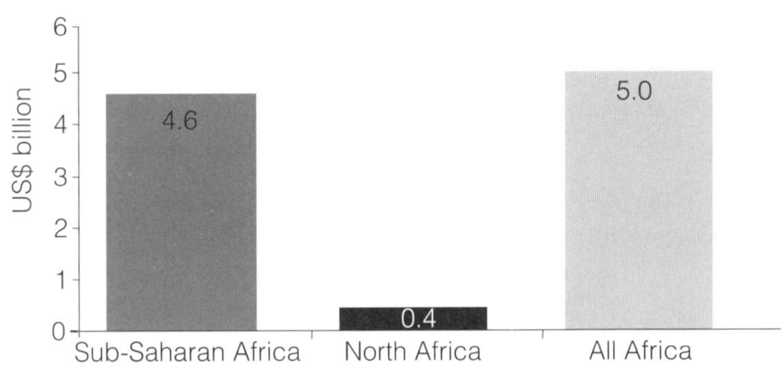

Source: IFPRI IMPACT simulations.

FIGURE 5—Cereal and meat output in Africa under "business as usual" and "vision" scenarios, 1997, 2020, and 2025

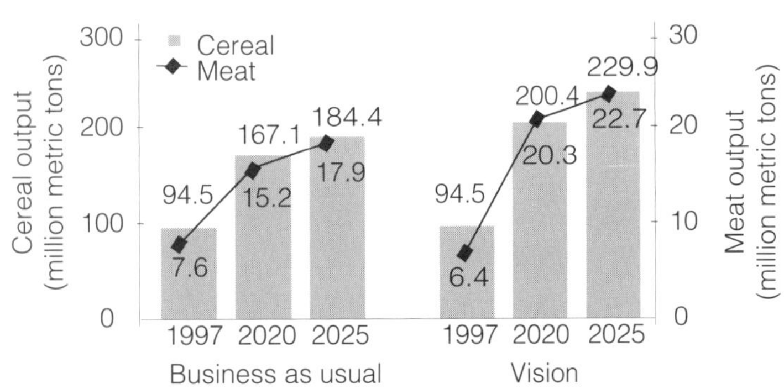

Source: IFPRI IMPACT simulations.

cereals in Sub-Saharan Africa increase from 12 million metric tons to 30 million metric tons and nearly double in North Africa from 23 million to 40 million metric tons. Given the relatively slow economic growth and the limited foreign exchange reserves in many countries in Africa, this kind of increasing trade deficit will put additional pressure on food security.

Figure 4 illustrates the results of the global "trade liberalization" scenario, showing the annual economic benefits derived from the elimination of subsidies and trade barriers both in the developed countries and in the African countries. By 2020 Sub-Saharan Africa will gain US$4.6 billion every year through the elimination of trade restrictions worldwide. About a third of that is due to the elimination of restrictions within Africa itself, and about two-thirds is due to developed-country policies. That US$4.6 billion represents almost 10 percent of value added in the commodities that we analyze here, so it is a significant benefit to agriculture. North Africa benefits somewhat less.

Let's compare production under the "business as usual" scenario and the "vision" scenario (Figure 5). Note that the "business as usual" scenario is not a highly pessimistic scenario—we project a doubling of meat production and about a 75 percent increase in cereal production by 2020—but that simply is not enough to provide serious inroads in food insecurity. In the "vision" scenario Africa achieves almost 50 percent more growth in both meat and cereal production between 1997 and 2020, thanks to those increased investments in research, infrastructure, and irrigation.

Now the crux of this story lies in indicators of food security and nutrition security. Figure 6 shows the number of people without access to clean water in Africa. The Millennium Development Goals set a target of reducing by half the percentage of people without access to clean water by 2015. To reach that goal, you need to reduce the number of people without access to clean water to about 170 million. Under current policies we are not only not approaching that, we are actually going to have significant increases in the number of people without access to clean water in Africa. The "pessimistic" scenario puts those numbers practically off the charts. Yet the "vision" scenario not only achieves that Millennium Development Goal, but also continues to dramatically reduce the number of people without access to clean water through 2020 and beyond.

Figure 7 is perhaps the most telling of all. Currently, about 37 million children in Africa are malnourished. That number will increase to 44 million and stabilize at about 42 million by 2020 under "business as usual"—clearly unacceptable. The situation is even worse under the "pessimistic" scenario. But once again, with the

FIGURE 6—People without access to clean water in Africa, 1995, 2015, and 2020

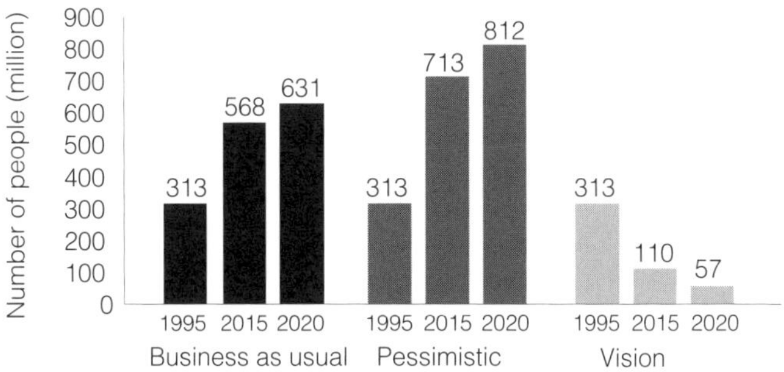

Source: IFPRI IMPACT simulations.

FIGURE 7—Alternative futures for African children, 1997, 2015, and 2020

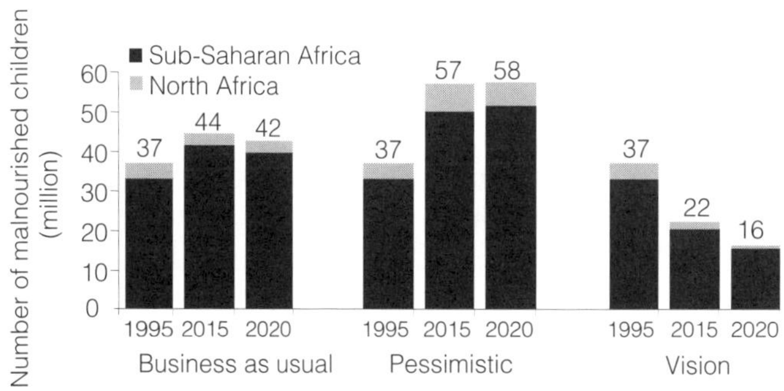

Source: IFPRI IMPACT simulations.

"vision" scenario, we can nearly achieve the Millennium Development Goals and reduce the number of malnourished children to about 16 million by 2020.

What exactly is involved in the "vision" scenario? Under "business as usual," investments in irrigation, clean water, education, rural roads, and agricultural research total about US$5.7 billion a year. To get to the "vision" scenario, we estimate that you would need to nearly double that to about US$10.3 billion a year (Figure 8). That is equivalent to increasing from about 15 percent of annual government expenditures in Africa today to nearly 30 percent. So US$10.3 billion is not a small amount, but it certainly seems achievable within the parameters of development aid, foreign direct investment, and the amount of money available within African countries today.

How do we see that breaking down? The biggest investment items under the "vision" scenario are rural roads and education (Figure 9). Out of a cumulative total investment of about US$237 billion over 23 years, about a third—US$74 billion—would go to roads, US$64 billion would go to education, about US$38–39 billion would go to irrigation and clean water, and US$22 billion would go to agricultural research.

To conclude, under current policies and investments we will not make any progress in terms of reducing food insecurity. Instead we'll have an actual increase in the number of children malnourished by 2020. But the choices we make today can make a huge difference. By increasing investments and improving policies, we can reduce the number of malnourished children to 16 million by 2020. In fact, our projections show that the kinds of policies and investment reforms we are recommending here could lead to the elimination of childhood malnutrition in Africa by 2030 to 2035.

FIGURE 8—Annual public investment in "business as usual" and "vision" scenarios, 1997–2020

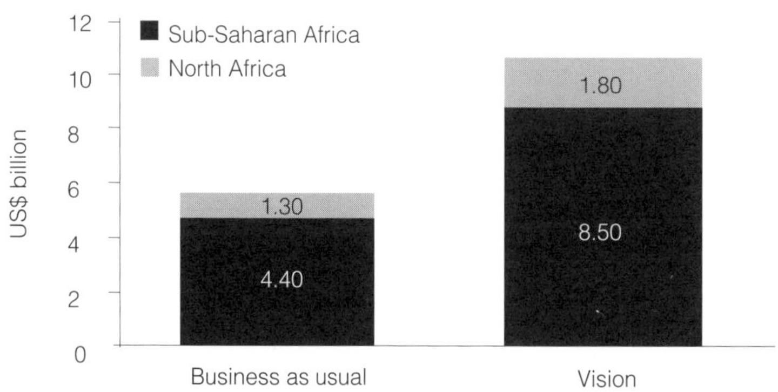

Source: IFPRI IMPACT simulations.

FIGURE 9—Cumulative investments by sector in "vision" scenario, 1997–2020

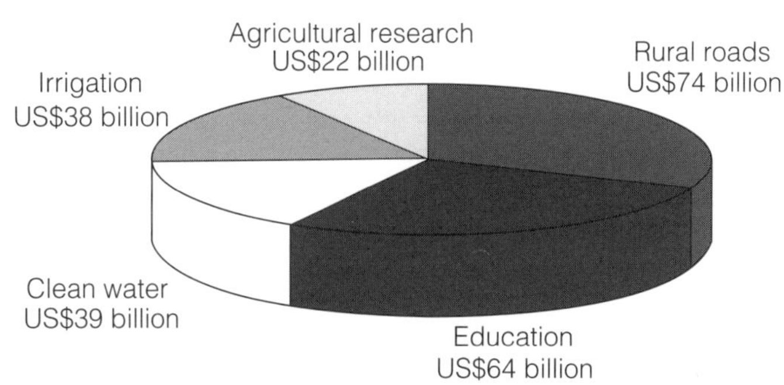

Source: IFPRI IMPACT simulations.

Excerpt 2: Looking Ahead: Long-Term Prospects for Africa's Food and Nutrition Security

Mark W. Rosegrant, Sarah A. Cline, Weibo Li, Timothy Sulser, and Rowena A. Valmonte-Santos

The projections generated for this paper are based on results from the International Model for Policy Analysis of Agricultural Commodities and Trade (IMPACT) for food supply, demand, net trade and malnutrition and from the IMPACT-WATER model for water resource projections.

IMPACT Business as Usual (BAU) scenario projections indicate that food security in Africa will not improve substantially over the next 20 years, with modest growth in agricultural production by historical standards expected over this period. Between 1997 and 2025, the IMPACT BAU projects annual cereal production growth rates in Africa of 2.3 percent for maize, 2.4 percent for other grains, 1.9 percent for wheat, and 2.5 percent for rice. African root and tuber production growth is projected to average a relatively high 2.7 percent per year between 1997 and 2025. In Sub-Saharan Africa, projected 2.7 percent cereal production growth is slightly below the 3.6 percent annual increase in production achieved in the region between 1982 and 1997, while projected annual root and tuber production growth rates also decline from their average annual growth rate of 4.3 percent between 1982 and 1997 to 2.7 percent between 1997 and 2025.

The IMPACT BAU projects that crop production in Africa will continue to expand onto unused land, with percentage increases of the area under cereal and root and tuber cultivation in Sub-Saharan Africa ranging from 27 percent in Nigeria to 40 percent in Central and Western Sub-Saharan Africa, although area expansion over the projection period will be slow compared with historic rates. North Africa is projected to experience a smaller percentage area increase: 14.3 percent for Egypt and 12.9 percent for other West Asian/North African countries.

African cereal yield growth is expected to average 1.4 percent per year between 1997 and 2025. North African cereal yields are projected to grow at a lower rate than in Sub-Saharan Africa, at 1.0 percent in Egypt and 1.3 percent in other West Asian/North African countries. Cereal yield growth across Sub-Saharan Africa is higher, however, and is projected to average 1.7 percent annually between 1997 and 2025, essentially doubling the yield growth achieved between 1967 and 1997. A number of considerations and assumptions underlie these mildly optimistic growth rates. Sub-Saharan African yields are very low by other developing-country standards, indicating that significant growth should be possible if countries in the region move toward appropriate technologies, policies, and programs. According to Boserupian theories of induced technological innovation, growing population pressure can be expected to lead to higher yield growth rates as low-input agriculture increasingly ceases to be a viable option. The BAU scenario projects total cereal and root and tuber harvested area in Sub-Saharan Africa to decline from 0.16 hectare per capita in 1997 to 0.11 hectare per capita in 2025. Of course, higher population densities do not guarantee rapid innovation. Even as populations throughout Sub-Saharan Africa are losing their ability to practice shifting cultivation because of high population densities, they also continue to practice other elements of extensive cultivation, including low levels of technological and capital inputs, traditional land tenure and land husbandry practices, and traditional methods of resource acquisition. Moreover, harvested area grows at a slow rate in most regions over the coming decades under the BAU scenario. Given that a high proportion of land suitable for agricultural use is already being harvested and given other factors such as urbanization, slow growth in irrigation investment, and soil degradation, additional growth of harvested area will be hindered in the future. Declining real cereal prices also influence harvested area expansion, making it unprofitable to expand harvested area. The slow rate of area expansion means that production growth comes primarily from yield improvements, which are also slow in this scenario.

This has been excerpted from the draft discussion paper prepared for the 2020 Africa Conference; the final version will be available in 2005.

Chapter 3 Why Has Africa Not Yet Achieved Food and Nutrition Security?

Chair: Richard Mkandawire
Agricultural Advisor, New Partnership for Africa's Development (NEPAD) Secretariat, South Africa

We continue to be bombarded by images in the media of starving populations and emaciated children in the Horn of Africa, in Southern Africa, and in other regions in Africa. Those images are perhaps much more telling than the statistics in illustrating the deteriorating human condition of the majority of Africans over the past four decades.

It is in this context that the heads of state and government in Africa, particularly under the framework of the New Partnership for Africa's Development, are saying that this situation cannot continue. Something drastic must be done. And the heads of state and government in Africa, as we heard this morning, are truly committed to doing something about the situation.

Agriculture, food security, and road development, alongside infrastructure and health, have been prioritized as key sectors under NEPAD. This commitment is particularly reflected in the Maputo Declaration of 2003, where the heads of state and government committed themselves to increasing their budgetary allocation to agriculture to 10 percent within the next five years.

Why is this significant? We know that over the past two decades investments in the agricultural sector have been on the decline. So this is a good beginning. Alongside these commitments by the heads of state and government, there is a commitment to begin to address issues around governance in general, and more specifically governance within the agricultural sector. In fact, at the FAO regional ministers' meeting that took place in Johannesburg some two weeks ago, the ministers of agriculture made it very clear that issues of governance within the agricultural sector are critical and that they need to be addressed.

As our panelists provide us with insights into what has gone wrong, they also need to provide us with information: What has gone right? And what can we do collectively—as knowledge institutions, as scientists, as farmers, as politicians—to address these deteriorating human conditions of the majority of people on this continent?

Josué Dioné
Director, Food Security and Sustainable Development Division, United Nations Economic Commission for Africa, Ethiopia

Food security, as we have heard over and over, is an issue of income: either income in the form of one's own production of food or income earned from activities that might be related to agriculture or not and used to gain access to food through the market. Nutrition security, on the other hand, is very much dependent on education, on health, on hygiene, and on sanitation conditions. When we put the two together, food and nutrition insecurity are fundamentally a poverty problem. They are closely interrelated because of lack of education and lack of access to food. And all of those are components of poverty.

We have seen clear data showing that four decades ago, during the time of independence, we were more food secure than today. And even a decade ago, we were more food secure than today. What are the factors underlying this downgrading of the state of food security in Africa? One might cite natural disasters, including floods and droughts, epidemics like HIV/AIDS and malaria, and conflicts. But all of these factors can be characterized as factors aggravating the effects of a fundamental factor, which I would call the main actionable cause: inappropriate or inadequate policy choices and inconsistent policy choices. Through those inconsistencies, Africa has failed to engage and sustain a process of agricultural development and transformation.

Four decades ago, during the time of independence, we were more food secure than today.

— Josué Dioné

Why do agricultural development and transformation depend on all those variables? Everybody knows the statistics. About three-quarters of our population still lives in rural areas. Seventy percent of poor people in Africa live in rural areas. About 90 percent of the labor force among those people is employed directly or indirectly in agriculture.

We also know about backward and forward linkages between agriculture and other economic sectors: if agriculture does not move, we lose opportunities for creating employment, opportunities for income earning, and opportunities in other sectors that should normally be linked to agriculture.

In failing to develop agriculture, we trigger rural poverty, which in turn feeds urban poverty. And we all know the phenomenon of rural-urban migration. I used to argue with demographers who said, "The future of Africa is urbanization." I'd say, "It depends on whether we are on a path of sustainable urbanization or an unsustainable one." And we know what happens in the urban areas in terms of unemployment and other problems.

For agricultural development and transformation to take place, we need to go back to the policy explanations of the failure to engage in this process. I will give a short historical perspective.

Immediately after independence, many of our countries rushed to leapfrog directly to industrialization. This effort was combined with urban bias policies and state control policies. All those policies resulted in excessive taxation of agriculture, which never succeeded in creating any capital at its own level. We were not funding agriculture; we were taxing agriculture, without any sustainable productivity gains, and this cannot lead to sustainable transformation.

After that, we went into a phase of piecemeal projects that were not closely related to each other. We focused on single crops, on credit issues, on irrigation extension, but in a piecemeal manner without a comprehensive strategy or approach.

Then we went into integrated rural development projects. I happened to work at the African Development Bank for a few years, and we did a good evaluation of those projects. They succeeded in places where there was adequate institutional capacity, but because of the complexity of the projects, in the face of a lack of human and institutional capacity, they failed in most cases.

All these stages happened in the 1960s, '70s, and '80s in the context of a deteriorating structural and macroeconomic policy environment. Then, starting in the 1980s, we shifted gears and adopted structural adjustment and macroeconomic policy reforms. But in so doing, we forgot about central issues. We worked very well on the macro context, but when we look at the evolution of investment in agriculture, we start seeing the clear decline during that period. As a result, the agricultural sector in Africa is one of the most undercapitalized in the world today. The statistics, like percentage of area under irrigation, fertilizers used, and so forth, are well known to everybody. Because of this undercapitalization, we began to see low or declining productivity in agriculture. Africa is the only region in the world where per capita food production has been declining.

There is no miracle. In order to seriously attack food insecurity and nutrition insecurity, we have to come back to consistency. Coming back to consistency can be seen in two ways. We can look at it either in terms of technological, institutional, infrastructural, and policy requirements or in terms of different pillars within the agricultural sector.

One of the first pillars to work on is the market at the national, regional, and even global levels. We know that our markets are incomplete. They are poorly endowed with infrastructure, with information, and with market intelligence. On the world scene we are facing difficulties in accessing global markets, but we have not even developed our own markets. We should start by developing domestic and regional markets.

If we have markets functioning well, the second pillar is water. It is not by accident that the NEPAD Comprehensive Africa Agriculture Development Programme, which is estimated to have a cost of US$250 billion, devotes more than 50 percent of its cost to water management.

The agricultural sector in Africa is one of the most undercapitalized in the world today.

— Josué Dioné

The third pillar is land. There are not only soil fertility issues, but also serious issues of security of land tenure. Land tenure issues should be considered not only within countries, but also between countries, in the context of regional integration. If we want mobility of investment within Africa, we have to secure that investment.

Next is science and technology. Along those lines, some proponents at the Economic Commission support the idea of developing regional research centers of excellence. One other topic that has been touched upon is the HIV/AIDS pandemic, which is threatening the very survival of agricultural people. If we do not tackle this problem seriously, all that we are doing about markets, technologies, and so forth will fail. This pandemic presents us with a puzzle regarding technology. How can we decide whether to pursue labor-saving technologies or land-saving technologies if we do not know what is happening to the labor force in the first place? What kinds of technologies are we going to develop for the next generation of farmers? What will be the land-to-labor ratio? We have to think about these questions.

Rosebud Kurwijila

Commissioner for Rural Economy and Agriculture, African Union, Ethiopia

First, what is the most common cause of food and nutrition insecurity? It is inadequate food supply, brought about by low agricultural productivity. We all know the causes of low agricultural productivity: dependence on rain for our agriculture, a low level of knowledge about agricultural production practices, an insufficient supply of inputs, and the high cost of inputs. All of these bring about low agricultural productivity. But inadequate food supply is not the only cause of food and nutrition insecurity.

Inadequate distribution of and access to food are among the important causes of food and nutrition insecurity, and these causes arise from market failures and low household income levels. Market failures lead to inadequate distribution of and access to food by hindering food produced in one area from being supplied to another area. I will come back to access to markets in another point. And if you have low household income, you have income poverty, which reduces your purchasing power and prevents you from gaining access to food that you do not produce.

Nutrition insecurity, especially at the household level in rural areas, is exacerbated by several factors. One factor is ignorance about the right kind and combination of food served in the right environment—that is, with the right sanitation. Another factor is related to traditional cultural practices that prohibit the eating of certain kinds of foods, mainly by women and children. In communities where these practices are followed, women and children are the ones who really suffer from nutrition insecurity. Another factor is change in eating habits and diet. For example, when communities that are used to eating soybean nuts and cassava, which are drought-resistant crops and are available throughout the year, shift to eating foods like maize and rice, which are not always readily available, they may experience nutrition insecurity.

> *It is time for Africa to put the role of women in food and nutrition security high on the agenda of priorities.*
>
> — Rosebud Kurwijila

Most African countries engage in subsistence agriculture. We produce only for eating; we do not produce for the market. Commercialization of agriculture, even at the grassroots level, can eliminate income poverty and boost food security. Producing for the market can raise the income levels of households, so that they can purchase the foods they do not produce.

With commercialization of agriculture, we come to the issue of market access. This issue is also linked to production. With access to markets, farmers have an incentive to produce more because they know they have somewhere to sell their products. So market access is very important to food security.

Another issue is the role of women in food and nutrition security. Women are the producers of food. Women are the people who prepare food for their families. Women are responsible for the distribution of food at the family level. Yet women in many African countries do not have access to and control over land, and this limits the types of food crops they can grow. Because they do not own or control land, they cannot easily diversify their food crops in order to meet the nutritional requirements of their families. Women do not have the nutritional knowledge required to enable them to balance the quality of the food that they serve to their families. And women do not have access to technologies that enable them to process and preserve food to be eaten during times of food shortage. Moreover, women do not have access to independent income to enable them to buy the food that they do not produce. If women cannot buy food, it is difficult for them to

You need to be able to make farming into a business enterprise, which then generates more income and gives people more disposable money.

— Robbie Mupawose

balance the food they serve their family. It is time for Africa to put the role of women in food and nutrition security high on the agenda of priorities.

At the macro level, another point concerns the issue of political will. Some African governments are trying to devote sufficient resources to the agricultural sector, but in most African countries the national budget allocation to agriculture is very low. For this reason African heads of state pledged at the July 2003 Maputo Summit to allocate at least 10 percent of the national budget to agriculture, and they reaffirmed this declaration at the Extraordinary Summit on agriculture that took place in Sirte in February this year.

Another point at the macro level is the failure to translate macroeconomic policies to the micro, grassroots level. Many African countries now have poverty reduction strategies, for example, but how many of these strategies are translated to the grassroots level or even understood at the grassroots level?

There are other reasons why Africa has not achieved food and nutrition security, including rural-urban migration and the prevalence of HIV/AIDS, which erode the labor force for agriculture.

Robbie Mupawose

Chairman, Barclays Bank of Zimbabwe, Zimbabwe

Is it really food and nutrition we are concerned about? I am more concerned about the quality of life of our people, because that issue is more encompassing than the issue of food and nutrition per se. The quality of life of our people is decided by a number of factors, one of which is people's incomes. How can people end up with enough income to benefit themselves?

A family or a nation does not have to produce food to have food self-sufficiency. But if you do not have the means of purchasing food, then you have no choice but to produce. We lack activities that generate incomes for people to acquire food. As a result, they must produce their own food. Of course, we have had to import, for which you need foreign currency, and we do not always have that.

Those activities that can generate incomes for people are activities outside agriculture: industry, trade, tourism. One of the presidents gave a statistic this morning: 3 percent of Americans are involved in agriculture. So why must every African be a farmer? That idea must be killed in people's minds forever, because there are many people who have better occupations than farming. Farming is one of the hardest occupations you can be involved in—I know that because I am a farmer.

We need to get our governments to think more seriously about developing the economy overall. Agriculture will never survive and grow in an environment where there is no economic growth. Most of our farming is subsistence, not commercial. Farmers do not even keep records about, for instance, whether they produced more bananas this year than last year. You need to be able to make farming into a business enterprise, which then generates more income and gives people more disposable money.

A business base, an industrial base, or a trade base absorbs the productivity of agriculture. Without reasonable internal growth in a country to help absorb the products grown there, farmers must try to sell them somewhere else. So we need to increase the number of people who have enough income to be able to purchase produce.

How much time do rural people have to farm? Half the time they are being called to rallies and political meetings. And most of the farmers are women who must also bear children, carry water, and look for firewood. Yet they do not own the land in some of the countries we come from. The man owns the farm and he is never there, so the decisionmaking is left to somebody who does not actually know what goes on on the farm.

We need to find a way for the women, the entrepreneurs themselves, to decide and dictate. They need to be given the title to the land. Let those people who are operating on the land have rights to it. Why

Let those people who are operating on the land have rights to it. Why should I invest my own money or borrow money to invest in a capital asset that I do not own and that might be taken away from me the next day?

— Robbie Mupawose

should I invest my own money or borrow money to invest in a capital asset that I do not own and that might be taken away from me the next day?

Land must be marketable. Plots of land are too small for the rural people. In Zimbabwe, for example, we undertake a land reform in which we give farmers 5 hectares. But the real farmer wants maybe 20, 50, 100, 200 hectares. Can enterprising farmers acquire the land, buy their neighbors' land, and let their neighbors work for them? What's wrong with that? They become more productive and therefore contribute to greater growth.

There are also problems with the quantity, quality, and size of the land. We have had soil depletion and tillage problems. People till by the hoe. If you have a small plot of land, you cannot justify mechanization, you cannot justify growth. Economies of scale do not exist.

Horticulture offers an opportunity for growth that we should take advantage of in most of our countries, where markets are waiting.

We also need to find a way to develop linkages between business, government, and farmers and to develop entrepreneurship skills so that markets can supply the goods and the quality of produce demanded.

One area on which we spend little time is the quality of the farmer associations and the leadership of the farmers. They tend to be led by the politicians. We need to listen to the farmers. Governments do not listen to the farmers; they tell the farmers. Why don't the farmers lead themselves? We need to develop commodity associations of farmers so that the farmers can talk to each other and produce beyond subsistence.

We need to leapfrog from poverty to wealth, and biotechnology is one tool we need to take advantage of to do this. Some people say, "What about GMOs?" I am not scared of growing horns because I might eat GM products. The split of the atom showed the energy of the atom, and biotechnology has shown the strength of the cell. Why should we hang behind and wait for other people to leapfrog? We must use scientists to help us leapfrog to greater advances, more growth, and stronger markets.

Finally, if there is no peace and tranquility, if you are just fighting wars, there will be no production.

Mandivamba Rukuni

Program Director, W. K. Kellogg Foundation, South Africa

I would like to give you my interpretation of what has happened since 1960 when we started having the independence wave in Africa.

At that time, Africans actually thought we could skip certain stages of development and pretend agriculture was not very important in getting us into an urban industrial society. By 1980, however, when the Lagos Plan of Action was put in place, African heads of state had agreed that agriculture is important.

Our governments and our donors alike are still experimenting to find the research and extension models that will work in Africa.

— Mandivamba Rukuni

African governments at that time were spending less than 10 percent of their gross domestic product (GDP) on agriculture, but they agreed to increase it. By the new millennium, however, the figure still had not increased. The political will was there, or shall I say, although the spirit was willing, the flesh still was refusing to come forward, for various good reasons.

One reason was the difficulty faced in the 1980s by the old political parties that came to power with a political liberation agenda and found that economic liberation is even more difficult to achieve. With structural adjustment programs and other such efforts in place, it was not easy. The urban few in Africa are very powerful. If you subsidized their food yesterday and you remove the subsidy today, it doesn't matter that they are the minority—they can take you out of power.

So Africa is the only region in the world where the numbers of hungry and malnourished people continue to increase. Although the Millennium Development Goals say we will halve these numbers by 2015, Africa is the only region where these numbers are projected to grow. We have about 200 million hungry people today; by 2020, we are projected to have 300 million. So there is a time lag between wishing that we invested more in this area and actually finding means of doing it.

My second point is that the policy environment continues to be somewhat unfriendly to agriculture, although it has improved a bit. The macroeconomic policy environment is more or less stabilized in Africa, but too much effort was put behind the structural adjustment programs, getting the exchange rates right, and all that. These programs did not address the key problem of leveling the playing field for agriculture. That problem still remains.

The third issue is that those key institutions that support smallholder farmers in Africa through research, extension, and training are still weak. Even the capacity

My message here is that what we need is to modernize, not to Westernize.

— Mandivamba Rukuni

of the private sector to supply the needs and inputs of farmers is very weak. After decades of experimenting with different models, it is clear now that the colonial models do not work for our smallholder farmers.

The transitions over the last 20 or 30 years have been enormous. I can group them into four major transitions: a management transition from colonial models to local administrative systems; a scientific transition from expatriate-based science to indigenous scientists; a financial transition from spending on a large-scale, plantation-type, colonial economy to support from our governments and from donors; and a political transition from the powerful commercial farms to smallholder farmers, who may not be as politically powerful. At the end of the day, it is clear that our governments and our donors alike are still experimenting to find the research and extension models that will work in Africa.

The issue of security of tenure and property rights was raised, and I would like to add two points. First, the issue should be looked at broadly in terms of how African society can transition from a primarily agrarian society to an industrialized society down the road. History has shown that if the land tenure and property rights issue is not addressed properly, that transition can be very painful. In Africa the major issue is not whether our traditional systems of tenure should be replaced by colonial or Western types. I believe that the traditional tenurial systems are the best that we have. But we have not looked at them carefully; we have just done the same thing the colonialists did.

In my part of the world, the colonialists were the British. They did not understand what the Africans were doing. Somebody had a piece of land behind the hill, another one near the river; and the British thought this was crazy. In fact, the system works just as well as the Western system because it includes the four major rights that are to be safeguarded: the right for various uses of that land; the right to transfer that land to others in the family and in the clan; the right to ensure that others do not violate your rights; and finally the right to have the state enforce these rights on behalf of citizens. If local legal and administrative processes safeguard those rights, the traditional system of tenure can be just as secure as any other tenure. But most of us Africans have had a difficult time distinguishing between modernizing and Westernizing. My message here is that what we need is to modernize, not to Westernize.

Then, there is the issue of longstanding underinvestment in social and physical capital in Africa. This situation leads to centralization of the key economic infrastructure in the urban areas. The rural road infrastructure in Africa today is poorer than what India had even before the Green Revolution. Africa is a large continent physically, and we Africans are spread thinly. It is a continent that is a lot more difficult to supply with roads, electricity, telephones, and so on. The same applies to provision of health and educational assistance.

Sixth is the issue of technology to transform traditional agriculture. I will break it into two parts. What you might call "embodied technology" is technology embodied in some kind of physical attribute, such as machinery, seeds, or chemicals. We just do not have the industrial capacity to produce these things. Our "disembodied technology"—knowledge-based technology—is not too bad. But when you put everything together, we still badly need technology that is actually going to transform our agriculture.

Finally, there is the shortage of labor, which is another paradox in Africa. There is always an assumption that because we are so poor and so rural, labor must be in abundant supply. But as Isatou Jallow said this morning, actually there is no labor. The women, who do most of the work, are already overworked.

Someone told me an interesting statistic the other day. To educate an African to the level of a master's degree or Ph.D., as most of us here are, costs the equivalent of 150 peasant-years. That is how expensive we are. But once we get that education, we look at it as a means of escaping poverty in the rural areas and do not invest anything back there.

I strongly believe that as long as productivity in agriculture remains low because labor productivity is low and because educated people do not invest in agriculture, it is a self-fulfilling prophecy that people are going to remain poor for a long time.

To educate an African to the level of a master's degree or Ph.D., as most of us here are, costs the equivalent of 150 peasant-years.

— Mandivamba Rukuni

Excerpt 3: Development Strategies and Food and Nutrition Security in Africa: An Assessment

Franz Heidhues, Achi Atsain, Hezron Nyangito, Martine Padilla, Gérard Ghersi, and Jean-Charles Le Vallée

Two early responses to African socioeconomic development crises were the Lagos Plan of Action (LPA) and the Regional Food Plan for Africa (AFPLAN). These started from the premise that, given the limited size and capacity of the private sector, the states had to take on the dominant role in development. Thus governments drew up comprehensive five-year plans, invested in large state-run basic industries and market structures, and enacted pervasive regulations to control prices, restrict trade, and allocate credit and foreign exchange, all generally carried out with full donor support. Publicly funded programs in support of agricultural research and extension, fertilizer supply, export production and marketing, and food distribution were the essential components of this approach.

When by 1980 it had become apparent that Africa's crisis was deepening, the World Bank and IMF argued that a fundamental shift in approach was needed to stabilize African economies, increase efficiency of investment, and reinvigorate growth. Their new concept of structural adjustment programs (SAPs) implied a move away from state-dominated development to reliance on the private sector. Food and nutrition security were addressed only indirectly in these programs through the aims of improved economic stability and higher economic growth.

In response to concerns about the deleterious impact of SAPs on health services, education, infrastructure, rural support institutions, and employment, all of which had particularly affected Africa's poor, the approach of the World Bank and donor community shifted. The Comprehensive Development Framework (CDF) and the Poverty Reduction Strategy Papers (PRSPs) both emphasized the need to integrate cultural, social, political, and environmental considerations into development strategies, and to apply these considerations to reducing poverty and creating a framework for pro-poor growth. The emphasis on poverty in the CDF/PRSP concept implies that agricultural and rural development were envisioned as playing vitally important roles.

Building on the CDF/PRSP process, African leaders at the turn of the century developed the New Partnership for Africa's Development (NEPAD). This approach intended to combine African initiatives and ownership of the development process with neoliberal concepts. The NEPAD strategy seeks to produce agriculture-led development that eliminates hunger and reduces poverty as well as food insecurity.

SAPs and PRSPs have shaped regional approaches and country policies and their implementation throughout Africa. A significant number of African countries have carried out successful programs of macroeconomic stabilization and structural reform. Reforms and retrenchment of the public sector have been carried out in numerous countries, although often at the costs of increasing unemployment—and thus vulnerability to food and nutrition insecurity—and a decline in public services, even in essential areas such as health, education, and research and extension.

Many countries have formulated poverty reduction policies, with an increased emphasis on agricultural development. More progress is needed in key areas, however, such as in reducing social and economic discrimination against women. Similarly, in areas such as employment creation, natural resource protection, and governance reform, some countries have initiated encouraging measures, but much more progress is needed. The most successful reformers have been countries without war or civil unrest, and with reform processes characterized by strong political leadership and a commitment to reforms with wide domestic participation and ownership.

This has been excerpted from 2020 Discussion Paper 38, published by IFPRI, Washington, DC, 2004.

Part II | Priorities for Action: Perspectives from the Regions

Chapter 4 Southern Africa

Chair: Bongiwe Njobe
Director General, National Department of Agriculture, South Africa

Moderator: Tobias Takavarasha
Chief Executive Officer, Food, Agriculture, and Natural Resource Policy Analysis Network (FANRPAN), Zimbabwe

Rapporteur: Andrew Temu
Visiting Research Fellow, International Food Policy Research Institute (IFPRI), USA

Johann Frederick Kirsten

Professor and Head, Department of Agricultural Economics, Extension, and Rural Development, University of Pretoria, South Africa

Agriculture, industry, and trade have experienced a serious crisis in Africa since 1980. This crisis can be traced back to the three pillars of the Washington Consensus, namely, fiscal austerity, privatization, and market liberalization, and to the related debt crisis in Africa. In Southern Africa climatic shocks such as recent floods in Mozambique and the 2002 drought in most countries led to short-term food security crises.

The February 2004 Southern Africa Development Community (SADC) Food Security Update summarizes Southern African food security as follows:

> The combined effect of poor rains and reduced area planted to main crops is likely to result in a crop harvest that is lower than last season's output of 22.93 million tons. The SADC region will therefore not be able to cover its cereal requirement for the 2004/2005 marketing year. The current food security situation remains poor in most Member States, with the number of households running out of food continuing to increase as the region enters its lean period before the next main harvest.

Clearly, urgent action is required. In trying to list priorities for action, I am, however, weary of falling into the trap of just listing items that we all know and that often appear at the end of a presentation or in the concluding chapter of a report—that is, good governance, funding for agricultural research and extension, investment in infrastructure, access to credit, input and output markets, and so on. It is very easy to fall into this trap, as Steve Omamo showed in a 2003 paper. He argued that agricultural policy advice in Africa has generally provided these stereotypical solutions without determining why markets and systems are imperfect and not functioning. Before one identifies priorities for action and designs policies, therefore, it is much more important to focus on the questions "how" and "at what cost." Case studies and networking analysis can highlight the institutional architecture of subsectors by also showing how different actors behave or make decisions. These aspects are often critical in identifying the most appropriate actions for achieving food and nutrition security.

I argue that politics at the community level, within local and national government, in parliament, and within business is often responsible for the poor func-

Before one identifies priorities for action and designs policies, therefore, it is much more important to focus on the questions "how" and "at what cost."

— Johann Frederick Kirsten

tioning of systems, institutions, and markets and for the lack of business opportunities. Many of the challenges of food and nutrition security can be met if all role players and stakeholders are committed to a common vision and strategy. Ensuring that all stakeholders (government departments, politicians, farmers' unions and their leaders, traders, agribusiness, community leaders) are committed to achieving the vision of a food- and nutrition-secure continent would be one of the first priorities for action. Political will and commitment are sometimes necessary for interventions to bear any fruit, and if all stakeholders internalized the same vision and strategic plans, it would go a long way in assuring food and nutrition security in Africa by 2020.

As far as specific priorities for action, increasing domestic agricultural production remains the main vehicle to reduce food insecurity in countries, including SADC countries, in which agriculture is still a leading contributor to gross domestic product. First, we need to determine why domestic agricultural production is failing. What factors are inhibiting commercial production? Often they go beyond the obvious and relate more to institutional, sociological, human behavioral, political, and other "softer" issues that policy analysts usually ignore.

The needs of the poorest groups can be addressed effectively through vegetable and fruit gardens, which play an important role in improving the flow and composition of nutrition. But additional spending geared to this end should be carefully balanced against alternative approaches, such as boosting welfare grants or delivering more food parcels, both indispensable short-term measures. Investment in agriculture should yield sustained benefits in the long run, but achieving these benefits will require an equally sustained commitment by the public sector to spending and institutional restructuring. Reducing the constraints on food production faced by low-income households and convincing them of the returns to be had from devoting more of their own resources to agriculture is not a short-term task. Support systems and information are necessary to create a conducive framework from which productive agricultural activities will flow spontaneously.

Beyond measures to raise income and agricultural output, there is a need for both proactive and reactive systems to address acute food insecurity brought on by disasters such as droughts, floods, and political instability. Accessibility is a critical consideration. Although vulnerability assessment, early warning, and emergency distribution systems are all now being developed, they are still in their infancy. As clearly identifiable public

Conference participants Bongiwe Njobe and Mandivamba Rukuni confer between sessions.

goods or services with obvious positive externalities, these should be high priorities for public spending. But the challenge posed by this group of needs extends well beyond the allocation of additional fiscal resources: more than money, it requires closer communication, coordination, and collaboration between governments at all levels and between government, nongovernmental organizations, and the private sector.

Low-income households are particularly vulnerable to price increases, especially the kinds of sudden and often sustained increases that are not compensated for to some degree by a rise in nominal income. The incidence of such increases has grown markedly over the past decade with the deregulation of agricultural markets and the exceptional volatility of the South African currency, affecting food markets in the whole region. It is therefore a priority to consider the merits of a regional grain exchange or a strategic grain reserve to counter sharp increases and fluctuations in the prices of staple commodities. Whether grain reserves are the best way of achieving this remains a hotly contested debate.

In a region where development issues are a high priority, as in Southern Africa, it makes sense to try to join disaster management and development efforts wherever possible. Some shorter-term actions, including relief efforts and preparedness, are high-priority actions. These are essential, particularly when food stress is heightened by events such as floods and droughts. In the medium term, however, such actions need to be complemented with a longer-term, risk-reduction approach. This will require serious investments in enhancing the capacity of public institutions; interfaces between government and the public; research support; appropriate data collection, use, and sharing; and

The high cost of road transport between South Africa and its neighbors also affects food security in the region.

— Johann Frederick Kirsten

analytical capacity for strategy development, such as vulnerability assessments and livelihoods information systems.

Finally, efficiently functioning transport networks are important to any competitive economy and are the key to a successful food security strategy. Because of the inefficiency of the region's rail network (slow turnaround time, limited number of trucks), transport of most grains has gradually moved to roads, and this shift has contributed to increased raw material costs at the mill door or factory gate. The high cost of road transport between South Africa and its neighbors also affects food security in the region on a more macro scale. Improving the logistical aspects of rail and road transport in Southern Africa should therefore also be an important priority for action.

Finally, it should be noted that the efforts toward good governance and infrastructure development discussed here are meaningless without the elimination of agricultural subsidies and market access barriers in developed countries.

Ajay Vashee

President, Southern African Confederation of Agricultural Unions (SACAU), Zambia

To find solutions to "how," we must deal with strategy. To change from one state to a desired future state requires a course of action. This IFPRI conference is well timed to add to the growing chorus of voices agitating for a new deal for African agriculture.

We just completed a milestone event for farmer organizations in Africa—articulating a continental position on CAADP, the NEPAD plan for agriculture. We submitted a statement on behalf of all farmers in Africa at the FAO regional ministerial deliberations. Many of the insights and views presented here are drawn from the work done during the event.

Farming is inherently a rural activity affecting rural economies. We have an important role to play as producers, but we caution that looking to farmers as the panacea will ignore the contribution that nonfarming rural enterprises can make to alleviating the challenges of rural economies. Accordingly, farmers' organizations in Southern Africa believe that two complementary strategies should be pursued:

1. optimizing agricultural output by farmers—this has a national and regional dimension; and
2. ensuring that rural development policies and practices lead to the growth of rural areas—this is a likely impact of successful farming.

In Southern Africa in 2000, people faced food shortages in a region that technically has the agricultural potential to feed itself and produce net surpluses. Such an anomaly demands urgent attention.

Large historical disparities between white and black farmers are prevalent in South Africa, Namibia, and Zimbabwe. These disparities call for actions to redress the unequal access to land. This is a political process that needs to be implemented in a way that benefits all farmers without hindering agricultural output and investor confidence in the region.

Improving the technical ability of farmers is an imperative that needs no further justification.

Access to international markets is an absolute requirement for this region to reap the benefits of improved technologies and infrastructure upgrading. We cannot simply trade with each other, as we produce similar products. Empirically, it appears that the SADC Trade Agreement could result in a 10 percent improvement in trade volumes for Southern African farmers. Therefore, to harness the potential benefits of trade, the region's capacity to negotiate international trade must be improved. But at the same time, given the volatility of global commodity prices, coupled with large currency

Access to international markets is an absolute requirement for this region to reap the benefits of improved technologies and infrastructure upgrading. We cannot simply trade with each other, as we produce similar products.

— Ajay Vashee

swings, a price support mechanism ought to be developed for farmers.

Infrastructure for farming has been neglected in many countries as governments supported other economic priorities, primarily rapid urbanization. The drastic decline in public expenditures for agriculture is well documented. The casualty is rural infrastructure: roads, storage, electricity, communications, schools, and hospitals, with the concomitant lowering of production.

Even if farmers have ideal circumstances to produce, the impact on the rural economy will be marginal if other complementary strategies are ignored. We must think of the entire rural supply chain as an opportunity. We also have to invest time and money into researching the linkages that can be exploited to the benefit of the rural economy. Small manufacturing concerns that add value through agroprocessing have a big role to play in solving rural poverty.

Although we expect good governments to promote food security, this ideal often leads governments to pursue interventions that harm producers. Instances where food imports or food aid lead to the collapse of local commodity prices are common. This result not only leads to an inadvertent transfer of rural wealth to the urban areas, but also erodes sustainable productive capacities, rendering rural farmers worse off than they were. Therefore, it is important to balance the enhancement of sustainable agriculture against food security. We have to depoliticize the food issue and allow farmers a reasonable return for their efforts. Governments, donors, and other supporters all have important roles to play in contributing to this rural revival.

Health and welfare programs in rural environments have too few resources. HIV/AIDS has affected agriculture disproportionately. Because rural areas have few safety nets, rural producers are burdened with unnecessary social costs. The public sector has neglected schooling, care for the aged, and proper health services in rural areas and needs to become better at providing them.

Rural enterprise support in this context involves putting in place the enabling environment that can result in entrepreneurial development, and not just farming. But this growth is also dependent on stable macroeconomic fundamentals, where inflation, the exchange rate, and interest rates are reasonable.

Farmers' organizations can contribute at the policy, strategy, and operational levels to programs and projects aimed at rural poverty alleviation, provided they accept that for poverty programs in agriculture to be sustainable and successful, they have to use the market. This means farmers have to be business oriented. Few national organizations have the institutional capacity to take up the challenge, and most would need organizational strengthening. Assuming this occurs, and there is every likelihood that it could, farmer organizations are well placed in a few areas.

Our voice as farmers must be heard as we all grapple with creating a viable agricultural sector in Africa.

— Ajay Vashee

Starting at the operational level, farmer organizations are best suited to offer development services to existing and potential members. Many farmers' organizations offer training, business services, and technical support. This role can be extended to project management of larger infrastructure investments.

National agricultural policy is firmly in the hands of national governments. Farmers' organizations are important stakeholders and rely on government to fight for benefits for agriculture. We wish to be contributing stakeholders and can be a bridge between our members and the government. As we develop capacity as farmers' organizations, we become more skilled at presenting technically sound views and sophisticated arguments. At the very least, we expect any actor who is planning initiatives aimed at or affecting farmers to adopt an inclusive approach.

Our voice as farmers must be heard as we all grapple with creating a viable agricultural sector in Africa.

Discussion

The discussion centered on two broad themes: the basis for taking action to address food and nutrition security, and the key areas for specific action. Participants sought to better understand these issues and challenges, acknowledging the diversity of Southern Africa.

Issues related to markets and trade figured prominently in the discussions. Participants asked why domestic markets fail so often. They acknowledged transportation challenges, including those related to roads and railways, and the way in which they impose high trade costs. It was noted that transportation challenges buttress other marketing transaction costs, albeit differently in various localities. The strengthening of institutions, in the form of laws and regulations, was recognized as a means to cultivate incentives. Farmers' organizations were mentioned as a way to tap economies of scale, and it was noted that farmers act best as groups, despite the fact that policies have often undermined collective actions. The operational and market impacts of strategic food reserves were also mentioned.

Domestic government interventions in, for example, input and output markets and credit markets emerged as a concern. Given the ways in which market distortions send the wrong signals, leading farmers to make suboptimal investment decisions, participants noted the need to acknowledge past mistakes and look critically at the role of the public sector in these areas. Participants also discussed subsidies on inputs and noted that central to the debate of subsidies versus measures for equalization is the question of whether subsidies represent a socioeconomic transfer or a support to cushion the disadvantaged.

The challenges of an uneven playing field for trade, particularly protectionist agricultural policies and the divide between North and South, were raised and solutions discussed. The capacity to negotiate in international trade dialogues was also mentioned as a concern, and it was recommended that available capacities, as well as the negative effects and costs of deficiencies, be assessed. Participants also discussed the role of the NEPAD, emphasizing the need to ensure that it delivers the expected advancements in the area of trade.

It was noted that to serve and develop markets, a change in mindset is needed to overcome the inherent government mistrust of the private sector. Participants recommended looking further into patterns of private sector development and the potential for public-private sector collaboration in markets.

In terms of the key role of institutions and partnerships, participants pointed to the need for laws and regulations to govern agricultural marketing. They noted the important role of marketing organizations, especially grassroots farmers' organizations, and organizational relationships linking private sector organizations, philanthropic nongovernmental organizations, and public service institutions. The need to create partnerships and relationships, particularly between developed and developing countries, donors and donor recipient countries, and countries in the North and South, as well as among countries in the South, was recognized.

The hidden dimensions of the effects of food aid were also raised during the discussion. Participants commented that food aid often arrives too late, stays too long, and on certain occasions, acquires a political dimension, thereby depressing domestic markets. Food aid can hinder regional trade, and it is important to examine the past and future role of domestic governments in redressing, preventing, and mitigating its effects. The need to limit food aid to rational scales and to always be aware of its negative effects was highlighted. Other comments on food aid mentioned the need to take measures to mitigate its negative effects, to share information to better guide aid management, and to develop effective modes of delivering food aid.

Participants emphasized the importance of human capacity and human resources in enhancing agricultural productivity. The need for research and development of relevant technologies to enhance productivity in Africa was also high-

---

Owing to technical difficulties, the discussion in this session was not audio recorded. Certain elements of the discussion may inadvertently have been left out of this report.

lighted. Issues of natural resource management were brought up in the context of increasing agricultural productivity within sustainable water and land management paradigms. There were pleas for new visions and methods in agricultural research and for the scaling up of successes.

The linkages of HIV/AIDS to lowered productivity and food and nutrition insecurity were noted. Participants urged that special attention be paid to vulnerable groups and called for mainstreaming issues of women and youth.

Participants suggest several actions for the Southern Africa region:

- Invest in capacity building and public awareness through innovative approaches;
- Develop the best means to deploy land and water resources with a regional perspective;
- Provide cash instead of food aid;
- Design and build capacity within farmer organizations using innovative and intuitive methods;
- Design mechanisms to mitigate price fluctuations and stabilize prices;
- Strengthen capacity to prioritize actions, acknowledging that stakeholders are diverse;
- Instigate production planning for the region;
- Mobilize young, trained citizens to engage in agriculture;
- Finance both small- and large-scale water management systems for irrigation and agroprocessing;
- Map out and prioritize investments in cross-border routes to tap into intraregional trade potentials, making use of existing regional bodies;
- Strategically target youths as a key dimension of poverty;
- Undertake proactive and joint efforts and initiatives from within the subregion to penetrate markets in the North;
- Take stock of and document the effects of market distortions, beyond the first category effects on national income;
- Design better mechanisms to generate information in the areas of food aid, in order to create more dignified assistance during periods of food need, and articulate roles and modes of engagement for donors and governments in a different manner from the past; and
- Create regional clearing organs to oversee, authenticate, and sanction strategic reserves, technology, and knowledge and resource links, including patents.

Chapter 5 West Africa

Chair: Mamadou Kone
Minister of Scientific Research, Côte d'Ivoire

Moderator: Achi Atsain
President, West African Economic Association (WAEA); President Network of Ivorian Intellectuals for Peace, Democracy and Governance; and former Minister of Employment, Civil Service, and Social Welfare, Côte d'Ivoire

Rapporteur: Tidiane Ngaido
Research Fellow, International Food Policy Research Institute and International Center for Agricultural Research in the Dry Areas (ICARDA), Senegal

Rosanna Agble

Chief Nutrition Officer, Ghana Health Service, Ghana

In the opinion poll conducted just before this session, I was not surprised that the majority of people believe food security can be achieved by 2020, but not nutrition security. Nutrition security requires three main factors—food, health, and care—and these three have to work together if we are to achieve nutrition security.

What are the requirements to ensure a successful and sustainable food and nutrition program? We have heard a long list of reasons for our problems. My intention is not to go through that long list, but to look at the issues that we must address to ensure that we achieve nutrition security.

I have placed them under three different headings. First, there are technical issues. As we see, even in the representation at this meeting, there is a lack of personnel adequately trained in nutrition. In addition, there is a lack of understanding of nutrition issues among policymakers. People think nutrition is just putting a plate on the table and putting food on it, but nutrition encompasses more than that.

Moreover, nutrition has not been related to development issues, but is looked at as a humanitarian issue. Unless nutrition shifts from a humanitarian to a development issue, it will always fall through the cracks.

The perception of nutrition among the general public is also an issue because nutrition is complex: you have to look at food, health, and care in achieving interventions in nutrition. Because of its complex nature, it is difficult to implement these interventions.

Second, there are political issues that prevent nutrition programs from being achieved. Nutrition fits poorly within government structure. Sometimes people tell me, "Oh, nutrition—you belong to agriculture." Then somebody else will say, "Nutrition—you belong to health." Each sector has its own mandate, which does not include nutrition. Where are we? That is a major issue.

The policies at national and institutional levels usually do not take nutrition into consideration, much less allocate resources to nutrition. In the health sector—if nutrition is represented, it is in the health sector—there are so many other competing programs that nutrition gets what is left. If it is in the agricultural sector, the same thing happens. Nutrition is so heavily involved in production, but we fail to outline the nutrition issues that should be addressed in agriculture.

Next, nutrition does not come with visible achievements. Any politician will say, "I built a school for my

People think nutrition is just putting a plate on the table and putting food on it, but nutrition encompasses more than that.

— Rosanna Agble

community" or "I built hospitals." You do not see nutrition that way.

Under the third heading are institutional problems, and these concern mostly partnerships. We need strong partnerships between the sectors of food, health, and care. I am not talking about the sort of partnership where you sit around a table, agree on a program, and somebody says, "Find me the money, and I will do it." We need partnerships where people are convinced to go back to their sectors and to implement programs that have been outlined.

There is little partnership between the nutrition sector and the agricultural sector. Because of the very set-up of these two disciplines, they often do not work in unison, but instead sometimes even see themselves competing.

Partnerships are also needed between nutritionists and other sectors, such as education. In my country we are always talking about the low levels of education, and we are always quick to blame teachers, lack of textbooks, and other things. But have we looked at the children—these children who go to school hungry, who are anemic, who have lower IQs because of iron deficiency? Maybe they are absorbing to their fullest capacity and because of these nutritional issues, we are not seeing the real benefit of education.

Partnerships are needed with other professionals in the health sector, such as doctors, nurses, and health educators, and with professionals in the agricultural sector. We also need partnerships between nutritionists and researchers. We have enough research telling us what the problem is. What we need is operational research that will move us forward, and results packaged in a way that is user-friendly to policymakers.

Partnerships between the private and public sector are useful for nutrition education, and by partnering with existing community structures and cultural traditions, nutrition can also address the human capacity issues in the region.

What are some of the priorities for moving forward? There is a need to build strong political support and relate nutrition to development. There is a need to build effective collaborations within and among sectors. And there is a need to identify strong, visionary leaders in nutrition and advocates at national and subnational levels. Not only nutritionists, but also people in other sectors and disciplines can be advocates for nutrition. And finally, there is a need to set up a proactive agenda in nutrition that includes the marketing of nutrition.

There are opportunities, both at the country level and at the regional level, to ensure that the institutions with which we are working move forward. The nutrition profiles that many countries in the subregion are working on are very strong advocacy tools. The decentralization in many countries in our subregion also offers opportunities, if we advocate at all levels.

There is a need to identify strong, visionary leaders in nutrition and advocates at national and subnational levels. Not only nutritionists, but also people in other sectors and disciplines can be advocates for nutrition.

— Rosanna Agble

We need to look at nutrition issues and relate them to other existing programs. We also need to identify and train people in nonformal structures. In our subregion, when people are sick, they often first use herbal medicine, or women may use traditional birth attendants. We have to look at ways of incorporating nutritional knowledge into these practices. We need to use available media in all of our countries to promote nutrition.

All of the countries in the subregions have agreed to the Millennium Development Goals. In each of those eight goals, there are opportunities to integrate nutrition. The poverty reduction strategy papers in all the countries also give opportunities to integrate nutrition into programs.

The regional structure ECOWAS (Economic Community of West African States) comprises the heads of state in the region and offers a forum where we can advocate for nutrition. Within ECOWAS, the West African Health Organization houses the nutrition focal points. These heads of nutrition in the subregion meet annually to look at nutrition programs and learn from each other on how to move forward.

Last but not the least, an Africa Nutrition Capacity Building Initiative is also being implemented in the various subregions on the continent.

All of the issues I have raised were raised during our nutrition focal points meeting. The heads of nutrition within the subregion and others have identified these as some of the main issues affecting nutrition. These are among the issues we have to address if we wish to make progress on nutrition in West Africa and achieve nutrition security by 2020.

The West African market is big enough to support a whole series of economic activities that generate income, increase buying power, and improve supply, thus reducing food insecurity.

— Michel Benoît-Cattin

Michel Benoît-Cattin*

Associate Director for Economics and Social Sciences, Scientific Direction, French Agricultural Research Center for International Development (CIRAD), France

It has already been said 50 times, but I am going to say it again another way: By reducing food and nutrition insecurity, we increase the probability that one day each person in West Africa will have access to quantitatively and qualitatively satisfying food, whether it comes from his own production or from the market. The problem is complex, and solving it requires many elements.

The subregion faces some conditions that are historically unique. More and more consumers are urbanized and not producing. Although there are more and more producers, they have to feed more and more people. This is a new equation in the history of mankind. Moreover, producers have to feed more people out of resources, particularly soil and water, that are more and more limited, and hence overexploited and even degraded.

I am going to propose some steps in the area of public or collective action that concern the various groups of stakeholders represented at this conference.

The first concerns agronomic research. Whatever technical path is envisaged to improve productivity for food farms in a lasting way, research must continue. Research organizations must also become more involved in partnerships with producer organizations, public services, and private operators, particularly in the area of fertilizers and seeds.

Another point rarely addressed, which I feel strongly about, is the enormous manipulation of data. We all know the state of agricultural statistical systems and even demographic systems in our countries, and it is normal, at least for researchers, to have some doubts about these figures, whose source is never cited. When someone cites "FAO 2003," where do the FAO figures come from? If we want to seriously and correctly identify nutrition and food problems and accurately assess the economic and agronomic programs associated with them, we must set up a lasting system of observation, information, and analysis. We need to think about a partnership between research, the administrations concerned, professional organizations, and of course the FAO, which has as one of its mandates the collection and analysis of data. This implies a long-term commitment of these stakeholders in human and institutional capacity building (supported by international donors).

In relation to the challenge of food insecurity, West Africa is large enough to allow for evening out food supply and demand imbalances between regions. Crop years are never bad everywhere: some regions have surpluses, while some have deficits. What is more, West Africa can also support a market for other products and other activities, which will themselves help improve the standard of living and the buying power of all consumers. The West African market is big enough to support a whole series of economic activities that generate income, increase buying power, and improve supply, thus reducing food insecurity. For these market arrangements to work better, the region must be protected to allow people and products to circulate within and between the different countries.

Next, as has been mentioned, public investments in infrastructure must be relaunched, because structural adjustment, local conflicts, and other factors have caused interruptions in infrastructure development.

In addition, laws and credit regulations must encourage private investment in trade, transportation, and product transformation. There is no need to expect the Japanese or the Brazilians to come and invest in these activities in Africa. The Africans also have investment capacities, and they must be mobilized and encouraged to invest in their own economies. To help make this work, the regional economic and monetary integration underway must continue.

Finally, it is important to improve governments' ability to come up with coherent national policies and regional policies that can be defended outside the region. This involves increasing and improving the training of government officials, based on good analysis and good research.

The job of improving policies has started, but it must continue, for it is a priority—indeed, an absolute necessity.

* This presentation was originally given in French.

Uzo Mokwunye
Director, The United Nations University, Institute for Natural Resources in Africa, Ghana

The cheapest and most appropriate way to begin to restore the capital of our soils is to apply sufficient quantities of phosphorus.

— Uzo Mokwunye

Insufficient food production is a major cause of food insecurity in West Africa (Table 1). If we want to restore food production to the point where food insecurity is no longer a problem, we have to invest in the most important natural capital that a farmer has at his disposal—the soil.

The cheapest and most appropriate way to begin to restore the capital of our soils is to apply sufficient quantities of phosphorus. Why phosphorus? More than 90 percent of the soils of West Africa are short of this nutrient. The shortage is so severe that when the small amount of phosphorus in some seeds like millet and sorghum is used up, the seedlings die.

Over the past 20 years phosphorus is the one nutrient that has declined in the amount we apply to the soil (Table 2). If we were in bad shape 20 years ago, we are in worse shape today.

In the absence of phosphorus, the more expensive nitrogen fertilizers are inefficiently used in West Africa. So if we want to use nitrogen fertilizers, which we buy and use in large quantities, we must first correct the phosphorus content of the soil.

Many people, particularly the ones who want to engage in organic farming, say, "Oh, grow leguminous trees and plants," because they fix nitrogen so you do not have to buy mineral nitrogen. But in the absence of phosphorus, those plants do not have the capacity to fix nitrogen. So if you want to go organic, you have to go inorganic first, by putting phosphorus into the soil.

Phosphorus—unlike nitrogen, for example—also has residual effectiveness. That is, when you apply phosphorus to the soil, the plant takes what it needs, the soil microbes take what they need, and the rest stays in the soil for the next crop. We can take advantage of this factor not only for the current crop, but also for subsequent crops.

Applying phosphorus is the cheapest and the most appropriate action because we do not even have to go outside of West Africa to get the phosphorous we need. West Africa has abundant supplies of phosphate rock; nearly every country in West Africa has a deposit (Figure 1).

If we can mine the phosphate rock, grind it, and spread it around, not only on the farmers' fields, but also on the grasslands and the homesteads—everywhere in West Africa—we can change the environment in West Africa within 10 years. We will make West Africa more productive.

TABLE 1—Food consumption and production in West and Central Africa, 2002 (million metric tons)

Region	Consumption	Production	Surplus/deficit
West Africa	37.04	33.42	–3.63
Central Africa	13.40	12.65	–0.75

Source: FAOSTAT.

TABLE 2—Nutrient application in West Africa, 1981, 1991, and 2001 (million metric tons)

Nutrient	1981	1991	2001
Nitrogen (N)	143,302	281,634	254,571
Phosphorus (P)	119,997	146,414	114,568
Potassium (K)	93,492	133,391	103,043

Source: FAOSTAT.

FIGURE 1—Phosphate rock deposits in Sub-Saharan Africa

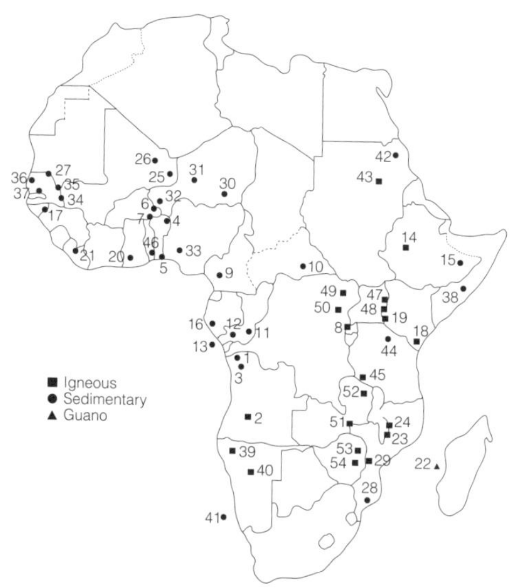

Source: G. H. McClellan and A. Northolt, "Phosphate Deposits of Tropical Sub-Saharan Africa," in A. U. Mokwunye and P. L. G. Vlek, *Management of Nitrogen and Phosphorus Fertilizers in Sub-Saharan Africa* (Dordrecht, the Netherlands: Martinus Nijhoff, 1985); P. van Straaten, *Rocks for Crops: Agrominerals of Sub-Saharan Africa* (Nairobi: International Center for Research in Agroforestry, 2002).

Must a Green Revolution in Africa necessarily follow a Western model of agrarian change? The answer is no.

— Kanayo Nwanze

Kanayo Nwanze
Director General, WARDA–The Africa Rice Center, Côte d'Ivoire

My hypothesis is simple. Agriculture is the backbone of Africa's economic development. Agricultural development requires appropriate agricultural technologies. Agricultural technologies require science and technological breakthroughs. It's "A plus B equals C." Science and technology were the mainspring of the Green Revolution that transformed Asia from a land of hopelessness into a world of economic growth and prosperity.

Question number one: Why did this same transformation not happen in Sub-Saharan Africa? First and foremost, the Green Revolution depended on homogenized environments and high inputs, irrigation, and fertilizers. Poor African farmers can scarcely afford these inputs.

Question number two: Must a Green Revolution in Africa necessarily follow a Western model of agrarian change? The answer is no. Our approach must be different; it must take into consideration physical, socioeconomic, and cultural realities and the large disparities between our regions.

West Africa, for example, faces unique challenges. It is Africa's most populous region and home to the most populous country: Nigeria. By 2020 West Africa's population will be close to 450 million inhabitants. This is a major challenge to food security. West Africa is also in the belt of coups d'état and has been devastated by more than three decades of civil strife, recurrent droughts, and the increasing onslaught of HIV/AIDS. Our countries are ranked at the bottom of the human development index. Our economies are predominantly agricultural, but dependent on exports of one or two commodities that are severely affected by agricultural subsidies in industrialized countries.

Even with these statistics, West Africa has seen some spectacular breakthroughs in science and technology that are bringing hope to farming communities. For example, improved technologies have boosted maize production in the subregion from about 3 million tons in 1980 to about 10 million tons in 2000—close to a 400 percent increase. Another example is cassava, which is feeding about 200 million Africans. The technological breakthrough against cassava pests brought benefits worth more than US$2 billion to farmers.

Millions of West Africans survive on plantains. In East Africa, banana is a major food crop. The recent tissue culture of banana technology has not only increased banana yields, but also shortened the maturity of the crop.

Closer to home, the New Rice for Africa, NERICA, is now a symbol of hope for millions of rice farmers and consumers in Africa. What makes NERICA stand out among technological breakthroughs? Its unique selling proposition lies in a remarkable combination of traits: higher yields, shorter duration, and reduced labor. In principle, these characteristics should eventually reduce imports and increase farmers' incomes and well-being. Moreover, there are hundreds of varieties of NERICA. And NERICA varieties are being developed not just for rain-fed agriculture, but also for irrigated systems.

What are the immediate impacts of NERICA in West Africa, which accounts for 70 percent of the total rice-growing area in Africa? Demand for rice in West Africa is growing at more than 6 percent per year (Figure 1). To meet this soaring demand, the subregion of West Africa imports about US$1 billion worth of rice every year. This represents 25 percent of the total food imports of the subregion.

FIGURE 1—Rice trends in West and Central Africa, 1961–2002

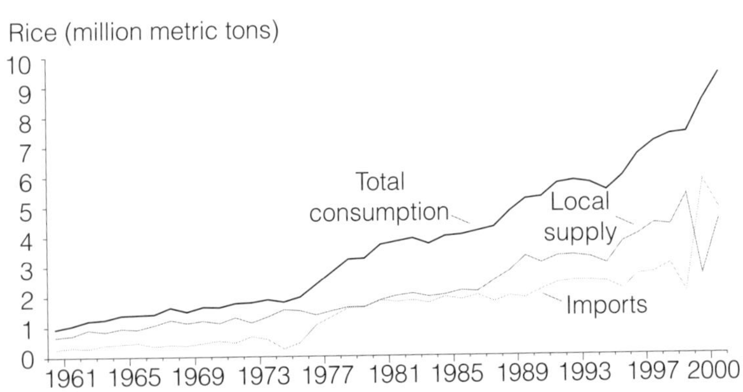

Let us look at what has happened in Guinea, for example. With NERICA, in 2003 that country was able to save over US$13 million of rice imports. Today the Guinean rice farmer grosses about US$65 per hectare with minimum inputs, and about US$145 per hectare with a moderate level of inputs.

Now NERICA is spilling over into East Africa, where rice is not a food crop, but a commercial crop. Within three years of NERICA's introduction, Uganda was growing 6,000 hectares of NERICA.

Today donors and international nongovernmental organizations (NGOs) are collaborating with African governments to help disseminate NERICA. They are convinced that NERICA has tremendous potential. The African Development Bank is already funding a US$30 million NERICA dissemination project.

What are the factors that make NERICA an outstanding success? One is sustained funding by the CGIAR members. Technologies do not emerge without sustained funding. Next, there are committed partnerships at all levels, led by Africans: partnerships in research, partnerships with development agencies, and partnership with farmers. Most important, NERICA is adapted to local farming conditions. Unlike the Green Revolution, we have not modified the environment to fit the technology; we have developed a technology that fits the environment.

Farmer participatory approaches, selection of varieties by farmers, and novel approaches for seed production using community-based systems have also helped in the spread of NERICAs.

Branding the product is also important. Before 2001, NERICA-1 was WAB-HP-1-plus-B-minus-F. But everybody can relate to a name like NERICA.

Finally, political support at the highest level was crucial.

I have described some impressive technologies that have high potential to contribute toward boosting agricultural productivity in Africa. But why have our efforts not led to large-scale agrarian transformation in Africa? To transform these technologies into effective instruments for an African agricultural revolution, it is imperative for our African leaders and policymakers to move from rhetoric to action. We have had too much of rhetoric. They should take ownership of the technologies and not wait for assistance from outside.

If African countries and governments cannot achieve political and social stability, favorable agricultural policies, removal of unfair subsidies, better infrastructure, active involvement of the private sector, price incentives for quality products, access of farmers, particularly women, to credit, massive promotion of local products, strong producer-processor-trader-consumer linkages, competitive local and regional markets, and political commitment at the highest level, we will never capture the benefits of NERICA.

What I have shared with you is not just the role of science and technology in the transformation of African agriculture. It is much more than that. We have shown the capacity of an African institution, managed by Africans and staffed by Africans, to develop technologies that can contribute to Africa's agricultural revolution.

To transform these technologies into effective instruments for an African agricultural revolution, it is imperative for our African leaders and policymakers to move from rhetoric to action.

— Kanayo Nwanze

Discussion

In his opening remarks, the chair, Mamadou Kone, pointed out that although 3 million Africans die of hunger each year, the intellectual and material means to escape this cycle do exist, and he encouraged participants to identify specific technical, institutional, and political limitations that prevent West Africa from achieving food security and to propose priority actions to be taken. Kone referred to discussions that took place earlier in the year in Bamako, Mali, in a lead-in workshop called "Food and Nutrition Security Policies for West Africa" (see Box 2). He mentioned that the following topics were considered in Bamako: the problem of food and nutrition security in West Africa and regional strategies to guarantee it; the effects of migration on rural development and food security; the role that technological, institutional, and political options play in food security and poverty alleviation; the management of natural resources for food security; the role of infrastructure and water management on rural development, food security, and poverty alleviation; and the effects of conflicts on food security and the struggle against poverty.

The moderator, Achi Atsain, also raised key messages emerging from Bamako. At that workshop, said Atsain, participants noted that most African countries have strategies to counter hunger and malnutrition at the national level, but despite these programs, there is still a lack of continuity in action. The Bamako participants felt that because of government or structural changes and unforeseen situations, programs that are begun are often abandoned or priorities are changed over time. Another important issue raised in Bamako was the question of access to markets, in particular the legal hurdles to creating effective regional markets, the ability to negotiate, the question of public governance, the effects of conflict and migration within this framework, and above all the failure to implement at the national level protocols that were signed at the subregional level. The discussions in Bamako emphasized the need to invest in infrastructure, the importance of sound management of natural resources, and the challenge of creating institutions that can effectively implement planned actions. Decentralization was a subject of much discussion, with participants pointing out that conditions must be created in order for West African farmers to be able to make their voices be heard. Decentralization was seen as a mechanism for consultation with farmers and for their participation so their needs are taken into account in policies at the micro and macro levels. Atsain continued that the workshop in Bamako began to develop a research program. He hoped that the discussion in the current West Africa session would address how to strengthen regional cooperation effectively in West Africa, harmonize customs and trade policies, and coordinate subregional programs, including affirming political involvement.

The subsequent discussion covered a wide range of topics, including consumer participation, the promise of new technologies, food as a human rights issue, and gender considerations.

A participant expressed concern about reproducing traditional models when engaging in research partnerships and stressed the need to take into account consumers' perceptions of the products that will be offered. While research must be undertaken in partnerships, as it often is with producer organizations, economic operators, and public powers, the participant noted, above all it should also include the consumers. This issue might also partly explain the success of NERICA, since its development involved the use of a participatory method that brought farmers and women, who would be doing all of the work with the product, into the research process.

Asked why the promising technologies of NERICA and phosphorus rock fertilizer were not more widely used and supported, panelist Kanayo Nwanze responded that NERICA alone is not a panacea to food insecurity—it is only one of a number of areas to be addressed by governments and other actors. He continued that if those other aspects are not

---

Part of the discussion was conducted in French. It was translated into English and subsequently edited.

It is important to stress gender, but that in doing so it is necessary to take into account both women and men.

addressed, no matter what technologies are available, they will not make an impact. Panelist Uzo Mokwunye added that governments and donors often fail to promote beneficial new technologies, even when they are made aware of these benefits, and cited examples from Mali and Burkina Faso. In Mali, Mokwunye explained, research has shown that there is a phosphate rock deposit that, when applied as is, is just as good as the manufactured phosphate fertilizer on any crop that is grown in the country. He noted that the government and development community are aware of the potential benefits, but over 90 percent of the soils in the region are deficient and today Mali still imports compound fertilizers from outside. In Burkina Faso, Mokwunye continued, a center was set up to show how phosphate rock could be used for agricultural production. When a World Bank specialist visited, he reported that in the year of application phosphate rock does not produce as much as super-phosphates and is therefore not economical. Mokwunye stated that as a result the Government of Burkina Faso could never get funds to begin to mine or apply phosphate rock, despite the value of being able to invest in and draw upon the country's own natural resources.

During the discussion about the potential of new technologies and crops, a participant pointed out the potential of *florido*, a plant species from South America, to be multiplied in different regions to help contribute to food security. It was suggested that the region should promote "poles of excellence," in which, for example, Senegal would provide the region with peanuts, Guinea and Côte d'Ivoire would provide bananas, and Mali and Burkina Faso would provide millet and rice. The value to West Africa of deepening its research, and if necessary, enacting new laws regarding genetically modified organisms, as was done for computer and communications technologies, was also raised. Another participant pointed out that agricultural scientists in the region must send samples abroad to get product analyses and noted that this does not make sense for a region that is seeking technological solutions to its food problems. This participant suggested that creating a regional analysis center for West Africa would save scientists time and money, particularly given that conditions for entering into foreign markets are increasingly difficult for Africans.

Access to food of sufficient quality and quantity and to sufficient nutrition was identified as a basic human rights problem. It was also pointed out that it is important to stress gender, but that in doing so it is necessary to take into account both women and men—both are partners, and when setting policy, it is necessary to take into account the involvement of both. The participant continued that this then becomes a question of political choice and political will. If both women and men are taken into account throughout the process as projects are developed until they are completed, development can truly be participatory and integrate women fully.

Box 2: Laying the Groundwork for the 2020 Africa Conference

Two lead-in events in Africa fed directly into the discussions that took place at the 2020 Africa conference. First, in December 2003, more than 60 high-level policymakers, senior researchers, and representatives from farmer groups, the private sector, and international development agencies met in Pretoria, South Africa, for an international conference, "Successes in African Agriculture: Building for the Future." The conference was jointly convened by NEPAD; Internationale Weiterbildung und Entwicklung (InWEnt); Centre Technique de Coopération Agricole et Rurale (CTA); and IFPRI.

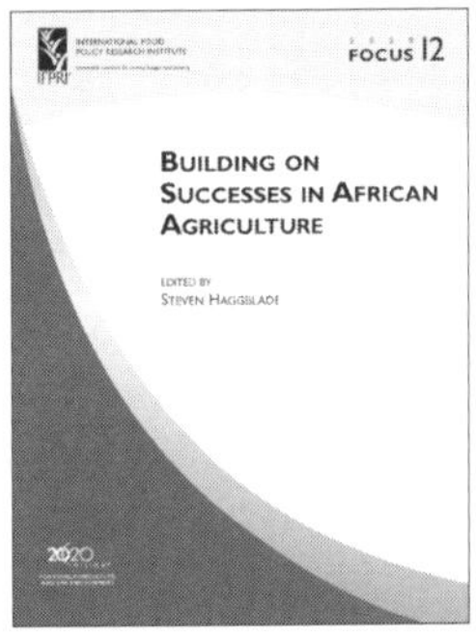

Some exciting efforts of African farmers and researchers have significantly raised agricultural productivity in certain countries and for certain products. These successes, however, have not been numerous, continuous, or important enough to achieve food security for much of the continent's population. To help extend and multiply African successes, conference participants examined the processes that produced successes and assessed the domestic and international policy environment within which African leaders formulate and implement agricultural policies.

The outputs of the conference include a set of 2020 Focus policy briefs compiled into *Building on Successes in African Agriculture*, which describes some of the main cases studied and the conclusions drawn. It also contains the Pretoria Statement on the Future of African Agriculture, a shared statement of findings by conference participants, identifying priorities for future policy action necessary to trigger and sustain agricultural development on the continent. (The 2020 Focus is available at http://www.ifpri.org/2020/focus/focus12.htm, and the Pretoria Statement can be found in Excerpt 7 in this volume).

The second lead-in event to the 2020 Africa conference was the regional workshop "Food and Nutrition Security Policies for West Africa: Implementation and Research Agendas," held in January 2004 in Bamako, Mali. The workshop drew about 70 participants representing a wide range of stakeholders, including policymakers, policy advisers, researchers, and civil society actors. It was jointly organized by IFPRI/2020 Vision Initiative, Centre de coopération internationale en recherche agronomique pour le développement (CIRAD), and l'Institut d'économie rurale (IER), in cooperation with Sécurité Alimentaire Durable en Afrique de l'Ouest Centrale (SADAOC Foundation).

At the workshop, participants discussed a range of issues concerning food and nutrition security in West Africa, including conflict; migration; natural resource management; public spending; technological, institutional, and policy options; and high-priority research areas. Participants agreed that the chief goals for the future are to advance research and disseminate results, stabilize and liberalize commerce, improve market information systems, apply technical standards, raise funding, and extend nutrition education.

A synthesis of the conclusions from the workshop was presented at the 2020 Africa conference in Uganda, and the full proceedings of the workshop, in English and French, were subsequently published and are available at http://www.ifpri.org/2020africaconference/events.asp.

Chapter 6 East and Central Africa

Chair: Newai Gebre-ab

Chief Economic Advisor to the Prime Minister, Ethiopia, and Director of Ethiopian Development Research Institute (EDRI), Ethiopia

Moderator: Isaac Minde

Coordinator, Eastern and Central Africa Programme for Agricultural Policy Analysis (ECAPAPA), Uganda

Rapporteur: Steven Were Omamo

Research Fellow and Regional Network Coordinator, International Food Policy Research Institute (IFPRI), Uganda

Asha-Rose Migiro

Member of Parliament and Minister of Community Development, Women, and Children, Tanzania

Tanzania has adopted numerous international conventions and declarations on gender equity and equality, but the situation there is still somber. Women are still disadvantaged when it comes to issues like participation in decisionmaking, distribution of domestic workload, accessing resources, and appropriating incomes accruing from various household economic activities like agriculture. This situation perpetuates the problem of malnutrition and food insecurity in the country.

The current status of food security in Tanzania is generally satisfactory at the aggregate or national level. At subnational levels, however, particularly in some districts and households, food insecurity persists, with about 20.4 percent of the population falling into the category of the food poor.

In developed countries, food is always available in supermarkets; what one needs is money to buy it. In Tanzania, however, the rural population and a considerable number of urban dwellers have to produce food for themselves. Therefore, food production and agricultural activities are of paramount importance to the livelihoods of most Tanzanians. But agricultural activities face numerous challenges that need to be addressed in order to attain food security. They include:

- *Dependence on rainfed agriculture coupled with hand hoe cultivation.* This system of cultivation is susceptible to weather variations and drought. Moreover, it prevents farmers from cultivating enough land area to guarantee food security for the nation.
- *Lack of incentive structure to encourage agricultural growth.* In Tanzania there are no arrangements to provide subsidies and loans to small farmers. In developed countries like Britain and France, farmers are given loans and subsidies. There is no way our farmers can ensure food security in the absence of such arrangements.
- *Men's appropriation of incomes accruing from agricultural activities.* Agricultural activities are normally undertaken by women and partly by the youth. Men spend most of their time on leisure and nonagricultural income-related activities. As heads of families, however, men appropriate the income derived from farming. This trend needs to be reversed for the sake of guaranteeing sustainable food production and food security.

For food security to be attained in Tanzania, agriculture must be intensified.

— Asha-Rose Migiro

- *Heavy workload for women.* Women in typical Tanzanian communities bear an inordinate family workload. They invariably have to care for the children and sick family members (especially victims of HIV/AIDS), prepare food for the family, and participate in agricultural activities to sustain their families. Their workload is made even heavier by inadequate access to improved water supplies and excessive dependence on increasingly scarce wood fuel as a source of domestic energy. All of these factors have a negative bearing on guaranteeing food security.

For food security to be attained in Tanzania, agriculture must be intensified. The country cannot continue relying on rainfed agriculture coupled with application of inappropriate technologies. It needs to explore all avenues for transforming agriculture, including irrigation. After all, recent studies have shown that irrigated agriculture provides 40 percent of the world's food production from 17 percent of the cultivated area. In regions of water shortage, yields on irrigated land are often two to three times that of rainfed agriculture. Nonetheless, in a country like Tanzania, where more than 82 percent of the population live and eke out a living in rural areas with agriculture as the mainstay of their living, irrigation alone cannot be a solution to food insecurity. It has to be accompanied by improved gender relations among the actors involved in agriculture to bring about meaningful transformation that can guarantee food security.

It would be interesting to examine the 2004 budgets of the countries that have signed the Maputo Declaration to see what they have actually earmarked for agriculture and rural development.

— Kankonde Mukadi

Kankonde Mukadi*
Professor, Protestant University of the Congo, Democratic Republic of Congo

Heads of state and African governments must make a firm commitment to fund scientific research in general, and agricultural research in particular. To do this, they must allocate a certain percentage of their national budgets. African leaders have already done this for the agricultural sector. At the African Union Summit in July 2003, they decided to devote at least 10 percent of each country's national budget to agriculture and rural development over the next five years. It would be interesting to examine the 2004 budgets of the countries that have signed the Maputo Declaration to see what they have actually earmarked for agriculture and rural development.

Real collaboration should take place between Central and East African research centers. The activities undertaken by the Eastern and Central Africa Programme for Agricultural Policy Analysis (ECAPAPA) and the Association for Strengthening Agricultural Research in Eastern and Central Africa (ASARECA) should be well distributed geographically. We need to have a regular exchange of information and researchers. For example, a research project carried out in an East African country could make use of the expertise of one or more researchers from Central Africa and vice versa, in accordance with available means. Universities, especially faculties of agricultural science, should be actively involved in IFPRI's research projects.

The selection of research subjects should involve close collaboration with civil society, NGOs, the private sector, and federal representatives. All research projects focusing on development, and particularly on food and nutrition security, should adopt a participatory approach. Giving the general public access to research results is an indispensable part of ensuring the impact of the research in the field.

Examples of research directions that could be considered include the domestication of wild animal and plant species; farming techniques that can produce long-lasting agricultural output, such as agroforestry and crop rotation to solve problems like soil fertility, water management as a production factor, family fish farming, and short-cycle animal husbandry; appropriate processing and storage technologies for small-scale producers; and nutrition education for urban and rural populations, especially targeting women.

It is crucial to coordinate the actions of the various federal technical departments concerned with food and nutrition security. These departments include Agriculture

* This presentation was originally given in French.

(to increase food production), Health (to improve public nutrition education, especially for women), Environment (for the rational use of wild animal- and plant-based foodstuffs, Education (for nutrition education in the public school system), Research (to improve agricultural productivity), and Commerce (to ensure the exchange of products that are profitable for all participants).

We should establish partnerships for food and nutrition security on three levels: the national level, the regional level, and the pan-continental level. An effective, fruitful partnership means that each partner has something to offer. The skills and know-how required for the partnerships should be forged at the national level. Without this, it will be impossible for partnerships to develop at the other two, broader levels.

The partnerships would involve three key participants: the state, civil society—especially those farmers, both male and female, who are the main producers of foodstuffs—and researchers. Leaders should look past their personal egos and encourage farmers to join forces so that they can, collectively, become a partner that is able to engage in dialogues with the state and researchers. Indeed, civil society constitutes the weakest segment of the partnership triangle.

At the pan-continental level, the fight against food and nutrition insecurity must become a high-priority issue for the African Union.

— Kankonde Mukadi

At the regional level, decisionmakers should look past national egos and enter into agreements that are profitable for the entire region. These individuals should come together in solidarity to fight food and nutrition insecurity, doing everything possible to combat any hatred among the different nations of their region.

At the pan-continental level, the fight against food and nutrition insecurity must become a high-priority issue for the African Union. This fight must take place through concrete acts of solidarity that encompass not only scientific and technological research, but also trade.

Discussion

The key issues raised during this session included markets, food aid, smallholder and gender issues, investments, and the role of the private sector. Markets emerged as the key priority area. Concern was expressed that the region has focused for too long on production issues. Once farmers have increased their productivity, a participant said, they have no market outlets for their returns, and they often get discouraged and do not buy fertilizer or adopt other recent technologies. Domestic markets need to be developed so that produce can be moved from where it is produced to where it is needed. He noted that it is not uncommon to see one part of a country with surplus production, where the farmers do not know how to store the excess produce, and another part where people are starving to death. There is a need to remove internal and cross-border barriers to trade in the region and to address built-in international barriers to trade that punish farmers in the region.

It was noted that local producers of food for food aid purposes have come to represent an important spur to market development. In Uganda, for instance, explained a participant, the World Food Programme (WFP) now gets more than half of its resources in cash and therefore focuses on local purchases. He said that in the previous year WFP had bought more than 106,000 tons of Ugandan commodities, spending almost US$25 million, which served to stimulate production.

School feeding programs were offered as an example of a way to stimulate and keep up local production. A participant remarked that Uganda's school feeding program will expand from the current 350,000 children to 2.5 million children, all supported with locally purchased food, and it will take place within the government's poverty action fund framework, where general budgetary support is applicable and school health can be linked with it. It was suggested that school feeding programs are a win-win-win proposition to break the vicious nutrition cycle at school with local food.

The smallholder farmer was another key topic of discussion. A participant highlighted the importance of strengthening farmers' organizations as a way to improve markets and stressed the need for strong farmers' associations that are integrated from production to market. Along similar lines, the need to create an enabling environment for smallholders and peasants was mentioned. It was felt that it is not right to eliminate the smallholder just because the smallholder is the food-insecure one, especially since the smallholder represents such a large segment of the farming population in the region. On the other hand, another participant remarked that traditional practices in agriculture represent a major hurdle to increased food security and claimed there is widespread ignorance and lack of education. Concern was expressed that farmers should be accorded more dignity. It was also mentioned that research and extension services must be given higher priority than they are at present.

Gender issues were also discussed. A participant argued that women's empowerment is crucial to achieving the required increases in agricultural productivity but added that there is also a need to take steps to bring more rural men into agricultural production processes. Although income security was identified as a critical way to address nutrition, it was noted that it should be accompanied by financial management. In this context, participants asked who manages the household budget and controls which proportion goes to food, and they stressed the need to consider these intra-household factors when discussing such issues.

Another key group focused upon was the youth. Participants asked what the future is for young people in agriculture. It was suggested that because many young people do want to be in the rural areas, where they have status, cultural roots, and families, a solution might be to think seriously about how to enrich their quality of life in rural areas—by investing in those areas that relate to modern life and technology.

An additional investment considered important was that of improving access to productivity-enhancing inputs. It was acknowledged that critical inputs for increasing agricultural productivity, such as improved seed, fertilizers, and chemical protection, have been unable to get from researchers into the hands of the farmers. A participant highlighted the need for a distribution system to ensure that these technologies reach farmers but explained that there is no single bank that considers agriculture an attractive investment. Therefore, it is the role of governments or development partners to put up the money for this sector, at the very least to get productivity-enhancing inputs to the farmers, since the private sector is not willing to take the risk. The participant proposed an intervention such as an agricultural investment fund to create access to finance for increasing agricultural productivity.

Other issues related to the private sector were also raised. Participants pointed out that the seasonality of agriculture creates important, unexploited opportunities in agribusiness, especially in storage and processing. It was suggested that the fact that poverty levels and food insecurity have been increasing could be a result of a rapid change of policies from government-led standards to private sector-led ones. How can policies be harmonized so that the private sector is supported by the government in areas of strategic intervention that were previously government led?

The Maputo Declaration that commits governments to a 10 percent target for public investment in agriculture was viewed as a positive development revealing a high-level of political commitment to agricultural development. However, a participant asked, what would be the best opportunities for investment within the agricultural sector? The need for country-by-country analyses of returns to investments in agriculture was stressed. Participants raised the questions of how "agriculture" would be defined and whether there would be a uniform approach by African countries.

Concern was expressed about the long-term management of natural resources and whether statements made during the discussion represented the same exploitative approach to the environment and the agricultural base as in the past. The chair added that for far too long, Africa has been mining its soils and that given this fact, together with the climatic changes that have been taking place, it is now facing food insecurity as a structural problem, as a built-in factor.

The importance of learning from experiences from other regions of the world was also raised. A participant cited the example of microfinancing in southern India and emphasized the potential of South-South exchange.

At the end of the session, the chair, Newai Gebre-ab, reported that among the most central challenges in the region were:

- How will the Maputo Declaration, which commits governments to allocate at least 10 percent of budgetary resources to the agricultural sector, be implemented?
- How can rural women gain more power and influence in agriculture, and how can rural men become more involved in agricultural production processes?
- What are the most fruitful roles for domestic and regional trade in agricultural development, and what kinds of investments are needed?
- How can credit be made more accessible and affordable to farmers?
- How can improved natural resource management be built into agricultural development approaches?

How can policies be harmonized so that the private sector is supported by the government in areas of strategic intervention that were previously government led?

Chapter 7 Northern Africa

Chair and Moderator: Mohand Laenser
Minister of Agriculture and Rural Development, Morocco

Rapporteur: Martine Padilla
Scientific Administrator, International Center for Advanced Mediterranean Agronomic Institute/Mediterranean Agronomic Institute (CIHEAM/IAMM), France

Mohammed El Mourid
Regional Coordinator for North Africa Regional Program, International Center for Agricultural Research in the Dry Areas (ICARDA), Tunisia

Speaking on behalf of **Adel El-Beltagy**, Director General, ICARDA

Like the rest of Africa, the countries of North Africa—Mauritania, Morocco, Algeria, Tunisia, Libya, and Egypt—face severe food deficits leading to food insecurity. Their production systems are highly fragile because all of them have large areas under desert conditions.

Agriculture in North Africa takes place within a diversified environment of which a substantial proportion is classified as "less-favored," that is, where agricultural production is significantly constrained by factors such as moisture stress due to low and highly variable rainfall, extremes of temperature, short cropping seasons, shallow soils, soil nutrient depletion, steep slopes, lack of infrastructure, and inadequate policy support. In view of the prevailing shortage of arable land and water resources, sustainable increases in agricultural production will necessarily have to come from increases in productivity per unit area, in particular through a significant improvement in water-use efficiency at the farm level. Significant investments in agricultural research, technology transfer, and extension are required to enable North Africa to meet the challenge.

Over the past two decades, the world has gone through dramatic changes that have set the path for economic globalization, with significant political, social, and economic implications throughout the planet. Moreover, the economic and institutional reforms stemming from structural adjustment programs have shaped a whole new environment, characterized by the global, and often abrupt, opening of markets. In the wake of such fundamental changes, agricultural development must be seen as the strategic asset for overall economic growth and poverty alleviation in North Africa.

Sustainable food security is a fundamental objective of all countries in North Africa and is linked to grain production. Yet in most countries the consumption-production gap for cereals has widened. The region is a net importer of cereals and the world's largest durum wheat importer (50 percent of the world market). Per capita production of wheat, particularly durum wheat, has been declining in most countries during the past 30 years. The same trend is observed for food legumes, for which the region turned from being an exporter to a net importer in the 1990s.

ICARDA has a program for North Africa with a regional office in Tunisia to serve the research and training needs of Algeria, Libya, Mauritania, Morocco, and Tunisia. Another regional program, based in Cairo, serves the needs of Egypt, Sudan, Ethiopia, and Eritrea. These regional programs carry out special projects and conduct research and training according to the needs of each country.

Agricultural development must be seen as the strategic asset for overall economic growth and poverty alleviation in North Africa.

— Mohammed El Mourid

The region is facing a number of converging trends that threaten the future of livelihoods of the poorest sector of the society.

— Mohammed El Mourid

Chair Mohand Laenser reflects upon the deliberations.

The region is facing a number of converging trends that threaten the future of livelihoods of the poorest sector of the society. First is global climate change and persistent drought. North Africa is predicted to become warmer and drier with reduced crop productivity compared with other regions; cereal production is projected to decrease by 10 percent. Second, the region is threatened by water scarcity and inefficient water use. North Africa (with West Asia) is already one of the most water-scarce regions, and water scarcity is predicted to worsen markedly over the next 25 years. The limited water resources continue to be mined, causing depletion of water tables and salinization of good agricultural lands. Third, land resources are limited, and desertification continues. Arable land constitutes only 5 percent of the total land area in North Africa. Moreover, over 45 percent of the area dedicated to agriculture and rangeland is experiencing some form of degradation. Fourth, poverty is a major threat, especially in the rural areas where 60–70 percent of the poor are concentrated. Fifth, there is insufficient investment in science and technology in agricultural research. As a result, insufficient and at times inadequate production and protection technologies are available for transfer to farmers, including improved cultivars of various commodity crops. Finally, the policy environment is inadequate. Technology alone will have limited impact if not supported by an enabling policy. Science and technology should be backed by policy research giving policymakers options for appropriate national policies that would have a positive impact at the farmers' level.

In an era of increasingly open markets and constant communication and information revolutions, the fate of the agricultural sector in the region will undoubtedly depend on its capacity to "grow in place"—that is, its capacity to adopt a regional research and development approach that creates the right conditions and incentives to significantly improve agricultural productivity while preserving the environment. Agricultural and rural development in the region should focus on (1) fostering broad-based rural economic growth; (2) improving social well-being, managing and mitigating risk, and reducing vulnerability; and (3) enhancing sustainability of natural resource management. The aim should be to devise and implement strategies that would ensure reasonable complementarity between the goals of growth, equity, and preservation. Such strategies should include technology and management options for high-potential areas, technology and management options for less-favored areas, people-centered development, investments in science and technology, and building of regional and international partnerships.

Sustainable development in North Africa will depend on commitment, capacity, and good governance by the key actors. A focus on improving the well-being of rural people and reducing rural poverty in the widest possible sense will mean improved quality of life, not just increased average income of rural populations. Investing in agricultural research will always pay off. At the same time governments must invest in education, health, clean water, and rural infrastructure. Policies should provide incentives for sustainable natural resource management, such as secure property rights for smallholders. Above all, poor people must participate in making decisions and implementing programs that affect them. Finally, policy research is required from the household to national levels to help farmers cope with global changes and challenges.

Mustapha Guellouz*

Director General, President of the Board of the Enterprise, Livestock and Pasture Office, Tunisia

Food security remains a challenge in developing countries. Guaranteeing food security involves intensifying agricultural production and adjusting domestic and foreign marketing channels so that everyone can have physical and economic access to essential basic foods all the time. In North Africa, however, agriculture is essentially dependent on rain. Drought must be considered the rule, and good years, the exception.

Managing rangeland also poses a real problem after the dislocation of tribal life. Conflicts of interest between communities result in the deterioration of rangeland. Whether rangelands can be rehabilitated is linked to how they are managed and to user behavior—for example, load per hectare.

In some countries, including those in the Maghreb, food security is achieved through food self-sufficiency. Self-sufficiency in milk and meat has become an important goal to be reached.

Animal production has an important place in the economies of North Africa. In Tunisia animal production accounts for 40 percent of the value of agricultural production. Milk production accounts for 9 percent of the value of agricultural production and 25 percent of the value of animal production, whereas meat production accounts for 16 percent of the value of agricultural production and 50 percent of the value of animal production.

Tunisia's consumption of milk and milk products (in milk equivalence) rose from 71.6 liters per inhabitant per year in 1997 to 96.0 liters in 2002. In Morocco, consumption of milk was 37 liters per inhabitant per year in 2000. Tunisia actually achieved 100 percent self-sufficiency in drinking milk in 2002, up from 55 percent self-sufficiency in 1997. In 2000 Morocco had 80 percent milk self-sufficiency.

In terms of numbers, Tunisia had 203,600 purebred livestock in 2000 and 200,990 in 2003 (Figure 1). The country had 278,500 local cross-bred livestock in 2000 and 249,320 in 2003.

Farmers face a number of limitations to greater productivity and production. These include the small size of farms; parceling; lack of water resources, equipment, inputs, services, and land; and financial constraints.

Tunisia also has a negative balance sheet for animal feed. Animals need 5.5 billion forage units, but in a dry year only 4.0 billion forage units are available, and even in a good year only 5.0 billion forage units are available. In the face of this negative balance, the policy question is, should the numbers of livestock continue increasing? Or should productivity per hectare and per animal be improved?

The agrarian structure is mostly made up of small farms (Table 1). Fifty-three percent of farms are smaller than 5 hectares; 73 percent of farms are smaller than 10 hectares. Only 3 percent of farms are larger than 50 hectares. Herds are also small. In Tunisia 76 percent of bovine herders have herds of fewer than 3 cows, and in Morocco 85 percent of bovine herders have herds of fewer than 3 cows. In Tunisia 95 percent of herders hold fewer than 10 cows, and in Morocco 99 percent of herders have herds of fewer than 10 cows. Fragmentation of parcels is also a problem, and the phenomenon of landless animal owners creates difficulties as well.

The small herd size and the agrarian structure are linked to problems with transfer of technologies related to

FIGURE 1—Change in the number of cattle in Tunisia, 1992–2003

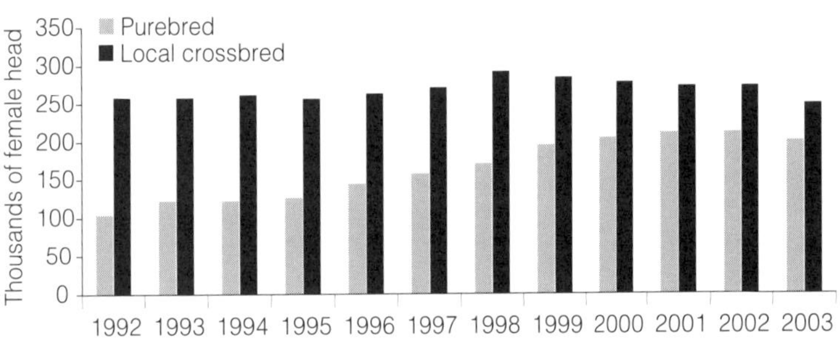

TABLE 1—Agrarian structure

Farm size (hectares)	Number	%	Area (thousands of hectares)	%
<5	251,000	53	471	9
5–10	92,000	20	643	12
10–50	114,000	24	2,235	42
50–100	10,000	2	645	12
>100	4,000	1	1,301	25
Total	471,000	100	5,295	100

* This presentation was originally given in French.

artificial insemination, performance monitoring, high-yield forage, and fertilization, as well as to low productivity.

Agricultural credit is very limited. Only 1.8 percent of small farmers have recourse to short-term credit in Tunisia, and only 9.2 percent of small farmers have recourse to medium- and long-term credit. This low penetration is due to lack of titles to land, requirements for security deposits, lack of self-financing, and the impossibility of having a good revolving fund.

Other problems are the rudimentary work tools and the use of bran and hay instead of concentrate, green forage, and silage.

In sum, farmers view the cow as a piggy bank, not as an economic project.

The professional organizations related to agriculture, like farmers' organizations, service cooperatives, and breeders' associations, are inadequate. Organizations have been created from the top down, there is a lack of human and material resources, management leaves something to be desired, the presence of professional organizations in the regions is weak, and membership in professional organizations is low. Only 20 percent of producers are covered by professional organizations.

There are also problems with adequate supplies of inputs and lack of strategic stock.

Add to all these constraints the sometimes contradictory and inconsistent government policies. For instance, the same farmer may be subject to several contradictory aid programs (range development and fruit trees, for example). And laws and regulations are often not enforced, leading to illegal practices such as clandestine slaughtering, peddling, and other such activities.

All of these constraints lead to a social agriculture that is not performing, a precarious self-sufficiency situation, and poor product quality. These conditions lead in turn to fragile agricultural systems and a lack of competitiveness, which in turn lead to a lack of sustainability.

El-Sayed Zaki

Former Minister of Finance and Economic Planning, Sudan

In my presentation, I will identify priorities for action to achieve food and nutrition security in three countries in North Africa: Egypt, Morocco, and Sudan.

North Africa is characterized, with some exceptions, by a high rate of population growth; high population density along narrow strips of inhabited land, especially in Egypt and Libya; frequent and prolonged droughts, especially in Morocco and Sudan; decreasing agricultural land in absolute and relative terms, leading to decreasing per capita productive land; serious water problems in terms of quantity (per capita consumption), quality, and efficiency of water use; and a profound government role and share in investment in agricultural and food production as well as in product and input markets.

In sum, farmers view the cow as a piggy bank, not as an economic project.

— Mustapha Guellouz

Food security is generally defined as physical and economic access to food. In the absence of effective interregional and international trade, adequate production of food is a prerequisite for food security. In the past, availability of grains or other staples was the main indicator of food security. Recent studies, however, have identified other crucial indicators besides food availability: food consumption as a proxy for access, and nutritional status as a proxy for food utilization. These indicators have direct implications for the individual and household levels in terms of availability from the market or from own farm production and in terms of diversification of food consumption and nutrition. In the presence of efficient product and input markets, income levels determine food security status. Given that rural economies are increasingly monetized, household earnings have become a determinant factor in food security.

At the national level, some countries in the region continue to confuse the issue of food self-sufficiency with that of food security and consequently devote scarce resources to food production. The irony is that such confusion often leads to less than optimal resource allocation and hence renders the economies more vulnerable to food deficiencies. It violates the principle of comparative advantage and could result in reduced producers' income. In some cases it jeopardizes the monetization of the local economy. In some situations, like the grain-producing semi-mechanized farming in the mid-plains of Sudan, this approach has resulted in serious environmental degradation that reduces future capacity to produce food and other agricultural products. For strategic reasons, Egypt continues to reclaim land and expand agricultural production in marginal lands. Libya has adopted similar policies and

At the national level, some countries in the region continue to confuse the issue of food self-sufficiency with that of food security and consequently devote scarce resources to food production.

— El-Sayed Zaki

executed the Great River Project for the utilization of underground water in agricultural and food production.

Dependence on cross-border trade to meet the food needs of the countries of the region is viewed with suspicion, especially by the general public. In Egypt, Sudan, and probably Morocco, there is an outcry for production of wheat (a proxy for food security in urban communities, in particular) within national or regional borders. As a response to this public demand, countries have devoted scarce land and water resources to this task, attempting production in marginal areas with low productivity for both inputs.

Would full integration of these economies into the world economy—the most neutral definition of globalization—ensure their food security? How would globalization, with its free flow of goods (including food), services, technologies, financial flows, investments, labor, information, and cultural goods, affect the allocation of resources and the efficiency of national markets?

Answers to these already complex issues are further complicated by technological advancements in the field of gene engineering and the production of genetically modified food products. To date, there is a significant psychological barrier, as well as political resistance, to genetically modified foods, but these barriers will eventually be overcome and cheaper products will flood the markets. Powerful transnational corporations that control the production and marketing of these high-tech products will facilitate this shift.

Until the present, food security at the household level in the region has been dependent on smallholder production with accessible local markets and some significant cross-border trade. In an environment of increased globalization and highly competitive food products, smallholders are not likely to be able to compete. Thus, the countries of the region are likely to depend more rather than less on globalized markets for their food needs.

In the past the governments of the region adopted food security policies that supported the food consumption of the urban population through large subsidy programs. Egypt was constrained by the large budgetary resources it devoted to this effort, which may have gone to people who were not very needy. Sudan had a similar policy—cross-subsidies from wheat producers to urban consumers of bread were common—but it was gradually phased out. It is important to avoid distortions in resource allocation and to ensure that the national market forces are working and providing the right signals.

National markets should be developed, and product and input market failures should be avoided. Unless small subsistence producers have confidence that the markets can satisfy their consumption needs, they will not transform into commercial producers. Hence, integration of small producers into the economy through appropriate policies, strengthening of institutions, and physical and road links should receive high priority. It is essential to enhance their coping strategies through diversification of crops and enterprises, pro-poor and pro-small producer adaptive research, produce insurance, marketing loans, and other such actions.

It is also important to enhance integration into international markets. Better productivity, marketing services, standardization of products, and differentiation of markets are needed. Adaptive production research to improve returns to unit inputs of land and water and to enhance comparative advantage is a prerequisite to competition in the world, and particularly African markets. Special effort should be made by African countries to encourage their markets, given that Africa's share of world markets is negligible—1 percent.

Dependence on cross-border trade to meet the food needs of the countries of the region is viewed with suspicion, especially by the general public.

— El-Sayed Zaki

Discussion

The chair, Mohand Laenser, opened the session by reviewing the objective, which was to propose concrete actions to strengthen commitment to achieving food security. He called upon session participants to define steps, facilitate complementary partnerships, propose actions that could be leveraged, and reach consensus about the actions required and the various actors' roles in implementing those actions.

During the subsequent discussion, participants noted that human resource development is often primarily intended for professionals. Concern was expressed that the agriculture sector, however, is made up of farmers who are still for the most part illiterate. Basic training for these farmers, as well as for rural women, was identified as essential. These measures, along with measures to improve access to education and health, were seen as a means to improve the well-being of those living in rural areas.

Rural infrastructure, in particular electricity, roads, and potable water, was also discussed. Noting that the unfavorable agroecological environment in North Africa poses a key constraint to food production, participants identified the need for the region to improve management of water in all its uses: agriculture, tourism, and urban uses. The role of investment in research and technology, particularly in water-saving technologies and species varieties, was highlighted.

Participants acknowledged that despite the unfavorable environment, agriculture is and will remain strategic for economic growth and poverty reduction, given that poverty is 60 to 70 percent rural. Problems related to land parceling and pastoral land use were identified as major reasons for the agricultural deficit. It was noted internal marketing channels must be improved and productivity increased in order to prevent encroachment into excessively sensitive areas.

The need for farmers to diversify their crops was highlighted, and it was noted that agroforestry may offer such an opportunity. Participants felt that North Africa should insist on tree crops rather than on grain crops when diversifying, in order to provide farmers new sources of revenue. Biodiversity development could be achieved through the diversification of good-quality agricultural products.

Participants emphasized the urgent need to improve governance by reconsidering the policy and legal environment. The variety of different policies in place creates incoherence, and at the same time laws and regulations often go unenforced. It was also noted that trade organizations are at present established from the top down. Participants felt governance methods should be reviewed and a participatory approach encouraged so that the grassroots can be involved in decisionmaking processes, which are very hierarchical at present. In particular, professional organizations, still weak, do not participate enough in decisionmaking.

Another comment was that partnerships are needed in the region, not only between the public sectors of different countries, but also between the public sector and the private sector. An enabling political environment would be required for these partnerships to be established.

Owing to technical difficulties, the discussion in this session was not audio recorded. Certain elements of the discussion may inadvertently have been left out of this report. Part of the discussion was conducted in French. It was translated into English and subsequently edited.

Chapter 8 Plenary Panel Discussion on Perspectives from the Regions

Chair: Per Pinstrup-Andersen
Chair, Science Council, CGIAR; H. E. Babcock Professor of Food and Nutrition Policy, Cornell University; and 2001 World Food Prize Laureate, USA

Will the 2020 Vision for Africa be achieved? In other words, will every African achieve food and nutrition security by 2020? What we have heard today is: It is possible. Whether it will happen depends on the actions taken. In other words, are the rhetoric and the plans going to be translated into appropriate action? If that happens, we can see a year 2020 where every African has access to enough food for a healthy and productive life.

There is a great deal that we from outside Africa can do to make this happen. However, I want to quote H.E. President Museveni in his statement on the front page of the program for this conference: "We Africans are the ones who must act to meet our food and nutrition needs in a sustainable way."

With support from outside, I have no doubt that Africa will solve its own problems. But we from the outside must support Africa, and we must, at a minimum, get out of the way. That means we must get our agricultural and trade policies in the OECD countries straightened out so that we stop penalizing low-income people and low-income countries, while at the same time telling them, "Trade is the solution to your development." We must follow our rhetoric with appropriate action.

But it is, as I said, Africa that will solve its own problems. It is therefore a tremendous pleasure for me to chair a panel of four outstanding Africans who will report on the discussions in the parallel sessions and who will give their own perspectives as well.

Bongiwe Njobe
Director General, National Department of Agriculture, South Africa

I would like to start on a point of hope. To quote the winner of the youth contest, Nelisiwe Mbali Mtsweni, "By 2020, instead of an Africa that's malnourished, we'll see an Africa that will have flourished." What would be the elements of that flourishing Africa? First of all, young people would be farmers. People would be able to exercise a choice with respect to food. And incomes and employment would be remunerative. Investments, savings, and innovations would be encouraged. And they would build on the human capital that we would have developed. We would have an improved quality of life.

In the session on Southern Africa, we tried to answer the question, "How will we get there?" Getting there will involve dealing with issues of markets and trade, food aid, productivity, and institutions.

First, we need knowledge generation systems and allocation of resources to increase productivity. A very interesting study by the InterAcademy Council changes our assumptions about the best way to increase productivity. It will be a challenge for us to confront those conclusions.

Second, we need wisdom—which is knowledge acquired through experience—and high-quality products. These will help us respond to the market that we know

We from the outside must support Africa, and we must, at a minimum, get out of the way.

— Per Pinstrup-Andersen

is there. Not only are there national markets, but there is an amazing opportunity within the region to service each other's markets. And then, of course, there is international market demand.

Third, we will get there through good governance. Good governance is not just an African issue; it is also an industry issue and a developed-country issue. We need information, systems, and dialogue to ensure effective monitoring, evaluation, and feedback on policies and programs and their impact on our societies. On the issue of the northern subsidies, it just makes good governance sense for taxpayers' money not to be wasted on subsidies.

Then, of course, we will get there when we have common clarity of purpose. We need a common vision among farmers, governments, and the private sectors in each of our countries and then, of course, a common vision across the continent, which we have in the form of NEPAD.

We ended up with a long list of actions under these four titles. First, we have a 16-year time horizon until 2020. Sixteen years is not a very long time to close the food and nutrition insecurity gap. So we need commitment on the part of all actors. The African political commitment has been shown through NEPAD. Industry needs to show its commitment to good governance and to working with governments to ensure the success of the transition to market economies. Donors must commit to changing the food aid options on the table and developing food aid alternatives that have exit strategies. Developed-country governments must commit to removing the subsidies that currently harm African agriculture. And I would like to add one more: all practitioners should personally commit to lobbying for free and fair trade, as we were challenged to do by President Museveni.

The second concrete action is developing a critical mass of clever people. And I am deliberately saying "clever people," because they have to be clever. They have to operate within the environments of developing states. They have to apply their knowledge to the real problems they face. And they have to design and implement strategies involving both strong governments and markets. They need to create an enabling environment within which sound policy management can occur.

Third, we need better institutional alignment. To what extent is each of our organizations, especially the public sector institutions, aligned to address the pressing development challenges? Have we stuck with inherited institutional forms even though they have not yielded results in terms of prosperity? To what extent have the incentives for private sector and academic success aligned with the challenges of development?

> *We need to transmit the message that it is good to be in agriculture—in fact, it is cool to be in agriculture—so that we close this disconnect with the sector that we rely upon for our prosperity.*
>
> — Bongiwe Njobe

The group also raised the issue of the importance of the ability to be organized, especially for farmers—and I would add the ability to have informed consumers. If African consumers exercised an informed choice, they might even predetermine what the market trends would be immediately and in the future.

Partner institutions in developed countries need to be aligned toward the emerging transformation of African leadership, accepting it, responding to it, and not expecting the traditional donor-recipient relationship to continue.

We had a lot of discussion on markets and trade, including subsidies. What is our message regarding subsidies? Is it my government or is it your government that has to drop the subsidies? Are subsidies interpreted as farmer support, or are they helping consumers? We need to agree on the message around these issues and communicate that message effectively.

Two additional proposals were made. First, we need to transmit the message that it is good to be in agriculture—in fact, it is cool to be in agriculture—so that we close this disconnect with the sector that we rely upon for our prosperity. Second, in response to the rationales given by the European Union and the United States for their subsidies, we should say to them, "You may wish to support your rural development agenda, but your choice of instrument is wrong. You have other options to deal with your rural development initiatives; do not use instruments that impede our opportunity to grow and prosper."

Finally, we need to invest in infrastructure: on-farm infrastructure, off-farm infrastructure, and infrastructure that links countries in the region, particularly linking high-potential agricultural land with markets in our region.

Is it possible for Africa to attain food security within the confines of subsistence agriculture–that is, without commercialization?

– Newai Gebre-ab

Newai Gebre-ab

Chief Economic Adviser to the Prime Minister of Ethiopia, Ethiopia

Seven points emerged in our session on East and Central Africa. First was an appreciation of the Maputo Declaration of NEPAD. The 10 percent target for government budget allocations to agriculture was considered an important point of departure. Two questions were raised. One, what is the definition of agriculture? Where does it end? And two, where is the best return within agriculture for this 10 percent investment?

Second, we need to empower women. Women conduct the major part of agriculture, yet they do not have decisionmaking authority. This needs to be redressed, if agriculture is going to be made efficient. Equally important, the male labor force is not as actively engaged in agriculture as it could be, and this is not a sustainable situation.

The third point raised revolved around trade–trade within the countries, trade within the region, and internationally. Surpluses may arise in local markets, and yet the country as a whole may still face the problem of food insecurity. This situation underlines the importance of transport and marketing facilities to enable the proper flow of goods. In relation to trade, the possible negative role of food aid was raised, but one of the donors reminded us that several donors are now being flexible about allowing food aid in the form of cash rather than just in kind. That would have a salutary impact both for food security and for maintaining prices at a level that would provide an incentive to farmers.

Fourth, credit is extremely important to small farmers. Farmers must have access to credit, and they must be able to afford it. I want to add that affordability is a critical question for Africa. Since the liberalization of interest rates, interest rates on the lending side tend to be extremely high. I wonder how we can reconcile the macro policies that we have undertaken and the need for credit for the small farmers.

Fifth, we need to improve natural resource management. For far too long we have been mining Africa's natural resources. No wonder the soil is degraded and its fertility down. This needs to be redressed if we are to tackle the problem of food insecurity on a sustainable basis.

Sixth, we must enhance coordination among the various agencies that work on issues of food security, including government agencies, the private sector, and communities.

Finally, we need partnerships between the public and private sectors, NGOs, and donors.

I would like to add two more questions of my own–fundamental questions that arise when we consider food security. First, is it possible for Africa to attain food security within the confines of subsistence agriculture–that is, without commercialization? This is a complex issue. It raises the question of whether the domestic market is large enough, and if not, it raises the importance of access to external markets and all the issues that we have been addressing regarding trade with the North. It seems to me that commercialization of smallholder agriculture is very important, for it is difficult to imagine the possibility of attaining food security within the context of subsistence agriculture.

My second question is, is it possible to attain food security within the confines of rainfed agriculture? The examples we have seen of addressing food insecurity through a Green Revolution clearly indicate the need for irrigated agriculture. In some cases it might be possible to take the water needed for irrigation to where the farms are located. In other cases it might be necessary to move people from one area to another area–often the lowlands–that can be suitably irrigated.

Mamadou Kone

Minister of Scientific Research, Côte d'Ivoire

For West Africa, achieving food and nutrition security by 2020 will require action. Prior to this meeting in Kampala, representatives of West African countries met at a workshop in Bamako, Mali, to prepare for this meeting. Our conclusions about key priorities for action are based on this workshop in Bamako.

First, we need better integration between food and nutrition issues–they must be addressed together. Second, we need an enabling environment that determines the roles of all the stakeholders and promotes synergies in their interaction.

For action to take place, there are some political requirements, some institutional requirements, and some technical requirements. We emphasize political commitment instead of political will. We need to move from rhetoric to action. We need capacity building for better policies and more timely implementation. This means we need to train decisionmakers to make the right decisions at the right time. It is also important to create the conditions for promoting successful technological breakthroughs that have been tested, like phosphorus rock fertilizer and NERICA [New Rice for Africa]. And we must advocate for effective implementation of action and intervention.

We also face technical requirements. We ought to strengthen agronomic research. The only discipline that will change the destiny of Africa is research. The next breakthrough will be in our knowledge. We need to improve our capacity to add value to traditional dry cereals. We also need better linkages between research and education and better communication of research findings, so people will know how researchers are advancing humankind.

There are also institutional requirements. We need to enhance public and private investment in material and financial infrastructure. We should pursue regional integration to facilitate trade. We want to reemphasize decentralization. And governance must be improved. Conflict, migration, and political instability are not good for the continent.

Finally, we need partnerships in the areas of financial commitment, research, policymaking, and implementation.

Mohand Laenser*

Minister of Agriculture and Rural Development, Morocco

In the parallel session on North Africa, we heard three speeches that focused on the limitations the countries in the region face in terms of achieving food security, but also examined those countries' opportunities and advantages.

There was a consensus that the major problem of food insecurity in North Africa is local unavailability of food products in sufficient quantities, particularly grains. Agriculture, however, is and will remain strategic for economic growth and for overcoming poverty in the region, given that 70 percent of the poor live in rural areas. This rural poverty is due to a permanently unfavorable agroecological environment, characterized by the scarcity of water and arable soil. It is also due to

Good water management is essential, for water is the biggest limitation and will be an even bigger limitation in the future.

— Mohand Laenser

land problems, which are at the basis of the agricultural deficit: the parceling of land, the small size of farms, and the use of pasturage land, for example. Lastly, it is due to farmers' lack of access to credit for modernizing.

There was also a consensus on the need for investment in research and technology, especially research on fuels, varieties, and water-saving technologies.

Good water management is essential, for water is the biggest limitation and will be an even bigger limitation in the future. It is important to improve agricultural production and productivity, and this means improving rural people's well-being—their education, their access to health care, and their access to potable water. It is also important to raise rural people's incomes, and that requires diversifying production and jobs in rural areas.

Since farmers participate little in decisionmaking, it is necessary to review modes of governance and encourage a participatory approach.

The professional organizations related to food security tend to have few members, for they give the impression of being created from above and not from below. Strengthening these organizations will involve training, popularizing knowledge, and raising literacy, because illiteracy rates are very high in rural areas.

Special attention should be given to marketing domestically. There are trade limitations on domestic markets, as well as regionally and abroad.

There is also a problem of consistency between policies and failure to enforce laws and regulations. The judicial and legal system must be reviewed and improved; this is one of the most important reforms for assisting agriculture in North Africa.

Food security cannot be created without a partnership on two levels: a regional and interregional partnership within Africa, and a partnership between the

* This presentation was originally given in French.

private sector and the public sector. The legal, judicial, and economic environment must allow these public-private partnerships.

Lastly, we believe that this forum should be continued, perhaps at the subregional level, to deepen the focus of discussion and to set up an agenda for applying and implementing steps and decisions on which there is consensus.

Discussion

Panel chair Per Pinstrup-Andersen opened the discussion by highlighting the key issues emerging from the panelists' presentations: markets, trade, and infrastructure; good governance, including political commitment and good policies; emphasis of action over rhetoric and plans; the promise of NEPAD, along with the acknowledgment that NEPAD needs to move very quickly toward action; partnerships, including public-private partnerships and partnerships across countries; more appropriate agricultural research to generate appropriate technologies for small farmers that are compatible with sustainable use of natural resources; productivity increases going hand-in-hand with natural resource management; better water management; and specific subregional, national, and community-level priorities. He provoked the audience by reiterating the two questions posed by panelist Newai Gebre-ab: Is it possible to attain food security in Africa without commercialization of agriculture? And can we achieve sustainable food security within rain-fed agriculture?

One participant quickly answered "no" to the first question, claiming that Africa cannot achieve food security without commercializing agriculture. Spirited discussion ensued, however, on the second question. Whereas one participant believed that Africa could achieve sustainable food security within rain-fed agriculture, another disagreed, saying that Africa could not achieve food security without irrigation. A different participant pointed out that rainfall and irrigation are not mutually exclusive.

Much of the subsequent discussion focused on vulnerable groups, such as youth, farmers, and women, after a participant raised the need to give special attention to these groups, as they are the people who are going hungry and risk falling through the cracks in the system. A participant noted that unemployment is high among youth. Youth are educated at agricultural colleges for jobs in ministries of agriculture, but when they graduate, the jobs are not there. Can these youth be mobilized as the farmers of tomorrow, the new hope for combating hunger? Another participant said that in discussions of commercialization, small farmers, who form the largest percentage of African farmers, are often ignored and risk being left behind, while big farmers, who are commercially oriented, are targeted. Policies should address the needs, difficulties, and constraints of both large and small farmers. A participant also raised gender issues, arguing that empowering women means educating women. There is a crucial need to educate rural women, who handle the bulk of work in agriculture as well as shouldering many social problems.

Part of the discussion was conducted in French. It was translated into English and subsequently edited.

Participants met in both parallel and plenary sessions during the three-day conference.

Diverse livelihoods and energy needs were two other topics mentioned during the discussion. Noting that rainfall is bound to fail occasionally, a participant suggested that while waiting for irrigation, farmers should be encouraged to pursue more diverse livelihoods so that agriculture is not their only source of income. The chair added that the rural poor are not all farmers and that many of them have different income sources and opportunities for income diversity.

Another participant noted that in discussions of infrastructure, neither energy nor power had been mentioned. Without adequate energy, African agricultural goods would not reach European markets or even regional markets. The participant noted Africa's large potential for creating energy and said that some African countries have the capacity to supply low-cost energy to the continent.

Given the many issues mentioned, the importance of sequencing, or prioritizing, the necessary actions was pointed out.

Part III | Leading to Implementation

Chapter 9 Constraints and Opportunities

Chair: Godfrey K. Binaisa

Former President of the Republic of Uganda

For how long will food and nutrition remain one of Africa's fundamental problems? This is not a melodramatic question posed in a feverish emotion, but a brutal query from the lips of 200 million people who call Sub-Saharan Africa their home. They are all victims of undernourishment and are everlastingly hungry, scratching out a living of less than one U.S. dollar a day. Unless drastic measures are taken now to think about new ways to tackle this formidable task, the future of our continent is very bleak indeed.

Emphasis has been given to markets, but I would like to add that whereas markets are important, production is equally important. The two have to go hand in hand. It is a question of the egg and the hen, when you come to thinking about production and markets. You cannot take anything to market if you haven't got it, even if the market is open to you.

Second, no mention has seriously been made of legislation concerning land ownership and land tenure in Africa. We have to look at a country like Costa Rica, where the coffee farmers have lots not exceeding five acres. But they handle it in such a way that they are producing as much coffee as the farmers who have big tracts of land.

We also have to think about the need to go back to our colonial past and pick up certain things we can use today—for instance, having prizes for small farmers who are doing a good job across Africa. We should not concentrate too much on the big farmers because they have enough capital to invest; it is the small guy who needs our help most.

And here I must come to the question of management. Today Africa has too many economists and too few managers. We should concentrate not on acquiring degrees only in economics, for degrees in business management are equally important, if not more crucial. Most of the shortcomings we have today are not due to a lack of economists. In many cases, economists are too theoretical, whereas business managers are very practical.

Lastly, from my own experience in government and elsewhere, I have come to conclude that African leaders do not delegate enough. They accumulate too much power, and they want to do it all by themselves. I have seen this in many countries in Africa. This is one of the reasons why no deliveries are made, or if they are made, they are made late: everybody is waiting for the minister to give the marching orders. The junior people below the minister are afraid of taking a risk and doing something before the minister sanctions it.

Keynote Address: Mitigating, Preventing, and Ending Conflicts in Africa

Graça Machel

President, Foundation for Community Development, Mozambique; former Expert of the Secretary General of the United Nations on the Impact of Armed Conflict on Children; and former Minister of Education, Mozambique

I have been asked to offer some reflections on the impact of conflict on our continent and its relationship with food security. I will begin by giving an overview of how the continent has been affected by conflict in the

African leaders do not delegate enough. They accumulate too much power, and they want to do it all by themselves.

– Godfrey K. Binaisa

past 20 years so that we have an idea of the dimensions of the issue.

Among the main reasons for food insecurity in Africa are civil strife, which leads to refugees and internal displacement of people as well as economic disruptions; climate change, which has provoked droughts or floods; deforestation; and more recently, the impact of HIV/AIDS on households and communities, particularly its impact on women, who are producers of food, and men, who are breadwinners. Conflict, refugees, internally displaced people, and food security are closely interlinked.

Let me give an example. In the 1980s my country, Mozambique, had one of the biggest emergencies on this continent due to armed conflict. Half of the population was displaced internally. A quarter of the population became refugees in neighboring countries. And we are still one of the countries most severely affected by land mines. Beyond the loss of life and the maiming of people, the impacts of conflict go deep, especially in rural areas, and they leave very deep scars in the human capital of a country.

The impact of conflict occurs not only in the country in conflict, but also in neighboring countries. Again, during the period of conflict in my country, our small neighbor Malawi had the burden of about 3 million Mozambican refugees. Tanzania had an equal number of refugees. And even today Tanzania has refugees from Burundi and Rwanda. Kenya has the burden of refugees from Burundi, Rwanda, Somalia, and Sudan.

We can categorize conflicts as "high-intensity conflicts," which include countries or areas engaged in civil war or experiencing continuous violent armed conflict, and "low-intensity conflicts," which include high tension or sporadic violent conflict or clashes (Table 1). Then we have countries that have recently emerged from violent conflict and may be experiencing low tension, if any.

Conflict, refugees, internally displaced people, and food security are closely interlinked.

— Graça Machel

From the Atlantic to the Indian Ocean, the continent is broken in the middle by a dense area of conflict. Angola, which is now "out of conflict," has only recently reached that stage. Until recently, Angola had one of the longest conflicts on the continent. Sudan is now the longest conflict on the continent. Fortunately, Rwanda is now out of conflict. Uganda is still experiencing a bit in the northern part of the country.

Even countries that never experienced conflict directly—Botswana, Zambia, Tanzania—bore the burden of conflicts during the 1970s and 1980s, when countries like Mozambique, Angola, South Africa, and Namibia were fighting for their liberation. So the whole of Southern Africa, directly or indirectly, has been under influence of conflict. We can say without doubt that two-thirds of African countries have directly or indirectly experienced conflict.

In March 2003 an NGO based in the western state of Sudan was reporting that 40,000 households had missed crops because of displacement. In Angola, according to CARE, 50 percent of rural households are headed by women who have recently come back from refugee camps. And many of them are still displaced.

TABLE 1—Conflict sites in Africa

High-intensity conflict	Low-intensity conflict	Out of violent conflict
Democratic Republic of Congo (DR Congo)	Namibia (Caprivi Strip)	Mozambique
Sudan	Zimbabwe	Sierra Leone
Burundi	Ethiopia/Eritrea	Angola (excludes Cabinda Enclave)
Angola (Cabinda Enclave)	Republic of Congo	South Africa
Uganda (North)	Chad	Lesotho
Somalia	Côte d'Ivoire	Rwanda
	Western Sahara/Morocco	Liberia
	Central African Republic (C.A.R.)	Malawi
	Algeria	Nigeria

We can say without doubt that two-thirds of African countries have directly or indirectly experienced conflict.

– Graça Machel

What is the implication of this? Not only are there movements of people, but people have lost land, they have lost everything they had, they have lost even the strength and the capacity to work because they have been in a debilitating situation for many, many years.

In those countries, we also have to account for the impact of land mines. Today Angola is the country with the highest rate of people disabled by land mines. Even when the arms get silenced, land mines continue to kill and maim. It will take decades to de-mine and to make the land free for agriculture. Because of land mines, Mozambique had a district of 22,000 square kilometers go without being able to produce for eight years.

TABLE 2—Countries facing food insecurity in Africa

Country	Reasons for food emergency
Angola	Returnees, IDPs
Burundi	Civil strife, IDPs
Cape Verde	Drought
Central Afr. Rep.	Civil strife, IDPs
Congo, Dem. Rep.	Civil strife, IDPs, and refugees
Congo, Rep. of	Civil strife, IDPs
Côte d'Ivoire	Civil strife, IDPs
Eritrea	Civil strife, IDPs
Ethiopia	Drought, IDPs
Guinea	IDPs and refugees
Kenya	Drought in parts
Lesotho	Adverse weather in parts
Liberia	Civil strife, IDPs
Madagascar	Drought in southern parts
Mauritania	Drought
Mozambique	Drought in southern parts
Sierra Leone	Civil strife, IDPs
Somalia	Civil strife, drought in parts
Sudan	Civil strife, drought in parts
Swaziland	Drought in parts
Tanzania, U.R.	Drought in parts, refugees
Uganda	Civil strife, IDPs, drought in parts
Zimbabwe	Drought, economic disruption

What drives conflict? I am not going to be exhaustive but just give some examples. We have a proliferation of small arms on this continent. In certain places, it is much easier to get a pistol or an arm than to get a book for a child. We have severe environmental conflicts related to, for example, drought, deforestation, famine, global warming, and floods. We also have governments who are failing to create a nation-state that ensures that at least a basic sense of belonging is given to every citizen. We have religious intolerance. We have inequitable distribution of national resources, which leads to competition for power, because power will allow control of wealth. We also have competition for investment in markets.

Some examples of states that face food insecurity due to civil strife are the Democratic Republic of Congo (DRC), Sudan, Burundi, the Congo, Côte d'Ivoire, Madagascar, Liberia, Central African Republic, Somalia, Sierra Leone, and Guinea (Table 2). We also have a group of countries with a combination of strife, or sometimes refugees and internally displaced people, and climate problems, like drought or floods. There is hardly a subregion of our continent that is not being affected by food insecurity, in one way or another, because of one or a combination of these reasons.

Then we come to HIV/AIDS and food security. In certain countries, up to 40 percent of the people between ages 25 and 35 are infected at the most productive time of life. A high level of AIDS-related deaths and prolonged illness has seriously undermined the ability of households to produce food. HIV/AIDS affects the more productive members of households, who are unable to tend to their fields. And the health of HIV-positive individuals is deteriorating more quickly than usual because of poor nutrition. More important, governments are obliged to spend more resources on health care and less on food production.

We cannot plan how to escape food shortages and improve the nutritional state of our citizens without concentrating our efforts on resolving conflicts. As you

We have a proliferation of small arms on this continent. In certain places, it is much easier to get a pistol or an arm than to get a book for a child.

– Graça Machel

know, the newborn African Union has given a high priority to conflict resolution, conflict management, and peace building. Although these institutions are still in the making, we have the Security Council, created precisely to oversee situations of conflict. And we also have an emphasis on issues of governance.

So we are quite aware, as Africans, that none of our projects to change the status of this continent is achievable without resolving conflict. And in the past two to three years, we made progress in the DRC. There are still pockets of conflict here and there, but a transitional government is in place. Angola is in peace. Sudan is also on the way to peace.

But now we need to reprioritize our resources toward development. Resources that were concentrated on armies, on so-called "security," must now be diverted to human security, one of whose basic aspects is food and nutrition.

We have sometimes witnessed our leaders make commitments, but the political will to implement development initiatives has not been great. We are delighted to realize that we have a new crop of leaders who are trying to move from being assessed by what they say to being assessed by what they do.

I see NEPAD as the development agency of the African Union. The heads of state meet at least four times a year to make sure that every quarter they follow how decisions are being implemented. This strong mechanism of follow-up and accountability is a shift in African history.

Of course, governments are the main actors responsible for implementing decisions, but we are also engaging the private sector, civil society organizations, and especially the international partners who are now structurally involved in helping to implement NEPAD. So we seem to be moving in the right direction.

But we Africans still have a serious problem of ensuring access to resources, especially education and information, for all our citizens. How many of our citizens are informed about decisions being made by our parliaments, our governments, our decisionmaking institutions? Citizens feel alienated; they feel they are not part of what's happening. We need to empower citizens and make sure that they feel they are the ones who drive the processes of democratic institutions.

I want to speak especially of women, youth, and rural populations. Why? Because these are the majorities of our nations. In any African nation the majority of the population is young people, the second majority is women, and the third majority is the rural population.

In any African nation the majority of the population is young people, the second majority is women, and the third majority is the rural population. But these three categories are precisely those who are not involved in the decisionmaking.

— Graça Machel

But these three categories are precisely those who are not involved in the decisionmaking. How many young people do we have in our parliaments? How many women do we have? How many rural people are asked when we discuss agricultural policy and decide on strategies for the next 5 or 10 years? So our democracies are failing to bring the majority to the center of the decisionmaking process.

By extension, if you go to the subregional and regional bodies, the majority of people there are my age. They may bring the experience of life, of course, but they will fail to dream and to think what is going to happen in 30 years. Because young people are the majority, it's in their vested interest to dream and to take over from us. But they are not in the decision-making process. And sometimes nations have minorities that also feel alienated.

Redistribution of resources has also been one of the problems African nations face. There is a certain degree of concentration of ownership of national resources that are not going to the majority of our people. And that has been one of the reasons for conflict.

How do we act now to prevent conflict? I am going to say something I am sure is not very popular: we need strong states. In a situation like ours, markets alone cannot solve the problems of development. You need a combination of a strong state that regulates, directs, and is able to invest in those areas where the market does not because they do not bring immediate profit. The state has to be there to tackle the pockets of poverty.

We must have a separation of powers. We have to have checks and balances under which we can talk then of transparency, accountability, and inclusiveness.

In many of our states, we have two systems. We have the modern system, but the majority of our people run their lives on the basis of traditional rule. We have

> *We need much more tolerance regarding differences.*
>
> — Graça Machel

Graça Machel highlights the links between conflict and food and nutrition insecurity.

to integrate our traditional way of doing things into the modern state. In other words, the two systems must meet in the middle, because that is what is going to bring all the majorities, especially the rural people, into the decisionmaking arena.

We need to create platforms for citizens to voice their grievances. This is one of the problems that lead to conflict. They have grievances, they try to make them heard, but there is no mechanism of dialogue and communication. And in a situation of accessible arms and land mines, people then resort very easily to violent conflict.

We need small—and I am underlining "small"—but well-trained and professional militaries, under civilian accountability. Many times our citizens wake up and find out they are at war. There is no information about why. Then women and children are caught to be killed without even knowing the reason for the conflict. That is why it is important to have civilian accountability of our armies.

We need leadership that encourages democracy, inclusion, and negotiation. By this, I mean we need strong social structures and alternative means of political participation so that opposition will not be tempted to resort to violent conflict.

And here I have to insist that we need much more tolerance regarding differences. We need to accept that, "Yes, I hold power today. Because I hold power, I've been entrusted by the majority to run civil life. But I don't own the nation." Flexibility and dialogue with opposition are of extreme importance if we are to prevent conflict.

We also need a functioning private sector that is sustainable, independent, and diverse. We need a patriotic private sector that invests and gives a hand to public life to build our nations. And it must be independent to prevent the sort of promiscuity where someone in public life is at the same time a businessman. How is he going to be independent in parliament if his own interests are invested in decisions he has to make? So we need to develop this sense of powers that are separated, connected, and mutually supportive, but each one in his or her place.

We need a strong, vibrant, and independent civil society. Many of our organizations on the continent are still very weak and dependent on the extent of funding. This makes them vulnerable to a failure to set agendas that are nationally driven and that respond to national priorities.

We need mechanisms to monitor and control the flow of small arms and land mines to drastically reduce their cheap and easy availability.

We know from experience that those who pay the highest price in conflicts are women, children, and rural populations. In peace building we have to make sure that we involve women in negotiations and in the drafting of new, transitional constitutions. We have to make sure they bring their own aspirations and feelings into the transitional rebuilding period of our nations. Women and children have to become a much more visible priority in reconstruction and rehabilitation programs when we seek to mitigate conflict.

It is extremely important, as we plan for the decades to come, to understand that the impact of conflict still exists in a country even when the arms have silenced. So we must take into account the human impact and help to rebuild human capital. Finally, with HIV/AIDS having come to stay for some time, no plan of food security and nutrition will succeed without integrating the component of controlling HIV/AIDS in the decades to come.

> *It is extremely important, as we plan for the decades to come, to understand that the impact of conflict still exists in a country even when the arms have silenced.*
>
> — Graça Machel

Excerpt 4: Breaking the Links Between Conflict and Hunger in Africa

Ellen Messer and Marc J. Cohen

In February 2004, United Nations agencies calculated that over 45 million people in developing countries experiencing or recovering from conflict were in need of food and other emergency humanitarian assistance. More than 80 percent of those affected lived in Sub-Saharan Africa.

Conflict causes food insecurity and, under most circumstances, depresses production and income from cash crops and livestock. This reduction in production and income further decreases food security and reduces the coping capacity of those dependent on these sources for their livelihood. According to the Food and Agriculture Organization of the United Nations, conflict cost Africa over $120 billion worth of agricultural production during the last third of the 20th century. Given the importance of agricultural livelihoods to overall economic well-being, especially in conflict-prone countries in Africa, these losses were devastating. The United Nations Children's Fund reports that conflict countries have also failed to make much improvement in child malnutrition and mortality rates, in part because of the destructive violence and in part because of underinvestment in health, education, and nutrition programs relative to military spending.

By contrast, the ways in which food insecurity currently contributes to conflict are less well understood, including the circumstances under which food insecurity triggers conflict. Recent theories of civil war, for example, ignore the linkages between the agricultural sector, which employs the majority of people, and other primary-commodity sectors, which are usually implicated in funding arms and troops—and in funding their warring political leaders.

Conflict in developing countries stems from a constellation of factors, including ethnic rivalries and environmental scarcities, as well as intergroup competition over resources such as land, water, and development aid. In conflict situations, there is usually some combination of perceived unfairness in resource distribution, injury to a group's sense of cultural identity, struggle for control over access to high-value primary resources, and a precipitous decline in household incomes due to a natural disaster or a plunge in the price of key mineral or agricultural commodities.

Studies of the economic correlates of war—or of the motives and opportunities of the combatants—rarely investigate food insecurity directly, although they often find that conflict is strongly associated with factors closely related to food insecurity, for example, high infant mortality, destitution, inequality, and declining per capita incomes.

In postconflict countries such as Mozambique, the consequences of previous wars exact a toll on food security and economic development long after the end of fighting, as combatants deliberately destroyed agricultural production capacity, markets, health posts, and human and social capital. Despite more than a decade of peace and favorable economic growth, Mozambique is still hampered by landmines and unexploded ordnance that continue to kill and maim agricultural workers and make land hazardous to farm. Roads, schools, and teachers, all decimated by conflict, remain in short supply, and the country, like all of Sub-Saharan Africa, now faces the additional labor and food security challenge of HIV/AIDS.

Most of the conflict and postconflict countries in Sub-Saharan Africa are home to substantial numbers of food-insecure people. In most cases, the population in need of food and other emergency humanitarian assistance accounts for only a small share of the total food-insecure population. Hence, African conflict countries are zones of high, *chronic* food insecurity.

This has been excerpted from 2020 Africa Conference Brief 10, published by IFPRI, Washington, DC, 2004.

Keynote Address: Will Food Security in Africa Be Achieved by Sustained, Increased, and More Effective Aid?

Poul Nielson
European Union Commissioner for Development Cooperation and Humanitarian Aid, Belgium
Speech delivered by **Sigurd Illing**, Head of Delegation of the European Union, Uganda

Food aid is not an appropriate instrument to foster long-term food security.
— Poul Nielson

Let me first of all convey to you very best wishes from the European Commissioner for Development and Humanitarian Aid, Mr. Poul Nielson, who very much regrets not being present in person. He forwarded me his message, which I have the honor of reading to you:

"Assuring Food and Nutrition Security in Africa by 2020" is the subject of this conference, and I, as European Commissioner for Development Cooperation and Humanitarian Aid, have received the invitation to address this audience. Will food security in Africa be achieved by sustained, increased, and more effective aid? I would like first to reflect on the concept of food security.

Food security encompasses many dimensions: trade, agriculture, environment, health, and employment. To increase their access to food, people require broader employment opportunities. Individual food security depends on addressing consumer and health issues. Environmental threats, limitations, and opportunities must be considered to ensure sustainable food production. Trade opportunities are key incentives for growth and for the integration of African countries into the global economy. All these aspects are fundamental blocks in a comprehensive fight against hunger.

Yet other important elements need to be taken into account for the eradication of poverty: the elimination of inequalities, the building of democracy and good governance, respect for human rights, and the creation of peace and security. The mutually reinforcing relationship between poverty, food insecurity, and natural resource degradation on the one hand and social and political instability and conflict on the other has yet to be fully recognized. Addressing hunger and nutrition requires considering the complex nature of food insecurity.

The mutually reinforcing relationship between poverty, food insecurity, and natural resource degradation on the one hand and social and political instability and conflict on the other has yet to be fully recognized.
— Poul Nielson

What is the role of development aid in meeting this complex challenge? If we look at official development assistance (ODA) in global terms, we realize that its financial volume is lower than remittances from migrants and lower than private investments. It represents roughly one-third of what OECD countries spend in support of their domestic agriculture.

ODA, however, still matters, and very much so for many developing countries. Our task, then, is to fulfill the commitments reached in Monterrey for increased resources—to make ODA more relevant and more efficient by harmonizing donors' procedures and more cost-effective by, among other things, adopting the principles of untying of aid, including public procurement and food aid. These are issues that the European Union (EU) is championing in international fora.

Your task as African leaders is to find African solutions for the problems Africa is facing. We can only support your own efforts. This is why the concept of partnership and ownership are two of the pillars of our relations with countries in the African, Caribbean, and Pacific Group of States (ACP).

Let me now introduce the Commission's policy and approach to food security. For the Community and its member states, food insecurity is fundamentally a dimension of poverty. It requires a broad-based policy approach for sustainable development while tackling the root causes of the problem. It is essential to simultaneously address the issues of food availability (that is, production, strategic reserves, trade), access to food (that is, economic growth, employment, income), and response to crisis situations and nutritional problems.

The important role of women for food security must also be recognized. Farmers are still perceived as males by policymakers, development actors, and those who deliver agricultural services. Women have less access to resources such as land, water, credit, and training, hindering their production capacity and their role in promoting increased food security.

Agriculture and the rural economy constitute the engine of economic growth in most African countries and the basis for their integration into the world economy. However, to contribute effectively to poverty reduction and food security, agriculture must become an integral part of a wider rural development strategy encompassing nonagricultural elements of the rural economy, as well as the social sectors.

Trade expansion plays an important role in fostering broad economic growth. Both developing countries and countries in transition need to be integrated in the world trading system to reap benefits from economic growth.

The European Commission (EC) reiterates its commitment to achieve these goals along the lines agreed in the Doha Development Agenda. Comprehensive negotiations are to be pursued on the three trade pillars—market access, export subsidies, and trade-distorting domestic support—while nontrade concerns are to be taken into account. Special and differential treatment for developing countries needs to be an integral part of the negotiations, to be operationally effective, and to take account of their development needs, including food security and rural development.

The EC is the world's largest importer and second-largest exporter of agricultural and food products. In particular, the EC is the largest buyer from developing countries, to a large extent as the result of granted trade preferences. All imports—except arms—including all raw and processed products from the 49 poorest countries have unlimited and permanent duty-free access to EC markets. We call on similar regimes to be applied by other developed countries.

A few words now on how we see the role of food aid within our food security policy. We in the Commission are convinced that food aid is not an appropriate instrument to foster long-term food security. As a result, we have reduced our supplies of food aid-in-kind to emergency interventions. Contrary to other donors, we strongly support the decoupling of food aid provisions from the use of grain surpluses in our countries, and we encourage the purchase of food in the surplus-producing areas in developing countries.

This is not to say that food aid does not remain important in emergency food shortages and postcrisis situations, as well as a component of safety net strategies for vulnerable sections of the population. The EC has a budget of roughly EUR 450 million annually for food aid and food security interventions targeted to a limited number of countries, most of them in Africa. The European Community is the second-largest donor to the Food Aid Convention.

Let me now turn on the specific challenges facing Africa. If we look at the percentage of undernourished population in the developing countries, we see that, with the exception of Sub-Saharan Africa, these have decreased during the last decades in most regions. On the other hand, life expectancy has declined as a result of HIV/AIDS, the worst-affected countries being in Sub-Saharan Africa.

At the same time, emergencies continue to have a significant impact on progress toward halving the number of people suffering from hunger. And natural disasters still have a devastating effect in many regions. Thus, the challenges facing Africa in meeting food security are enormous.

This brings me to the conclusion that our approach to food security in Africa needs to be different. Our dialogue needs to be more relevant, and our conferences need to deliver concrete outputs. And today, the African Union makes the difference that we believe will bring new hope for Africa.

Development, finally, depends on developing countries' own actions. Implementing sound policies and improved governance, fighting corruption, and improving human rights are essential for progress. We have, therefore, warmly welcomed the NEPAD initiative, and even more so the launching of the African Union (AU). You all know how keen the European Union is to support the AU and engage in a meaningful EU-Africa dialogue.

The AU has already gone a long way. The AU Commission has been elected, and its new vision and mission have emerged under the leadership of President

Contrary to other donors, we strongly support the decoupling of food aid provisions from the use of grain surpluses in our countries, and we encourage the purchase of food in the surplus-producing areas in developing countries.

— Poul Nielson

If agriculture is to fulfill its promise of being the driving force of economic growth, it needs greater attention in development policy and priorities.

— Poul Nielson

Konare. We share common goals regarding the region's security and prosperity, and we have the financial and technical means to work jointly toward these goals. These issues were discussed last week in Brussels between the whole of the EC and the AU Commission.

The abilities of the AU to deal with peace and security are crucial for the future of Africa. Conflicts are damaging the image of Africa and hindering prospects for development. Armed conflict and civil strife not only cause humanitarian crises for millions of internally displaced persons and refugees, they also cause agricultural output losses and increased food insecurity. The fact that the number of food-insecure people living in complex political emergencies is growing is a major constraint to reducing hunger.

Similarly, the AU sees agriculture as an important driving force for social and economic development across the continent. I commend in particular the commitment taken by the African heads of state in Maputo to channel 10 percent of national budgetary resources to agriculture. If agriculture is to fulfill its promise of being the driving force of economic growth, it needs greater attention in development policy and priorities.

Africans are entitled to adequate food and greater opportunities to rise out of poverty, and they have the right to better education and health care. We can, and must, put an end to hunger, ignorance, and pandemics. For these legitimate expectations to be met, we need to see action, and action starts at the country level.

Although international and regional dimensions are important—in particular, as concerns trade, management of shared resources, research, and early warning systems—the interventions needed in support of food security have primarily a national dimension. Therefore, the implementation of national poverty reduction strategies needs to rely on a variety of instruments capable of addressing the multifaceted nature of food insecurity. There will only be more resources available to fight food insecurity if African countries make this goal a priority in their own national development strategies. Coordination and cooperation between partners in Africa in this respect are essential for success.

It is my sincere hope that this conference will help us to better understand and identify key actions for improving food security in Africa and help us to mobilize the political will required to see these priorities implemented. Our plans have to build on the work of recent years, starting with the Millennium Development Goals and the agendas we set for ourselves in Doha, Monterrey, and Johannesburg.

Keynote Address: Achieving Sustainable Agricultural Growth in Africa: Lessons from Experience

Norman Borlaug

President, Sasakawa Africa Association and Nobel Peace Prize Laureate, Mexico

Let me begin by giving you some feel for where I came from and from where I speak. I was born on a very small farm in northeast Iowa. I am a product of a one-room country school for my first eight years. I am probably only one of two people present at this conference who went through the utter economic chaos of the Depression following the collapse of the stock market in 1929. I know what a "dollar-a-day" job means—I have worked them, when I could get one. Most of you think that the United States was always in a good economic position. During that period, I was not sure it would survive without a revolution.

I joined the first foreign technical assistance program to help a food-deficit nation. That program was sponsored jointly by the Mexican government and the Rockefeller Foundation. I joined it in 1944, and in one way or another ever since have been affiliated with trying to develop science and technology and to transfer

Use the organic fertilizer that is available, and use it where it fits—close to urban areas, for vegetable production, or for high-value crops. But do not give the impression that the world can be fed by the use of organic fertilizer alone.

— Norman Borlaug

and apply it across disciplines to try to change food production in some parts of the world.

One person does very little alone. But if I have contributed anything of major importance, it is to bring information from disciplines together, to demonstrate what that can do on farmers' fields, and then finally to connect it to economic policy.

And I have been surprised by some of the things that have happened. One person did not do it. It was a team of international young people that made the Green Revolutions of India and Pakistan. Young people, selected by FAO and financed by the Rockefeller Foundation, were brought to Mexico in large numbers in the 1960s, trained across all of these disciplines, and put in contact with farmers' co-ops so that they saw how the co-ops operated—co-ops for credit, especially—with the irrigation commission and with the seed organizations. And farmers made many of the contributions.

There were some who said at that time, "Forget about it." Some of the best minds in academia said, "There's no solution to the food problem in India. Maybe in Pakistan something can be accomplished." But when this effort was transferred from Mexico—not a very likely place for wheat technology to emerge to have an impact around the world—we succeeded.

In India production went from 11 million tons, stagnant over five years, to self-sufficiency in about seven years, and to 74 million tons in the year 2000. It spread from Pakistan to China, first to remove hunger, but hopefully to produce more, to become a part of the economic community by sales.

But there are many who have no land and who are unemployed. And so at the same time there have to be some food-for-work projects. In my early career in those dismal years in the 1930s, I was trained as a forester. I led an emergency work program on soil conservation and forestry, working on roads and trails built by hand by unemployed people. These are the things that can stave us over in hard times and get this ball rolling.

Now, what are the products? They have to be basic foods. By and large they are maize; sorghum in the drier areas; cassava, also in drier areas but warmer climates; one of the legumes, perhaps cowpeas; and some others.

There is plenty of potential. Figure 1 shows what has been done by the Sasakawa Africa Association, sponsored by the Nippon Foundation. It is an extension program—we were never in research. But once in a while when we would see a bottleneck, we would take some of those extension funds to support agents to clear the bottleneck.

Nobel Prize winner Norman Borlaug urges participants to act before it is too late.

These graphs show what that potential is. The graphs are based on several hundred thousand quarter- to tenth-hectare plots on farms throughout 12 different countries. You can see that countries with an asterisk show the highest yields; these are where hybrids were used. But with a good open-pollinated variety, you can achieve great benefits. It is not the magic of the variety alone—it is restoring soil fertility, it is handling weed problems, it is conserving soil moisture. All of this together is the package of technology that has to be transmitted to farmers' fields.

Among the types of maize being introduced is quality protein maize (QPM), which is particularly important because of its nutritive value. It is very important to populations where there is little or no milk and meat is very scarce. This is one of the problems we are addressing

FIGURE 1—Sasakawa Global 2000 maize demonstration yields

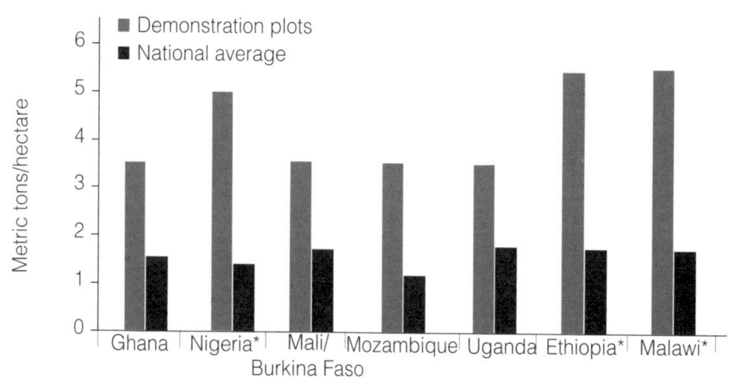

Source: Unpublished data from Sasakawa Global 2000; FAOSTAT.
* Primarily using hybrids.

To me, the lack of roads and infrastructure is the curse of Africa.

— Norman Borlaug

with QPM, which has protein quality approaching that of skimmed milk. Ghana has led the way in QPM research and development in Sub-Saharan Africa. QPM varieties and hybrids are now grown on at least 300,000 hectares in eight countries (Ghana, Mozambique, Uganda, Ethiopia, Malawi, Burkina Faso, Mali, and Guinea), and the number of countries and total area are expanding quite rapidly.

The soil fertility problem, or infertility, has to be approached through on-farm experiments in which you determine what levels of different kinds of fertilizer are needed, and then wide demonstrations on small plots to convince the small farmer.

If you are going to put a new technology across, it has to produce a large magnitude of improvement. For an increase of 10 percent, forget about it—this might be the difference from one year to the other in rainfall or temperature.

FIGURE 2—Fertilizer nutrient consumption per hectare of arable land in selected countries, 2000

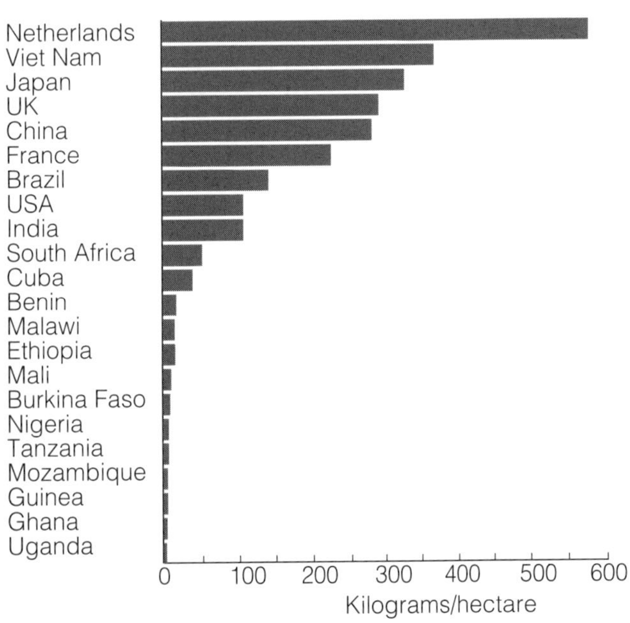

Source: FAOSTAT, July 2002.

Now take a look at soil fertility. Figure 2 shows Viet Nam up near the top now, China very near the top with more than 200 kg of nutrients per hectare, and India at about the same level as the United States. Had this chart been made 30 years ago, the Asian countries would be where the Sub-Saharan African countries are today, where you can barely see on the figure the amounts of nutrients used.

We have to be realistic—I dislike seeing people from affluent countries who do not understand the complexities of soil fertility coming and advising heads of state and ministers of agriculture that they can solve their problems with organic fertilizer. This is just misleading people. Use the organic fertilizer that is available, and use it where it fits—close to urban areas, for vegetable production, or for high-value crops. But do not give the impression that the world can be fed by the use of organic fertilizer alone. It cannot be done. If we were to try to replace the current global consumption of nitrogen from chemical fertility—which stands at about 80 million metric tons—with cow manure, for example, we would need 50 times that amount.

We have to do something about the resource base, the land. In parts of African countries, it is deplorable. The only way erosion can be ameliorated and reduced is through planting trees and grass, forest technology, and agroforestry. A lot of this will have to be accomplished by food-for-work types of operations, where food-insecure farmers are hired to take part in eco-rehabilitation projects in many of the major watersheds. These areas are the worst-eroded, and something has to be done to turn the situation around. Without social investments the job will not get done. Farmers are too poor—and often too weak—to reclaim these environments on their own.

And we need to do something about water in many areas. We can produce enough food now to feed Africa from rain-fed areas, but in some areas it is possible to capture runoff, and this should be done. Many water-harvesting technologies are low-cost, labor-intensive, and not high in capital investment. Some of our Sasakawa programs in several countries are teaching farmers to capture water in ponds and to use drip irrigation.

To me, the lack of roads and infrastructure is the curse of Africa (Table 1). We had a case in Ethiopia three years ago with excellent maize crops in mid-elevation areas. Two hundred kilometers away, at a slightly lower elevation, people were starving and unable to move the crops from one place to the other. Roads are necessary not only for bringing in inputs, like fertilizer, but for moving additional grain to market.

More important in the long run, from my point of view, is that a road brings a school. You cannot get teachers to go into the backcountry where there is no school. So that road brings the school. Soon thereafter, there is a public health officer or a doctor or nurse. And soon there will be a beat-up old bus carrying people, crossing ethnic and linguistic barriers, reducing fear between people who cannot communicate because of language difficulties or different cultures. All of these consequences are indirect, but they are vital to the further development of Africa.

From the standpoint of adults, there is tremendous neglect: 140 million adults in Africa are illiterate. There are nearly twice as many illiterate women as men (Figure 3). Another 50 million children of primary school age are still out of school. School lunches are one thing that will help—both to improve nutrition and to get kids into school. Basic education in the medium term will turn things around, indirectly. It will also slow population growth, because family size automatically decreases with education, and more attention is given to each child's survival.

I agree with the four basic thrusts of the comprehensive agricultural development strategy for Africa being advanced by NEPAD. But we have to win the leadership of the people in government. Prime ministers and presidents—people of that stature—have to decide that they are going to change things.

The things that changed India and Pakistan were four people that had the determination. Who were they? Prime Minister Indira Gandhi, because of her support for C. Subramaniam, the minister of agriculture. And he had the courage. In Pakistan it was President Ayub Khan and his minister of agriculture, Malik Khuda Bakhsh Bucha. The world owes them a debt. They did what many of the best brains in our Western universities said was never going to happen.

Not only did it happen in India and Pakistan, but wheat technology moved to China, by way of Pakistan. It got there eight years before I first got there in 1974. They knew how to grow it and where to grow it, where it fit and where it did not. Of course, you all know what has happened to food production in China in the last few years. It is the number one producer in rice, as it always has been, but it is now also the number one producer in wheat and the second-biggest producer in maize. Here, Chou En-lai and Deng Xiaoping were critically important leaders.

Modernization of agriculture and rural enterprise development in China have permitted the tremendous

TABLE 1—Kilometers of paved roads per million people in selected countries

Country	Kilometers of roads
USA	20,987
France	12,673
Japan	9,102
Zimbabwe	1,586
South Africa	1,402
Brazil	1,064
India	1,004
China	803
Guinea	637
Ghana	494
Nigeria	230
Mozambique	141
Tanzania	114
Uganda	94
Ethiopia	66
Congo, DR	59

Source: *Encyclopedia Britannica*, 2002.

FIGURE 3—African adult illiteracy

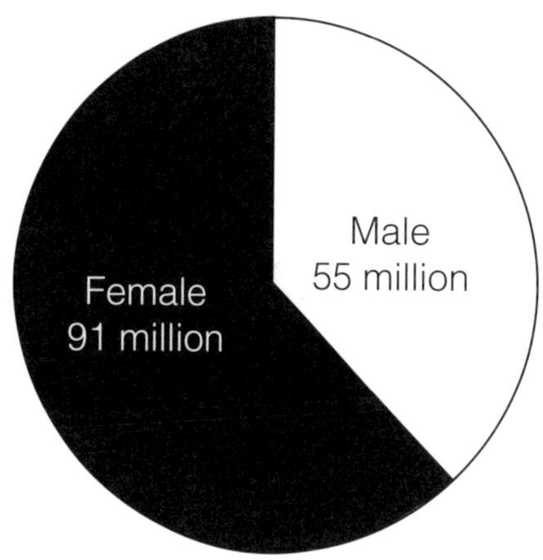

Souce: UNICEF, *State of the World's Children 2003* (New York, 2003).

I want to see two or three leaders here in Africa decide that they are going to do something dramatic in the direction of agriculture-led industrial development.

– Norman Borlaug

industrialization that is going on today. Rising incomes have also led to a revolution in meat demand. At the present time, China is importing something on the order of 16 million metric tons of soybeans from Argentina, Brazil, and the United States for pork and poultry production. Everything is changing. I want to see two or three leaders here in Africa decide that they are going to do something dramatic in the direction of agriculture-led industrial development. And it can be done.

The science and technology for most of the basic food crops are here to produce what is needed, and certainly to begin the process of agricultural transformation. How to distribute the increased production more equitably is another matter, but first we have to produce. I have never been interested in equitable distribution of poverty. I want to produce something worth distributing equitably, and what is a more worthy commodity than food in a food-insecure region such as Africa?

And how does the world spend its money? Nine hundred billion dollars go to military budgets. I am sorry to say that the United States spends slightly more than half of that, but there is altogether too much spent everywhere. We do this to protect ourselves—or try to—against all sorts of things, but certainly we cannot expect tranquility and peace with this gap growing greater between the poor countries and the rich. John Boyd Orr, the first director general of FAO, said it beautifully when he said, "You can't build peace on empty stomachs." To which I add, "and human misery." This has to change.

I am late in life. I will probably never see a Green Revolution in Africa happen. But I hope there are two or three leaders of African countries who are going to go for this goal. They may think, like India and Pakistan did, that they do not have the resources. But if agriculture starts changing and improvements are made, funds start to flow from many different sources.

So this is the challenge. Where are the leaders? Time is running out for me—I am now 90 years old—and I want to see it happen.

Box 3: Announcement of the World Food Prize 2004 Laureate

Robert Havener
President Emeritus, Winrock International; and Member of the Council of Advisors of the World Food Prize Foundation, USA

Shortly after Dr. Borlaug received the Nobel Prize in 1970, he began an effort to create a Nobel Prize for agriculture. Unfortunately, the Nobel Committee did not find the arguments persuasive, because they had closed the door to new prizes. So we set about developing a World Food Prize for people who had made an outstanding contribution to increasing the quantity, quality, and availability of food throughout the world. Thus far, we have recognized a number of people, at least two of whom are in this room—Pedro Sanchez and Per Pinstrup-Andersen—for their outstanding work. Dr. M. S. Swaminathan from India, who helped Dr. Borlaug initiate the Green Revolution in India, was the first recipient of the World Food Prize.

But the most recent recipients of the World Food Prize are two, for their outstanding work related to rice. The two people honored this year are Yuan Longping from China—the father of hybrid rice, which has dramatically increased rice production in China—and Monty Jones, rice breeder at WARDA–The Africa Rice Center. They will receive the World Food Prize in October in Des Moines, Iowa. On that occasion, Dr. Jones's citation will read:

> *Dr. Monty Jones, working in the most difficult environments for rice production, led a pioneering effort at WARDA to develop New Rice for Africa, NERICA.*
>
> *In an unprecedented achievement, he captured the genetic potential of the traditional African rices by combining African and Asian rice types, dramatically increasing the yields under Africa's growing conditions, and offering great hope to millions of poor farmers in Africa and around the world, and is a catalyst for agricultural transformation in major parts of Africa.*

There are a few other people who ought to share this prize, in spirit if not in fact, including Eugene Terry, formerly the director general of WARDA; Peter Matlon, then WARDA director of research; and Kanayo Nwanze, the current director general of WARDA. All have been great supporters of this work.

2004 World Food Prize winner Monty Jones gives thanks for the recognition of his achievement.

Monty Jones
2004 World Food Prize Laureate; Executive Secretary, Forum for Agricultural Research in Africa (FARA), Ghana

On Saturday, the 27th of March, I got a call from the president of the World Food Prize Foundation, Ambassador Kenneth Quinn, who informed me that I had won the World Food Prize. So this award came as a pleasant surprise to me. The award will mean a lot to me, to my family, and to my country, Sierra Leone. It will mean a lot to my current institution, the Forum for Agricultural Research in Africa. This is a new institution, created when I became its first executive secretary about 18 months ago. FARA has an important role to play in African agricultural research for development, because FARA's mandate is to coordinate and facilitate agricultural research for development in Africa by focusing on advocacy for support to agricultural research, developing partnerships and strategic alliances, and collating and disseminating relevant information.

The award will mean a lot to the Africa Rice Center. Dr. Terry has been mentioned earlier, and Dr. Peter Matlon is also here. He was my director of research when I proposed going into interspecific breeding of African and Asian rice species. He believed in my vision, and this is the reason Eugene Terry and Peter Matlon allowed me to go into this controversial subject at that time. Dr. Kanayo Nwanze, the current director of WARDA, also helped to promote the NERICAs vigorously after we obtained fertile interspecific progenies between the African and Asian rice species.

This award will also mean a lot to a number of collaborators worldwide. I would like to mention a few, like Dr. Brah of IRRI; Dr. Susan McCouch of Cornell University; and Dr. Alain Gesquire of the Institute of Agronomic Research in Montpellier, France. And I must mention the national programs of West and Central Africa that contributed a great deal in the wide-scale evaluation of the NERICAs.

The award will bring recognition of the African contribution to science and technology. It will also help to put together elements that will lead to food security and poverty alleviation in Africa by the year 2020. And it will also serve as a stimulus to young scientists, showing them that if they redouble their efforts, they will reap the benefits.

Box 4: The Voices of Youth

The young Africans of today are the ones who will be living with poverty, hunger, and malnutrition for years to come if no progress is made toward achieving food and nutrition security. To hear from these young people, IFPRI's 2020 Vision Initiative launched an Africa-wide youth writing contest on the theme "A Full Food Basket for Africa by 2020," in association with the conference. More than 200 young people from about two dozen countries from Morocco to South Africa, from Senegal to Ethiopia, sent in poems, stories, and essays in English and French expressing their analysis, insights, and hopes. In their writing, the entrants shared a human perspective on the sad realities of hunger and malnutrition, voiced their confidence that hunger in Africa can be overcome, and uttered a collective demand for action.

The winner of the grand prize, selected by an international panel of judges, was Nelisiwe Mbali Mtsweni of South Africa, a 17-year-old girl whose story "Emancipation from Emaciation" featured a "disco-king fairy godfather" who speaks in rhyme. Runners-up in the contest were Yoda Jean Paul, age 18, of Burkina Faso, for his poem "The Last Bit of Bread," and Oladayo Osunjaiye, age 17, of Nigeria, for his open letter to an African president. These winning entries and those receiving honorable mention were published in a booklet called *A Full Food Basket for Africa by 2020/Un Plein Panier d'Aliments pour l'Afrique d'ici 2020*, which was made available at the conference.

In a special ceremony at the conference, the 12-year-old Omukama (king) of Tooro Rukirabasaija Oyo Nyimba Kabambaiguru Rukidi IV, Uganda, presented the grand prize to Mtsweni. "I wish to tell the young people that we are the future of this great continent, Africa," said the king. "Very soon, we shall take over from the adults today, to tackle and solve the same problems they are discussing now. Let us learn eagerly from them and get involved in agricultural production, to have enough food and better nutrition."

Mtsweni then read her story in its entirety, inspiring the assembled conference participants.

The King of Tooro, Oyo Nyimba Kabambaiguru Rukidi IV, presents the grand prize for the youth writing contest to Nelisiwe Mbali Mtsweni of South Africa.

Emancipation from Emaciation

Once upon a time (we're talking eons ago), Gaya (Mother Earth) and her children lived as one big happy family. They coexisted impeccably and wanted for nothing. But after some time, the children felt the urge to leave their nest called Pangaea to explore their "wide futures." So they each went their separate ways and went on to bear their own offspring.

Inevitably, they each had their fair share of triumphs and tribulations, but the one who bore the brunt of it all was Africa. She was trapped in a perpetual web of distress over her ailing children. They were plagued by war, fatal epidemics, lethal pandemics, and famine. The latter was most prevalent. Famine had mutated into an invincible monstrosity that was ravaging more than half of Africa's children. It was so notorious that it had aliases like Hunger, Dearth, Starvation, Barrenness, Malnutrition, and Deprivation, and it had a sidekick named Poverty. This ruthless antagonist knew that once Africa had fallen prey to its insatiable appetite, it would almost be inconceivable to free it from its clutches. Almost?

The only thing that kept Africa's children alive was a tiny glimmer of hope that they refused to discard. It resided deep down in the pits of their stomachs. It was so minuscule that it could easily be engulfed in their stomach-ripping hunger pangs and be forgotten for a while.

Nelisiwe Mbali Mtsweni recites her prize-winning story, inspiring conference participants.

But it was there nonetheless. It was this tiny spark of hope that initiated the revolution. To Famine's future dismay, Africa's children were able to dig deep and channel that glint of faith, just enough to give them strength to ask for help one last time. All those millions of microscopic glimmers of hope put together created quite a formidable force. Gaunt, emaciated, and with hunger emblazoned in their eyes, they sent out a cry so loud that it drowned out the deafening sound of their collective rumbling stomachs.

Gaya heard them. She felt their pure anguish and unadulterated sincerity, and her heart almost imploded. After extensive deliberation, she resolved to bequeath to them what she knew would undoubtedly redeem Africa from this scourge. If this failed, Africa would be doomed, for Gaya's well of solutions had run dry.

Africa's children feared that their cries had fallen on deaf ears, as their calls hadn't yet been heeded. Starvation was in its element as it forcibly lacerated every last atom of their hope while they wept. Their gushing tears felt like excruciating acid rolling down their dry, discolored, paper cheeks. Little did they know that as each tear touched the scorched earth, a ripple effect was created. All their tears combined sent forth a colossal ripple that vibrated through the earth. The ground quaked vigorously. Thick black storm clouds rolled in from nowhere. Thunder exploded. Lightening slashed the sky. A gargantuan tornado approached from the horizon at the speed of thought. Yet, the most uncanny and inexplicable phenomenon was that during all this apocalyptic weather the children could have sworn that they heard the 70's Bee Gees hit "Staying Alive" blaring in the air. Psychedelic disco lights flashed everywhere. Glitter fell from the sky. Had the mind-numbing involuntary fasting forced their sanity to abandon them?

Then, just as abruptly as it all began, it came to a screeching halt, except for the song, lights, and glitter. The dust finally settled. There he stood in all his glory, too bright to look at with the naked eye. The children couldn't believe their eyes when they'd miraculously adjusted to the blinding shimmer. What in the entire universe was this apparition before them? Posing in 10-inch platform shoes, glittery sky-blue bell-bottoms, multicolored polka-dot shirt, and electric pink, star-shaped sunglasses, he held up the peace sign with his fingers above his awe-inspiring afro. After retrieving her jaw from the ground, one of the children mustered up the courage to ask, "What kind of angel are you?"

The figure replied,

"I ain't no angel, child, or a pixie or an elf.
I'm your fairy-god father, sent to help you by Gaya herself."

A 70's, disco king, fairy-god father that spoke in rhyme wasn't quite what they'd expected, but they were desperate. "What should we call you?" they asked.

In his animated manner of singing and dancing to everything he said, he replied,

"Well, I'm here to nullify Starving,
so you can call me Marvin.
For too long now, every African nation
has suffered from hunger's emasculation
I'm here to give you emancipation
From goiter, kwashiorkor, and emaciation!
With human kindness and education,
We'll declare an embargo on starvation.
I promise to get rid of Famine,
So we can all be carefree and jammin'!

The children of Africa were skeptical. This idealistic image that Marvin had described sounded like an unattainable Utopia. They asked him,

"In a world where unemployment, poverty, and hunger are rife,
How can you expect anything but hardships and strife?"

Marvin replied,

"Hey, if I can make you speak in rhyme,
I can do anything. You'll soon see in time!"

And before the children could open their mouths to retort, a whirl of purple wind suddenly engulfed Marvin, and he disappeared. All that could be heard was a fading voice in the distance singing,

continued

"By 2020, instead of an Africa that's malnourished,
we'll see an Africa that will have flourished!"

As the saying goes, charity begins at home. So Marvin entered the homes of billions of people around the world during breakfast, lunch, dinner, and snack times. He made himself invisible and whispered little inspirations in people's ears while they stuffed their faces. He'd whisper things like:

"Listen up, dude.
Here's some food for thought.
While you're being fussy about your food
There are people without grub of any sort!"

Or he'd say,

"Dealing with having nothing to eat is one major feat.
While you scoff down junk food in your comfy seat,
millions in Africa can't afford meat, or even dry wheat!"

He'd also whisper,

"Just before you take that bite,
Picture this unappetizing sight:
A child with kwashiorkor is dying and its mother has no might,
To fix the situation because there's no food (a basic human right).
So don't just sit there with your heart closed up tight,
Open it up to the less fortunate and to their lives add some light."

People all over the world suddenly had the impulse to rectify the hunger crisis in Africa and in their own communities. It started small. People stopped throwing food away. Schools organized monthly nonperishable food drives, where each learner had to bring one food product every month. Then companies started to do the same. NGOs admired this initiative and donated tons of staple foods. The movement grew. Celebrities used their fame and status to hold fundraisers. It grew even more when the governments got involved. First-world countries abolished the debts of the third world. They encouraged trade and invested in health, education, and agriculture. Medication was sent over to treat diseases like goiter, anemia, kwashiorkor, and AIDS, and the people were also educated about their prevention. Technological farming equipment was donated for commercial agriculture, and people were taught how to be self-sufficient through subsistence farming. A huge emphasis was put on education, especially for girls, so that the number of working professionals would increase, therefore enriching the economy. African governments included fiscal policies for agriculture in their annual budgets. Famine was no longer nobody's business. Everybody was concerned, and it became a priority of big news networks to report on the progress of the food drive. An International Food Council was established, which was responsible for organizing funds, research, giving aid, and ensuring that all donations were distributed accordingly. Although it was still a very controversial issue, people became a bit more susceptible to the idea of genetically modified food. And though it took some time, the warring countries finally reached mutual resolutions, and all refugees, who made up most of the world's hungry, returned home and were incorporated into the new economies.

Marvin's course of action had produced phenomenal results. Famine, Dearth, Starvation, Deprivation, Hunger, Barrenness, Malnutrition, call it whatever you like, was now a former notorious invincible monstrosity. Even its sidekick, Poverty, was keeping a low profile. Gaunt flimsy skeletons usually seen roaming or vegetating aimlessly were no longer the norm. The words, "I'm FAMISHED!" which people would bellow in agony, had now been reduced to a mere "I'm feeling slightly peckish." Marvin quietly disappeared back to where he came from and was soon forgotten or brushed off as a typical hallucination caused by extreme hunger. But what he accomplished was never forgotten, as they were faced with it everyday.

People's generosity and selflessness,
Was the unfaltering recipe for success.
The world was once filled with doom and gloom,
Now everywhere you looked, a smile would bloom.
And thus ends the story, ladies and gents,
Africa's children lived ever joyfully hence.
The world was gorged with pure elation,
As they'd acquired their emancipation!

An African dance troupe entertains participants at a reception following the youth award ceremony.

Chapter 10 Strategies and Options

Chair: Courage Quashigah
Minister of Food and Agriculture, Ghana

It is clear that we cannot, in the near future, phase out the more than 96 percent of farmers who operate on a small scale in Sub-Saharan Africa. In spite of the fact that they produce the bulk of our food, the majority of them are still poor. Malnutrition is also common among them since they do not have the means to introduce the required nutritional balance into their diet. Given that hunger is one of the most visible consequences of poverty, our pro-poor development strategies must include presenting farmers with technological options for increasing their production.

Nutrition is not a new element being introduced into food security. It has always been a part of many definitions of food security. The World Food Summit in Rome in 1996 agreed that "food security exists when all people, at all times, have physical and economic access to sufficient nutrition and safe food to meet their dietary needs and food preferences for an active and healthy life." The Ghana Food and Agricultural Sector Development Policy document defines food security as "good quality, nutritious food, hygienically packaged, and attractively presented; available in sufficient quantities all year round; located at the appropriate places at affordable prices." Most people, however, continue to interpret food security in terms of food sufficiency and access to it in terms of location and purchasing power.

But awareness is now growing that malnutrition, particularly vitamin and mineral deficiencies, are causing a range of health problems ranging from a weak immune system, anemia, and blindness to lower IQs. Eating for good nutrition is not just feeding the stomach with any food, but with the right balance of carbohydrates, proteins, lipids, vitamins, minerals, and water to enhance growth, development, and maintenance of the body. Nutrition is aptly defined by the Council on Food and Nutrition of the American Medical Association as "the science of food, the nutrients, and substances therein, their action, interaction, and balance in relation to health and disease, and the process by which the organism ingests, digests, absorbs, transports, utilizes, and excretes food substances."

This is a life or death issue, and it must take center stage when we are talking about food security. Nutrition in food security is like leadership in management. You ignore leadership, you write your bankruptcy report; you ignore nutrition, you sign your death warrant. A food surplus will not automatically translate into food security. I am particularly happy that nutrition has finally been pulled out from its hiding place into the full glare of discussions, because it is precisely nutrition that presents the greatest difficulty in achieving 100 percent food security.

We must all take drastic measures to ensure that the generations behind us are well nourished so they can develop into the strong, healthy, and intelligent work force required to carry on the fight against poverty and hunger. In recognition of the importance of nutrition, which is criminally ignored, particularly in

Nutrition is not a new element being introduced into food security. It has always been a part of many definitions of food security.

— Courage Quashigah

Sub-Saharan Africa, I have decided to set up a working group comprising research scientists, nutritionists in the health and education services, food processors, agriculturists, and others to expose the nutritional values of our local foods and compose a nutritious diet menu for schools in Ghana using our local food items. We will enforce the use of this menu to improve the feeding program of our children. This will increase demand for local food items and create a much-needed market for our farmers.

> *Nutrition in food security is like leadership in management. You ignore leadership, you write your bankruptcy report; you ignore nutrition, you sign your death warrant.*
>
> – Courage Quashigah

FIGURE 1—Prevalence of undernutrition, 1999–2001

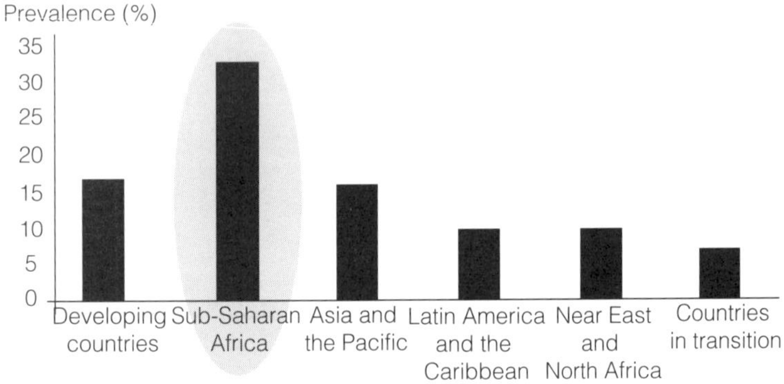

Source: FAO, *State of Food and Agriculture 2003* (Rome).

FIGURE 2—Number of undernourished people, 1999–2001

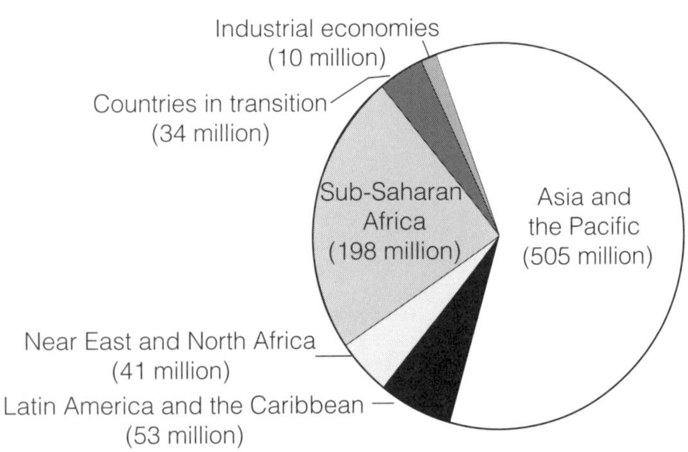

Source: FAO, *State of Food and Agriculture 2003* (Rome).
Note: Total = 842 million.

Keynote Address: Strategies for Improving Food and Nutrition Security in Africa

Victoria Sekitoleko
Subregional Representative, Food and Agriculture Organization of the United Nations (FAO), Subregional Office for Southern and East Africa, Zimbabwe

The theme of this conference is very important, as we are faced with the continuing paradox of a planet that experiences agricultural surpluses but at the same time has 842 million people without access to adequate food to meet their basic nutritional requirements. Globally, Sub-Saharan Africa has the highest percentage of undernourished people, with more than 30 percent of the population undernourished—an estimated 200 million people as of 2001 (Figures 1 and 2). Worldwide, more than 2 billion people still subsist on diets that lack the essential vitamins and minerals required for normal growth and development and for the prevention of premature death and disabilities such as blindness and mental retardation. At the same time, hundreds of millions suffer from diseases caused or exacerbated by excessive or unbalanced dietary intakes or by the consumption of unsafe food and water. Although the proportion and absolute number of chronically undernourished people has declined worldwide, progress has been uneven among developing countries. The challenge we face now is to build upon the progress that has occurred and accelerate the processes that improve food and nutrition security.

Today, on behalf of FAO, I would like to present strategies along three major lines to assure food security and nutrition in Africa:

1. enhancing political commitment and resources;
2. increasing agricultural productivity; and
3. addressing the complete food and nutrition cycle to reduce hunger and undernutrition.

First and foremost, there is a need for political will and commitment of resources to carry out new and existing programs and strategies for food and nutrition security. Fortunately, awareness of food and nutrition issues appears to be growing, as evidenced by the various global, regional, and national commitments to address food security and nutrition as major development issues. As you are all aware, FAO, along with key partners, has embarked on a number of interrelated initiatives and programs over the past few years to address problems of hunger, food insecurity, and malnutrition. For example, in 1992 FAO and the World Health Organization (WHO) jointly held the International Conference on Nutrition (ICN) in Rome, at which participating countries adopted a goal of eliminating acute malnutrition and substantially reducing chronic undernutrition.

The 1996 Rome Declaration on the World Food Summit, and the World Food Summit: five years later (WFS:fyl) in 2002, reiterated the ICN goals, emphasizing access by all individuals to safe and nutritious food to meet their dietary needs for an active and healthy life. Participating countries committed themselves to reducing the number of undernourished people by half no later than the year 2015.

The WFS:fyl debates also led to several documents and programs that helped to sharpen the focus on and linkages between poverty and hunger. Contrary to conventional thinking at the time, hunger is often as much a cause as an effect of poverty, and programs to reduce chronic hunger could play an important role in reducing poverty, especially extreme poverty. Eradicating hunger is not simply a moral imperative, but it is also justified on economic grounds. If large parts of the population are effectively excluded from the development process because of hunger, then sustainable economic growth is unattainable.

Africa is also one of the regions in the world most affected by poverty, with around 45 percent of the population, or 300 million people, living on less than US$1 per day. Two-thirds of Africans live in rural areas, and smallholder farmers account for 80 percent of the African poor. Long-term responses to reverse this situation must focus on the role of agriculture in improving food security, alleviating poverty, and promoting economic growth, as well as on improving preparedness for food security crises.

It was against this background that the Anti-Hunger Programme (AHP), a twin-track approach to hunger reduction, was developed by FAO in 2002. AHP combines longer-term investments in rural development and pro-poor policies with shorter-term targeted measures to broaden immediate access to adequate food for the poorest people.

The causes of the historical decline in food security in Africa are multi-faceted and complex, but at the heart of the problem remains the vulnerability of poor communities to land degradation and climatic variability, particularly drought.

— Victoria Sekitoleko

The WFS:fyl also led to the establishment of the International Alliance against Hunger (IAAH). The IAAH is expected to encourage dialogue and facilitate supportive action between global and national governments, civil society, and donors to help them approach hunger eradication in a concerted and vigorous way. This effort would include supporting countries as they update their policies and strategies for agriculture, food security, and nutrition in order to achieve the WFS goals by 2015.

Most recently, FAO and others have been assisting the NEPAD Secretariat in developing the CAADP, which recognizes that "until the incidence of hunger is brought down and the import bill reduced by raising the output of farm products ... it will be difficult to achieve the high rates of economic growth to which NEPAD aspires."

Over the past two decades, and specifically over the past six months, many global, regional, and national resolutions and calls for action have been made, but progress remains painfully slow. More needs to be done to rapidly implement these good ideas and intentions into concrete actions. Recall some of the major challenges faced by food and nutrition security in Africa:

1. external assistance to agriculture has decreased;
2. external assistance to agriculture does not reach the most food-insecure countries;
3. cereal production, and agricultural production in general, has stagnated;
4. the prevalence of undernutrition in Sub-Saharan Africa is more than 30 percent; and
5. there has been an increase in the number of emergencies, most of which are increasingly caused by humans (Figure 3).

FIGURE 3—Food emergencies by cause, 1986–2003

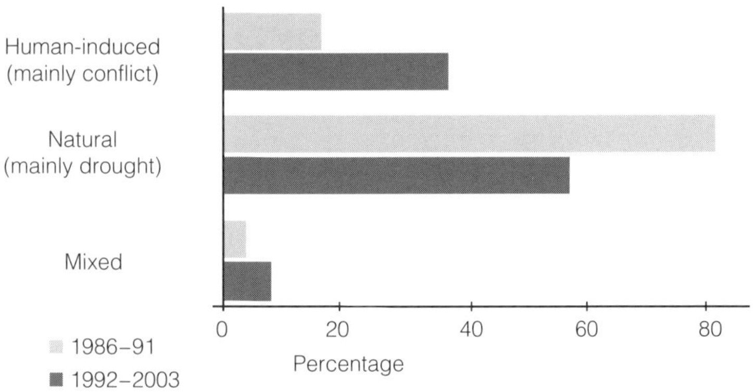

Source: FAO, *State of Food and Agriculture 2003* (Rome).

In addition, nutrition improvement needs to be a central, explicit objective of development, as articulated by recent political commitments and resource allocations. We therefore call for commitment and resources for policies and actions that:

1. put people at the center of development;
2. aim explicitly to improve nutrition;
3. focus on improving household food security;
4. recognize that sustainable improvements in food security are best achieved when they are addressed within the context of livelihood security;
5. take into account social, cultural, environmental, and health considerations (such as gender issues, HIV/AIDS, water usage, food safety), as well as economic ones; and
6. promote the equitable participation of people in the development process.

Yields from irrigated crops are three times higher than yields from rainfed crops, but agricultural activity on 93 percent of Africa's arable land is dependent on extremely erratic rainfall.

— Victoria Sekitoleko

The second strategy I want to highlight is that of increasing agricultural productivity. The causes of the historical decline in food security in Africa are multi-faceted and complex, but at the heart of the problem remains the vulnerability of poor communities to land degradation and climatic variability, particularly drought. The situation has worsened with the destabilizing impact of the HIV/AIDS pandemic, compounded by a range of policy and institutional factors, as well as civil unrest and conflicts in some countries.

A growing population in Africa has increased the continent's demand for food, and food imports have risen in general. But in spite of the inherent fragility of Africa's soils, the continent's climatic variability, and the distribution and availability of both surface and subsurface water resources, there is substantial untapped potential for the development of the continent's water and land resources for increasing agricultural production.

FAO estimates that only 7 percent of Africa's cropland is irrigated, compared with 40 percent in Asia. If we exclude Morocco, Egypt, Sudan, Madagascar, and South Africa, Africa's rate drops to 3 percent. Africa fails to make good use of its water resources—it only uses 4 percent of its water reserves available for irrigation, compared with 17 percent in Asia. In the absence of deliberate steps to accelerate progress, the amount of irrigated land in Africa is expected to grow at less than 1 percent over the period from 1996 to 2030, at which time the amount of irrigated land would be barely 20 percent of the potential area. Substantial public and private investments in developing and improving the management of these land and water resources will be essential for African countries to reach the levels of agricultural production required to meet the targets for poverty alleviation, food production, and economic recovery by 2015.

FAO estimates that about 75 percent of the projected growth in crop production in Africa between 1996 and 2030 will come from intensification in the form of yield increases (62 percent) and higher cropping intensities (13 percent), with the remaining 25 percent coming from arable land expansion. Yields from irrigated crops are three times higher than yields from rainfed crops, but agricultural activity on 93 percent of Africa's arable land is dependent on extremely erratic rainfall.

The productivity of the poor and food-insecure also needs strengthening. Because access to food is a function of both food availability and incomes, issues such as home gardening, postharvest handling, and especially off-farm employment should also be addressed.

The continent as a whole is susceptible to highly variable climatic conditions, putting the agricultural sector and food security at risk of natural disasters. According to a World Bank report, periodic droughts still pose the most serious threat to agricultural production and food security in Sub-Saharan Africa. Highly variable levels of rainfall are becoming normal events, and drought conditions can be expected somewhere in Africa in most years (although fortunately, it is rare for whole regions to be drought stricken at the same time). This situation, coupled with increased environmental pressures on already marginal lands and limited irrigation capacity, severely constrains the economic, social, and environmental well-being of the continent.

Variable rainfall and recurrent agricultural drought are among the risks of farming and lead to unpredictable levels of crop and livestock production. Some crops and grazing systems are more vulnerable than others, although increased exposure to drought conditions reflects the fact that current agricultural and livestock practices are out of equilibrium with the prevailing climatic conditions. Farmers' strategies are a step behind in responding to generally deteriorating internal and changing external conditions.

Land degradation—physical, chemical, and biological—is also a significant factor in many African countries because of, among other things, intensive cultivation and overstocking, high population densities on fragile lands, and inappropriate and unsustainable farming practices and soil management and conservation technologies. The cumulative effects are loss of organic matter and declining soil fertility, salinization, increasing erosion and desertification, decreasing vegetation cover, and declining crop yields and off-take rates of the livestock herds.

The negative impact of erratic rainfall on food production is exacerbated by the resulting pressure on fragile land in semi-arid environments. In times of drought, soils rapidly lose organic matter and experience a breakdown of soil structure as grazing and cultivation practices push land capacities to the limit. Governments have encouraged a variety of drought mitigation initiatives, including small-scale irrigation, water harvesting, food storage, and research on drought-tolerant varieties. Compared with those in other regions of the world, however, these efforts have been grossly inadequate or poorly implemented.

A range of policy and institutional factors have also contributed to reduced agricultural productivity and investment in the agriculture sector in Africa. Tractor usage in Sub-Saharan Africa is much lower than in other parts of the developing world (Figure 4), and even within Sub-Saharan Africa, usage is concentrated in a small number of countries (Figure 5). The reliance on inefficient parastatals and unsustainably high subsidies from the 1960s to the 1980s led to heavy financial burdens on government budgets and distorted prices and incentives throughout the agriculture sector. The market reform policies of the late 1980s and 1990s were often only partially implemented and based on unrealistic expectations of the role that a very weak private sector could play in providing agricultural services and food staple production. The lack of private sector response has led to a drastic reduction of support services and inputs to many farming systems. At the same time, in some countries the absence of land tenure security, rural financial institutions, market infrastructure and information systems, and appropriate farmer advisory services seriously inhibited long-term investment and the development of sustainable production systems in the smallholder sector.

FIGURE 4—Number of tractors in use in different continents,1961–2000

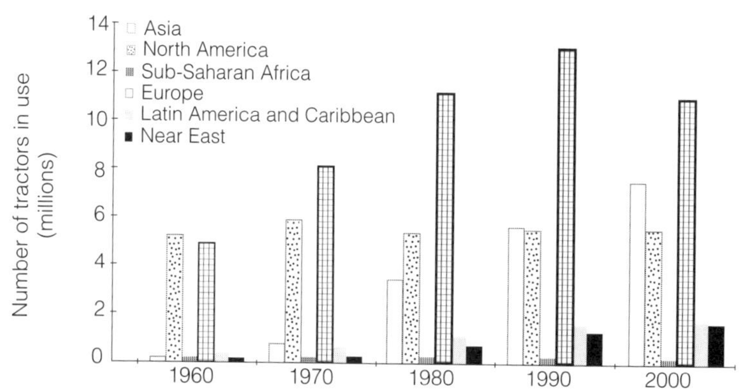

Source: FAO, Agricultural Support Systems Division.

FIGURE 5—Proportion of tractors in use in Sub-Saharan Africa, by country, 2000

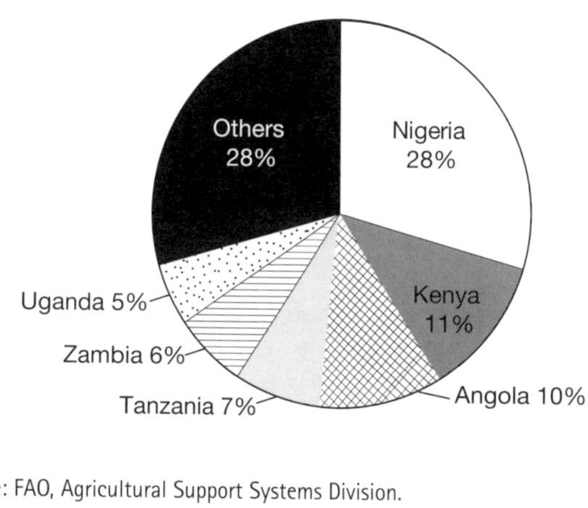

Source: FAO, Agricultural Support Systems Division.

Clearly considerable improvements in food security could be achieved by intervening to improve water and sanitation. Interventions should target the poor, who bear the greatest burden of water-related diseases.

– Victoria Sekitoleko

It is becoming increasingly evident that urgent attention to the HIV/AIDS pandemic is critical to reverse its negative impacts on agriculture, food security, and nutritional status for Africans. For example, Southern Africa has some of the highest HIV prevalence rates in the world, ranging from 15 percent in Malawi to 33 percent in Swaziland and Zimbabwe and up to 39 percent in Botswana, with the poorer socioeconomic groups worst affected. Almost 15 million people were living with HIV in Southern Africa in 2001, and an estimated 1.1 million died of AIDS, the majority in their productive years. HIV/AIDS undermines the sustainability of development, threatens food security, and undermines agriculture through a decrease in the agricultural labor force; a loss of agricultural knowledge, practices, and skills; an acute decline in household incomes; changes in the household composition; a disruption of household production; imbalances in the age and sex composition of populations; and degradation of public services.

Given the central importance of women farmers in Africa, gender issues should be addressed forthrightly. Gender inequality is one of the driving forces behind the spread of HIV. Access to productive resources, including land, credit, knowledge, training, and technology, is strongly determined along gender lines, with men frequently having more access to all of these than women. With the death of her husband, a wife may be left without the access she had gained through him or his clan, and her livelihood and that of her children are immediately threatened.

The Rome Declaration on World Food Security and the World Food Summit Plan of Action, adopted by heads of state and government in Rome in November 1996, acknowledged the fundamental contribution of women in achieving sustainable food security for all. In particular, governments committed themselves to foster equitable participation of women and men and to adopt legislation guaranteeing women access to and control of productive resources. In this context, they further recommended that there is a need to improve the collection, dissemination, and use of gender-disaggregated data in agriculture, fisheries, forestry, and rural development.

Women's work in the agricultural sector often remains invisible because the products of their labor are for the largest part intended for household use and do not reach the market economy. This results in an underestimation of women's contribution to agricultural production and an undervaluing of their potential part in reducing hunger and malnutrition and in achieving food security. The reality in most African countries is that more than 50 percent of the active female population works in agriculture, reaching 93 percent in Burkina Faso, 87 percent in Angola, 98 percent in Burundi, 96 percent in Malawi, and 92 percent in Mali and Tanzania. This percentage is, however, low in a few countries like Botswana (3 percent), Kenya (25 percent), and South Africa (16 percent).

During the past few years, the United Nations secretary general has sent several special envoys to Africa to review the humanitarian situation and ongoing relief efforts, to raise international support and awareness, and to provide recommendations to improve the response. Some of the recommendations from these missions include:

1. enhancing the market response to food needs by accelerating adoption and enforcement of policies to liberalize markets and encouraging private sector participation;
2. clarifying the role and use of genetically modified and biotech foods;
3. encouraging agricultural interventions and programs—seeds, fertilizers, conservation farming systems—that are more cost-effective and have longer-term effects than continuing food aid distributions;
4. building awareness and developing innovative responses to reduce the impact of HIV/AIDS;
5. enhancing support for nutritional interventions, such as emergency and supplementary feeding programs to improve the nutritional status of school-age children, lactating mothers, orphans, the sick, and the disabled;

6. ensuring linkages and mutual support between the immediate emergency response and longer-term programs;
7. promoting advocacy and resource mobilization toward immediate and longer-term needs; and
8. enhancing coordination efforts between the various partners involved—governments, the UN, NGOs, civil society, and the private sector.

The third main strategy for food and nutrition security is to address the complete food and nutrition cycle (Figure 6). Undernutrition is worsening due to HIV/AIDS and poor economic prospects. It is going to be difficult to achieve the World Food Summit goal of halving the number of undernourished people in developing countries by 2015 because rates of undernutrition have been declining only slowly. An alarmingly high proportion of children in the developing world suffer from undernutrition—that is, stunting, underweight, and wasting resulting from a range of inadequate food intake and diseases such as diarrhea that prevent proper digestion and efficient utilization of the food. Inadequate food intake in most communities is mainly a consequence of low food production due to agroecological conditions and poor access to agricultural inputs.

The vicious cycle between undernutrition and disease, especially diarrheal diseases, is very common in the developing world and is the major cause of child morbidity and mortality there. The death rate among undernourished children suffering from diarrhea is far higher than among their better-nourished counterparts. Thus, ready access to safe water for drinking and cooking is important for good health, food and nutrition security, and overall economic development. Clearly considerable improvements in food security could be achieved by intervening to improve water and sanitation. Interventions should target the poor, who bear the greatest burden of water-related diseases.

Africa's success in freeing its people from hunger and promoting prosperity will require action by both public- and private-sector stakeholders principally at the national level. It will also call for complementary initiatives requiring cooperation among countries. NEPAD's CAADP provides a framework for the convergence of national priorities, under which, when properly applied, countries singly and in cooperation can work to reverse the crisis situation in agriculture.

NEPAD also provides a mechanism for cooperation between regional economic communities to promote international convergence on high-priority investments to raise agricultural production. It can also invigorate existing regional early warning systems, upgrade and better link food storage facilities, and ensure more effective use of transport corridors to rapidly mobilize food distribution for emergency response. NEPAD can also promote the effective use of trade as a tool of food security among the countries of Africa.

FIGURE 6—Food and nutrition security cycle

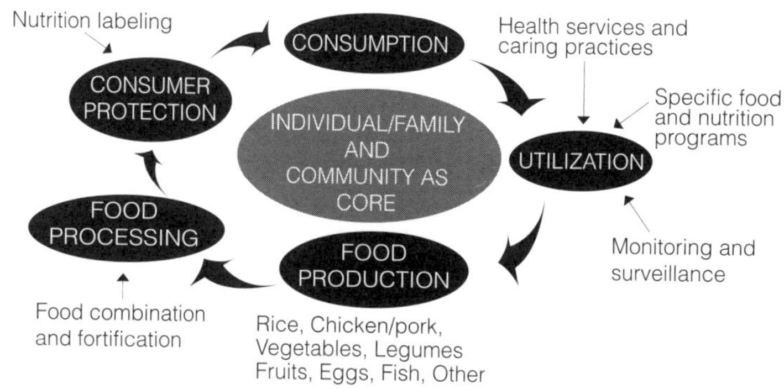

Source: FAO, *State of Food and Agriculture 2003* (Rome); Institute of Nutrition, Mahidul University, Thailand, 1998.

Support to regional programs for food security should also be enhanced through programs designed to:

1. strengthen capacity of African states to respond to natural disasters;
2. develop and expand the use of appropriate and drought-tolerant crop varieties;
3. expand the development of irrigation systems;
4. strengthen regional cooperation in controlling transboundary animal movements and related disease transmission;
5. favor livestock marketing in the drought alert phase and restock after the drought;
6. help develop emergency feeding schemes;
7. support collaboration on information collection, dissemination, and sharing;
8. strengthen harmonized policy formulation and analysis capacities;
9. enhance collaboration on policy, product, and standards harmonization to facilitate trade in agricultural products; and
10. expand regional cooperation in the development, management, and utilization of shared natural resources.

Improvements in health and nutrition status can only be based on preventive, sustainable, population-based approaches in which agriculture plays a key role.

— Victoria Sekitoleko

Special emphasis should also be focused on creating an environment for profitable private-sector investment in agriculture (including public investment in cost-reducing infrastructure and yield-enhancing water management); on reinforcing actions to address the issue of political and economic governance; and on utilizing appropriate laws and policies to accelerate the process of economic growth and development. Corresponding to national policy actions, concerted attention will be needed to build up local institutional capacity to support emerging commercial farmers, small- and medium-scale agroenterprises, commercial service providers, farmer organizations, and agricultural input and output marketers.

To help increase agricultural productivity in the medium term, rain-fed production systems need to be improved and stabilized and small-scale water control needs to be developed or extended to promote income generation to guarantee food security, particularly in remote, highly vulnerable areas. In the longer term, investment in irrigation development, including human capacity development in water management and irrigation, needs to follow where there is comparative advantage in producing food staples and cash crops for regional and international markets.

Stabilizing rainfed systems should also include improved resource management technologies to exploit the available soil moisture, especially where water control and small-scale irrigation schemes are more challenging to implement. This would include improving farmers' access to and adoption of more drought-tolerant seed and rotation options. It would also involve close attention to enhanced soil moisture conservation, such as through conservation agriculture. This concept, which is based on the maintenance of a permanent crop residue cover, zero tillage, direct seeding, and improved rotation, has already been shown to be highly effective in Zambia (under FAO supervision for emergency response).

Investment in water control is critical to closing the gap between production and demand for food. Water control is conceived as the key component in FAO's Special Program for Food Security. The program's water component functions as the entry point to intensify crop production and diversify farm income. Substantial production increases can be achieved only if conditions of optimal water supply can be secured through the introduction of appropriate technologies for irrigation, water conservation, and drainage and flood control. Through a process of participatory consultation with smallholder farmers, the program identifies water management constraints and water control techniques and implements suitable low-cost solutions and technologies.

The vast majority of the world's nondeficient population gets its nutrients from the food it eats, and the majority of the undernourished population experiences chronic inadequate dietary food intake. Thus, if we are to accelerate and sustain the progress that has been achieved so far, we must turn increasingly to other approaches and especially to food and nutrition security approaches.

In accordance with the World Declaration and Plan of Action arising from the ICN and WFS conferences, FAO, in close cooperation with the countries present, agreed to implement a number of food- and agriculture-based actions, including:

1. diversification of crop and animal production;
2. improving food preservation and storage to alleviate seasonal food shortages at the household level;
3. research to enhance bioavailability of micronutrient content in majors crops;

Given the high prevalence of poverty, food insecurity, and undernutrition in Africa, strategies to address the current crisis should aim to bridge the continuum between provision of appropriate short-term emergency relief-to-recovery assistance and longer-term development.

— Victoria Sekitoleko

4. promotion of home gardens, fish ponds, and poultry-rearing;
5. food and nutrition education and training; and
6. food fortification.

Improvements in health and nutrition status can only be based on preventive, sustainable, population-based approaches in which agriculture plays a key role. Such approaches are fundamental to achieving the recognized human right to adequate food and nutrition, and they are a basis for achieving sustainability and for empowering people to take their health and nutrition status into their own hands.

FAO's experience over the years has shown that programs to improve food and nutrition security can be successful only if macro contextual factors, community-level factors, program design features, and sustainability factors are taken into consideration. A strong policy environment can also have a positive impact on food and nutrition security. Active intersectoral collaboration, with clear definition of each sector's responsibilities, and strong partnerships among international agencies, the private sector, NGOs, and academic and research institutes have also rendered major projects successful. This is in line with the theme of this conference—"Prioritizing Actions, Strengthening Actors, and Facilitating Partnerships."

Similarly, the World Food Day theme for 2003 was "International Alliance Against Hunger," emphasizing the need for global mobilization to create the political will to eradicate hunger. The Alliance brings together many different groups, including food producers and consumers, international organizations, governments, agribusinesses, scientists, academics, private individuals, policymakers, religious groups, and NGOs.

Governments must also make a significant financial commitment to food and nutrition security. This may come in the form of investing in capacity-building activities and prioritizing food and nutrition security activities in long-term plans. Sustainable programs have been put in place where there was strong political support, use of existing community structures, community empowerment, and institutionalization of activities. Policies to reduce hunger, such as nutrition surveillance programs, better primary health care, and community-based actions to increase the supply of more nutritious food with activities linked to nutritional education and cultural habits, are also important ways of reducing undernutrition in our communities.

Success mostly depends on having the conducive policies, adequate institutions, improved market infrastructure, social safety nets, and most important, peace and stability, and all of these must be sustained over time.

— Victoria Sekitoleko

What is the way forward? Given the high prevalence of poverty, food insecurity, and undernutrition in Africa, strategies to address the current crisis should aim to bridge the continuum between provision of appropriate short-term emergency relief-to-recovery assistance and longer-term development. To attack the root causes, balanced, broad-based, pro-poor, growth-oriented programs are required that emphasize both the need to increase agricultural productivity and rural income in general and the need for special targeted programs to alleviate hunger. These should include enhancing the political will and financial commitment to implementing existing global, regional, and national initiatives, increasing agricultural productivity and access to food, and reducing undernutrition.

These are some ideas for strategic responses to address high-priority food security and nutrition, poverty reduction, and economic growth targets in a progressive and sustained manner. Reducing food insecurity requires a strong focus on rural people and their empowerment, on agricultural development, and on increased investment in agriculture and agricultural trade. Thus, all players in these sectors need to forge strong partnerships in order to play a more significant role in improving food and nutrition security. With consistent political commitment and availability of resources to both agriculture and rural development as well as the use of integrated approaches that are people centered, agricultural productivity will increase. In this way the complete food and nutrition cycle can be addressed to reduce hunger and undernutrition. But success mostly depends on having conducive policies, adequate institutions, improved market infrastructure, social safety nets, and most important, peace and stability, and all of these must be sustained over time.

Excerpt 5: Reforming Land Rights in Africa

Tidiane Ngaido

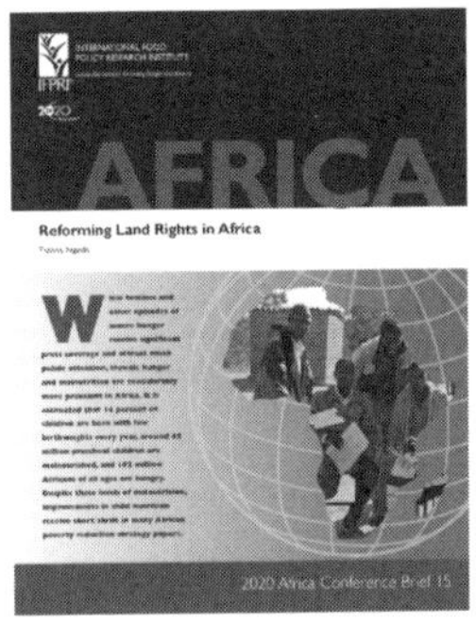

There is no doubt about the need to reform customary rights to alleviate the multiple constraints farmers face in accessing input and credit markets. In response, African countries have enacted plenty of laws and implemented a wealth of land reform processes. Yet many of these laws and reform processes are inappropriate, especially the new policy agenda that attempts to generalize land titling and market mechanisms while bypassing different land rights and evolving market processes. It is critical to account for the capabilities and possibilities of poor households, to target land rights and the markets under which these rights operate, and to set up a process linking all these rights and markets. Moreover, it is essential to recognize the administrative and legal processes associated with different approaches and the capacity of governments to support those processes.

Reforming customary land rights and institutions

One can improve the efficiency of resource allocation and meet the demand for inputs and credit by simply registering customary rights. Once these rights are registered, they can more easily be traded between community members and even outsiders. This reform approach involves very low transaction costs because it relies heavily on existing local institutions. Complementary investments consist mainly of setting up a simple recording system that can be used later to develop a cadastre.

Improving the performance of land redistribution programs

Most land rights established by land redistribution programs fall outside formal land markets and constrain farmers' capacity to sell their lands and invest in other productive areas. Two pathways may improve the system. The first option is to maintain the system but allow these rights to evolve into private property. In Morocco, agrarian reform lands evolved into full private property once holders paid the costs of their field. The second option is to create cooperatives or associations whose members own shares of all the resources. Members who want to quit farming can sell their shares to the cooperative or to farmers who wish to join the cooperative. These approaches would avoid maintaining inefficient farmers and would provide poor farmers with capital to invest in other activities.

Balancing equity and legitimacy in market-based agrarian reform approaches

High land values have been the main constraint to balancing equity and legitimacy concerns in market-based agrarian reforms. The main differences between the land under customary rights and farms operated by white and black elites are land titles and investments made to improve the land. Consequently, to reduce the overvaluation of land, a clear distinction must be made between improved and unimproved land. On improved land, land prices will include productivity and collateral values, whereas on unimproved land, prices will consist mainly of collateral values. In unimproved areas devoted to grazing or forests, however, land value could be calculated using the value of the feed contribution or timber productivity and its collateral value. Such an approach would allow landowners to recover the full value of their investments on improved lands and give many poor farmers access to unimproved lands at a cheaper price. Moreover, it would reduce Southern African governments' cost burdens for acquiring these lands for redistribution. This valuation approach could be also applied in dry areas, which have low cropping potential, but the redistribution process in dry lands in particular must favor group ownership and be accompanied by an insurance scheme that would service group loans during drought or bad seasons. This would prevent groups from risking loss of their land.

This has been excerpted from forthcoming 2020 Africa Conference Brief 15, published by IFPRI, Washington, DC, 2005.

Keynote Address: Technological Options for Africa's Small-Scale Farmers

Gordon Conway
President, The Rockefeller Foundation, USA

Africa stands at a crucial moment. New choices and technologies offer promise, but the challenges faced by poor farmers suggest caution.

I intend to address three questions:

1. What are the current and potential technological options appropriate for African farmers?
2. How can African farmers gain access to them?
3. What are the implications for human capital development?

Before I tackle these questions, I would like to say a few words about psychology. As some of you know, I have worked on development and technology questions for 40 years. I have seen a dramatic shift in perspective from the great optimism and confidence about technology of the 1960s to the pessimism of the current era. I believe pessimism as an approach is deadly—a road that leads to nowhere. There is a joke that it is better to be a pessimist, because then at least you get to hope you are wrong. It may be easier to be a pessimist, but it is a mistake. Let us choose to be pragmatic and committed instead.

Now let me address the first question: How can technology help African farmers? I want to begin by reminding ourselves of the power of technology in the past. The Green Revolution was one of the great technological success stories of the 20th century.

Of course, the Green Revolution was not all success. It was, perhaps, too reliant on pesticides and fertilizers, and it bypassed many of the poor, particularly in Africa. But it was revolutionary in its effects on yields and the prices of staple cereals. Countries like India and China no longer suffer from famine. For those who remember the 1950s and 1960s, when many believed there was no hope for India or China, this is a remarkable achievement, of which we can all be proud.

Here in Africa, today, I believe we are seeing the beginning of a new Green Revolution. I have called it a Doubly Green Revolution. That is, a revolution as productive as the old Green Revolution, but also more equitable, more sustainable, and more environmentally friendly.

Let me illustrate my point with a representative African farmer—a woman with perhaps one hectare or less of land with erratic rainfall and no irrigation. Over the years her land has lost its nutrients. Fertilizer is prohibitively expensive. Urea in Western Kenya is US$400 per ton versus US$90 per ton in Europe. On average, African farmers use only 10 kilograms per hectare of fertilizer—and many use none at all—while European farmers use more than 200 kilograms per hectare.

> *Technology by itself is not enough. Any new technology has to be accessible, and to be accessible to the poor in particular.*
>
> — Gordon Conway

Her farm faces numerous pests, crop diseases, and environmental stresses. Potentially she can harvest two tons of produce from her hectare, but by the time of harvest she has been afflicted by:

- mosaic virus and mealybugs on her cassava;
- borers and streak virus attacking her maize;
- numerous pests on her cowpeas;
- fungal diseases that shrivel the pods of her beans and lower nitrogen fixation;
- black Sigatoka, nematodes, and weevils attacking her bananas; and
- the twin scourges of drought and the weed *Striga.*

At harvest she will gather in less than a mere ton (Figure 1), and her family will be malnourished and sick.

FIGURE 1—An insecure farm

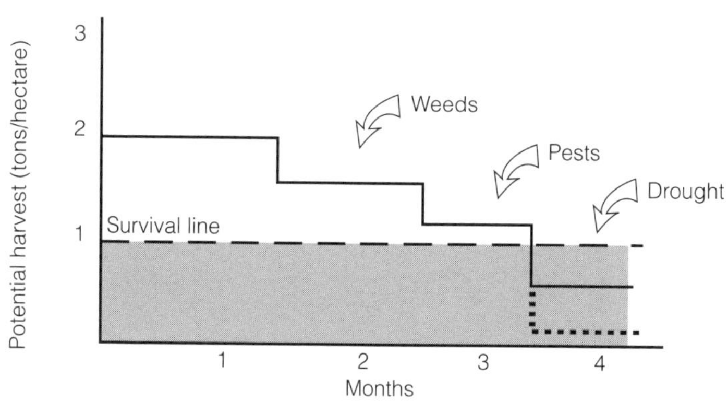

Source: G. Conway and G. Toenniessen, "Science for African Food Security," *Science* 299 (February 21, 2003): 1187–88.

> *The rise of a sophisticated global intellectual property system covering many building-block technologies has meant that public researchers have little access to new ideas and tools in their field.*
>
> – Gordon Conway

But technologies to help her are at hand:

- Biological control, using an imported parasite from South America, is reducing mealybugs on cassava.
- New virus-resistant strains of cassava have been developed.
- New maize varieties resistant to pests and diseases and tolerant of drought are being produced.
- Maize and legume intercropping is producing higher yields of both while improving soil fertility.
- Intercropping of Desmodium with maize is resulting in some control of Striga.

These are successes of conventional technologies, but biotechnologies are also already playing a significant role: In Uganda, tissue-cultured bananas developed by African scientists are being produced free of pests and disease and yielding more than 50 tons per hectare. The new rices, the NERICAs, also products of tissue-culture technologies and developed by African scientists at WARDA, are being grown with great success not only in West Africa, but also in Uganda. Yields are up to 3 tons per hectare with little or no fertilizer.

TABLE 1—Bt cotton production in South Africa, Makhathini Flats, 1999–2000

Indicator	Conventional	Bt
Yield (kilos/hectare)	261	417
Value (Rand/hectare)	568	905
Seed cost (Rand/hectare)	91	197
Pesticide cost (Rand/hectare)	116	72
Gross margin (Rand/hectare)	361	638

Source: Y. Ismael, R. Bennett, and S. Morse, "Farm-Level Impact of Bt Cotton in South Africa," *Biotechnology and Development Monitor* 48 (2001): 15–19.

Marker-aided selection is also playing an increasing role in transforming conventional breeding into a more precise science, producing new varieties in as little as two to three years. African maize-breeding programs are beginning to show results in developing resistance to streak virus and in boosting high-quality protein in local varieties. These are real achievements, many of them funded by the Rockefeller Foundation, that are already benefiting the farmers of Uganda and of Africa as a whole.

But many of Africa's food production problems can only be partially solved by these means. For these problems, that other product of biotechnology—genetic engineering—holds considerable promise. So far GM crops are being grown only in South Africa, but elsewhere in Sub-Saharan Africa a new generation of bright, highly trained African scientists are setting up laboratories to develop GM crops for the most intractable of Africa's problems. The practical success of new varieties produced by tissue culture and marker-aided selection in public laboratories shows the potential of biotechnology in general.

We can also be encouraged by the success of Bt cotton in the Makhathini Flats of South Africa (Table 1). The cotton has been grown by some 5,000 small farmers over the past five years, with results that mirror those in China, Brazil, and Mexico. Farmers are gaining higher yields and greater returns, and, most importantly, they no longer have to rely on the backbreaking and hazardous spraying of their cotton crops. As a result pesticide poisoning is declining.

Now let me turn to my second question: How can African farmers gain access to these new technologies? To stress the obvious: technology by itself is not enough. Any new technology has to be accessible, and to be accessible to the poor in particular. This has several dimensions. First, we have to ensure that new technologies, in particular proprietary technologies, are available to African plant breeders for their breeding programs. In the past we relied on publicly funded research and development. Today much of the advanced agricultural technology innovation takes place in the for-profit sector—a sector dominated by five very large multinational corporations. And for them, there is no profit from investing in expensive research on new products that

> *If we do not invest in training new scientists, we are like farmers who fail to invest in seeds.*
>
> – Gordon Conway

can be purchased only by African subsistence farmers. They are not focused on improving such crops as millet, sorghum, cowpeas, yams, or cassava. The result is not just missed opportunities. The rise of a sophisticated global intellectual property system covering many building-block technologies has meant that public researchers have little access to new ideas and tools in their field.

As a partial response, the Rockefeller Foundation has helped launch the African Agricultural Technology Foundation (AATF). It is an African-led organization that is set up to gain access to new proprietary technologies and make them freely available to African plant breeders.

The second aspect of access is affordability. In Africa today, markets are not working for the poor. The price of inputs is out of range, owing to inflation, devaluation, and poorly functioning markets. Poor roads also make it difficult for those in marginal areas to have access to inputs. In Malawi, for example, farmers travel an average distance of more than 20 kilometers to get inputs. The inputs are also not available for farmers in small sizes that they can afford.

These conditions, however, are changing. With Rockefeller Foundation support, the Citizens Network for Foreign Affairs (CNFA) and Appropriate Technology, working in Uganda, and CARE International in Malawi, Uganda, and Zimbabwe are helping to create a rural network of input traders who bring seeds, fertilizers, farm equipment, and extension advice right to the doorsteps of poor farmers. These so-called agro-dealers are connected to major input suppliers by a credit guarantee scheme. In many areas, they have grown to become the most important source of inputs for the rural poor. However, they still need access to working capital to be able to expand the range and volume of agricultural inputs they can sell.

Finally, I want to briefly refer to the implications of the foregoing for the development of human capital. It is clear that without more and better-trained African scientists, the cycle of poverty and inadequate technological responses will continue. Yet we are not doing enough. A review by the World Bank of its expenditures on agricultural research, extension, and education from 1987 to 1997 revealed that out of US$4.8 billion in global investments, about 98 percent went to agricultural research and extension and a mere 2 percent went to agricultural higher education.

If we do not invest in training new scientists, we are like farmers who fail to invest in seeds. We at the Rockefeller Foundation have been helping to train new researchers for decades. In 1992 we initiated a program called the Forum on Agricultural Resource Husbandry. I am happy to announce that this year we will be adding more than US$3.5 million in new money to the effort to help train new scientists.

Let it be Africans and African governments that determine what technology is right for them and how best it can be accessed.

— Gordon Conway

We are also helping to initiate an effort in Africa to develop a new generation of skilled professionals to develop better agricultural policies and institutions. An African-led Agricultural Economics Education Board (AEEB) has established a collaborative program for training graduates at the master's level in agricultural and applied economics. Over the first five years of the initiative, some 700 students will be trained in agricultural policy and trade, food and agribusiness management, rural development, and natural resource economics.

But what we are doing in training is not enough; we need partners. And we all need a commitment to stay in this area for a long, long time.

Let me conclude with a plea for greater tolerance and a constructive dialogue in the discussions about science and technology for Africa. I have laid out a case for a much more serious investment in science and technology to help farmers. Others may suggest a different approach. Certainly there are real environmental and social questions that can be raised. But too often when discussing issues like genetically modified crops we have forums that tend to generate more heat than light. These arguments are excellent fodder for the news media and provide a healthy living for public relations specialists on both sides, but they do not do much for poor African farmers. Let us remember, it is them we have to serve. Most importantly, let it be Africans and African governments that determine what technology is right for them and how best it can be accessed.

The potential exists to find and harness technology to help millions of people, but we have too often failed in the past.

An American writer named Margaret Fuller once wrote, "If you have knowledge, let others light their candles at it." That is, I believe, how we will solve this problem.

Excerpt 6: Making Information and Communication Technologies Work for Food Security in Africa

Romeo Bertolini

Knowledge and information are important factors for accelerating agricultural development by increasing agricultural production and improving marketing and distribution.

The telephone is the only information and communication technology (ICT) used (if any) by the majority of farmers in Africa. Empirical research in rural Ghana shows that the proportion of households using public community call offices—where available—is around 60 percent, and average household telephone expenditure is over 5 percent of monthly household income. The same research indicates that, in terms of agricultural production, prices of inputs such as seeds, fertilizers, and pesticides are the most frequently telecommunicated information.

Beyond that, more sophisticated ICTs could make the greatest contribution by shortening the distance and reducing the cost of interactions between stakeholders. National and international policymakers and organizations dealing with rural development and agriculture require, generate, and provide information relevant to agricultural production. ICTs enable the exchange of information about innovations in crop varieties, pest control, manuring, weather forecasting, irrigation, and efficient monitoring methods.

Capacity building is another area of opportunity. ICTs, for example, have enabled the World Bank to initiate its Global Distance Learning Network with 50 learning centers around the globe, and the Commonwealth of Learning (COL), the Consultative Group on International Agricultural Research, and the Food and Agriculture Organization of the United Nations (FAO) have also promoted distance learning and ICT applications within their training programs.

The most important ICT applications for addressing malnutrition relate to educating personnel and enabling efficient networking. The FAO's Food and Nutrition division, for instance, provides online training materials on many nutrition-related topics. Relatedly, given that health- and nutrition-related information is usually disseminated to the general public via mass media, ICTs have the capacity to enhance the accuracy and timeliness of information flowing to journalists.

Monitoring nutrition status—including reacting to large-scale threats—is a particular area of assessment and analysis that depends on ICTs. Food insecurity and vulnerability information and mapping systems (FIVIMS) are increasingly implemented to assemble, analyze, and disseminate information on who the food insecure and malnourished are, where they are located, and why they are at risk.

The links between food security, markets, and ICTs are obvious when it comes to integrating farmers into regional, national, and international trade systems. ICTs improve the ability to search for information and increase the quantity and quality of information available, ultimately reducing uncertainty and enhancing market participation. Answers to questions such as, "How do buyers and sellers find each other, and what prices can be achieved?" and "Is it better to store the produce or sell it immediately?" open opportunities, support the functioning of markets—and hence the availability of food—and increase income.

It is widely agreed that the availability of appropriate information is an effective means of averting famine. Information on the variability of food production, for example, is needed to plan and accumulate food stocks. Further, the difficulties of moving food into isolated regions can be overcome if limited transportation facilities are used more efficiently, and the costs of food imports will be lower if there is sufficient time to purchase food on regional or world markets and to arrange for inexpensive shipment to the affected areas. Finally, government action can be better coordinated to respond to shortages. Again, ICT-based systems such as the Famine Early Warning System (FEWS) and the Global Information and Early Warning System (GIEWS) for food and agriculture are means of leveraging action to avoid disasters such as famines.

This has been excerpted from 2020 Africa Conference Brief 11, published by IFPRI, Washington, DC, 2004.

Keynote Address: Implementing Action to Reduce Hunger: Learning from Mali's Experiences

Oumar Ibrahima Touré*
Delegate Minister for Food Security, Mali
Speaking on behalf of **Seydou Traoré**, Minister of Agriculture, Livestock, and Fisheries, Mali

Oumar Ibrahim Touré offers lessons learned from successes and failures in Mali.

Mali is a landlocked country in the heart of West Africa. It has a semi-arid tropical climate with a very long dry season and a short rainy season. Rainfall is very low and varies considerably between the different regions of the country (from 200 millimeters in the north to 1,200 millimeters in the south).

According to FAO data from 2000, the cultivated area represents 3.9 million hectares, or 9 percent of the 43.7 million hectares available for agriculture and livestock. The main crops are millet, sorghum, peanuts, corn, rice, cotton, acha, catjang, and various tubers. The main food staples are grains: millet, sorghum, rice, and corn. Livestock production and fisheries play an important role in the economic life of the country. Together with cash crops such as cotton, they generate most of the resources from exports.

Mali does not currently have substantial mining resources. The economy therefore depends on the development of agriculture as a source of raw material for the country's processing industries as well as a source of foreign currency to finance imports. This explains the position and the weight given to agriculture in the economic and social development strategies that have been prepared by successive governments.

Hunger alleviation and the efforts to achieve sustainable food security, defined by the World Bank as "access by any individual at any moment to enough food to lead an active and healthy life," have always been among the main priorities of the government of Mali. Strategies and actions have thus been implemented to satisfy the following conditions necessary to guarantee sustainable food security:

- ensuring a secure food supply;
- ensuring the stability of the supply in time and space; and
- ensuring that all individuals can afford the food staples.

Mali has carried out agricultural development and food supply strategies since the time of the First Republic, when farmers' cooperatives were established. This trend continued with the implementation of development and marketing policies through state entities such as the Société Malienne d'Importation et d'Exportation (SOMIEX—Mali Import and Export Company) and the Office des Produits Agricoles du Mali (OPAM—Agency for the Agricultural Commodities of Mali) before the launching of structural adjustment programs. These programs began in 1981 with the Cereals Market Restructuring Program (PRMC), developed by the Government of Mali in conjunction with its main food aid donors. The adoption of a national food strategy in 1982 helped define the conceptual framework for the PRMC.

The PRMC emerged out of the following realities: a state monopoly in cereal marketing, chronic food deficits, balance of payments deficits, and public finance deficits. It represented a consensus between the state and 11 donors. The strategic objectives of the PRMC were to liberalize cereal trade; to divide activities between the public and private sectors; to increase producers' prices; to reduce state costs; to refocus the OPAM mandate toward supplying poor zones and managing food aid; and to make cooperative structures more dynamic.

The PRMC has gone through six phases:

- Phase 1: 1981–87, dismantling of state monopoly begun;

* This presentation was originally given in French.

- Phase 2: 1988–90, role of the private sector intensified;
- Phase 3: 1991–93, continued promotion of the private sector;
- Phase 4: 1994–96, food security improved through modernization of the cereals market;
- Phase 5: 1997–99, food security system reinforced; and
- Phase 6: 2000–04, new risks linked to new urban poverty taken into consideration

The reforms have had many positive results. The state was disengaged from cereal marketing, trade was liberalized, an environment favorable to the promotion of the private sector was created, food supplies for destitute populations were assured, national stocks were available in case of crisis, and operators showed a marked interest in technical aspects such as transforming and adding value to their goods. In addition, state-controlled structures were reformed, villages were encouraged to develop stocks, circulation of transparent and reliable information improved, income in rural areas rose, and fluidity of trade increased.

In 2002 Mali adopted a national strategy to ensure food security by 2015. This strategy focuses on promoting productive agriculture; developing and integrating subregional markets; sustainably improving access to food and basic social services; improving prevention and management of economic crises; and reinforcing the capacities of actors and promoting good governance for food security.

At the national level, the strategy conforms to the goals of the food strategy of 1982—that is, increased and diversified agricultural production, improved income of the population, and transformation of local products. Nationally, the institutional framework for this national food security strategy consists of a national food safety council, a technical committee for coordinating food security policies, and a technical secretariat. At the regional level, there are regional food security committees, technical secretariats, and local and municipal food security committees.

There are a number of weaknesses remaining in Mali's current food and nutrition situation. Rates of malnutrition are high among preschool children. There is a chronic energy deficiency among pregnant women. Deficiencies of iron, iodine, and vitamin A remain problems.

Nonetheless, Mali's experience offers important lessons. First, political intervention is needed to manage food problems. Second, a fundamental awareness of actors' responsibilities in managing food problems is required. Third, it is crucial to construct a real partnership with sponsors. Fourth, there is a need for an intersectoral approach to problems of food security. Fifth, developing agricultural production requires a sector-based approach. Sixth, there must be an oversight system. Seventh, questions of nutrition security must be addressed directly.

The challenges Mali still faces are to free agriculture from climatic risks, to increase the transformation of agricultural products, to improve the nutrition security of the population, and to open the country internally and externally.

Chapter 11 Improving Implementation: What Can Lessons from Successes and Failures Teach Us?

Chair: Hamid Narjisse
Director, Institut National de la Recherche Agronomique (INRA), Morocco

Peter Hazell
Director, Development Strategy and Governance Division, International Food Policy Research Institute (IFPRI), USA

Too often agricultural development experts have sought success through "magic bullets," meaning one-dimensional interventions that are expected to single-handedly transform African agriculture. Some of the magic bullets recently tried in Africa include macroeconomic policy reform; technology fixes such as improved crop varieties, soil management, treadle pumps, and organic agriculture; microfinance; market information systems; and market chain integration. Some of these interventions are important and have the potential to make a real difference. But our analysis of past successes in African agriculture shows that successes are more complex and multidimensional phenomena. Magic bullets work when they are part of a critical mass of several essential and interlocking ingredients that are required for agricultural growth.

In thinking about the requirements for success, it is useful to think in terms of market chains. These extend from "plow to fork," as my IFPRI colleague Ashok Gulati likes to put it.

Market chains begin with the production process. For this, farmers need access to land and labor, appropriate technology, key inputs like seed and fertilizer, credit, knowledge, and market incentives. When all these things come together and click in the right ways, then on-farm productivity can increase.

The next step in the chain is postharvest handling and storage, leading to marketing activities. Marketing must include working arrangements for collection of farm products, wholesaling, agroprocessing, retailing, and exporting. Key requirements here are infrastructure and transport systems, market information, trader credit, quality and safety standards, contract enforcement, arrangements for handling price risks, and a stable and conducive policy environment. When all these things come together and click in the right ways, then farmers have an incentive to produce, and processors and traders have an incentive and means to provide key marketing and processing services.

Successes arise when all the parts in a market chain function. Any major gap or bottleneck in the chain can cause failure, regardless of how magical some parts of the chain may be.

Market chains are failing many small farmers in Africa today. Some market chains have worked well in the past, especially market chains for traditional export crops like cotton, coffee, and cocoa. But these market chains are increasingly challenged by their privatization, by persistent downward trends in world prices, and by consumers' increasing demands for higher-quality products.

Ironically, the best market chains in Africa are for agricultural imports, and these chains can undermine African farmers. Some of these chains successfully bring canned fruit juices from farms in Thailand and other Asian countries to tourist hotels in Africa, crowding out inferior local products. Food aid and world grain markets are also very efficient at bringing subsidized grains from farms in Europe and the prairies and Great Plains of North America to crowd out locally produced food staples in Africa.

Recent years have seen some remarkable growth in market chains for nontraditional exports from Africa, especially for horticultural products, fish, and some processed foods. These chains have been developed and driven largely by the private sector and have made some important contributions to agricultural growth in Africa. But they are still relatively unimportant and anyway are

Successes arise when all the parts in a market chain function. Any major gap or bottleneck in the chain can cause failure, regardless of how magical some parts of the chain may be.

— Peter Hazell

biased toward larger, capital-intensive commercial farms that can meet high standards. Despite some successes, they are not reaching small farms anywhere near the scale needed to make a dent in Africa's poverty statistics.

Market chains for domestic and intraregional trade in food staples are still struggling and are a serious constraint on small farm development in Africa. They also make it difficult for African farmers to compete with subsidized food staple imports from the rich countries. The value of Africa's food staple consumption—food grains and livestock products—accounts for some two-thirds of total agricultural production, and it is projected to double by 2015. Market liberalization programs have proved disappointing, and many small farms have less access to credit, key inputs, or marketing services than before the reforms, and they are also now fully exposed to the vagaries of world market prices. At this stage of Africa's agricultural development, the private sector is not likely to play a large role in the market chains for many food staples, as it does for some higher-value products. Fixing these market chains needs to be one of the highest priorities for African policymakers.

In thinking about market chains for food staples, it is useful to look at the experience in Asia during the Green Revolution era. Different agents have key roles to play in market chains, and it is now fashionable among development experts to think that the private sector and producer organizations can perform most market chain functions. In this new paradigm, the government's role should be limited to creating an enabling environment, such as setting and regulating grades and standards, ensuring food safety, and registering and enforcing contracts. But I am impressed by the key role that the public sector played in food staple market chains during the early years of the Green Revolution in Asia.

There the public sector went far beyond a facilitating role and provided most key services itself, including research and development, extension, improved seeds, fertilizer, credit, storage, and marketing. Moreover, government intervened to stabilize prices for producers and consumers alike and provided subsidies for many key inputs to encourage their uptake.

IFPRI's new work on India shows these interventions played a key role in launching the Green Revolution. They also helped ensure that small farmers were able to participate, and this contributed greatly to the levels of poverty reduction achieved. Our calculations show that most of these policies and interventions had favorable benefit-cost ratios in the early years, but these ratios worsened over time once the interventions had served their primary purposes. Unfortunately, once they were institutionalized, it has proved very difficult to remove these interventions, and as input use increased, the costs to the governments soared. Today, for example, India spends about US$10 billion per year on unproductive subsidies.

The international development community is now so obsessed with post–Green Revolution problems that it is asking Africa to launch its own agricultural revolution without these kinds of public interventions. Africa is being asked to rely almost exclusively on the private sector and producer organizations. Is the international development community asking for the impossible? Is it drawing the right lessons from Asia?

There is hardly any credible evidence to suggest that the private sector can take the lead in market chains for staple foods during the early stages of agricultural development. As farmers struggle with low productivity and high subsistence needs, low input use, low incomes, poor infrastructure, high risks, and the like, the amount of profit to be made in market chains for food staples remains low and unattractive for much private investment. There is also a growing body of studies showing that important institutional and market failures are to be expected at that level of development. It is a singular fact that no Asian country shifted its food staple agriculture from a subsistence to a market

We need a much better understanding of those aspects of public intervention that really worked in Asia and why. Then we can draw the right lessons for developing new institutional innovations to bring those essential ingredients to Africa.

— Peter Hazell

orientation without heavy public intervention in the market chains. But then nor have any other developing countries, or indeed most rich countries (and almost no rich countries in the past half century)! Africa has suffered from the imposition of many inappropriate development paradigms in the past, and we may now be seeing the emergence of another.

I am not advocating a return to costly and inefficient parastatals or to hefty and poorly targeted subsidies. Nor am I arguing against a strong role for the private sector where the private sector can work, such as in many high-value market chains. But we need a much better understanding of those aspects of public intervention that really worked in Asia and why. Then we can draw the right lessons for developing new institutional innovations to bring those essential ingredients to Africa.

Hezron Nyangito

Principal Policy Analyst, Kenya Institute for Public Policy Research and Analysis (KIPPRA), Kenya

Speaking on behalf of **Franz Heidhues**, Professor, Institute for Agricultural Economics and Social Sciences in the Tropics, University of Stuttgart-Hohenheim

African countries have had numerous strategies, policies, and programs. Indeed, each African country has been assisted by an average of about 30 institutions in coming up with strategies and, most important, actions for implementation. We define "implementation" as clear formulation, a conducive policy and institutional environment, a wide consensus, capacity to implement, and financial resources.

What lessons do we learn from evaluating the strategies, policies, and actions that African countries have used in implementing development strategies? First, we learn that most actions in food security and nutrition in Africa have been donor-driven. Basically, the implementation of various programs was mostly determined by the conditionalities of the World Bank and other donors, particularly the structural adjustment programs (SAPs) and, in recent times, the poverty reduction strategy papers (PRSPs).

This does not mean that Africa has not had its own programs and actions: the Lagos Plan of Action was an African initiative and so, more recently, was NEPAD. The Lagos Plan of Action was not implemented very well because of a lack of commitment. We do not have much to say yet about NEPAD because it has just begun, but the formulation gives us some hope, if there is political commitment.

> *Most actions in food security and nutrition in Africa have been donor-driven.*
>
> — Hezron Nyangito

The SAPs and PRSPs have largely shaped regional approaches and country policies and their implementation. A significant number of countries have carried out successful programs, in particular macroeconomic stability and structural reforms through liberalization of international trade and domestic price controls, and public sector reforms. However, because of the associated sudden unemployment, vulnerability to food and nutrition security, and decline in public subsidies, this is not good news for food and nutrition security.

What is the issue? The issue, we believe, is that in Africa there is need for a strong private sector to take over some of the government functions that the government is not required to do. And this is not occurring. Therefore the issue is: How do you develop the private sector to take over the role of government?

On agriculture, even though there is a forecast by analysts of eventual development, much more is required. For example, there should be a focus on reducing social and economic discrimination, and issues such as land access, credit, inputs, and output markets should be emphasized.

Another lesson is that peace and security are key for success in implementation. Therefore, restoring peace and establishing rule of law is a priority for Africa.

Strong leadership and political will are also needed. Where there is weak leadership and lack of political will, there is no serious effort to address food crisis issues. This problem is made worse by internal resistance that hinders implementation of programs.

The other lesson concerns governance and the rule of law. Reliable and independent judicial systems, community involvement, and privatization that encourages private sector initiatives, entrepreneurship, and ownership by locals lead to success in implementation of various programs.

Country ownership is important. This has been attempted through the PRSP process, which is a noble idea, but participation needs to be institutionalized. When you look at the plans on paper, they may appear quite participatory, but who participates? A number of tech-

The capacity at the ground level to implement, or even to question the implementation of various policies, is lacking.

— Hezron Nyangito

nocrats and politicians assume that they represent the local people, and then the plan is claimed to be participatory. However, there should be a meaningful institutional framework that can turn ownership over to the citizens.

Capacity building is also an issue. It is needed at all levels—purchasing, financial accountability, policy formulation, local administration, and project management and evaluation. Indeed, the capacity at the ground level to implement, or even to question the implementation of various policies, is lacking.

Another lesson is that agricultural development initiatives should be given a high priority. More programs should focus on agricultural innovations and productivity and farmers' involvement. However, these are activities that require specialized agricultural expertise that can help local programs. Agricultural research and extension policies should also focus on supporting farmers.

Agricultural productivity should be linked to support programs. In most cases agricultural productivity strategies ignore other programs, such as those on rural health, empowerment of women, and access to education, land, water, production factors, and markets.

Another issue is coherence. There are so many programs and actions where there is no coherence between donors and governments. Where there is coherence, there is success.

Finally, there is lack of attention to micro-level conditions. Indeed, where policies are clearly linked to such conditions, there is success.

There are successes in different parts of Africa, but they are isolated. We need to scale them up.

— Wilberforce Kisamba-Mugerwa

Wilberforce Kisamba-Mugerwa

Minister of Agriculture, Animal Industry, and Fisheries, The Republic of Uganda

The successes in African agriculture have derived mainly from adoption of recommended practices. Most of these recommended practices—seeds, stock, planting materials, and techniques in soil and water conservation—have been generated through research. But underlying all these successes is access to markets. In Uganda, for instance, until we created the Uganda Grain Traders to enable us to export, it was impossible for farmers who were adopting new technologies to succeed, but now we are becoming the food basket of this region. At a conference on agricultural successes held in South Africa in December, we enumerated the successes in Africa, and among them were cotton in Mali and cassava in Nigeria and even here in Uganda. In fact, in Nigeria cassava is now becoming an industrial crop.

So there are successes in different parts of Africa, but they are isolated. We need to scale them up.

There are also failures. For some countries, failure to attain sustainable feeding of their population is generally related to drought. Many of the countries in Sub-Saharan Africa cannot sustain growth for even a short duration. In Uganda, if the rains stop for three weeks, people plant and all the crops fail.

In some cases, studies by IFPRI and others show that we have low adoption of technologies, and hence low production.

Poor extension services are also a problem. All the models that have been tried for delivering extension services have been largely unsuccessful in reaching farmers and empowering them. As a result, farmers do not get proper guidance in adopting and implementing various technologies.

Infrastructure is a problem—not only rural infrastructure, but also market infrastructure and roads and railways. When Malawi and Zambia had a bad maize harvest, we could not get maize to them. It was cheaper for Malawi to get maize from the United States than to get it from Uganda.

Natural resource degradation is also obviously a serious concern. In Uganda, we have managed to achieve 5 percent agricultural growth. But the population is chasing this achievement, growing at a rate of 3.5 percent, so agriculture is growing at just 1.5 percent in real terms. Although we have nominally achieved 5 percent growth, we are aiming to reach Nigeria, where President Obasanjo said agriculture is growing at 7 percent.

If you don't have proper policies and institutions, it becomes very difficult to implement anything.

— Wilberforce Kisamba-Mugerwa

Conflict is another issue preventing us from scaling up in order to implement success. In some districts here in Uganda, people are very strong and have expansive pieces of land, but for the past seven years they have not been productive in agriculture because of conflict. Thus, it becomes difficult to think of success.

Another important task is creating an enabling atmosphere, in terms of policies and institutions, to facilitate increased productivity. In some cases, you may know where you could have success: research, extension, sustainable use of natural resources, rural finance, promoting agroprocessing. You may even have the political will, as shown by the Maputo Declaration. But if you don't have proper policies and institutions, it becomes very difficult to implement anything. In this era of liberalization, privatization, and decentralization, ministries must create an enabling atmosphere in order for the farmer to respond and adopt the technologies and in order for the private sector to invest in farmer input systems.

For example, who should be investing in tractors? We may think that the private sector should invest in them, but they are not responding quickly. In Uganda, you can see private coaches used for public transport—they cost about 180–200 million Ugandan shillings, but the private sector is investing in them. But when it comes to a tractor of 35-50 million shillings, none of them has invested in it.

Finally, we have taken a sectorwide and multisectoral approach. The private sector, the public sector, and civil society and NGOs must each play the right part.

All of these efforts require funds. Some activities are in the private sector, and some are in the public sector. In some cases, where the private sector is weak, we need to approach a private good as a public good, and we need strategic investment. But strategic investment needs money. Despite our talk of the 10 percent increase in spending on the agricultural sector, most of the Sub-Saharan African countries are experiencing budgetary constraints, so we need to increase the tax base. Then we can make the strategic investments that will help us increase productivity. As a result, it will be easier to implement the policies that will lead us to food and nutrition security.

Hans-Joachim Preuss

Secretary General, Deutsche Welthungerhilfe, Germany

German AgroAction (Deutsche Welthungerhilfe) is implementing food and nutrition security programs not only in Africa, but in many countries of the world, and we are doing this with local partners from community-based organizations. I would like to draw on some of our experiences in the past to offer lessons from successes and failures.

Food and nutrition security are achieved only if adequate food is available to, accessible for, and satisfactorily utilized by all individuals at all times to achieve good nutrition for a healthy and happy life. This concept incorporates the availability of adequate food for the public, the access to food that is achieved when households and individuals within those households have sufficient resources to obtain appropriate food, and, last but not least, the utilization of food that is influenced by the ability of a human body to ingest and metabolize culturally adapted food.

The nutritional status of an individual (see Figure 1) thus depends on his or her food intake and nutritional status. For adequate food intake, food availability through production, purchase, or donation and the caring capabilities of the respective households are

FIGURE 1—Nutritional status at household level

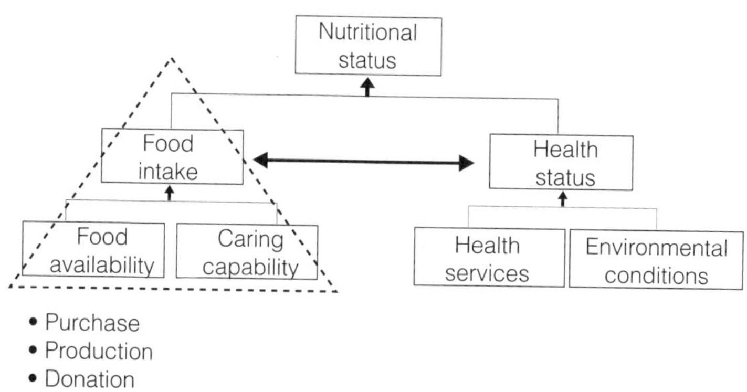

Source: Adapted from R. Gross, H. Schoeneberger, H. Pfeifer, and H.-J. Preuss, "Four Dimensions of Food and Nutrition Security: Definitions and Concepts," *SCN News*, no. 20 (July 2000): 22–27.

> *When people come from abroad, they often have good intentions, but sometimes they do not know what the local potential is and what is really needed at local levels.*
>
> — Hans-Joachim Preuss

crucial. Adequate nutritional status depends on the existence of health services and environmental determinants such as housing and other environmental conditions.

This is the situation that implementers find when leaving important meetings and conferences. Moreover, we face a much more complex situation in the field, depending on the level of self-help capacity of a given population and a given region when we start food and nutrition security programs.

Figure 2 shows the continuum of stages of food and nutrition security related to the self-help capacity of the different populations that require differentiated mixes of interventions. Beginning on the left, the first stage after a natural or a man-made disaster, when services and infrastructures are malfunctioning, is emergency aid, accompanied by the free provision of commodities. Then, if self-help capacity grows after a natural disaster, we can apply more sophisticated instruments until the technical cooperation instruments can be applied. This model is a simplified one because it reflects only one target group in one given region. Implementing agencies are facing very different conditions and very different situations among hungry people. This sometimes very complex situation must be considered at the meso- and micro-level when implementing programs.

What have we learned from past failures and successes? Our experiences show, first, that international donors, implementing agencies, and even NGOs do not believe in the self-help capacities of populations. They do not believe that even in cases of natural disaster, local people can do a lot for themselves. We find that even in disastrous situations, local people are able to contribute physically and financially to the success of programs. This means that the assessment of local capacities is a crucial issue. Local participation is more helpful than good intentions. When people come from abroad, they often have good intentions, but sometimes they do not know what the local potential is and what is really needed at local levels.

The second lesson from our experience concerns government versus private services. Donor agencies, international NGOs, and governments have a tendency to take over all necessary responsibilities for development. Fertilizer supply, credit schemes, market operations—all these can be run by private services if attractive terms are given over a longer period. Extension and health services can be provided by NGOs, sometimes more efficiently and effectively than by government bodies. The government, however, must set rules and regulations. So experience shows that external funds should be used to a greater extent to attract private business or NGOs. Government activities are to be limited to supervision and balanced coordination. Balanced coordination means that we should not try to take control of all the different activities.

Next is donor competition versus coordination of effort. We talk a lot about coherence and development cooperation. These do not always occur. Coordinating the efforts of various actors must be done in a certain way. Coordination cannot be done by a paramount institution. We tried that approach with large rural development programs in the past, and it proved to be unsuccessful. You must create a coordination body composed of those who are acting in the field, and they must prove that they have established interfaces to the other organizations.

Next, we find that as an NGO partially funded by donors, we tend to focus on fast delivery. We have to give results within two or three years. They want us to write reports and so on, and we have to exert the same

FIGURE 2—Stages of food and nutrition security

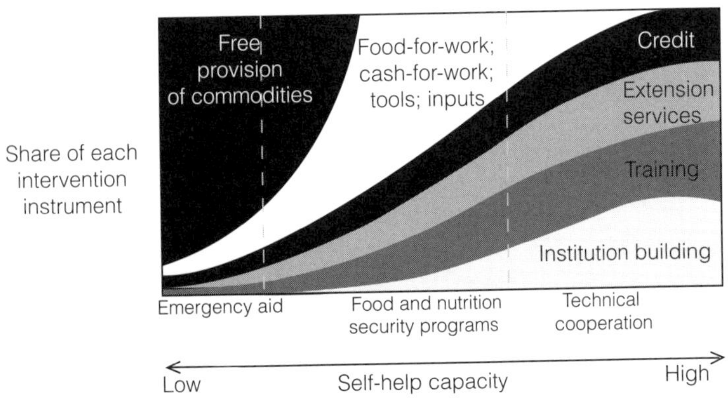

Source: Adapted from R. Gross, H. Schoeneberger, H. Pfeifer, and H.-J. Preuss, "Four Dimensions of Food and Nutrition Security: Definitions and Concepts," *SCN News*, no. 20 (July 2000): 22–27.

pressure on our local partners. But community-based development is not quick; it takes years. And an NGO working in this area is not responsible for executing all these activities over the long term. This is up to the local people, and it takes some time for them to take over the behavior and institutions at this level. So my fifth recommendation is that more flexible administrative behavior is necessary to address the specific requirements of food and nutrition security programs.

The last area concerns short-term funding versus long-term orientation. We have heard that development and food and nutrition security are long-term objectives. But the funding for meeting these goals is related to short-term, sometimes annual, budgets of donor countries and governments. So programs need a longer lifetime to institutionalize these activities.

Let me conclude with a plea for complementarity. If taken seriously, complementarity will lead to a division of labor. Rational division of labor means that different actors could stick to their comparative advantages. National governments have important roles to play in ensuring security, providing the legal framework that enables people to produce, and creating the institutions that facilitate and supervise private initiatives and community-based activities. Much of the rest can be done by local communities themselves.

Discussion

The discussion on improving implementation centered on the proper roles of the public and private sector. Some participants pointed to the need for clear policies delineating the roles and responsibilities of the two sectors, as well as proper ties between them so they can work together. One participant noted that when African governments liberalized, nothing was done to form effective links between the public and private sectors. For example, in Uganda, it was stated that the government has adopted interventions to help poor farmers but has not linked up with the private sector to show how it could profitably supply poor farmers with tractors. Another comment concerned the need to clarify the role of government versus that of NGOs. NGOs, the participant noted, often receive public funding from abroad, and therefore their governments are indirectly involved. Mechanisms to ensure the involvement of community-based organizations in policymaking are also needed.

Government policies, another participant argued, need to be periodically evaluated and, if necessary, adjusted, and a mechanism to provide for checks and balances should be put in place. The government's role, or lack thereof, in correcting for market failures was identified as a concern.

Keeping long-term needs in perspective when creating short-term goals was highlighted. A participant recommended that a long-term program be worked out and that short-term programs that contribute to the long-term objectives then be nested within it. So far, programs have had a short-term focus, whereas the problems and needs are long term in nature. Drawing attention to the heavy pressure to respond to short-term needs and problems, and to do so quickly, a participant called for balancing short-term perspectives with long-term perspectives.

Several participants mentioned the need to help farmers better organize themselves and to create powerful farmers' organizations. One participant said that small farmers, if well organized, could form a viable commercial unit. They should also be encouraged to engage in contract farming, through a legal framework that would protect them against exploitation. Another pointed out that with strong organization and means to secure funding, small-scale agriculture can be profitable and highly competitive, potentially even more so than large-scale commercial farming.

Excerpt 7: The Pretoria Statement on the Future of African Agriculture

On December 1–3, 2003, the New Partnership for Africa's Development (NEPAD), Capacity Building International, Germany (InWEnt), the Technical Center for Agricultural and Rural Cooperation (CTA), and the International Food Policy Research Institute (IFPRI) assembled a group of experienced agricultural, trade, and finance specialists from government and the private sector and from across Africa to help review, summarize, and distill conclusions from the case studies of African successes. Together, these 70 specialists produced a shared statement of findings identifying priorities for future policy action necessary to trigger sustained agricultural growth in Africa.

Evidence from a series of successful episodes in African agriculture suggests two fundamental prerequisites for sustained agricultural growth as well as a number of promising specific opportunities:

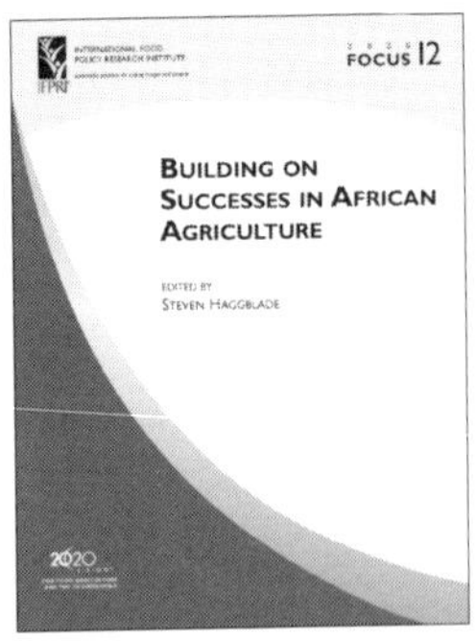

FUNDAMENTAL PREREQUISITES

• *Good governance.* High-level political commitment has consistently proven essential to improving the welfare of farm households. It translates directly into favorable policy environments and budget allocations to agricultural support institutions and related infrastructure. Effective farmer organizations remain central to improving the communication and articulation of farm sector needs to government.

• *Sustained funding for agricultural research and extension.* Virtually all of the successes we have identified involve some form of improved technology: biological, agronomic, mechanical, or organizational. Therefore, governments must elevate funding for agricultural research and extension. Furthermore, it is important that farmers' innovations be mainstreamed into the research agenda.

PROMISING OPPORTUNITIES

• *Soil and water conservation.* We have been impressed with the number and range of innovative efforts by farmers and researchers to sustain soil fertility and water resources in response to increasingly degraded natural environments. Therefore, further testing of these models across national borders merits additional examination and support with the aim of refining and scaling up successes in restoring and sustaining soil fertility. This will require interaction among formal researchers, farmers, and their supporting institutions.

• *Replication of proven commodity-specific breeding and processing successes.* We are impressed with the importance of upscaling cassava breeding and processing research to meet food security, livestock feed, and industrial uses. Strong complementarities across regions suggest that regional cooperation and sharing of biological and mechanical technologies will magnify returns. Tissue-culture bananas and NERICA rice offer further examples of commodity-specific replication potential. NEPAD and leading centers of technology development should take the lead in initiating this exchange.

• *Marketing and information systems.* Mechanisms for aggregating and improving the quality of the products of smallholder farmers and providing relevant and timely market information will enhance market efficiency. This will prove necessary in enabling them to compete in increasingly concentrated domestic, regional, and global markets. A variety of models exist—contract farming among cotton and horticulture producers, dairy marketing groups, and others—for grouping smallfarmers into economically viable market entities.

• *Vertical supply chains.* To improve efficiency, raise value added in production and processing, and ensure improved coordination between producers and final markets will require increasing attention to supply chain management rather than an exclusively production orientation. Successes in cotton, horticulture, dairy, and maize all reveal the importance of vertical farmer-to-market coordination.

• *Regional cooperation in trade and agricultural technology.* Regional trade offers significant potential for moderating food insecurity through cross-border exchange. Harmonization of trade regulations on a regional basis will prove necessary to facilitate these commodity flows. In research as well, countries along common agroecological zones mean that regional technology and information exchange offers significant opportunities for sharing research and development overheads, expanding benefits, and reducing costs. This cross-border technology exchange has proven vitally important in the cases of cassava, maize, and natural resource management technologies. For this exchange, capacity building is necessary. NEPAD and the regional economic organizations remain uniquely suited to facilitate such exchange.

This has been excerpted from 2020 Focus 12, "Building on Successes in African Agriculture," edited by Steven Haggblade and published by IFPRI, Washington, DC, 2004.

Box 5: Participants Polled on Food and Nutrition Issues

A highlight of the conference was the digital voting system, used to survey participants and get instant feedback on topics related to food and nutrition security in Africa. Using hand-held electronic voting devices, participants periodically responded to questions about their views on food and nutrition issues and on approaches to overcoming hunger and malnutrition in Africa. Poll results were presented to the assembled participants immediately.

Were participants hopeful about prospects for food and nutrition security on the continent by 2020? Most saw achieving food security as possible but not likely, whereas less than half viewed achieving nutrition security as possible, and the vast majority believed nutrition security would not be attained. All of the digital voting results appear below.

J. J. Otim, Wilberforce Kisamba-Mugerwa, and former Ugandan President Godfrey K. Binaisa submit responses electronically to digivote questions.

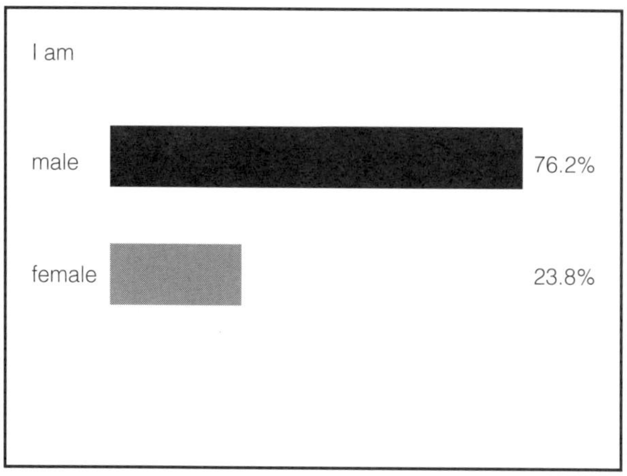

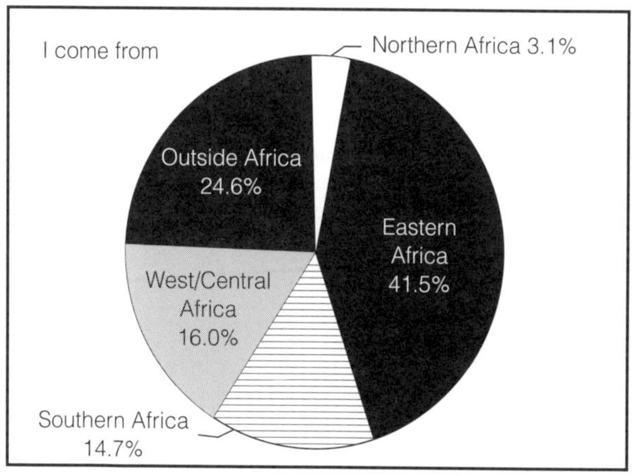

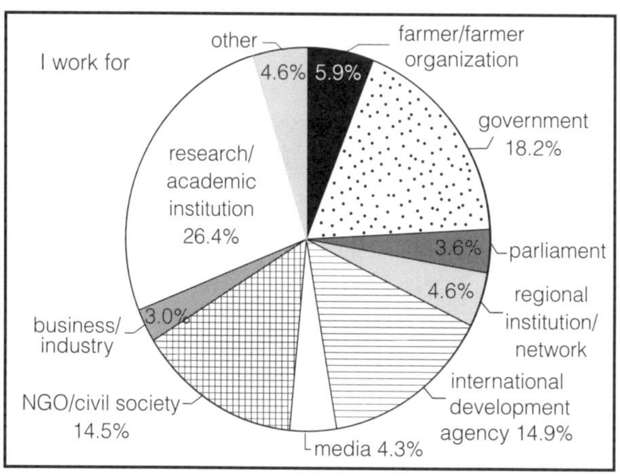

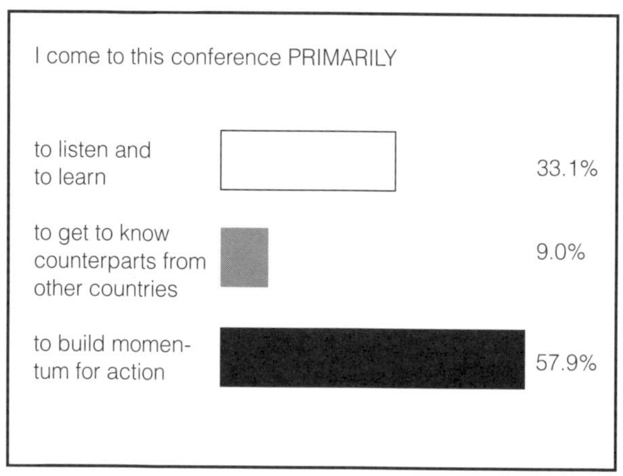

continued

Conference participants give feedback on the key questions of the day during a digivote session.

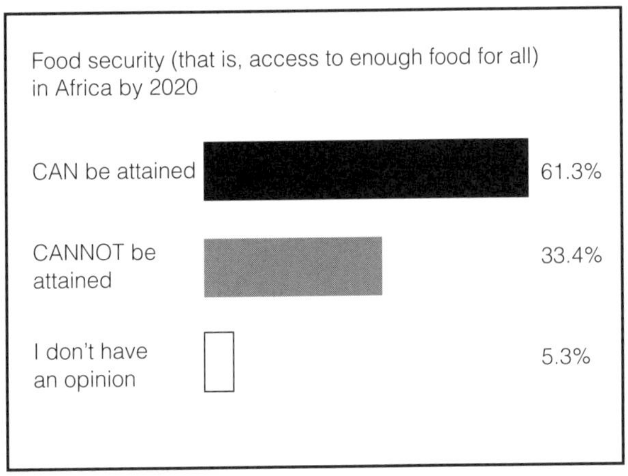

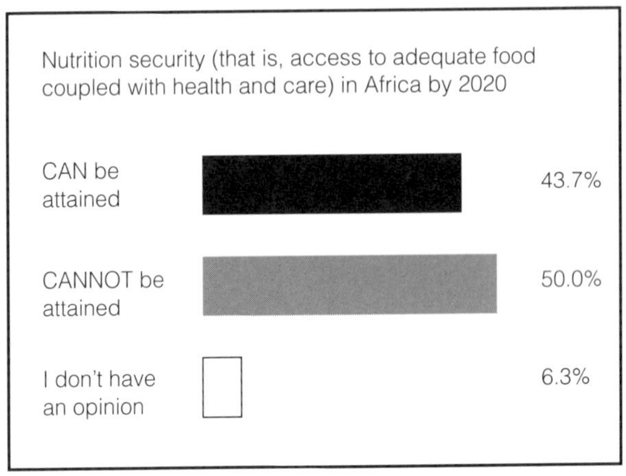

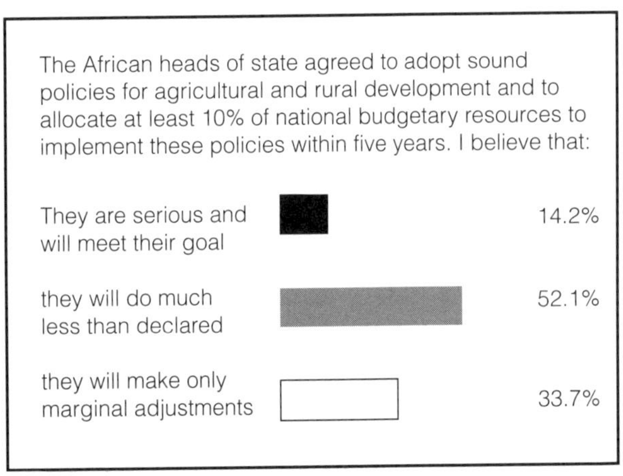

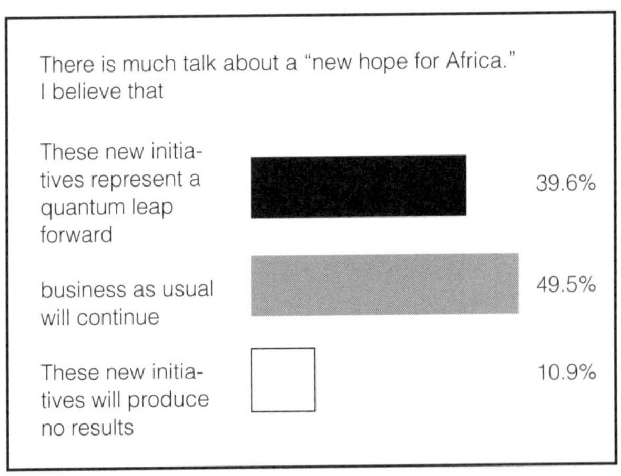

Klaus von Grebmer, IFPRI's director of communication, enthusiastically conducts the electronic voting.

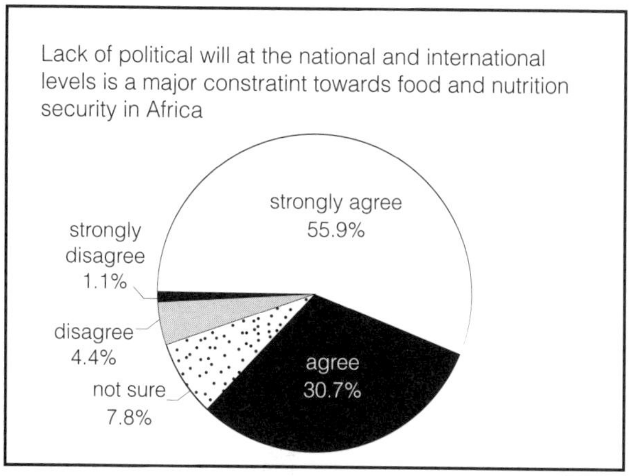

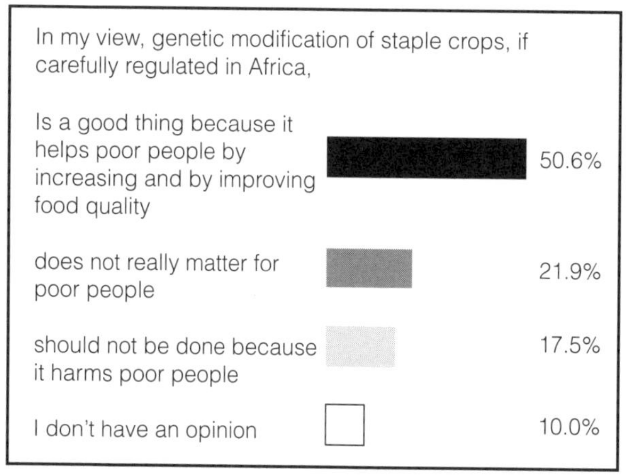

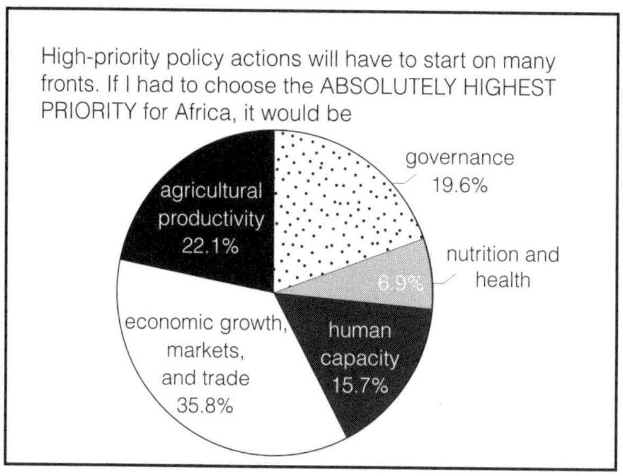

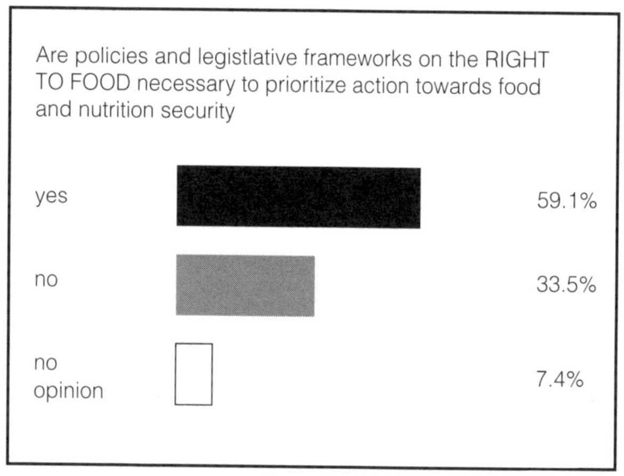

continued

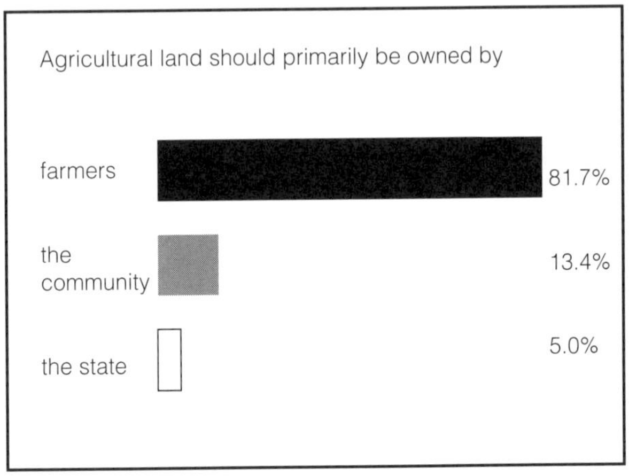
Agricultural land should primarily be owned by
farmers
81.7%
the community
13.4%
the state
5.0%

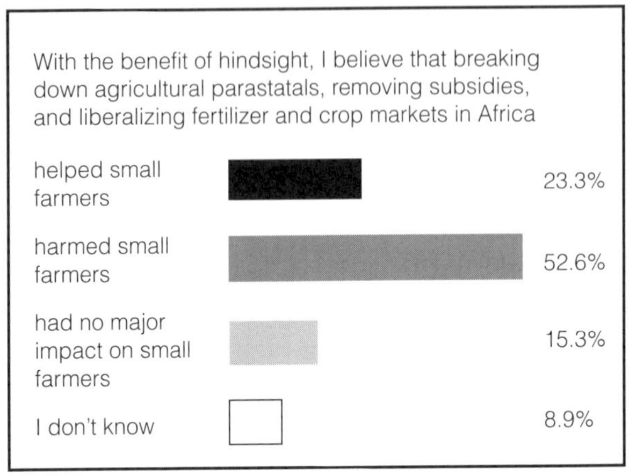
With the benefit of hindsight, I believe that breaking down agricultural parastatals, removing subsidies, and liberalizing fertilizer and crop markets in Africa
helped small farmers
23.3%
harmed small farmers
52.6%
had no major impact on small farmers
15.3%
I don't know
8.9%

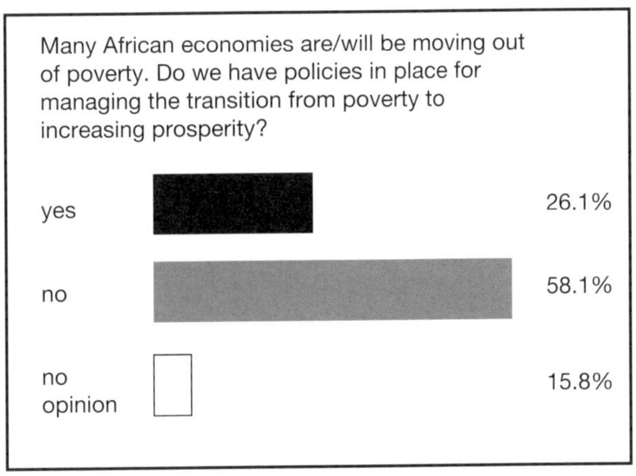
Many African economies are/will be moving out of poverty. Do we have policies in place for managing the transition from poverty to increasing prosperity?
yes
26.1%
no
58.1%
no opinion
15.8%

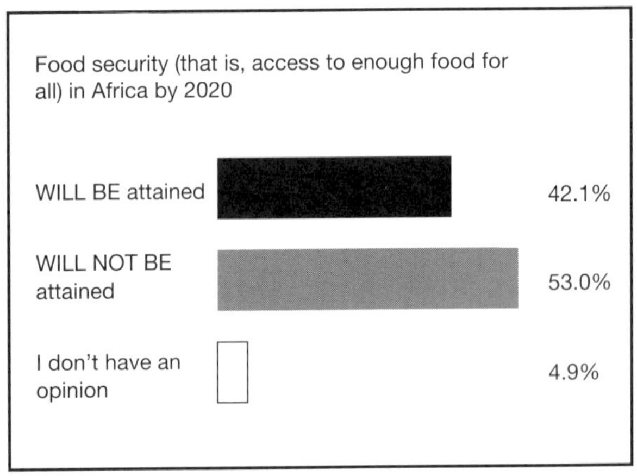
Food security (that is, access to enough food for all) in Africa by 2020
WILL BE attained
42.1%
WILL NOT BE attained
53.0%
I don't have an opinion
4.9%

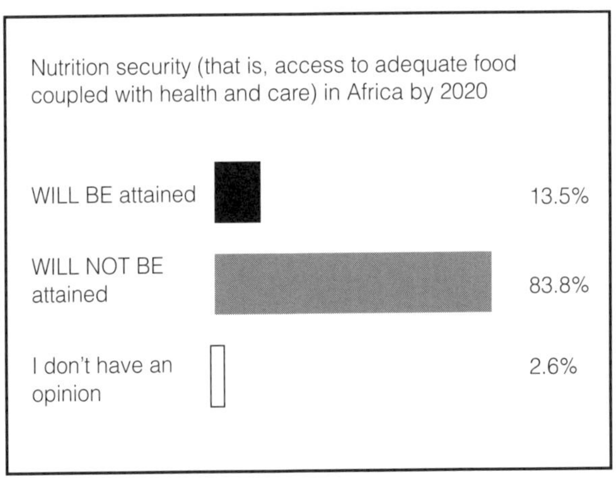
Nutrition security (that is, access to adequate food coupled with health and care) in Africa by 2020
WILL BE attained
13.5%
WILL NOT BE attained
83.8%
I don't have an opinion
2.6%

Part IV | Implementing Action in Key Areas

Chapter 12 Raising Agricultural Productivity

Chair and Moderator: Monty Jones
Executive Secretary, Forum for Agricultural Research in Africa (FARA), Ghana

Rapporteur: John Pender
Senior Research Fellow, International Food Policy Research Institute (IFPRI), USA

Glyvyns Chinkhuntha
Executive Director, Freedom Gardens, Malawi

My question for the educated of Africa is: Why did we go to school? In most cases, as President Museveni said yesterday, Africans went to school to avoid the soil. We went to school to run away from the soil because we thought it was too dirty. In fact, our parents told us, "If you guys don't go to school, you will be like that farmer." So most of us actually went to school to avoid farming.

For any national economy we need educated people to catalyze economic operations. If the issue is food security in Africa, we can only do that through the hands that do the job. Education should mean building capacity to marshal natural resources more wisely than the person who has not been to school, in order to create national wealth, national growth, and mechanisms to alleviate poverty.

But the educated left the rural communities and went to look for white-collar jobs. Education, therefore, has meant that our society has been dissected into one sector into which educated people have streamed and one sector from which educated people have streamed away. The sector that has lost the hands empowered by education to produce food security for Africa has been deserted. We need to find a way to attract these men and women of Africa back to where they should be applying their education—to increasing food productivity on the continent.

Let me share with you a model that I have developed (Figure 1). The donors have been pumping a lot of money into Africa over the past 30 or 50 years. With all the favorable factors on the continent, rivaled by few other continents, we should be champions in food production. Why is it then that we have grown hungrier and poorer on the continent? What I suggest is misallocation and translocation of the capacities to produce food.

Agriculture in Africa can be dissected into two subsets: agriculturalists are in one subset, and farmers are in the other. All the capacity building—and nations have spent billions to invest in these young people—is concentrated in the left-hand circle representing agriculture and agriculturalists. In the right-hand circle, where food production is taking place, there is not so much

FIGURE 1—Model of agriculture in Africa

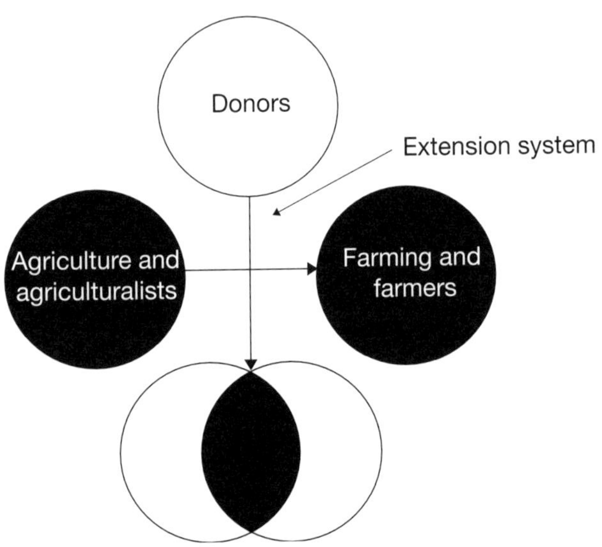

Glyvyns Chinkhuntha emphasizes the importance of reaching out to farmers.

capacity. There is no education there. There is no empowerment of any kind. Even credit access is nil.

Now, how do we expect farmers in the right-hand circle, without the capacity, to produce all the food they need and all the food to sell to those who are enclosed in the ivory towers in the left-hand circle? They cannot.

There is a maxim across Africa and elsewhere I have always heard in conferences like this: Let us put our money where our mouths are. And I say, no, that is wrong, because if you put your money where your mouths are, you will be creating consumer economies to take us nowhere. Let us put our money rather where our hands are, because then we will be empowering the hands that will produce the food that Africa needs.

We have the donors, sometimes with very good intentions, at the top of the diagram. They give money for lifting the farmers out of hunger on the right-hand side, but look at the route the money follows. From the donors it first lands in the left-hand circle, and from there it takes a long conveyor belt to reach the people that need the support on the right-hand side. And some of you know as well as I do what happens to that money along the long chain. People draw on it through project proposals, symposia, and consultancies to evaluate and monitor whether the project has worked or not. And most of them are declared successful without results on the ground.

There is a whole armada of extension service people. They have let us down. Now we need to look elsewhere, to the innovative, creative, and entrepreneurial power that exists at the grassroots level. Farmers are so innovative, so creative, and so entrepreneurial. They know what to do. They know where to do it and when to do it. What they lack is recognition.

In fact, the people who have avoided farming and have gone into the left-hand circle have sometimes turned their backs on and despised farmers. We need a reversal of this situation. Let us make farming so attractive to our youth that when they compare farming with white-collar jobs, they see more benefits and a better life in farming.

This is what innovative farmers are seeing right now. I am one of them. I was a public servant, I have been in the private sector, and now I am on the ground. What I say here, I say from experience.

We have innovative farmers all around us. These are the natural leaders you find in every community who have lifted themselves up from almost nothing, marshaled resources within the community, and shown that we can feed ourselves and generate economic welfare for our families just by mobilizing our natural resources and pulling the right strings together.

Now, we know that this left-hand circle has a frontline, which is extension service. But the communities also have a frontline—that small group of innovative and creative actors. Rather than go through the extension service to reach farmers in the communities, why can't we for once go through the innovative frontline of farmers? These innovative farmers are the ones who live with other farmers, work with other farmers, and generate employment for other farmers. This would be a more effective entry point for interacting with and supporting the grassroots communities.

This approach requires your support in certain areas. To promote innovation and entrepreneurship in African farmers, we need support in forming innovative farmer networks. We have talked of farmer associations and farmer cooperatives. These have failed. We need to look at farmer networks, where farmers retain their individual capacity, their individual commitment, and their individual responsibility, which drives them to personal success.

Farmers are so innovative, so creative, and so entrepreneurial. They know what to do. They know where to do it and when to do it. What they lack is recognition.

— Glyvyns Chinkhuntha

Let us make farming so attractive to our youth that when they compare farming with white-collar jobs, they see more benefits and a better life in farming.

– Glyvyns Chinkhuntha

We need support to empower farmer networks through capacity building to enable them to demand their farmers' rights and benefits.

We need support for product promotion, which includes processing at the cottage level and also calls for energy accessibility.

We need support for market infrastructure development, so we can develop outlets connecting us to supermarkets in a more effective and farmer-friendly way.

We need support for institutional development to give us the capacity to replicate our experiences and our methods and spread them to other farmers that need them.

We need support for lobbying and advocacy for policy reform. Current policies favor grouping actors in, for instance, clubs at the community level, but innovators are individuals. So we need policies that will also look at individual capacities and will help build and improve those capacities, even before farmers are grouped together.

All is not lost. Tremendous achievements have been made. Let us not throw away even our failures. They are our resource—we have a lot of things to learn from past failures.

The future holds a lot for the continent, but it is all dependent on whether we can change our mindset, especially among the youth. We need to hold dear to our hearts farming and the land.

Seyfu Ketema
Executive Secretary, Association for Strengthening Agricultural Research in Eastern and Central Africa (ASARECA), Uganda

Agriculture is the world's largest single industry. It employs about 1.3 billion people and produces US$1.3 trillion worth of goods per year. Over the past 40 years, per capita world food production has grown by 25 percent. Between the 1960s and 1990s, average cereal yields grew from 1.2 metric tons per hectare to 2.5 in developing countries, and total cereal production grew from 420 to 1,176 million tons per year, according to FAO.

Despite this increasing productivity, the world faces a fundamental food security challenge. At the turn of the century, there were an estimated 790 million people hungry and lacking adequate access to food, and 25 percent of these were in Africa. The World Food Summit pledged to achieve food security for all and eradicate hunger in all countries, reducing the number of undernourished to half their present level no later than 2015. Some enhancements in food security will be achieved by 2015, but the World Food Summit target is far from being reached. Studies from FAO suggest that it may not be accomplished even by 2030. So this is a big challenge.

Over the years leading up to 2030, intensity of use and pressure on resources will continue to build up, including pressures associated with degradation. Arable land per person in developing countries shrank from 0.32 hectare during 1961–63 to 0.21 hectare during 1997–99, and it is expected to drop to 0.16 hectare by 2030. Land quality is declining—nearly 40 percent of the world's agricultural land is experiencing serious productivity reduction due to soil degradation. And extreme poverty and hunger will push people even further onto marginal lands and more fragile ecosystems characterized by drought and low soil fertility. So poverty will cause even more degradation. How are we going to face up to this challenge?

Over the past four decades we have produced 25 percent more food per person globally, but 7 percent less food per person in Africa. In Africa, millions are on the brink of starvation. Agriculture will remain the backbone of most African countries, but African agriculture is largely rainfed; only 4.1 percent of the land is under irrigation. African agriculture is characterized by smallholder farms, and most smallholders do not produce

African agriculture is characterized by smallholder farms, and most smallholders do not produce enough. Studies show that in fact they purchase 40 percent of their own food—far from feeding themselves and the rest of the population.

– Seyfu Ketema

enough. Studies show that in fact they purchase 40 percent of their own food—far from feeding themselves and the rest of the population.

The competitiveness of African agriculture presents a challenge. Africa has lost important export markets for some agricultural commodities. Yields in agricultural production are well below world norms, and this is a challenge to both policymakers and agricultural researchers.

Some important issues will need to be addressed. In the coming years there will be less water, less arable land, natural resource degradation, and less labor because of HIV/AIDS and other diseases. We are going to face climate change. Agricultural science and technology will be challenged to produce the diversity of crops, livestock, fish, forests, and commodities needed over the next 50 years in an environmentally and socially sustainable manner; address water deficit and soil fertility problems; improve the nutritional quality of food; combat new and emerging agricultural pests or diseases; and reduce postharvest losses.

Major international commitments to address some of these issues have been made at the World Food Summit in 1996, at the World Food Summit on Sustainable Development in 2002, and by the New Partnership for African Development. So how can agricultural research networks in Africa contribute to raising agricultural productivity and improving food and nutrition security? In each of our countries, the research budget is shrinking. We all complain in different forums that in Africa we have a lack of capacity. Investment in research is low and declining.

One solution is to network so that we bring together the region's human resources, financial resources, and institutions. Agricultural research networks can take into consideration the issues mentioned and contribute to raising agricultural productivity by identifying the goals to be achieved, developing well-defined themes or strategies, identifying the existence of potential sources of technologies and ideas, and harmonizing organizations where appropriate. Networks can facilitate the participation of scientists at the global, regional, and subregional levels, provide technical leadership and policy direction, and facilitate the free exchange of results and methodologies, education, and training opportunities.

Pedro Sanchez

Director of Tropical Agriculture, The Earth Institute at Columbia University; Co-chair, Millennium Project Hunger Task Force; and 2002 World Food Prize Laureate, USA

The work of the Millennium Project's Hunger Task Force, which is co-chaired by M. S. Swaminathan and myself, is to figure out a business plan on how the world can cut hunger in half by 2015. A business plan means not only what should be done, but also how it will be done, who is going to do it, how much it is going to cost, where it should be done, and what the benefits are. This exercise is the most daunting one I have undertaken in my career.

Why is Africa in such bad shape? If we look at the climate and soils, at the continental level they are okay. They range from good to bad, but in that range there is basically no difference from the climate and soils in Latin America and Asia. So that is not the problem.

Africa also has, however, an unusually large human disease load—HIV/AIDS, malaria, and others. Why should Africa, of all continents, have that? As an agronomist, I know that when you grow plants at their center of origin, they are accompanied by a suite of diseases and pests. The center of origin of rubber is in Brazil, and Brazil cannot grow much rubber, but when rubber was introduced in Malaysia, it became extremely productive. Africa happens to be the center of origin of our species, and perhaps the same situation applies. It certainly has a very large human disease load.

Also, Africa is plagued by poor policies and poor governance, although both are improving dramatically. Africa has a large rural inland population in sharp contrast with Latin America and Asia, which have large coastal populations, a situation that allows for more trade.

Even though Africa has huge rivers like the Nile, the Congo, and the Zambezi, unfortunately, the basins are not very suitable for irrigation. Yesterday when someone asked whether rainfed farming can be made profitable and sustainable, I said a very emphatic "yes." Certainly

Africa has had tremendous quantities of nitrogen and phosphorus taken out of the soil—through crop grains, crop residues, and soil erosion—that have not returned.

— Pedro Sanchez

we should irrigate whatever we can, but the situation in Africa is very different from that in Latin America and Asia, which have much larger irrigation resources.

Africa has felt little impact from the Green Revolution. Hans Gregersen at the University of Minnesota and Bob Evenson of Yale University have looked at the contribution of improved varieties of 11 major food crops—including not only maize and wheat, but also cassava and beans and others—to yield increases in the past 40 years. They found that in Asia these improved varieties were responsible for 88 percent of the yield increases; in Latin America, 66; in the Middle East, 69; in Sub-Saharan Africa, 28. Why? There has been a lot of work on crop genetic improvement in Africa.

There are many reasons, including policy and governance issues. But there is one overwhelming biophysical reason, and that is soil fertility depletion. Unlike other continents, where soil fertility depletion has been tackled by applying fertilizers, and in the case of the United States and Europe, applying them excessively, Africa has had tremendous quantities of nitrogen and phosphorus taken out of the soil—through crop grains, crop residues, and soil erosion—that have not returned. Pioneering work at Wageningen University led by Eric Smaling showed that a total of 132 million tons of nitrogen, 15 million tons of phosphorus, and 90 million tons of potassium, worth US$11 billion a year at current prices, has been lost from cultivated land in 37 African countries during the past 30 years.

FIGURE 1—Factors limiting crop growth in the rainy season in the Sahel

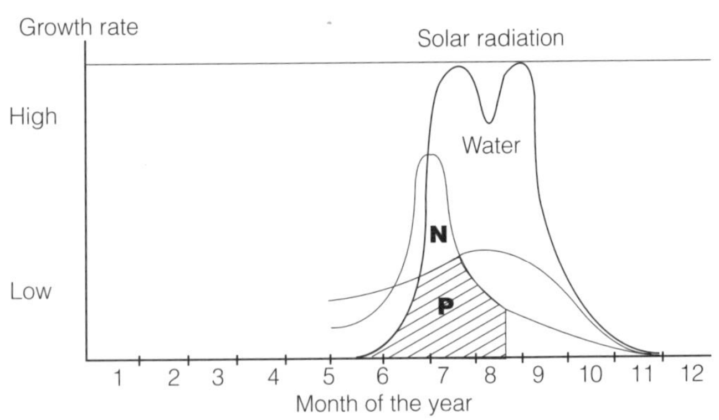

Source: InterAcademy Panel 2004.
Note: During the rainy season in the Sahel, phosphorus becomes limiting first, then nitrogen, then water, and finally solar radiation.

FIGURE 2—Synergistic investments in hunger hotspots

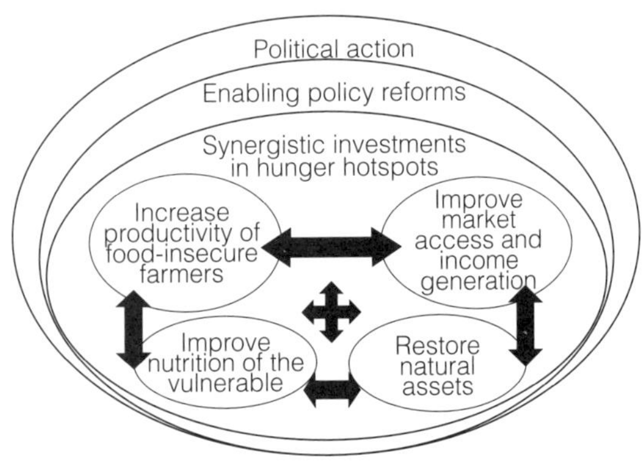

Source: Author.

This is the fundamental biophysical constraint, very similar to the need for upright Green Revolution–type varieties in Asia 40 years ago. If you do not tackle the fundamental biophysical constraints, no matter how much fertilizer you used in Asia before the Green Revolution, no matter how good the varieties we have here in Africa are now, it is not going to work. So first things first, and this is a major one.

Another major biophysical factor, almost as important as soil infertility, is the problem of too much and too little water. There is a lot of argument about which is more important—soil fertility or water. I think finally the answer has come for the Sahel, which is certainly semi-arid, in a study about to be released from the InterAcademy Panel (Figure 1). This graph shows the main limiting factors for the Sahel. Month six, June, is when the rainy season starts. Before anything else, the first limiting factor is phosphorus, the second is nitrogen, and the third is water. Eventually, the fourth biophysical limiting factor is solar radiation. So even in the more semi-arid areas, nutrient problems come first.

The Hunger Task Force is developing a set of recommendations at three different levels. We are talking about political action worldwide; we are talking about enabling policy reforms; and we are talking about four synergistic investments in hunger hotspots (Figure 2). By "synergistic," we mean things that have to be done together and that help each other out.

The first investment is increasing the productivity of food-insecure farmers, in addition to increasing the productivity of food-secure farmers. Let's focus on the food-insecure farmers because the farming population accounts for half the hungry people in the world. The second investment is improving nutrition of vulnerable people: pregnant and lactating mothers and children less than two years old, schoolchildren, and people affected by HIV/AIDS or excluded for racial, tribal, or other reasons. The third investment is making markets work for the poor and improving opportunities for income. And the fourth one is restoring natural assets that have been degraded by agriculture.

I will focus now on the first investment. Increasing productivity for food-insecure farmers has four major components: investing in soil health, small-scale water management, better germplasm and seed delivery systems—whether through genetic modifications or conventional breeding—and, in the case of Africa, reinventing extension.

Investing in healthy soils is what Jeffrey Sachs calls a prima facie case. He developed a thought paper for the Hunger Task Force that said that plant nutrient inputs in African small farms are disastrously below levels needed to ensure food security, and posed different investment options.

You can augment household income to achieve food security in different ways: you can provide food aid, which may not augment household income but could provide food security; you can provide income transfers, as the Zero Hunger Project in Brazil is doing; or you can work on overcoming the fundamental biophysical obstacles, which is what the Green Revolution did in Asia 40 years ago with improved varieties.

Investing on the input side, in natural capital—in this case soil and water—will be less costly than investing in food aid or income transfers. And it certainly will provide higher returns than investing in the output side.

The components of soil health investments in Africa, then, are several: accessing nutrients at the lowest possible cost, whether they are inorganic or organic; returning crop residues to the soil, which is generally not done in Africa at all; conservation tillage; soil erosion control; small-scale water management; and policy and political support.

Accessing plant nutrients at the lowest possible cost is the number one issue, and there are several options. One is fertilizer trees, nitrogen-fixing leguminous trees that capture the nitrogen from the air. We live in an atmosphere of 78 percent nitrogen, and the legumes are the only family of plants that can capture it. With the fertilizer trees, the captures are large—100 to 200 kilos of nitrogen per hectare per year right in situ. Other options are cover crops, green manures, and mineral fertilizers. It would be very foolish of the development community to say that mineral fertilizers are bad or organic sources are bad. We need both. There is nothing wrong with mineral fertilizers when properly used. The plant does not care whether the nitrate and the phosphate ions that it uses come from decomposing urea granules or from a decomposing piece of manure or a plant.

It would be very foolish of the development community to say that mineral fertilizers are bad or organic sources are bad. We need both.

— Pedro Sanchez

Fertilizer use needs to increase by an order of magnitude. Now fertilizer use is less than 10 kilograms per hectare per year, whereas countries like Viet Nam use about 100.

The problem with fertilizers is their high cost. They cost around US$400 to US$700 per ton—using urea as the standard—in inland areas like Malawi and Uganda, owing mainly to high transport costs. In my view, when the farmgate price is less than US$250 per ton of urea, which is about the world market price, then use it. In coastal Ghana, for example, that is the price of fertilizer, and that price is reasonable. The problem arises when transport costs are added. In addition, if you use fertilizers rather than agroforestry technologies, you must sell enough crops to pay for the cost of fertilizer. Other technologies require fewer cash inputs.

We must use mineral fertilizers for correcting phosphorus depletion. The organic fertilizers may help a little bit, but they cannot solve it. But when it comes to nitrogen, we can talk about organics versus inorganics.

Sasakawa Global 2000 and many other organizations in Africa have done good work in setting up demonstration crops using fertilizers, and about a million farmers have benefited from demonstration crops, usually with excellent results. They may have problems selling their crops to markets and paying off loans, but there is no question that fertilizers work effectively. We need to do it for the 80 million farmers in Africa, not just 1 million.

Transport costs are a major problem. As Norman Borlaug mentioned yesterday, Africa's road density now is less than India's was at the start of the Green Revolution. On the Mombasa-Kampala road, the Trans-Africa Highway, trucks go through innumerable checkpoints and potholes. The road is in such bad shape that this is clearly one of the first priorities to solve.

To move one ton of fertilizer 1,000 kilometers costs about US$15 in the United States, about US$30 in India, but about US$100 in Africa. To move one ton of maize

To move one ton of fertilizer 1,000 kilometers costs about US$15 in the United States, about US$30 in India, but about US$100 in Africa.

— Pedro Sanchez

from Iowa to Mombasa, a distance of 13,600 kilometers, costs US$50. To move that same ton of maize from Mombasa to Kampala, a distance of 900 kilometers, costs US$100.

Smallholder farmers can access nutrients at a lower cost. Farmers are using indigenous medium- to high-reactivity phosphate rocks. There are good deposits and plenty of them throughout Africa—Minjingu in Tanzania, Tororo in eastern Uganda, Tilemsi in Mali. You can also transfer biomass from hedges into fields with the Mexican sunflower, which has the ability to accumulate enormous quantities of nutrients. Transport costs are less in that case, but labor costs are significant. Finally, you can access nutrients at zero transport cost by using fertilizer trees. There are 250,000 farm families using this agroforestry technology in East and Southern Africa, and they all report high and consistent results. This is much fewer than the number of farmers using fertilizers, and both should go together. Fertilizer trees also provide fuelwood, help preserve woodland biodiversity, and decrease women's labor, which is very important.

After accessing nutrients, the second major soil problem is that all the crop residues are taken away to feed cattle or make live fences, like the fences in the Sahel made of sorghum and millet stems. Or crop residues come into the city for firewood. Or worst of all, animal dung is used for cooking, eliminating all possible nutrient cycling. Crop residues are taken away not because farmers are stupid, but because they need those resources. So a major part of soil health will be returning crop residues while making provisions for fodder for cattle, such as improved grasses and legume species, and for live fences, for instance, instead of dead fences in the Sahel.

Another major component of soil health is conservation tillage. Hand hoeing the soil is hard work. But research on conservation tillage in very small farming systems that do not involve mechanization might give us some good answers there.

Finally, soil erosion control is crucial. In places where erosion is advancing, the landscape is destroyed. There are certainly proven erosion control mechanisms. In the Kabale region of southwestern Uganda, the slopes have been totally controlled with contour leguminous hedges.

Small-scale water management, whether it consists of diguettes, zai holes, stone terraces, biological terraces, or other systems, are also key.

Now, let us turn to the policy and politics. This applies not only to investing in soil health, but also to the other recommendations of the Hunger Task Force. The hungry countries must develop national strategies that work, changing the PRSPs so that there are strategies in agriculture, in nutrition, and in markets. That is top-down action. We also now have the concept of Millennium Villages, which is based on bottom-up action. How about working with specific villages to accomplish all the Millennium Development Goals (MDGs) in five years? What do the villages need? What kinds of investments are needed?

Good governance is absolutely essential. We should not be working with countries that are poorly governed. We should begin with countries like Ethiopia, Uganda, Kenya, and Ghana because these countries are reasonably well governed. We must also increase national budgets for agriculture, nutrition, and markets.

Now, some rich countries have committed themselves to join what is called the G-0.7 club. Those are the countries that provide 0.7 percent of their national budget in development assistance. We must make development assistance much more effective. With the Government of Ethiopia, we are hosting an African high-level agricultural seminar in Addis Ababa on July 5, where we expect the secretary general to issue a major call to action on eliminating hunger in Africa. The Millennium Task Force has also been doing country planning exercises in Senegal, Ghana, Kenya, and Ethiopia at different levels, from farmers to heads of state.

Finally, the idea of the Millennium Village is a new one—how a village can accomplish all the MDGs in five years through community participation. This would involve, of course, not only healthy, well-watered soils, but also better germplasm; diverse crops, livestock, and trees; school lunches with locally produced foods in fully operational schools; malaria bed nets; AIDS antiretroviral drugs; safe water for drinking and sanitation; village vehicles; and energy platforms. They would have Internet access, clinics, banks, storage, products for storing their produce before it goes to market, product transformation, classrooms, and food-for-work for repairing infrastructure and environmental damage.

My conclusion is that cutting hunger in half by 2015 is possible—it is a global commitment and a political choice.

Carlos Seré

Director General, International Livestock Research Institute (ILRI), Kenya

Livestock is about a third of the whole agricultural sector in Africa, and it is very much linked to poor people and their livelihoods. About 70 percent of the rural poor have something to do with livestock. Some 200 million people have their livelihoods directly linked to animals.

Livestock, as you know, provides high-quality nutrition. We are making efforts to increase micronutrients in cereals, but animal products already have them, and small amounts of animal products have been shown to be extremely beneficial. Obviously, this is particularly important for people with AIDS, for example.

Crop-livestock links are diverse. Animal traction is a very important source of power for land preparation in Africa. Nutrients are cycled between livestock and crops. Livestock serve as a cash source for agriculture, and having some animals in agriculture plays a buffering role against climatic and financial risks. There are many more links, and these links are an intrinsic characteristic of African agriculture.

Obviously some people are exclusively dependent on livestock, like pastoralists, in many cases women, and landless people who produce milk with a cow fed with, for example, Napier grass grown along the road.

Livestock and the livestock economy have a number of dynamic aspects, and these need to be taken into account. Obviously, as population grows, demand increases. But as people move into urban settings and incomes gradually rise, demand for animal products grows much faster than demand for cereals. This implies that more and more of these animal products move to the cities. The supply chains for these products get longer, more complex, and riskier, which leads to changes in the rules and regulations governing how these markets function.

One important phenomenon is the rapid growth of supermarkets, which have clearly established policies on the types of products they want. This change in the way the markets operate has serious implications for smallholders. The changes are even greater for export markets. Regulations about safety, such as sanitary and phytosanitary rules, exclude lots of smallholders. Transboundary diseases such as Rift Valley fever and foot-and-mouth disease also affect trade. These changes are threatening the traditional role of smallholders.

TABLE 1—Net trade in livestock products in Africa, 1970–2030 (1,000 metric tons)

Product	1970	1980	1990	2000	2015	2030
Beef	119	63	-32	2	-5	-109
Eggs	0	-3	-5	-17	-9	-22
Meat	142	50	-110	-80	-283	-744
Milk	-913	-2,496	-1,785	-1,971	-3,605	-5,226
Mutton/goat	29	40	29	59	73	80
Pig meat	-4	-9	-21	-42	-71	-108
Poultry	-2	-43	-86	-149	-280	-606

Source: FAOSTAT 2002.
Note: Negative figures imply imports.

At the same time there is an enormous increase in demand. Projections for 2015 and 2030 show that the region will be largely a net importer of livestock products (Table 1). There is a market opportunity, and while Africa has a tradition in the production of animal products, if nothing is done to increase production, a large part of the demand will be met through imports.

I will now turn to key actions. In practical terms, many countries' PRSPs barely mention agriculture and rarely mention livestock, and they completely ignore livestock's important linkages. Addressing these topics in PRSPs is a key action because these papers determine what will be politically supported by national governments and by donors.

The second action is to work with the complex and rapidly changing value chains for livestock. We tend to feel that if you want to help farmers, you need to do something on the farm. In the livestock sector, however, if you manage to get supermarkets to buy from smallholders, you will probably have a much greater impact

As people move into urban settings and incomes gradually rise, demand for animal products grows much faster than demand for cereals.

— Carlos Seré

In the livestock sector, however, if you manage to get supermarkets to buy from smallholders, you will probably have a much greater impact than if you improve the calving rate by a few percentage points.

— Carlos Seré

than if you improve the calving rate by a few percentage points. We need to look at the whole value chain to understand where the inefficiencies are and where the opportunities are.

For example, ILRI did studies with the Permanent Interstate Committee for Drought Control in the Sahel (CILSS) in West Africa that showed that by custom, when live cattle are moved from the Sahel to the coast, you are charged informal taxes every time you cross a border. One analysis said small farmers would probably receive 25 percent more for their cattle if you could eliminate or reduce these informal taxes.

Because of disease and related problems, quality issues are also key in livestock. Capacity is needed in the public sector to develop and enforce policies. To trade, not only must you control foot-and-mouth disease, but the outside world—the World Organisation for Animal Health (OIE) in Paris—needs to know and believe that you are doing it.

Service delivery has been a serious problem in the livestock sector, as it has been in agriculture in general. Public veterinary services have been disbanded and not replaced. Moreover, there is a lot of regulation limiting the use of animal health assistants and people who are not veterinarians, and these regulations are hindering better service in the livestock sector. So service issues are also key.

Along these lines, which actors particularly need strengthening? Clearly, the regulatory capacity, the veterinary services, and the input quality control services need to be strengthened. But another important action in this very dynamic livestock market is strengthening collective action among smallholders. This is clearly the biggest challenge. Other regions of the world offer interesting experiences from which lessons can be drawn. Through India's Operation Flood, individuals deliver 8 to 10 liters of milk a day to a cooperative system that turns it into commercially viable products. Vertical integration is occurring very quickly, particularly in Asia, among small poultry producers. But we definitely need to strengthen the capacity of smallholders to participate in the market, to negotiate, and to get a fair share of the action.

Partnerships are crucial. Clearly a lot of players are needed in this dynamic sector. It is a question not of public versus private, but of strengthening the partnerships between them. The public sector, for example, frequently needs to regulate inputs. The private sector needs to produce those inputs. Delivering them to scattered smallholders is extremely difficult, but there the NGOs have the comparative advantage. So it is critical to understand how to orchestrate the interactions among these different actors to deliver the right services to farmers and livestock keepers.

The other element is agricultural research. While research has made many technologies available and is developing others, what is frequently lacking are links among all the actors in an innovation system. It is not good enough to have farmers and researchers talking to each other. For veterinary inputs, the private sector that is actually going to produce the product must be involved. The government sector, which is going to control the quality, must be involved. These people need to work together along the research-to-delivery continuum. Demand-driven research must be embedded in an effective innovation system.

Finally—and this follows what FARA and ASARECA are doing—research is clearly a public good in many cases and is much more effectively delivered regionally than nationally. Research partnerships within the regions are therefore essential. We are working, for example, to expand the nature of the services ILRI provides to the region in advanced biosciences. We will be upgrading and opening our laboratories to African partners to conduct their own biosciences research. This should provide access to advanced research equipment and technical backstopping to a range of African research institutions. We believe that research needs this regional focus to be cost-effective in Africa, particularly in the livestock sector.

Livestock is a neglected tool for addressing poverty in Africa.

— Carlos Seré

Effective partnerships must also be developed between the public veterinary services sectors of the different countries. Rift Valley fever or foot-and-mouth disease cannot be handled by an individual country when animals are moving across borders all the time.

I do not see many silver bullets. We are seeking to get very complex systems to work more effectively, and many things need to happen at the same time. Some are more important than others, but first of all, we clearly need policymakers and managers who understand the complexity of this sector. Coming from a research background, I believe that good research, looking not just at technology but also at policies and institutions, can enhance this learning process.

I would like to leave you with one message: livestock is a neglected tool for addressing poverty in Africa.

Eugene R. Terry

Implementing Director, African Agricultural Technology Foundation (AATF), Kenya

My remarks will cover three main areas: first, I will make some brief comments on the nature of the food security and poverty alleviation challenges that we face in Africa; second, I will give you an update on the start-up and project implementation activities of the new African Agricultural Technology Foundation; and third, I will comment on some intervention points with regard to raising agricultural productivity.

The problems we face are enormous and challenging because there are simply millions of very hungry and poor people in Africa. The most accurate estimate we have is that about 194 million Africans are today malnourished. Anywhere else in the world, this would be unimaginable and unforgivable. Imagine if half of all Americans were malnourished. Imagine if all of Australia, New Zealand, Canada, and tens of millions more were starving. In addition, around 40 million African children under the age of five are malnourished. Imagine if every child in every capital of the G-8 countries was malnourished.

These challenges should prompt us as Africans to affirm that we should, and indeed we must, find the best solutions. We must take ownership of our problems and their solutions. But hunger and poverty are symptoms, and we must first look at the causes.

In Sub-Saharan Africa, about 90 percent of the total labor force is in one way or another involved in farming. Agriculture contributes about 40 percent of the net export earnings of the continent. Yet a cold look at the data shows that between 1980 and 1995, Sub-Saharan Africa was the only region in the world to experience a decline in crop productivity. Crop yields increased by 27 percent in Asia and by 12 percent in Latin America, but fell by 8 percent in Africa.

> *We must harness all that science and technology can offer to help African farmers to grow more food.*
>
> — Eugene R. Terry

This problem is not likely to diminish in the near future because increases in population will continue to create food demands that will not be easy to meet. We must harness all that science and technology can offer to help African farmers to grow more food.

Before I describe how we can get there, let me address some of the doubts, perhaps unspoken, that many of you and others have about Africa's potential to feed itself. Three basic questions are sometimes asked indirectly because they are seen as politically incorrect or impolite.

First, does the African continent have the human potential or can it provide the human capital to make the advancements required to solve its agricultural and scientific problems? Second, are the nation-states of Africa so corrupt that they, in fact, constitute a hindrance to substantive economic improvement? And, third, are the enabling conditions for real economic progress present in Africa? Can the roads, markets, infrastructure, and policies be put in place to enhance our capacity for economic growth?

You might imagine that I would be affronted to be asked if Africa has the scientific capacity to improve its crop yields significantly. The story of WARDA and NERICA is becoming generally well known. We today have the pleasure and opportunity to have on the podium with us the young scientist, Monty Jones, who has just won the World Food Prize for that elegant piece of science.

With regard to corruption being one of the reasons for slow progress, let me state categorically that I condemn corruption and insist that we fix the problems of malfeasance in government. But if we can achieve dramatic increases in crop yields, our farmers and agribusiness entrepreneurs know how to sell their crops and get them to market. My answer, therefore, is that we can combat corruption by investing in healthy organizations.

Corruption thrives in the dark; let us, therefore, open up the process and support accountable and transparent systems.

With regard to the inextricably connected multiple parts of agricultural development—the policies, infrastructure, markets, capacity—they do not function as well as we wish. But if we know anything about free markets, it is that they work in complex ways but always seek profit. If we can increase output, we strengthen the incentives for roads and for middlemen in the marketing systems.

Let me be specific about why I think the AATF is such an important mechanism that will improve Africa's food security prospects. The activities of the AATF combine science and agriculture, and the organization is driven by the vision of a future in which Africa is self-sufficient and prosperous. But the work of the AATF rests on the concept of partnerships for gaining access to and delivery of technologies. The partnerships that we are promoting draw upon the best of academic, scientific, and business knowledge combined with the experiences and indigenous knowledge of the African farmer.

Unlike the rest of the world, Africa has not had effective mechanisms for negotiating access to and transfer of technology held by the public and private sectors. Partnerships are vital. We need access to industrialized countries' advanced agricultural science, and we need African scientists to adapt these advances to our circumstances. That is why it is important that the AATF is led and managed by Africans and focuses on African priorities.

We seek to identify opportunities for royalty-free transfers of technologies that would be helpful to African farmers, and we negotiate for access to these technologies. We then enter into contractual agreements that will facilitate deployment of these innovations. In other words, we are the responsible party. We deal with intellectual property management, regulatory regimes, liability, licensing, sublicensing, and freedom-to-operate assessments. We will ensure that technologies are appropriately and responsibly used across the value chain.

I am proud to report that the goal of creating an accountable, transparent, African-led scientific partnership with a wide range of technology holders, mostly from outside Africa but also within the continent, has come further than one could have reasonably hoped. After all, we have been operating in Kenya for only a year. In our first year we attracted support and recognition from corporate and nonprofit organizations as well as from regional and national institutions. We have an approved 10-year business plan. We have hired excellent, talented, and experienced senior staff.

I am particularly proud of our partnerships with local nongovernmental organizations, but we are also partnered with CGIAR centers, The Rockefeller Foundation, and African leadership groups including NEPAD and FARA. Our private sector partners include Monsanto, Dow Agro, Pioneer/DuPont, BASF, and Syngenta. We also have substantial support from two leading development agencies: the United States Agency for International Development and the United Kingdom's Department for International Development.

We have identified eight key problem areas for target intervention: the control of Striga in cereals, insect resistance in maize, nutritional quality improvement in maize and rice, increased productivity of bananas and plantains, increased cowpea production and utilization, drought tolerance in cereals, mycotoxins in food grains, and increased cassava productivity. These problem areas are crucial to food security. There will be more, but these are the current highest priority targets for the AATF.

All of you present at this conference are, or will be, prospective stakeholders and partners of the AATF. I look forward to working with all of you as we enter the implementation phase of our projects.

Florence Wambugu

Chief Executive Officer, A Harvest Biotech Foundation International, Kenya

At A Harvest our mission is to focus on using improved biotechnology tools, but in a holistic approach. Our strategy is to use the whole value chain, and especially to look at the downstream niche. We focus on grassroots mobilization, the downstream results. Our current activities include developing a pro-poor, tissue-cultured (TC) banana industry in Kenya through the whole value chain, focusing on market development; a project on reforesta-

Many, many projects start without looking at demand and supply. If you do not assess demand and supply, you can end up developing a research product that does not have a niche market.

— Florence Wambugu

tion, which is a major need in Africa; communication for development; and, most important, capacity building.

There are enormous concerted efforts toward fighting hunger and malnutrition in Africa. These efforts include UN bodies like the Millennium Project Hunger Task Force just described by Pedro Sanchez, of which we are a part; the CGIAR centers; NEPAD; and FARA. There is ASARECA and there are national programs, donor efforts, and NGOs. All these efforts are important and complementary. But I want to focus on the challenge of downstream delivery to the end users: farmers and markets. We should not forget that niche.

The process starts with an understanding of the challenges of the target community. Many, many projects start without looking at demand and supply. If you do not assess demand and supply, you can end up developing a research product that does not have a niche market.

I cannot say enough about applying the appropriate technologies. We cannot develop technologies in research centers and then fail to test whether they are appropriate for communities. We need to learn from the private sector, which first goes to the market to determine the need for a product before starting to develop it.

We need to identify and build the necessary human and institutional capacity. Next, we need to bring donors on board with us as development partners. More and more donors are interested in whether we are delivering to the target communities. And we need to apply an effective project implementation strategy.

The 6 "s" concept is useful. We need good *science*—that is, proven technologies and local knowledge. As we develop project implementation strategies, we cannot ignore the indigenous knowledge that comes from the rural communities. I would even suggest we need to start with it.

Next we need *selectivity*—areas of high impact—and *specificity* to the needs and conditions of the farming community. You get these when you do a needs assessment.

Then we need *sales*—making markets work for the poor calls for being sure there is a market for whatever product we bring on board. We need long-term *sustainability* of the project or initiative.

And last, but not least, we need *scaling up*. Can we scale up from a project to a community to a nation or even more to another country? Can we move a successful initiative like NERICA from West Africa across Africa?

If we are going to make science and technology work for the poor, we need an implementation strategy.

> *We say we are going to increase productivity in Africa, but where is the labor?*
>
> – Florence Wambugu

The essential components for a successful delivery are awareness creation, seedling availability and affordability, farm management, postharvest handling, and most important, marketing.

First, there must be awareness creation, sensitization, and information dissemination. For example, if we want to interest the youth in coming into agriculture, we must think of farming as a business. We cannot interest youth in farming in the old style. We also realized in Kenya that farmer-to-farmer extension is an effective strategy that works well in Africa. Before a farmer can accept something from a researcher, an outsider, there is a mental barrier that needs to be broken. We can use networking and farmer extension to share information. It is crucial that we go to the communities and talk to them and do it with them instead of doing it for them. It has to be a consultative effort.

Seedling availability and affordability are very important. Where are the seeds, whether they are hybrid maize, improved cassava, improved sweet potato, or bananas? Can the farmers get access to them? If they are biotransformed or tissue-cultured plantlets developed in laboratories, where can farmers find these materials? If a product comes from a CGIAR center, can the farmers get access to it? All the partners need to come on board to make this happen.

Most poor farmers cannot afford improved seeds, whether hybrid or genetically modified. If farmers cannot afford the seeds, is microcredit available? Transport and distribution systems also need to be in place.

Last year alone, our network mobilized 1.5 million improved seedlings for planting during the rains. My country, Kenya, has a serious deforestation problem. We have 1.7 percent forest cover. We are supposed to have 12 percent forest cover to meet the international requirement. It is a disaster. So Africa Harvest is involved in mobilizing improved tree seedlings, and even this effort cannot meet the current demand.

For TC bananas, there have to be nurseries, both large-scale and small-scale. This year, again, we are mobilizing 100,000 TC banana seedlings to small-scale farmers as well as 2.5 million improved tree seedlings, of which the greatest share will be planted by resource-poor, small-scale farmers. This is a challenge that we are ready to undertake.

I will not say much about GM issues, except to tell you that GM crop production is increasing (Figure 1). It is not just the United States that has adopted biotech crops; many more countries are involved, including Mexico, the Philippines, and some countries in Europe, like Spain (Table 1). GM has speedily become a global technology. So instead of just brokering information about the technology, we can see how it can benefit communities.

FIGURE 1—Global area of transgenic crops, 1985–2003

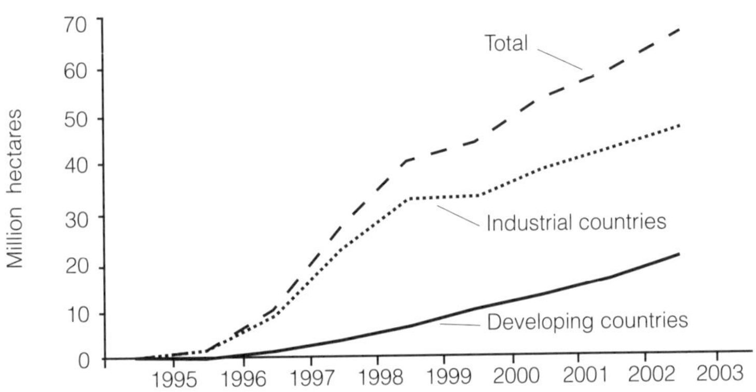

Source: C. James, *Preview: Global status of commercialized transgenic crops: 2003*, ISAAA Brief No. 30 (Ithaca, NY, USA: International Service for the Acquisition of Agri-biotech Applications).
Note: Increase of 15 percent, or 22.2 million acres, between 2002 and 2003.

TABLE 1—Global status of biotech crops, 2003

Country	Number of hectares cultivated with biotech crops
United States	42.8 million
Argentina	13.9 million
Canada	4.4 million
Brazil	3.0 million
China	2.8 million
South Africa	0.4 million
Australia	0.1 million
India	0.1 million
Romania	<0.1 million
Uruguay	<0.1 million
Bulgaria, Colombia, Germany, Honduras, Indonesia, Mexico, Philippines, Spain	50,000 or less

Source: C. James, *Preview: Global status of commercialized transgenic crops: 2003*, ISAAA Brief No. 30 (Ithaca, NY, USA: International Service for the Acquisition of Agri-biotech Applications).

With regard to growing and farm management, we need to be sensitive to issues of labor. Women have been the farmers, but they cannot continue to carry the load of increasing farm labor requirements. HIV is also taking a toll on labor. We say we are going to increase productivity in Africa, but where is the labor? Either we interest youth in farming, increase mechanization, or use some new methods.

In addition, in order to grow high-quality products and increase productivity, we must have soil fertility, water, and integrated pest management (IPM).

In high-yielding, small-scale banana orchards in Kenya, farmers are earning a lot of money for their produce. The smaller the land, the more a farmer needs to produce from that small unit of land. But small-scale farmers are working their way out of poverty. Some have even built stone houses from the earnings of very small units of land planted with bananas. We need to look at these successes and help scale them up.

A lot of products are lost after harvest. Thus postharvest management is crucial. Many products are perishable. It is important to think about seed treatment, transport to markets, and other areas of postharvest management. With bananas, for example, farmers earn a third of the value just through postharvest management. When the fruit is on the tree, you are capturing only part of the value. If you take it to the supermarket after harvest, you gain a lot more value.

Marketing and consumer acceptance are also important. For a crop like banana, we need to promote diverse varieties because a lot of farmers will not eat their own variety. Over 90 percent of food is consumed by the people who produce it. We need greater crop diversity to encourage consumption. Marketing studies and consumer feedback are required.

We need to make markets work for the poor. If production increases but there is no marketing intervention, we can fail. Farmers, even small-scale farmers, need to be able to access the supermarkets. That is where farmers can make $4 from every $1 investment. And marketing assistance can help them produce other products attractive to domestic consumers and even tourists.

There are still a number of broad challenges. We need assured markets as we think about larger-scale production. We need irrigation. We need a regulatory system to control quality in nurseries. For example, in Kenya flower production has a powerful regulatory system because we serve the European market, where there is quality control. For bananas and other crops, there is very little in-house quality control.

We need disease-indexing facilities. There is no disease indexing facility anywhere, except in South Africa, that can issue a phytosanitary certificate. Consequently, we cannot exchange material among Uganda, Kenya, Tanzania, and other African countries.

And finally we need government intervention in enhancing industry development through policy and infrastructure and through increasing funding, together with donors. We need policies that will help the products move from subsistence to commercial production.

NEPAD and FARA have adopted the TC banana project as a success model, together with NERICA and other crops that can be usefully scaled up. The message here is that if we are doing something good, we should ensure its success through the whole value chain so that it can be upscaled and moved to other regions. Together, I believe we can tackle or reduce the danger of wide-scale poverty and malnutrition.

Farmers, even small-scale farmers, need to be able to access the supermarkets. That is where farmers can make $4 from every $1 investment.

— Florence Wambugu

Discussion

Discussion in this session covered a range of issues, including sources of productivity increases, natural resource management, technology and crop choices, empowerment of rural people, and support for agricultural research.

Whereas some participants believed that productivity increases would need to come mainly from rainfed areas, others were skeptical about whether Africa could achieve food security without exploiting its irrigation potential. Africa must better harvest and store its water. Participants suggested investing in and adapting low-cost irrigation systems that conserve water, such as drip and sprinkler technologies. In Ethiopia, for example, rainfed systems are supplemented by water harvesting. A participant commented on the absence of fisheries in the discussion, noting that in Malawi aquaculture is linked to irrigation. Panelist Carlos Seré stated that interest in aquaculture is growing and there are opportunities for linkages to irrigation, but he also cautioned that there are many challenges related to food safety. Panelist Pedro Sanchez added that Africa must exploit whatever irrigation opportunities are available. A participant suggested that Africa should seek to reach a target of irrigating 8 percent of its cultivated land, up from 4 percent.

Besides water management, participants also discussed soil management. Nutrient management was identified as a key issue. A participant suggested shifting the emphasis from addition of inputs to management of the whole ecosystem to optimize production. Another participant called for providing fertilizer aid to Africa rather than food aid. Noting that investing in soil health includes fertilizer aid, Sanchez mentioned that subsidies for fertilizers, both organic and inorganic, are currently under discussion at the World Bank.

The discussion also covered technology issues. Although one of the participants decried the lack of investment in tractors, another argued that tractors were not necessarily important and that much could be done with improved tools and animal traction. Panelist Eugene Terry said that where agricultural technologies are not available to poor farmers, an effective mechanism is needed to negotiate for access on their behalf. Seré added that biotechnology is not only producing new crops, but also developing new technology for livestock. In response to concerns about intellectual property rights, panelist Glyvyns Chinkhuntha shared the experience of his enterprise, Freedom Gardens, which has no intellectual property rights restrictions, and noted that farmers must be able to share knowledge. He also raised the need for agricultural banks, for innovative farmers need financial resources. Energy needs on the farm were also highlighted during the discussion, with a participant calling for improved rural energy systems.

The issue of crop choice emerged. One participant argued that there is too much emphasis on growing maize and that Africans need to diversify their staple foods. Another said that each area should grow the crops best suited to its comparative advantage and then trade the surplus within Africa. The need to better integrate crops and livestock was identified by another participant.

Another topic of general agreement was the need for greater empowerment and organization of rural people. A participant mentioned the need to eliminate gender discrimination and empower youth and women. Another spoke of the importance of empowering communities and mobilizing peasants in farmers' associations, village associations, or cooperatives, which should not be mandated by government, but driven by demand. There is a need to examine why cooperatives have failed in Africa, the participant continued.

Participants also spoke of agricultural research, proposing more support to agricultural research, strengthened linkages between the centers of the CGIAR and national agricultural research systems (NARSs), and better linkages between on-farm research and agroindustrial research, particularly in the development of tools. Panelist Seyfu Ketema agreed that African governments should commit more resources to agricultural research and endorsed stronger linkages between NARSs and international agricultural research centers (IARCs).

Even as participants discussed modalities for raising agricultural productivity, they noted the linkages with markets and trade. A participant called for developed countries to reform their markets and agricultural subsidy programs in order to create a level playing field for Africa's farmers. Opportunities for expanding internal markets were noted, with a participant pointing to the growing significance of local purchases of food aid by donors such as the World Food Programme—in some countries, such local purchases *are* the local market. Sanchez concurred that school feeding programs using locally produced food can stimulate internal market demand. Panelist Florence Wambugu pointed out the need to focus not only on increasing productivity, but also on strengthening the whole value chain, including credit, farm management, and marketing. Seré noted that enforcing policy, not just enacting it, is important.

Excerpt 8: Investing in Sub-Saharan African Agricultural Research: Recent Trends

Nienke M. Beintema and Gert-Jan Stads

With political independence in the late 1950s and early 1960s, many African countries inherited the agricultural research infrastructure established by former colonial powers. Some countries inherited very specialized institutes that did not necessarily address their production needs, while other (often smaller) countries were unable to sustain their systems when financial resources and expatriate research staff were withdrawn. Research in the immediate post-colonial period focused mainly on export crops, and little attention was paid to the production problems of subsistence farmers. Hence, many countries were left with minimal physical, human resource, or organizational research capacity.

In the early years after independence, most countries focused on building capacity, specifically in terms of replacing expatriate staff with national researchers and enhancing research infrastructure, a process that was often hindered by political unrest and institutional instability. By the early 1980s, the focus of reform turned toward improving the effectiveness of national agricultural R&D, which involved amalgamating disparate research activities within a single agency, coordinating and developing national agricultural research plans, and improving management practices such as planning, monitoring, and evaluation. In more recent years, reforms in Sub-Saharan Africa (SSA) have focused on issues such as redefining the government's role in agricultural research, decentralizing decisionmaking processes, increasing farmer/stakeholder participation, identifying new funding sources and mechanisms, and strengthening system linkages.

Nonetheless, despite significant capacity expansion in the 1970s and 1980s, agricultural research in SSA remains heavily fragmented, with more than half the region's countries employing fewer than 100 full-time equivalent researchers each. In addition, the government still conducts the majority of agricultural research, having more than three quarters of total agricultural R&D staff in 2000.

Most of the growth in public agricultural research spending in SSA took place in the 1960s when real (inflation adjusted) spending increased by an annual average of 6.8 percent. During 1971–2000, real public agricultural R&D spending for our 27-country sample grew more slowly, at an average annual rate of 1.4 percent. Although expenditure growth appears to have been more evenly distributed over time than growth in researcher numbers, the annual growth rate declined from 2.0 percent in the 1970s to only 0.8 percent in the 1990s. As a consequence, average spending per scientist declined by about half between 1971 and 2000, though for many countries the decline was more extreme.

Total public spending as a percentage of agricultural output (agricultural GDP) is a common research investment indicator that helps place a country's agricultural R&D spending in an internationally comparable context. In 2000, Africa invested $0.70 for every $100 of agricultural output (in international dollars)—lower than the 1981 level of $0.95. Ratios ranged from 0.20 percent or lower in The Gambia, Niger, and Sudan to over 3.00 percent in Botswana, Mauritius, and South Africa. In 1995, the latest year for which global data are available, SSA's average agricultural research intensity ratio was slightly higher, at 0.79 percent—greater than the average ratio for the developing world (0.62 percent) but lower than the global average (1.04 percent).

There is no official recommendation on preferred intensity ratios for agricultural R&D investments. In the early 1980s the World Bank set a 2 percent target, which has been widely quoted since. Others, however, have found an intensity ratio of 1 percent to be a more realistic objective, but few countries in SSA have achieved even this lower target.

This has been excerpted from 2020 Africa Conference Brief 8, published by IFPRI, Washington, DC, 2004.

Excerpt 9: Strengthening Agricultural Research in Africa

Monty Jones

Recognizing that agriculture holds the key to Africa's development, and frustrated by insufficient progress, Africa's leaders have provided a framework for development through the New Partnership for Africa's Development (NEPAD). This framework, the Comprehensive Africa Agriculture Development Programme (CAADP), sets the broad objectives for agricultural research and development in Africa.

COOPERATION IN THE SUBREGIONS

There is now a widespread understanding of the need to achieve greater and more focused collaboration in agricultural research. Many constraints to agricultural development cross national borders, so national agricultural research systems (NARS) in Africa have formed subregional organizations (SROs) to raise impact through concerted actions. In turn, the SROs have formed the Forum for Agricultural Research in Africa (FARA) as an apex organization to provide continent-wide perspective on agricultural research for development. The Association for Strengthening Agricultural Research in Eastern and Central Africa (ASARECA) has concluded that collaborative agricultural research in East and Central Africa can address common constraints that cut across several countries; enhance complementarities and reduce duplication; increase the efficiency of agricultural research through the optimum use of human, financial, and other research resources; and facilitate the spillover and transfer of technology among cooperating countries.

POOR UPTAKE OF PAST AGRICULTURAL RESEARCH

The traditional linear process by which the products of research are passed on to extension services for dissemination to farmers has produced many important advances, such as the control of cassava mealy bug and of rinderpest. Much more common, however, are technologies that do not leave the research station shelves. Scientists have attributed this problem to the failure of the extension services, but such (real or perceived) shortcomings have not prevented farmers from adopting viable technologies such as hybrid maize, livestock vaccination, and smallholder dairying.

Now there is increasing recognition that some "solutions" remain on the shelves because, although they show technical potential, they are poorly adapted to the complex situations within which they are intended to be adopted. Farming systems research, which emphasizes on-farm experimentation, has had considerable success locally. With farmers involved in testing, many innovations have been shown to work on participating farms. But these innovations have typically failed to spread even to neighboring localities—as exemplified by the case of the ox-drawn broadbed maker in Ethiopia, which was designed to make raised seedbeds with intervening furrows that drain the land to permit early planting. With the right seed varieties and fertilizer, this method raises crop yields significantly. The implement was developed over many years of on-farm testing, but after initial promise it failed to be adopted as widely as had been anticipated.

One plausible explanation for the poor uptake of research products is the existence of critical gaps in the knowledge of research teams. If farming communities had been more involved in designing and validating the research on the broadbed makers (in addition to providing fields and labor), local farmers may well have predicted the poor uptake of this technology. They would have known about the unreliability of essential inputs such as fertilizer and the effects of market failures on the price of grain in case of local production increases.

This has been excerpted from 2020 Africa Conference Brief 9, published by IFPRI, Washington, DC, 2004.

Chapter 13 Fostering Economic Growth and Improving Markets and Trade

Chair: Benno Ndulu*
Research Manager, Development Economics Research Department, World Bank, USA

Moderator: Akinwumi Adesina
Associate Director, Food Security, The Rockefeller Foundation, Kenya

Rapporteur: Nicholas Minot
Research Fellow, International Food Policy Research Institute (IFPRI), USA

Eleni Gabre-Madhin

Senior Economist, Africa Region, World Bank, USA

I believe we are in the midst of a giant experiment. We in Africa are now in an era when we expect the markets to lead agricultural growth. This is a new paradigm. We have put markets in a central place. The fundamental question is whether we have learned how to create markets that will, in fact, deliver what we expect from them.

In a liberalized market economy, markets play a vital role as the clearinghouse of supply and demand. More is expected of markets than ever before for food security and for agricultural growth. Where growth must be demand-driven in the changing global agro-food system, markets must enable producers to respond to those growth opportunities. So we are starting with markets rather than ending with markets, and that is the paradigm shift that we have embarked upon.

This is a unique challenge. I had occasion to have a chat with Norman Borlaug about a year ago, and I asked him, how did the Asian experience proceed? What was the market situation during the uptake of technology in Asia? He put it very simply. He said, "In Asia, we just didn't worry about the market. There was absorption by the public sector, and we just didn't have that problem—in the way that we are now grappling with this market problem at the Sasakawa Global 2000."

I also recall a conversation with a senior Ethiopian official, who said, "We thought we were doing everything right. We liberalized our markets. We revamped our extension. We mobilized our farmers. We raised fertilizer use. We expanded our yields, and we had bumper harvests, so we thought we were doing well. But prices collapsed 60 to 80 percent in 2002 in Ethiopia. Farmers' incomes actually went down, and they were unable to pay their fertilizer loans." He put it very starkly. He said, "We are experiencing the failure of our very progress." These are fundamental issues that we have to think about.

Now, what is the relationship between markets and technical change (Figure 1)? The world described earlier by Norman Borlaug is that of the highly productive technology where, with well-functioning input markets and

FIGURE 1—Relationship between markets and technical change

* In addition to his role as panelist in this session, Benno Ndulu graciously agreed to serve as chair owing to unforeseen circumstances.

We need to get beyond the reform agenda, which was focused on getting prices right—and move to getting markets right.

— Eleni Gabre-Madhin

well-functioning, absorptive output markets, we are able to disseminate technologies that are very market dependent and that enable us to achieve highly productive agricultural transformation.

When markets are less effective, responses are different. I have heard it said, "Well, if we don't have input markets that work, if fertilizer delivery is not there, let's move into low-external-input agriculture, let's move into conservation farming." So that is one response. Of course, the other response occurs when the output side is functioning and you get price collapses and regression into lower-productivity agriculture.

The problem in Africa is that markets are just not delivering. Either a bumper harvest occurs, prices collapse, and everybody starts to shout, "What are we going to do?" Or the converse occurs, as in Southern Africa, where despite a significant price increase because of domestic shortfall, private markets did not respond by immediately importing grain into the region.

On the input side, there has been a decline in input use in many countries in Africa following market reforms.

FIGURE 2—Relationship between markets and technical change

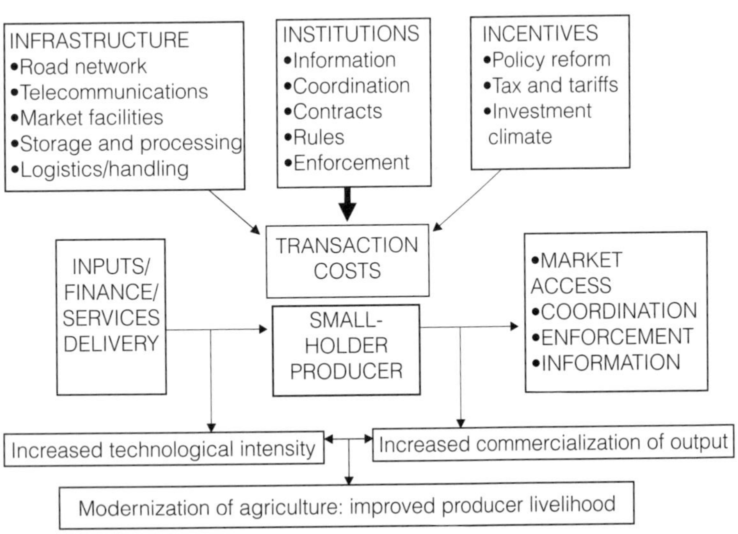

So why are markets not delivering?

First of all, we are not talking about atomistic, anonymous, impersonal markets. We are talking about markets that are embedded in human interaction. The humans that are involved in markets are boundedly rational, they are complex, and they are shaped by culture, history, and social forces. An emerging body of work is showing that social capital and what we call "trust" matter for economic outcomes.

Second, an emerging body of work is looking at the costliness of market interaction and the cost of coordination as a limiting constraint on market performance.

Third, market interaction requires enforcement. Not only are humans boundedly rational, but they are also opportunistic. They cheat each other. There is contract failure. So we have to work within those paradigms.

Finally, markets require human capital and infrastructure, so capacity is essential.

Over the past two decades of looking at markets, we have come to the conclusion that part of the problem is costs. Transaction costs are very high. Information is limited and asymmetric. Markets are uncoordinated. Often sellers do not know where the buyers are, and buyers do not know how to find the sellers. Contract risk is high; it is difficult to enforce contracts and legal enforcement mechanisms are lacking. Lack of finance also undermines the capacity of the private sector to invest in its trading enterprise and limits the scope and scale of market operations. In addition, smallholders lack market power and are unorganized. Markets are thin and seasonal. And market risk has increased dramatically.

We need to get beyond the reform agenda, which was focused on removing policy distortions and aligning prices—in other words, getting prices right—and move to getting markets right. Removing policy distortions is important and necessary, but it is not sufficient. Getting markets right involves the three "I's": *incentives*, which require policy reforms; *institutions*, which are the coordination and enforcement mechanisms; and *infrastructure*, which is bricks and mortar.

In his speech Norman Borlaug emphasized infrastructure. But my position is that neither infrastructure nor incentives alone will get us functioning markets if we do not also pay attention to institutions, which are at the heart of many of the problems. Finally, let's not forget the private sector, which is central to the three "I's."

Figure 2 tries to spell out the relationship between those three I's—infrastructure, institutions, and incentives—as they bear on the central issue of transaction costs. In turn, transaction costs have implications for both input delivery on the backward linkage side and output uptake on the forward linkage side. Ultimately these conditions have impact on smallholder incentives, production, and technology adoption.

What is the impact of high transaction costs (Figure 3)? In technical terms, a high level of domestic transaction costs essentially widens the import-export parity band. The wider a country's import-export parity band, the more its goods become nontradable. The reality is that to take maize from Addis Ababa—not even from the rural area, but from Addis Ababa—to the Port of Djibouti costs US$75 per ton, whereas it costs US$25 per ton to bring maize from Kansas to Djibouti. So it is not just about roads. A whole host of things create these very high-cost conditions.

Many of you are quite familiar with the issues regarding policy distortions and infrastructure. The third "I," institutions, is the least-addressed and the most pitiful in some ways. Institutions are, of course, the means of designing and enforcing the rules of the game and coordinating the market. So one of the roles of institutions is to reduce coordination costs, as well as to reduce risk, to enforce contracts, to increase participation, and to empower access.

The implication of weak market institutions—for example, the lack of market information and lack of grades and standards—is that buyers and sellers have limited capacity to respond to market signals with bargaining power. We have done empirical work to show that the lack of a grades and standards system in Ethiopia, for example, has a direct bearing on the number of times along the marketing chain that the grain has to be offloaded, visually inspected, and resacked. This has implications for economies of scale of transport and for the ability of the market to respond to price signals. It has implications for contract enforcement because people start to operate within very narrow networks. These factors ultimately have a direct quantitative impact on transaction costs and therefore on economic welfare.

FIGURE 3—Impact of high transaction costs

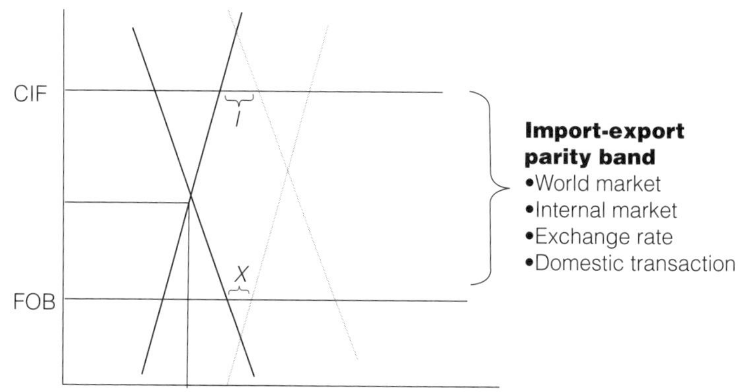

Lack of enforcement means that the market shrinks. It becomes even thinner because people work only with people that they know and trust. And the lack of intermediation means that coordination mechanisms are very inefficient.

To address the three "I's," we as development practitioners and as researchers have a rich agenda in front of us (Table 1). At the World Bank, we are looking at how we need to move beyond the initial agenda of incentives. We have to deal with food aid distortions, tax issues, the appropriate role of government, the investment climate, and other issues, as well as a whole host of issues related to infrastructure. On the institutional front, we need to deal with promotion of industry groups, the regulatory framework, legal reforms underlying market exchange, and the creation of hubs and exchanges.

TABLE 1—Addressing the three I's: A rich agenda

Incentives	Infrastructure	Institutions
Macroeconomy	Transportation links	Contract enforcement/ dispute settlement
Investment climate	Telecommunications/information and communications technologies	Grades and standards
Licensing regulation	Postharvest management/quality control	Market intelligence
Sectoral policies	Business management/training	Trade financing
High income tax and multiple levies	Storage capacity	Industry groups
Food aid distortions	Market-oriented agricultural extension	Producer groups
		Regulatory framework
		Legal reforms
		Commodity exchanges/auctions/hubs
		Warehouse receipts

You cannot push sorghum yields in West Africa without having an idea of how the product will be processed and whether consumers will buy it.

— Eleni Gabre-Madhin

In sum, can Africa achieve a market-led agricultural transformation? This is the key debate, and the answer is not obvious. The answer will depend first on whether we get markets right, which in turn depends on whether we use an integrative, holistic approach, rather than the somewhat narrow privatization policy reform agenda that we have espoused for the past 20 years as development institutions.

The answer will also depend on whether we can adjust to the fundamental paradigm shift, so that rather than thinking of market opportunities as an afterthought to production and productivity gain, we start to identify market opportunities as the initial step linking us to technology development and dissemination. In other words, you cannot push sorghum yields in West Africa without having an idea of how the product will be processed and whether consumers will buy it. Technology development and extension must be subsumed into the market approach.

Finally, we need an appropriate public role, not just for government, but also for donors and NGOs. This role involves working with and supporting the private sector, ensuring the necessary environment and strengthening the three "I's," and being pro-poor, which means paying attention to the access issues of smallholders and to safety nets because markets, whether or not they work perfectly, will remain highly risky. This role involves being strategic in handling the price stabilization question. I do not know whether the answer is insurance, contract farming, or some other solution, but we have to be strategic. And this public role involves managing donors. The example of Mali shows a country that managed its donors and, for that matter, the NGOs. There was a concerted donor strategy program in collaboration with the government. We need to move in that direction.

Hans Jöhr

Corporate Head of Agriculture, Nestec Ltd., Switzerland

My task is to describe what the food industry can do to link farmers to a food chain and a system that really contributes to food and nutrition security. Let me first introduce what we are doing. Nestlé has interacted for about 140 years with smallholders, starting in Switzerland with milk farmers. Today, we still interact directly with more than 350,000 smallholders around the globe, mainly because we need access to high-quality raw materials to build our products.

What are we looking for? We are looking for very long-term business relations with these suppliers and for very flexible structures because, at the end of the day, what we must do is match consumer taste preferences to their purchasing power.

In the food industry, agricultural raw materials are a key cost factor. High-quality raw materials are the base for building quality in the final product. The sourcing strategy obviously depends on availability and on specific requirements. We need to comply with standards for food quality and food safety.

In the United States we do not have a direct link to farmers because there are highly developed farms, and we get the raw materials from co-ops, for instance. But this is not the case in India or Pakistan or in many of the African countries where we have processing plants. In these countries we have very short supply chains in which we buy high-quality raw materials locally, process these raw materials, and serve mainly the local market.

To be successful and meet a long-term strategy, we need a sustainable supply of high-quality raw materials. This is why we started an initiative called the Sustainable Agriculture Initiative (SAI Platform) with other food companies, beginning with Unilever and Danone. Today, from three founding members, the Sustainable

We in the food industry want to contribute to improving people's access to affordable food and to consumers' being able to obtain food meeting their preferences, concerns, and needs.

— Hans Jöhr

Agriculture Initiative has grown to 18 members worldwide, in Europe, North America, and now New Zealand. All of us in the food industry are facing exactly the same problems. So this initiative is very pre-competitive.

Through the SAI Platform, we are looking at the next 20 years. Where are the future markets, and how can we serve these markets? How does this affect our sourcing strategies? We are looking at population growth. We are looking at expected diet changes, which may change with purchasing power. We are looking at doubling calorie outputs in about 20 years with the same natural resources available, such as land and water. This is a totally new approach by the food industry to address the issues of long-term sourcing of raw materials and interacting with rural economies and rural areas.

We need to make sure that we will still have access to high-quality, competitively priced raw materials 20 years from now, because we have to match the expected purchasing power of millions and millions around the globe. Productivity must occur in such a way that farmers use natural resources very efficiently and maximize profitability. We want to engage in a continuous improvement program to make sure that farmers can survive economically in the long term and provide these raw materials to us.

What have we done so far at Nestlé? We have been in many African countries for decades and have a number of private-public sector projects. In Côte d'Ivoire, for example, we interact with more than 800 farmers, most of them women, in about six or seven villages. From these women, we buy about 8,000 to 10,000 tons of cassava, which is used to produce starch for Maggi soups. It is not our area of expertise to do extension service at the farm level, so we engaged with GTZ (Deutsche Gesellschaft für Technische Zusammenarbeit) to set up this supply chain. We also worked with the agriculture research institute CSRS (Centre Suisse de Recherche Scientifique en Côte d'Ivoire) to determine the right varieties in terms of investment performance and productivity, to make sure that these varieties are really attractive for the farmers to grow.

Many different stakeholders are involved in linking farmers and communities to the food chain (Figure 1). Even before the farmer, there is the input industry. Then there is the farmer. Then there is trade, primary processing, and finally the food industry. But all of these processes have one purpose, and that is to serve the consumer.

We want to serve our customers as well as possible, and we must make very large investments, in things like factories, to do so.

— Hans Jöhr

We in the food industry want to contribute to improving people's access to affordable food and to consumers' being able to obtain food meeting their preferences, concerns, and needs. So everything is linked in the pocket of the consumer. From there, we define the needs and expectations in terms of quality requirements. From there, we go back to the rural areas. This market link creates a cash flow, and that cash flow creates new demand in the rural areas. Studies show that each dollar equivalent that flows to a rural area through this kind of scheme stimulates three to four more dollars' worth of economic activity there.

If you can link smallholders to such a scheme, then the system is sustainable because we want to stay in business as long as possible. We want to serve our customers as well as possible, and we must make very large investments, in things like factories, to do so. This entire approach is based on long-term thinking. We want stakeholders to participate in that value creation, but only those who really create value.

FIGURE 1—All stakeholders in the food chain

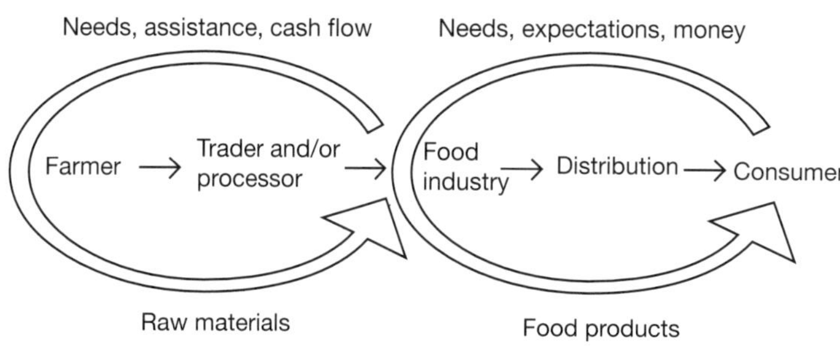

As much as we liberalize and say we are leaving everything to market forces, we still believe that our people cannot be fed on imports.

— Eusebius J. Mukhwana

Eusebius J. Mukhwana

Director, Sustainable Agriculture Centre for Research Extension and Development in Africa (SACRED), Kenya

I would like to present a case study of how we have tried to address food security in western Kenya through a project we call the Maize Marketing Movement.

Maize is of fundamental importance in Africa as a staple food, for economic development, and for political stability. Maize accounts for about 30 to 50 percent of the expenditures of low-income households in East and Southern Africa. If prices are high, then the poor are affected most.

The value of maize is very low in relation to transport costs. In Kenya it is sometimes more expensive to move one bag of maize than the value of that bag itself. As a result it is generally not possible to export maize within the region of East and Southern Africa, even when there is a surplus.

In addition, we have other problems, such as unreliable rain, low capitalization of smallholder agriculture, and stagnant or declining production. These factors have generally made Africa a net importer of maize.

Let me talk a bit about the politics of maize. After independence, most of our governments had two political priorities. One was food self-sufficiency, and the other was a guaranteed profit to farmers for their maize, regardless of how remote they were or the production costs they incurred. This was a sort of social contract that was accepted at independence.

Both before and after liberalization of maize markets, governments had difficulty accepting that producer prices can actually go very low, depending on supply, and that people can be fed through imports. Even today, we believe that somehow each country must be self-sufficient. And so, as much as we liberalize and say we are leaving everything to market forces, we still believe that our people cannot be fed on imports. This has implications for the policies we put in place and the way we implement those policies.

With many small buyers and producers and a high cost of production, our transaction costs are very high. But our social contract with farmers says that they will get a good price for their maize. And we have a social contract with consumers that says the price of food will stay very low. As you can see, these contracts are contradictory. As a result governments in Africa tried to subsidize grain marketing to the point where it was draining public resources. The liberalization that we undertook was forced on us by the World Bank, and we all know that. There were a lot of policy reversals, but in many places the legal framework for maize marketing was not changed. The policy says we are liberalized, but we are still using the preliberalization legal framework.

What are some of the impacts of liberalization? Per capita maize production has declined by an estimated 18 to 30 percent. Consumer prices are reduced—this is one positive impact we can acknowledge. There are high seasonal price fluctuations, sometimes as much as 80 percent in six months. There is the emergence of a large number of informal traders, who not only lack knowledge, but also lack capacity. Price transparency is limited, rewards for high grain quality are inadequate, and input supply systems are performing poorly. Before liberalization, input supply and credit were linked, but these two are now major problems. We also had strong cooperatives during the preliberalization era, but now when we need them the most, they are all collapsing. So generally we have increasing imports and increasing food insecurity in Sub-Saharan Africa.

In Kenya smallholder farmers are trapped in what we call the "good season/poor market" dilemma. Every time they have a bumper harvest, they end up with very low prices, a situation that discourages production the following year. Then prices go up, farmers produce more, and the price goes down again. This situation discourages technology transfer, as well as surplus production. Opportunistic middlemen, not farmers, dictate the price.

Farm storage losses of maize are increasing. Before liberalization, we used state stores and grain stores to store maize, but now there is increased farm storage. With the arrival of the larger grain borer, postharvest losses in the region are now estimated at about 40 percent.

Another problem is that our farmers were only used to producing. Before liberalization, they produced the cocoa and the government sold it. But now production is only half the job. Farmers also have to market it. Liberalization was done so quickly, without proper consultation of farmers, that the farmers were never prepared for it.

But for farmers to work in this liberalized market, they need capital, they need capacity, they need business acumen, they need strong producer associations, they need transport, and they need market information. All of these things are lacking. So how do farmers play a role in this kind of market?

We have started to implement a project in Western Kenya that is addressing some of these issues. The objectives of this project are (1) to assess and overcome market imperfections with today's transaction costs and risks for poor farmers; (2) to improve grain quality standards to help farmers access markets and receive better prices and to help farmers develop prototype cereal banks for collective banking, storing, and marketing their produce; and (3) to enable farmers to develop stronger institutional capacity for marketing farm produce by enhancing group cohesion and market objectives.

We have a research component, an extension component, and a marketing component (Figure 1). Under the research component, we have established a grain laboratory in the region and developed grain-processing protocols. We have a full-time grain quality specialist who trains farmers on how to improve the quality of their grain. We also have a socioeconomist who is establishing socioeconomic baselines and looking at what kind of subclass has been produced, which farms are involved, how much land farmers own, and how they produce maize. We have designed a marketing strategy and a way of documenting some of the impacts of this project. And we have established five community-based cereal banks and one central cereal bank that is setting recordkeeping standards and monitoring the activities of the community cereal banks. We have a full-time manager there.

The idea is to bring farmers together (Figure 2). We have a range of 40 to 100 farmers per group, and these farmers divide themselves into committees—one committee for training, another committee for buying, another committee for selling, another committee for auditing. They share the tasks so that they are able to deliver a high-quality product to the market.

Figure 3 shows industry standards for average quality of maize. We have seen that with basic training, farmers are able to go beyond those standards.

In the four months from October 2003 to January 2004, these groups were able to sell maize for a total of US$81,000. This is something they had never done before. They are selling to Unga Ltd., one of the largest mills, which offers US$202 per ton. If they had sold to the National Cereal and Produce Board, they would have received US$11,800 less, and if they had sold to a

FIGURE 1—Structure and responsibilities within the Maize Marketing Movement

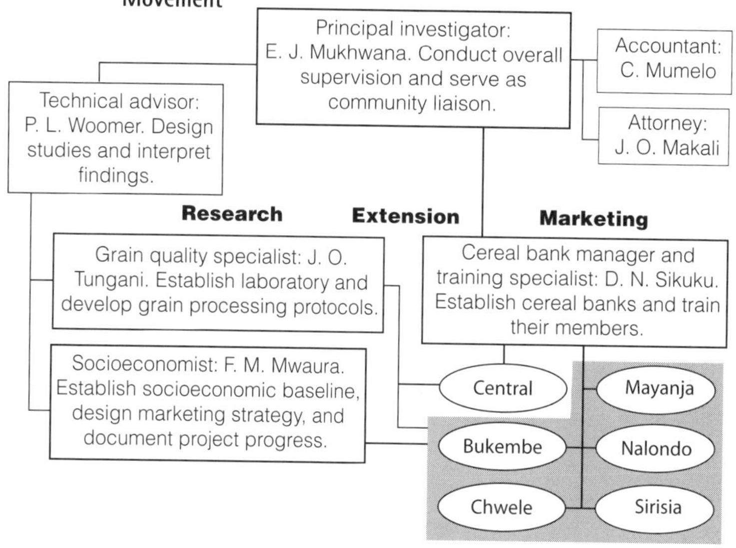

FIGURE 2—Maize marketing structure

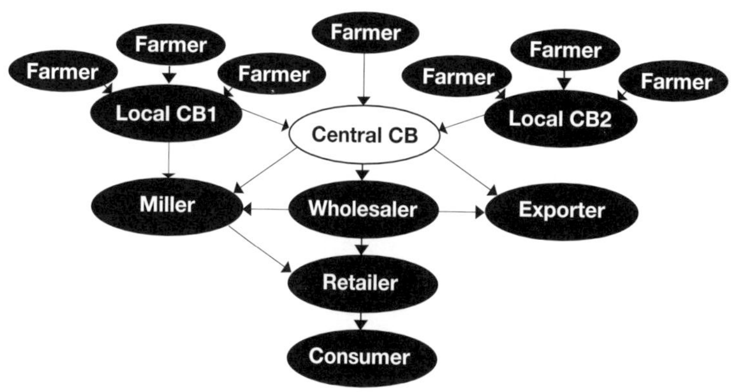

FIGURE 3—Industry standards for maize quality

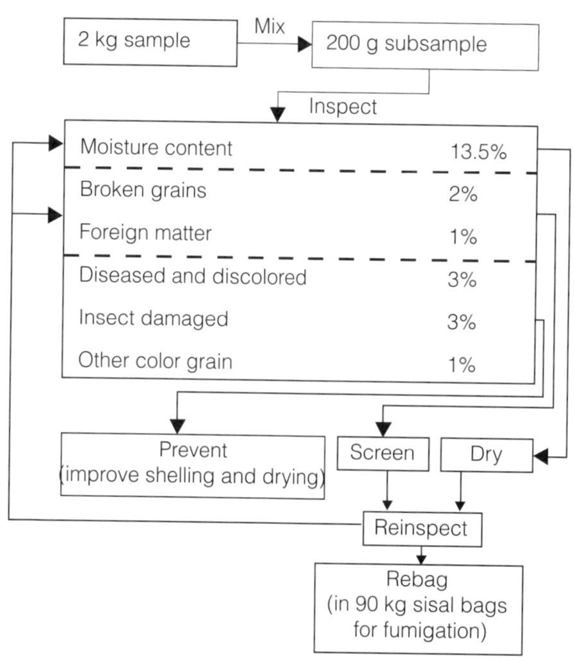

Owing to a lack of accurate information on supply and demand, our governments tend to make blind decisions.

— Stephen Njukia and Bernard Kagira

middleman, they would have received US$29,000 less. By coming together, improving quality, and producing high volumes, they were able to access a higher-end market that gives them a premium price and thus a good income from their maize.

For us, the Maize Marketing Movement is more than just a project. We are asking ourselves, how do we transform African agriculture from subsistence to this kind of scenario?

Stephen Njukia and Bernard Kagira

Regional Agricultural Trade Expansion Support (RATES) Program

Speaking on behalf of **Erastus Mwencha**, Secretary General, Common Market for Eastern and Southern Africa

In this part of the world, food is maize. Where there is no maize, there is no food. The demand for maize in Sub-Saharan Africa, according to IFPRI, is expected to increase from 27 million metric tons to 52 million tons by 2020. So we have to ask ourselves, can demand in East and Southern Africa be met by domestic supply and regional trade?

Even when a country is self-sufficient, maize is moving across borders. The people right along the border do not know that the border exists, and they are moving from one side to another. We would like to see the barriers to trade removed, and the barriers are not just the borders, but also trade policies and regulations and their implementation procedures.

We would like to see a "maize country" for this part of the world, where maize moves freely from surplus to deficit areas. The reason for cross-border maize movement is that when some countries are harvesting maize, others are experiencing the lean season and still others are trading. Maize deficits are actually seasonal deficits. Production and consumption may be balanced over the course of a year, but seasonally there will be a deficit.

Most of the trade taking place within the region is done by small-scale traders, although there are a few large-scale traders. The critical question therefore is whether government policy is helping this trade to take place, among either small-scale or large-scale traders.

Our research and conversations with traders have shown that there is a lack of information. We do not have growth forecasts. We do not know the level of supply and demand at any given time or the regional position. Owing to a lack of accurate information on supply and demand, our governments tend to make blind decisions. And when they make a blind decision, what happens? They impose export-import bans and high import tariffs. Tanzania, for instance, said, "We are not going to export maize in 2003 except from the southern highlands," but at the same time maize was moving across the border unofficially into Kenya.

The traders at the borders see demand across the border, and hence they move the maize for a profit. Because of barriers to formal trade, they are forced to engage in informal trade, which most of the time leads to corruption at border points or with police along the way. When a truck carrying maize reaches the border, it stops before crossing the border and the maize is offloaded and moved across the border using bicycles while another truck waits on the other side. These things bring about high transaction costs, and high transaction costs result in high consumer prices. So there is no food security based on commercial trade because of the high transaction costs.

At the Regional Agricultural Trade Expansion Support (RATES) Trade Office we are trying to facilitate trade using fax, telephone, email, short messaging system (SMS), and websites. Seventy active traders who frequently use our Trade Office form the core of our regional Maize Traders Network. A list of these traders is provided on our website, and anybody can access it. It identifies the traders within the Common Market for Eastern and Southern Africa (COMESA) with an emphasis on seven countries: Uganda, Kenya, Tanzania, Malawi, Zambia, Zimbabwe, and Ethiopia. We have another website—www.ratin.net—that gives the regional

One of the elements of addressing policy impediments to intraregional trade is development of a simplified customs entry document, which also serves as a certificate of origin.

— Stephen Njukia and Bernard Kagira

production and trade flow position of four countries: Uganda, Kenya, Tanzania, and Rwanda. RATIN stands for Regional Agricultural Trade Intelligence Network.

Another of our websites—www.tradeafrica.biz—links traders within COMESA, who use this platform as a marketplace, with buyers offering maize and sellers inquiring about sources from which to buy. We map these countries and see which has a surplus or a deficit at any given time of the season. The maps also illustrate in which direction the maize is flowing. For instance, you can see maize coming from Ethiopia to Kenya and from Uganda to Tanzania. Traders can also visit www.tradeafrica.biz to see daily prices. If they have maize to sell and they do not have access to the website, they can call our office and we put it on the website. More than US$18 million worth of maize trade has taken place since we started in October 2003.

If you want to promote trade, you will find that for each commodity, there are numerous policies and regulations. The focus so far in the region has been on tariffs, but there are many more trade regulations that impede intraregional trade. The RATES program, in collaboration with COMESA and the East African Community (EAC), is addressing this problem through stakeholder-led regional trade policy platforms. The process involves engaging the private sector and the policymakers in national and regional consultative forums. The trade policy platform is a private-sector-driven strategy for harmonizing commodity-specific policies and regulations across the COMESA and EAC region. RATES is presently targeting five commodities: maize, livestock, dairy products, coffee, and cotton and textiles. It is important to note that the process of policy harmonization is being guided by the regional integration framework, as enshrined in the EAC and COMESA treaties and the member states' commitments to cooperate in enhancing agricultural trade and to remove nontariff barriers to trade. What we are doing dovetails with this and helps the private sector to engage governments in meeting the commitments they have made.

Policy harmonization is a mandatory complement to the tariff reform program in both the EAC and COMESA. The significance of this intervention is underscored by the fact that although in the COMESA free trade area tariffs for imports are zero, trade is not taking place or it is taking place at very low levels.

One of the elements of addressing policy impediments to intraregional trade is development of a simplified customs entry document, which also serves as a certificate of origin. This will encourage informal traders to use official trade channels, which are much cheaper than informal routes. There are also efforts to address sanitary and phytosanitary regulations and quality standards on all of the target commodities, with maize being used as a pilot case.

In 1960 Africa was home to about 11 percent of the globe's extreme poor. By 1998 Africa accounted for 66 percent of the extreme poor.

— Benno Ndulu

In the case of maize, we have a vision. This vision was generated out of the studies that were done in seven countries. Over the course of five years, some countries had surpluses, whereas others had deficits. Representatives of the private sector in the region all agreed that the region can indeed trade in these commodities. There is a need for these countries to look beyond their national boundaries.

Preliminary work in the area of cotton and textiles and dairy products shows very low intraregional trade. We are therefore in the process of developing policy platforms to enhance regional trade and come up with a development agenda for those two sectors as well.

Benno Ndulu

Research Manager, Development Economics Research Department, World Bank, USA

I would like to highlight four aspects of the challenge of removing extreme poverty and hunger.

First, poverty and undernutrition are broadly prevalent, and this means that we require frontal action. It is not a case of dealing with marginal poverty and marginal safety net programs, but a case of fundamentally changing the purchasing power of the poor.

In 1960 Africa was home to about 11 percent of the globe's extreme poor. By 1998 Africa accounted for 66 percent of the extreme poor. While the rest of the developing world experienced strong reductions in poverty and undernutrition after 1970, in Africa poverty and undernutrition actually rose. The biggest difference between the two cases is growth. Over the long term, Asia has been able to reduce poverty and undernutrition by two-thirds, mainly based on robust and sustained growth. Africa has experienced periods of spurts of high growth, but not sustained high growth.

Asia has been able to reduce poverty and undernutrition by two-thirds, mainly based on robust and sustained growth. Africa has experienced periods of spurts of high growth, but not sustained high growth.

— Benno Ndulu

Second, African poverty, of course, is predominantly rural. Where subsistence is a major source of food consumption, vagaries of weather or any other disasters hit farmers from two angles: they lead to both income failure and food failure. In these situations, calamities are not solved purely by bringing in food; you must provide entitlements so that the rural poor also have a reliable income. Safety net programs must complement growth.

Third, urban poverty is becoming a major issue. Given the rapid pace of urbanization in Africa, projections show that the urban population is going to rise from about 24 percent of Africa's population currently to nearly half of the population in 2020. So, while the focus here is on agriculture and raising rural incomes, over time growth must create opportunities for both the rural and urban poor.

Finally, the poverty situation in Africa is also replete with problems of inequality, especially inequality in the capacity to exploit opportunities from growth. This reflects the unequal distribution of education, health, and other productive assets, like land.

Research has shown that the efficacy of growth in reducing poverty varies greatly across countries. Two countries may both grow at 6 percent, but one achieves a much higher rate of poverty reduction than the other. What makes the difference? Inequality is a key issue in terms of how quickly one can have an impact on poverty reduction.

Several actions are required for scaling up and sustaining broad-based economic growth.

First, we have to build on progress made during the past decade. We have to sustain the friendliness of the environment for growth in terms of macroeconomic stability and other components of the development environment.

Second, we need to improve governance and prevent or resolve politically motivated conflicts. The fact that NEPAD has endorsed governance as a key priority attests to a shift in the sense of importance. But it is not enough for individual countries to improve governance. Potential investors or holders of capital do not judge the region purely within national boundaries. They also judge the region's collective reputation and whether there is a critical mass of peace and good governance in the region. NEPAD's peer review system is an important part of making sure that this collective reputation is covered.

Third, infrastructure is crucial. The policy framework should rationalize movement and minimize unnecessary movements. But regional and coordinated action is also needed in developing infrastructure programs. Market integration and the connectivity of the region will be central in strengthening growth. Connectivity here refers not just to transportation, but also to energy and communication. It does not make sense to have countries that are load sharing and others that can sell power in the same neighborhood.

Fourth, it is important to diversify rural incomes and improve opportunities for urban poor to earn income. The issue is not just strengthening agriculture, but also seeing whether other sources of income can be generated within the rural areas.

Finally, collective engagement is needed with the global development community, both to improve market access and to be held accountable as a region for achieving results and therefore making a claim on a slice of international resource flows.

Even the peasants are in agriculture for purposes of having reasonable returns to their efforts.

Discussion

As the discussion opened, the moderator for the session, Akinwumi Adesina, remarked that instead of focusing on Africa's poverty, he hoped discussants would concentrate on how it might be possible to create wealth for all classes of people.

Strengthening markets was the most extensively discussed topic. It was initiatied by a participant who remarked that to prioritize actions, one must "unbundle" the nature of markets. There are three types of markets: local, national, and international. There is a long way to go before local markets can be integrated with international markets, partly because the rules of the game at the global level are set by actors who are beyond the control of the local level, the participant observed. As a result, within Africa it makes more sense to focus on solving the problems of local and national markets and on creating institutions that can reduce transaction costs there. He cited the example of Nestlé, whose integration of small milk producers into the vertical chain cut transaction costs by 80 to 90 percent. Panelist Eleni Gabre-Madhin responded that although a lot of attention is being given to linking local and national markets, there are a number of emerging successful initiatives to bring the local and global markets closer together. She cited the example of Kenya, where small farmers growing horticultural products are able to reach the global market partly because the Kenyan government does not meddle in buying and selling but instead focuses on developing producer associations and institutions for maintaining quality standards, which are crucial in integrating smallholders.

Another participant differentiated between two kinds of agricultural commodities, each of which requires different market arrangements and institutions. Bulk commodities like maize and sorghum may have high transport costs because they are bulky, but they do not have inherently high transaction costs, because people can store them. Perishable goods like fruits and vegetables have higher transaction costs because the risk is higher that the product is bad, so buyers like supermarkets prefer to buy these from sources they trust. This participant continued that since demand for these perishable goods is rising rapidly in Africa, particularly in urban areas, it is important to deal with the transaction costs and institutional needs of integrating small farmers into the very demanding markets for these goods. Gabre-Madhin noted that the appropriate institution depends on the commodity and market concerned. For a situation of many buyers and many sellers and a bulky commodity that can be stored, a commodity exchange would work best as the integrating and coordinating mechanism. With many sellers but only a few buyers, as for coffee or tobacco, an auction with bidding between buyers is the solution. For highly perishable goods, where timing, quality, and delivery matter very much, vertical integration may work best. Panelist Hans Jöhr added that the way in which a value chain and business system are set up can considerably reduce the costs from the farm to the factory to the consumer. He also added that trust is a crucial element in building long-term business relationships with developing-country producers.

Noting that markets for staple foods are incredibly thin and seasonal, a participant asked whether significant purchases in the marketplace could help to rebuild human and physical capital. The example of India was offered, where large numbers of women's self-help groups are getting food-for-work for road construction and their participation is making a big difference in their households' food security. Gabre-Madhin responded by referring to the crisis in Ethiopia, asking in particular whether the food price collapse was a question of poorly functioning markets or a function of the lack of entitlements and effective demand. While income-generation schemes would help to raise effective demand in the short run, something more sustainable and viable that enables people without means to actually enter the market is needed. Expanding the scope of demand itself, through intraregional trade, is another solution. One of the participants supplemented the discussion on the case of Ethiopia to call attention to the remedies taken by Ethiopian farmers themselves in organizing marketing cooperatives to assist in transporting products from surplus to deficit areas, to gain bargaining power, and to exploit export opportunities.

Participants noted that it is important to look at the whole supply chain, from the producer to the final destination of the product, whether it ends up in the region or outside the region. We need to understand how each of these links works. What are the policies that regulate these links in the supply chain? What is the relationship between the actors in each of these links? What policies need to be developed and what interventions will really make a difference in these links? Concern was expressed that regulatory frameworks often make value addition impossible. If any links are missing in the chain, the producers at the bottom are not going to be able to produce effectively and make the money they need to make.

The Ugandan experience with avoiding market collapse in the case of surplus supply, as happened in 2001, was shared. A participant noted that it is not a question of physical storage so much as a question of financing that storage to avoid farmers' being "switched off" again for production. He pointed to the need to engage commerce and banks in providing financial mechanisms for risk management.

Another participant added that public-private partnerships offer opportunities to bridge the gap between farmers and markets and to enrich value. If farmers and consumers all believe that they can benefit from the transaction, then the transaction costs may subside. Real public-private partnerships may provide the needed holistic understanding in order to achieve a win-win situation for farmers and consumers. Both the private and the public sector, the participant continued, have different roles, yet their interaction can be seamless.

The growing presence of supermarkets was noted, with a participant wondering whether the new arrangements between contract farmers and supermarkets are simply taking the place of the marketing boards that were eliminated in the 1990s. Another participant wondered how small farmers can be motivated to produce the products that are in demand and will reach the market. Trade issues were highlighted when attention was drawn to the minimal levels of intra-African trade and the urgent need for African countries to reduce barriers to trade within the continent. Bringing up the role of strategic food reserves, a participant asked how it is possible to reconcile private-sector efforts to increase cross-border trade with government efforts to control the movement of food, particularly maize.

The lack of investment in infrastructure was highlighted, with participants urging African governments to invest more in this area, including infrastructure for meeting sanitary and phytosanitary regulations for international trade. Panelist Gabre-Madhin noted the challenge of moving from an infrastructure strategy to a market strategy so that the infrastructure supports market development. Another participant encouraged a shift in perspective from the macro level to the problems of individual farmers. He offered the example of farmers in some areas of Cameroon, for instance, where roads are passable only in certain seasons; small farmers rely on middlemen who have trucks to get their produce to the market. Although there is concern about middlemen flooding the markets, what type of institutional frameworks could replace such middlemen?

The problem of postharvest losses, which remain very high in Africa, was raised. Participants noted that these losses contribute to high transaction costs and food shortages and impede regional trade of perishable items like milk and fish. It is vital to focus not only on food production, but also on food preservation and processing.

Food safety, food quality assurance, and food standards were also discussed. A participant emphasized that African countries need to give more attention to food safety, which affects not only international trade, but also the health of domestic consumers and thus the availability of productive labor. Markets cannot be developed and maintained without adhering to standards of quality and food safety. Jöhr agreed, noting that food safety and quality are crucial to the Nestlé business model, because reliable safety and quality save the company money and consumers will pay a premium for them; out of that premium, the company can pay more back to the farmer.

The chair of the session, Benno Ndulu, summarized the key points that emerged during the discussion:

- Get markets right to ensure that they function correctly.
- Focus on incentives, infrastructure, and institutions.
- Signal policy credibility.
- Grow the market.
- Deal with transaction costs, and make sure there is market integration and connectivity on a regional scale.

Underlying all of these aspects related to the market is the realization that even the peasants are in agriculture for purposes of having reasonable returns to their efforts.

Excerpt 10: Trading Up: How International Trade and Efficient Domestic Markets Can Contribute to African Development

David Orden, Hans Lofgren, and Eleni Gabre-Madhin

Market access has many components: linkages between farmers and local consumers, processors, and wholesalers; integration of rural and urban markets within geographical areas and among the various regions of a country; trade access among countries within the continent; and global flows of goods.

Policies affecting trade arise at three levels: in the multilateral forum of the World Trade Organization (WTO); within multi-country or bilateral regional trade agreements (RTAs); and in the unilateral decisions of nations. At each level, key questions can be asked, such as what are the highest African priorities for a new WTO agricultural agreement, how important are the tariffs and other barriers to trade among African countries, and what trade policies best serve a country? There is no silver bullet that will create optimal trade policy for nations in Africa or elsewhere.

In the Doha negotiations, African policymakers should focus on the developed-country policies that directly affect trade (tariffs and tariff-rate quotas or export subsidies) and therefore do the most direct harm. The domestic farm support policies of the developed countries can also distort markets, but there are differences in the degree of damage caused by alternative policy instruments. It is also crucial that any agreement on core trade issues be accompanied by efforts to help African countries break through the bottlenecks in their domestic financial, human, and institutional capacity that prevent them from benefiting more fully from international trade.

In addition to seeking reductions in support and protection by developed countries, African countries feel the effects of their own trade policies. Trade between SSA countries provides about 20 percent of their total agricultural imports. RTAs that lower trade barriers could increase the flow of goods within SSA, yielding benefits to producers and consumers. There are 14 RTAs between African nations, yet trade remains fragmented among member nations because in some cases the RTAs have partially overlapping memberships and in others conflicting objectives. Few of the RTAs have achieved substantial reductions in tariffs.

Researchers at IFPRI have identified more than 250 agricultural goods for which one or more SSA countries has a comparative advantage. Nearly one-third are goods—including such staples as livestock and livestock products, cereals, roots and tubers, and peas and beans—for which other African countries have a comparative disadvantage and are importers. Intraregional trade offers opportunities that complement trade with countries outside of the region. Increasing intraregional trade would provide opportunities for the rural poor and could help to partially alleviate Africa's food security problems.

Within the multilateral and regional framework, individual nations must decide on their own policies toward trade and national markets. Analysis shows what is at stake when developing countries reduce their own trade barriers *in conjunction with* the removal, as discussed above, of subsidies and trade barriers by developed countries. The research indicates that the gain in net agricultural exports and agricultural and agro-industry income in Africa and other developing countries would be somewhat reduced compared with the gain expected if the developing countries' policies remained unchanged. But internal reforms create a larger beneficial effect on total income in SSA and other developing countries. The gains to national welfare and total GDP are nearly doubled when these countries also reform their own policies.

This has been excerpted from 2020 Africa Conference Brief 5, published by IFPRI, Washington, DC, 2004.

Excerpt 11: Exploring Market Opportunities for African Smallholders

Xinshen Diao and Peter Hazell

Poorly functioning markets, weak domestic demand, and lack of export possibilities are major constraints on Africa's agricultural growth prospects.

Domestic and intraregional food markets are a potential source of demand for Africa's agricultural products. The current value of Africa's domestic demand for food staples is about US$50 billion per year, and this figure is projected to almost double by 2015. Only part of this output is actually sold (the rest is consumed on farm), but it still represents a large and growing market that ought to offer real income opportunities. Since Africa currently imports 25 percent of grain products such as maize, rice, and wheat, domestic production could potentially displace some imports.

Despite the promise offered by the production of food staples for domestic and regional markets, economy-wide simulations suggest that without increased demand induced by growth in other agricultural and nonagricultural sectors, even modest growth in grain productivity could depress domestic grain prices, given prevailing agricultural trade policies around the world and poorly functioning markets within Africa. This decrease in prices would benefit consumers and poor people in the region, but it would slow growth in agricultural income. Less than one-third of grain products can reach commercial markets, and linkages between grain and livestock production are extremely weak in most African countries. More promising scenarios would arise if African farmers were given better access to markets and if the productivity of the livestock and grain sectors could be increased in tandem. In the latter case, there would be an increase in the consumption of livestock products as well as grains, and an increase in the derived demand for feed grains. Agricultural income would then grow even while grain and livestock prices fell, leading to gains for both farmers and consumers.

One way for Africa to increase its competitiveness would be to invest in infrastructure and market development to reduce transport and marketing costs. This would reduce costs for a broad range of commodities, promoting trade and reducing domestic prices—with follow-on demand effects. A model simulation indicates that the combined impact of simultaneously reducing marketing margins and improving productivity across traditional and nontraditional export crops and the grain and livestock subsectors appears to hold the most promise for generating growth in income and food consumption. Per capita agricultural income would grow at 1.4 percent annually, twice the cumulative growth rate generated by targeting each individual agricultural sector separately.

Another way to accelerate growth in domestic demand for foods is by increasing incomes in the nonagricultural sector. Agricultural growth is one avenue for raising nonagricultural incomes because when agricultural incomes increase, rural people have more resources to spend on nonfoods. A second major avenue for increasing demand is through investments that increase productivity in the nonagricultural sector itself. Model simulations show that if productivity increases in both the agricultural and nonagricultural sectors (a two-engine growth strategy), demand for agricultural output can increase much more rapidly. For example, if productivity in the export (traditional and nontraditional) and the food (livestock and grain) subsectors grows at a rate of 6 percent and 1.5 percent per year, respectively, while productivity in some manufacturing and service sectors grows by 4 percent per year, then per capita agricultural income in Africa grows by 3.0 percent per year, per capita food consumption grows by 3.5 percent per year, and per capita agricultural exports grow by 8.0 percent per year more than in the baseline scenario; this is four times the cumulative agricultural growth rate obtained by focusing on the agricultural sector alone. These results show the high payoff of a two-engine growth strategy.

This has been excerpted from 2020 Africa Conference Brief 6, published by IFPRI, Washington, DC, 2004.

Chapter 14 Building Human Capacity

Chair: Angeline Kamba
Member of UN/UNESCO World Commission on Culture and Development, Zimbabwe

Moderator: Soumana Sako
Executive Secretary, African Capacity Building Foundation, Zimbabwe

Rapporteur: Willis Oluoch-Kosura
Program Coordinator, Collaborative Masters Program in Agricultural and Applied Economics, Kenya

Kwadwo Asenso-Okyere

Vice-Chancellor, University of Ghana, Ghana

In all circumstances an investment in human resources is a necessary precondition for national development. Not only does it promise a significant rate of return, but it also acts as a catalyst for a vibrant economy, society, and culture.

Although Africa abounds with natural resources, the continent lags behind world development in many respects. Moreover, the pace of Africa's development is so slow that it may not be possible to catch up with the rest of the world if something drastic is not done. Some have argued that the answer lies in accelerating the human resource development in Africa. Literacy and numeracy levels in Africa are low, and so they should be raised to get a critical mass of people to participate effectively in the development process.

But mere literacy and numeracy are not sufficient in the current knowledge economy. A tertiary education is a sine qua non for national development. A university education not only benefits African countries as a whole by developing a high-caliber workforce that is one of the greatest attractors for new economic investment, but it also prepares the continent to participate in the current global environment. A highly educated population and a dynamic research culture are vital to Africa's success in the new knowledge-based global economy and to improved quality of life for all Africans.

In Africa, however, only about 3 percent of qualified persons gain access to higher education institutions, according to conservative data estimates. Coupled with restricted access is the issue of quality of higher education, which must be upheld if African countries are not to lose out to the world competition. What strategies are needed to improve the quality of and access to higher education so that Africa can play a more meaningful role in world development?

Poverty is pervasive in Africa. Many households cannot even meet their daily nutritional needs. In a quest to gain funding, many higher education institutions have implemented cost sharing with students in the form of fees, but the poor are precluded from access to these institutions. Many households cannot afford the loss of income from members who spend so much time pursuing education. Although some attempts have been made to award scholarships to poor students, the absence of a process for means testing in many African countries has made this difficult.

The increasing incidence of HIV/AIDS has affected enrollment and retention of students in tertiary institu-

A highly educated population and a dynamic research culture are vital to Africa's success in the new knowledge-based global economy and to improved quality of life for all Africans.

— Kwadwo Asenso-Okyere

> *In Africa, only about 3 percent of qualified persons gain access to higher education institutions.*
>
> – Kwadwo Asenso-Okyere

tions in some African countries. Some of the faculty are lost to mortality from HIV/AIDS infections, and this has affected teaching in these institutions.

In some countries the low level of literacy and numeracy has relegated tertiary education to the background. In others, the few public tertiary education institutions are not enough to cope with the large number of applicants. For instance, for the 2003/04 academic year, the University of Ghana was able to admit only 52 percent of the 20,374 qualified persons who applied for admission.

Admissions are also skewed toward males. At the University of Ghana, despite a 20-year-old affirmative action policy aimed at achieving a 50:50 male:female admission ratio, enrollment is only 37 percent female. Conscious efforts to increase female enrollent and retention in tertiary institutions should be made. Special enrollment drives and financial assistance can be provided to female students to encourage them to enroll and complete their programs.

Many factors work together to reduce African universities' ability to admit large numbers of applicants. One of the most important limiting factors has been lack of adequate infrastructure in terms of lecture hall space, laboratories, and residential accommodation. In some universities some students must stand outside the lecture hall to listen to lectures. Such a situation compromises effective teaching and learning. Many of the buildings are not accessible by handicapped persons and therefore restrict their enrollment in the institutions. Appropriate housing around institutions of higher learning is scarce, and institutions are often unable to cope with the demand for housing, so some qualified applicants are not admitted. Inadequate and ill-equipped science laboratories hamper the development of science and technology education in Africa. Yet without science and technology Africa's development will continue to lag behind the rest of the world. It is crucial to demystify science and provide the facilities for its study so that many students can take it at the secondary and tertiary levels.

Another factor that restricts the number of applicants that can be admitted to tertiary institutions in Africa is inadequate qualified academic staff. This limits the range of courses that can be offered and the number of students that can be admitted.

In many African countries private universities are emerging. The high charges imposed by these institutions, however, preclude access to them by the poor. Many of the courses offered at these institutions are in the humanities and information and communication technologies, so courses in the sciences, agriculture, health, and engineering are left for the public institutions. It is about time some of the private institutions begin to look at areas that are critical for the development of Africa.

Distance education enables people to pursue education without the restrictions of time and location. African countries that want to expand access to tertiary education by a large number of persons should look at the idea of open universities and lifelong education. Most of the courses offered by universities can also be offered via distance education, through print and electronic media, to reach people who may not ordinarily find time to enroll in residential programs.

Many people complain that they do not have enough information about courses and entry requirements for tertiary institutions. Universities should set up websites that are maintained regularly to provide needed information to prospective applicants so that they can make the necessary preparations for university education.

Postgraduate enrollment is low in many African universities. Graduate programs should be expanded to provide the assistance required for undergraduate teaching and examining, and faculty research. Some of these graduate teaching and research assistants can be appointed as faculty on completion of their programs.

Attempts to expand access to higher education should not be done at the expense of quality. Increasing enrollment without also increasing resources puts pressure on available facilities and threatens quality.

> *It is crucial to demystify science and provide the facilities for its study so that many students can take it at the secondary and tertiary levels.*
>
> – Kwadwo Asenso-Okyere

Opening more institutions may not help since there may not be enough teachers for all of them. Quality must be upheld in existing institutions before new ones are established.

There must be sufficient space in terms of offices, lecture and examination halls, laboratories, and residential facilities to cater to the number of students enrolled. Information and communication technology must be available for teaching and learning, research, and administration. Access to the Internet enables both faculty and students to search for pertinent information for research and publications. One discouraging factor for Internet access in developing countries is the high charges demanded by Internet service providers. Arrangements should be made for broadband access to the Internet to reduce cost.

Up-to-date library facilities allow teachers to upgrade their knowledge on new literature and students to get access to references to augment classroom instruction. Library automation is the best way to serve large numbers of students. When the library is well automated and linked to other libraries, readers can have access to increased information and may be able to access the information from remote sites to reduce congestion in library facilities. The library is the heart of an educational institution, and every effort must be made to modernize it and increase its holdings in print or electronic form.

Government subsidies to tertiary institutions have been dwindling in real terms, and the situation may not improve in the short to medium term because of competing demands. Other sources of funding must be pursued to help maintain quality. Potential sources of funding are individuals and firms, alumni, student fees (supported by scholarships), foreign students (who may pay higher fees than local students), international donor agencies, research grants, and internally generated funds.

Student fees seem to be the most viable source of financing for tertiary institutions. But the extent of poverty and the absence of a means test to assist needy students make full cost recovery difficult.

Tertiary institutions can also increase the resources available to them by reducing their cost of operation. The institutions must concentrate on their core business and use transparent procurement practices. There must be prudential financial management with timely audit of accounts.

To make tertiary education relevant to changing needs, the curriculum must be revised from time to time. The curriculum must include relevant problem-solving science and technology to help produce the innovations needed to accelerate development. Besides leading to innovation, research should be used to enrich the curriculum and its delivery.

> *African higher education is in the crossroads. Faced with pressure to admit more students, higher education institutions are also challenged to maintain quality so they can survive the global competition in the knowledge economy.*
>
> — Kwadwo Asenso-Okyere

An adequately sized and highly qualified faculty is important for ensuring quality. Universities must recruit faculty aggressively and take measures to retain them. Conditions of service must be improved, tools of trade must be provided, and avenues for career progression must be created for faculty. Avenues for capacity building must be created as part of faculty development. Sandwich or split programs, which require undertaking one part of a degree program in one's country and the other part abroad, have been an effective way of counteracting brain drain among academic staff. Sabbatical leaves are essential for faculty to renew their energy, collaborate on research, prepare publications, and upgrade their knowledge and teaching skills.

Graduate research and teaching assistants can provide valuable assistance to faculty in their research and teaching programs. With a graduate research assistant to help with class tutorials and grading of assignments, a faculty member may be able to handle a large class. Faculty members who have been able to attract research funding and employed graduate assistants have been found to be successful in their research and publication programs. Graduate programs must therefore be expanded as part of a strategy to replace aging faculty and to assist in ongoing academic programs.

A tertiary institution must maintain integrity in its admission processes and examinations. Admission should largely be by merit denominated by scholarship. When an affirmative action policy is instituted to bring equity into the admission process, the rules must be clear to all and implementation must be transparent. Examinations should distinguish between bright and dull students.

African universities must cooperate among themselves in the areas of degree programs and research. This pooling of scarce resources allows African universities to obtain a critical mass of expertise required for the assurance of quality. For instance, the cooperative master of arts program in economics under the auspices of the African Economic Research Consortium allows faculty from other countries to teach modules of the courses offered. The continentwide master of arts program in economic policy management sponsored by the African Capacity Building Foundation brings students from other countries to one of the universities offering the program. In this case, proliferation of the course is avoided and resources are centralized to assure quality.

To ensure the maintenance of acceptable standards, new higher education institutions should be given accreditation before they are allowed to operate, and the programs of existing higher education institutions should be accredited from time to time. Such accreditation exercises may be carried out by reputable national accreditation boards set up for that purpose.

African higher education is in the crossroads. Faced with pressure to admit more students, higher education institutions are also challenged to maintain quality so they can survive the global competition in the knowledge economy. The imposition of cost recovery on students faces stiff opposition from politicians, students, and the citizenry because of widespread poverty and the fear that many qualified but poor candidates may be excluded from enrolling in higher education institutions. Yet other sources of financing are not forthcoming at a level that can ensure quality. This dilemma calls for ingenious ways of raising money to close the funding gap in higher education institutions so that internationally acceptable standards can be attained.

Suresh Babu
Senior Research Fellow/Senior Adviser, Training, International Food Policy Research Institute (IFPRI), USA

The capacity in many countries in Sub-Saharan Africa is inadequate. Almost 15 years ago, right after earning my Ph.D., I went to Malawi as a senior adviser for food security in the Ministry of Agriculture. When I went there, there were no collaborators. I was supposed to have a counterpart, but the position went empty for six months because no one could be identified for the position. So I started doing both jobs. Therein I learned the challenges of capacity at the national level, the sectoral level, the district level, and the community level.

Designing and implementing policies and programs at the national level will require overcoming a serious lack of capacity in many places. Even if capacity exists in some places, many of the institutions themselves are weak. Certainly there are some strong institutions with good leadership and capacity. But if they are not present, you face challenges.

Moreover, food and nutrition security are multidisciplinary subjects. Economists, agronomists, and others all have to come together, and bringing them together to solve problems is also a challenge.

Expatriates are not necessarily a solution, because they often do not have a fundamental understanding of what is going on. It takes two or three years to build that understanding, and by that time the expatriates have moved on to another country to learn about another contextual situation. The problem is not the presence of expatriates, but how we use them in building our own capacity and implementing programs.

How should we plan for the next generation of capacity? How do we build and keep adequate capacity, given that people move, people die, people get transferred, and people go into the private sector? We need capacity at global, national, subnational, and community levels.

We need to strengthen capacity for designing programs and policies in several areas. We need capacity to detect and diagnose signs of food and nutrition distress. In the past two years Southern Africa has been facing a food crisis, if not famine. But the crisis started with drought in Southern Africa. If you do not get rains in the second and third week of March, you are in trouble, and you can immediately start your planning process. We also need capacity for developing and executing food security programs and policies for emergency situations. How do you differentiate between a

To implement capacity-building efforts for food and nutrition security, we need to mainstream food and nutrition security into the national planning process.

— Suresh Babu

situation that calls for a short-term intervention and one that calls for a long-term intervention? You need to systematically monitor what is happening, who is eating what, where the food is produced, where the surplus is, and where the deficiency is. We had that kind of capacity in the mid-1980s and early 1990s, but it has eroded throughout the years.

Strengthening that kind of capacity requires collaboration among partners at the African Capacity Building Foundation (ACBF), for example, and partners in the country where efforts are being made to build that capacity. It is also important to bring in cross-country and cross-regional dialogue, but this is a challenge as well.

Coordination of capacity-building efforts at the national level is essential. Donors conduct different types of training programs. If a person goes to this training today and that training tomorrow and a different training the next day, there is not adequate support. And if you are building capacity, for example, at the M.Sc. or Ph.D. level, additional capacity is required simply to execute the program.

The kinds of training needed are constantly changing. When I was in Malawi, we said that whatever we needed at the moment, the University of Malawi was not teaching. The courses were good, the curriculum was broad, and the students came out with bachelor's degrees. But the expertise they needed when they came to the Ministry of Agriculture was not being taught.

To implement capacity-building efforts for food and nutrition security, we need to mainstream food and nutrition security into the national planning process. Wherever food security is taken seriously at the level of the president, minister of planning, or minister of finance, things tend to move very fast.

It is essential to build capacity for monitoring and evaluating programs and for linking that information with decisionmakers. We need to increase the capacity for data collection, processing, analysis, and communication with policymakers.

We also need to build capacity for food and nutrition leadership. Over the years we have seen that wherever there is a leader or a set of leaders who promote this cause, progress has been made. We need to identify such leaders at all levels and motivate them. We need to communicate information to the leaders and leaders must communicate it to policymakers to improve dialogue, awareness, resource mobilization, and good governance. One possible way to build this leadership is through executive programs for food security leadership.

We also need to build capacity for food and nutrition leadership.

— Suresh Babu

To build adequate capacity, we must begin by improving food security organizations—the organizations that plan for food security and are in charge of policymaking for food security. We also need to think about short-term and long-term training activities. We need to provide opportunities within countries to talk about problems as they come up, a practice that promotes democracy and good governance. The more you talk about problems, the more likely you are to find a way to address them. We also need to disseminate information effectively, engage local resources for attacking the problem locally, nurture and embrace capacity that is already there, and identify capacity gaps and fill them in a proactive manner.

We can address the problem of food insecurity and malnutrition on this continent. We have done so in many places. But to do so, we need the basic capacity. Even 10 people who really understand the problem can change things on the ground.

Carl Greenidge

Director, Technical Center for Agricultural and Rural Cooperation (CTA), The Netherlands

CTA's current approach to food security has been heavily influenced by recent advances in the analysis of famine, which recognize that famine is in part a social phenomenon. This understanding requires us to go beyond availability and geography to sector and farm-firm analysis. Attention must be paid to social forces and the role they play in exposing the resource poor and the institutionally disadvantaged to the risk of food insecurity.

This approach has implications for information and communication management (ICM). It is widely assumed, erroneously, that since the work of Sen et al., most problems of definition, analysis, and scope have been resolved. Recent work undertaken for the FAO, however, found that national analyses, as reflected in 25 Common Country Assessment reports and 50 PRSPs, were defi-

> *Little of value will be achieved in the struggle to improve food security without a systematic attempt to enhance capacity in the rural sector and related agricultural institutions.*
>
> — Carl Greenidge

cient. Measures aimed at addressing food security will fail if the analysis on which they are based is partial. Specifically, measures need to be underpinned by:

- the identification of poverty-specific groups or specific analyses of the extent and causes of insecurity and vulnerability;
- adherence to the priorities yielded by the analyses;
- recognition that institutional capacity is a key factor in the success of these programs; and
- significant commitment to a participatory approach.

The crucial importance of sharing information can hardly be exaggerated, but information and communication management needs to be tailored to the circumstances.

The right to participate has to be supported by the ability to contribute meaningfully to decisionmaking. This is the purvue of capacity building. At the same time the identification of at-risk and interested parties depends on the collection and analysis of data, appropriately stratified and disaggregated. Such analysis should in turn highlight the need for appropriate indicators. Thus capacity building will need to take several forms.

Gender is central in ensuring food security because of the quantity and nature of African farm labor and because of the traditional division of labor, as well as the evolving division of labor arising from the impact of HIV/AIDS. The key role played by women in child rearing, water conveyance, and food and nutrition, in addition to labor supply, means that their situation has a direct impact on the status of child nutrition. A considerable part of the capacity development effort therefore ought to be directed to women.

CTA's mission, set out in the ACP-EU Cotonou Agreement, is to support ACP rural and agricultural development by providing information and to develop the ICM capacity of ACP organizations. In seeking to meet this mission, CTA has fashioned three programs. Since 2000 these programs have worked to help establish an ACP agricultural knowledge network, with CTA as a major hub and with special attention devoted to facilitating ACP-ACP (South-South) exchanges. Traditionally, CTA has focused on delivering information and raising awareness, in addition to building capacity. The programs under Cotonou seek, in the jargon of ICM, to enable ACP actors to upload information that they deem important or useful.

The three programs are the following: First, Information Products and Services raises availability of information and heightens awareness of sources by providing information in a variety of forms, including print and electronic. Second, Communication Channels and Services enhances integrated ICM use, intensifies contacts and information exchange, and promotes and supports regional networks through information and communication technologies (ICTs), face-to-face exchanges, study visits, and seminar support programs. Third, ICM Skills and Systems strengthens capacity, partnerships, and participatory processes; provides integrated ICM support to local and national organizations; offers ICM training programs; raises awareness of science and technology in agricultural development; and encourages the development of appropriate science and technology-cum-innovation policies.

In fashioning its projects, CTA has devoted much attention to seeking a deeper understanding of the structural causes of poverty and identifying the vulnerable. At the same time it has attempted to help fashion appropriate means of supporting the various categories of players, as well as determining appropriate systems for meeting their information needs.

The projects may be classified according to whether they are intended to benefit individual actors or institutions, as well as their purpose in terms of ICM. For individuals, capacity-building efforts include raising awareness, building skills, and using platforms for dialogue. For institutions, they include networking, platforms for exchange of experience and ideas, and institution building. The most direct means of enhancing food security is to establish specialized information systems. CTA extensively supports such bodies on, for instance, early warning systems and management information systems.

Little of value will be achieved in the struggle to improve food security without a systematic attempt to enhance capacity in the rural sector and related agricultural institutions. The institutions charged with this task need to constantly review the evolving scenario in order to ensure that their interventions are relevant and effective.

CTA is ideally placed to support the efforts of ACP states to reduce food insecurity. Its annual programs involve extensive collaboration with a range of partners in approaching the challenge in an imaginative and comprehensive manner.

William M. Lyakurwa

Executive Director, African Economic Research Consortium, Kenya

The focus of this presentation is on designing and implementing an effective network for building human and institutional capacity in Africa. The African Economic Research Consortium (AERC), which primarily addresses building capacity for economic policy research and graduate training in economics, has achieved success but also encountered daunting challenges.

The first challenge is to build and retain capacity in African institutions so it can be used effectively for both policy analysis and advice, as well as for building other capacities in an effort to reach a critical mass. If this capacity is retained in African institutions, the next challenge is to identify the channels through which the capacity conveys the results of research and training to policymakers. Finally, to keep this capacity alive and active, there must be ways of replenishing it through training and an appropriate incentive system for research. In sum, the challenge is to build a network of individuals and institutions that are capable of tackling current problems in research and training with a view to applying the outputs in the policy context.

From our experience, several conditions help keep the network alive:

- The mission and objectives are clearly defined.
- An appropriate governance structure supports the mission.
- The management structure is responsive to and supports the network.
- The presence or continuous production of innovative topical issues for research keeps the research relevant to policy and enhances the visibility of the network.
- Research innovation driven by a peer review mechanism (and peer pressure) enhances quality, ensures delivery, and in turn strengthens the process of networking. This is the learning-by-doing research component of the thematic research in AERC.

There are enormous challenges that will need to be overcome before a success story of human capacity building in Africa can be told.

— William M. Lyakurwa

- Sharing the network's research and training outputs at either the national level or across countries strengthens the desire for networking and sharing experiences.
- Building a community of professionals with common ideals and objectives is in itself a strong incentive for networking.
- The presence of a dissemination strategy or a communication mechanism gives the network a higher profile and thus enhances its strengths.

These points may seem general, but they are important in trying to understand why capacity building in Africa has succeeded in some instances and failed in others. Perhaps we have less successful networks in Africa because of poor design and weak implementation, coupled with prohibitive dynamics, a few of which are the small pool of resource persons, a weak human and financial resource base, civil strife and a hostile policy environment, erosion of incentives, human and financial capital flight, and lack of policy receptivity.

The AERC networking experience suggests how to design and implement an effective network for human capacity building. AERC was established in 1988 to strengthen local capacity for economic policy research in Sub-Saharan Africa. The mission of AERC is to enhance the capacity of locally based researchers to conduct policy-relevant economic inquiry into economic problems facing the continent; promote the retention of such capacity in Sub-Saharan Africa and in relevant institutions in the region; and encourage the application of the capacity in the policy context.

This mission rests on two basic premises: Development is more likely to occur where there is sustained sound management of the economy; and such management is more likely to occur where there exists an active, well-informed group of locally based professional economists to conduct policy-relevant research.

African policymakers are not always open to using these researchers for policy advice and often follow the policies prescribed by donors. The problem is largely due to lack of ownership of the domestic policymaking process.

— William M. Lyakurwa

This should be regarded as a specific and limited intervention that targets the economics discipline and the local capacity of researchers to conduct policy-relevant economic inquiry into economic problems facing Sub-Saharan African economies. It shows that there is room to build networks in other disciplines that will address the lack of capacity in other policy-relevant areas.

Networking is the strategic framework for implementing AERC's activities. This framework links individuals and institutions in a knowledge-sharing experience. The AERC network functions through two main programs: research and training. The Research Program links individual researchers in the region so that they can carry out research pertinent to policy needs. This is learning-by-doing research. It breaks the barriers of professional isolation, encourages exchange of experiences, and creates peer pressure for enhancing quality. The other research activity, collaborative research, networks senior researchers to address pertinent policy issues.

The Training Program brings together 27 universities in 20 countries in Sub-Saharan Africa for collaboration on both master's and Ph.D. training. This approach rationalizes the use of limited teaching capacity, attains a critical mass of students, offers a larger menu of electives, and jointly enforces higher standards for graduate training in economics. In addition, these standards are translated into high-quality research via the Research Program, and thus these two programs support and augment each other. The two programs are also supported by outreach activities that ensure that AERC's research outputs are published and disseminated in a timely and cost-effective manner in both print and electronic formats.

The AERC network operations in the research activities are an example of designing, facilitating, and implementing an effective network. The Research Program's four principal objectives are to build a credible local capacity for policy-oriented research, generate research results for use by policymakers, promote links between research and policy, and promote the retention of high-quality researchers on the continent.

The strategy of the AERC Research Program has three elements. First, the program offers small grants to groups of individuals drawn from both academia and policy institutions to conduct research on a limited number of pertinent themes. Second, it establishes a support system for research in the form of peer review, methodology workshops, and access to relevant literature. Third, biannual research workshops provide a way to monitor the quality of research on a continuous basis, create effective peer pressure, foster interaction among the researchers themselves and with resource persons, and enforce scheduled delivery of reports. The Training Program features the Collaborative Master's Programme (CMAP) and the Collaborative Ph.D. Programme (CPP). CMAP currently brings together a network of 21 universities in 17 African countries. CPP involves eight degree-awarding universities, two in each subregion of Africa—West Africa, Francophone Africa, Eastern Africa, and Southern Africa.

One of the innovations aimed at disseminating research findings directly to policymakers is the senior policy seminar. Six such seminars have already been held. These events were designed to provide a forum to discuss policy-oriented syntheses of AERC research and to obtain feedback from policymakers on the relevance of the Consortium's research agenda for policymaking. The senior policymakers are drawn from governments, nongovernmental organizations, and the private sector.

Finally, research output is published in several series of papers designed to reach the research and policy community, as well as a website and two periodicals.

It may appear from the AERC example that networking is a panacea for capacity building in Africa. But there are enormous challenges that will need to be overcome before a success story of human capacity building in Africa can be told, and AERC's experiences point to a few of the challenges.

First, over the past few years, there have been significant changes in higher education in Africa. To counter dwindling government support for higher education, African universities have had to come up with innovative ways of raising additional resources. These have included, but are not limited to, charging fees for higher education, privatizing services at universities, running parallel programs that rely on full fee recovery, and initiating fundraising strategies to augment available resources. One result has been declining teaching capacity in the face of very high enrollment rates. For AERC, the shift of human resources to parallel degree programs has eroded personnel for the regular degree programs that AERC depends on for CMAP and CPP.

Second, although there has been a significant reduction in the unit cost of the master's program, from US$26,000 to a little less than US$15,000 per student per year, few individuals can afford to pay full fees for the program. AERC must continue to provide scholarships for the needy and thus must strive to raise additional resources. Universities are encouraged to approach their traditional funders to supplement AERC resources, although this has not been well implemented and in most universities has not been implemented at all.

In the Ph.D. program, AERC could provide for only 21 of the 80 students who required scholarships. Of the remaining 59, 4 students obtained scholarships from other institutions. The resource constraint will be aggravated as the profile, visibility, and success of the CPP filter into the wider academic and policy domain.

Third, even though AERC has attempted to build a stock of knowledge in policy-relevant areas, African policymakers are not always open to using these researchers for policy advice and often follow the policies prescribed by donors. The problem is largely due to lack of ownership of the domestic policymaking process.

Fourth, retention of human capacity depends largely on the institutional structures, reward system, and incentive structure in a particular country. AERC's intervention cannot be termed comprehensive in any way. The main responsibility for retention rests heavily on institutions and governments in the region, and AERC's capability in this area is limited. Without AERC, however, and given the new environment in which the private sector increasingly plays a major role, there would be few professional economists remaining in academia and conducting policy-relevant research.

In summary, networks are effective tools for building human capacity, and the AERC example is vivid proof of this. Although the challenges are daunting, the lessons learned may offer solutions to some of them and will strengthen other networks in the important role of capacity building and as reservoirs for policymakers in Sub-Saharan countries.

Jim Ryan

Visiting Fellow, Economics Division, Research School of Pacific and Asian Studies, Australian National University, Australia

For the past 18 months or so, I have been associated with an exercise conducted by the InterAcademy Council, at the request of Kofi Annan, to look at how we can better harness science and technology for improving agricultural productivity and food security in Africa. The study was conducted over a period of 18 months and involved a panel of 18 eminent scientists. Before preparing the report on the study, which is currently being published, we conducted a series of consultative workshops with subregional organizations throughout Africa and commissioned background papers and the like.

The question was asked, Why hasn't Africa had a Green Revolution like South Asia? The panel identified at least 11 distinctive characteristics of Africa that may help explain why. Many of these characteristics are very familiar to you. In contrast to South Asia, Africa does not have a dominant farming system on which food security largely depends. It depends on many different farming systems. There is a lack of functioning markets, and weathered soils of poor inherent fertility predominate. The other distinctive characteristics are a relative underinvestment in agricultural research and development, education, and infrastructure; poor economic and political enabling environments; the large and growing impact of human health on agriculture; low and stagnant labor productivity in agriculture; the importance of women in food production and food security; minimal mechanization; and the predominance of customary land tenure.

These distinctive characteristics have two types of implications. They certainly influence the options that might be available in science and technology. They imply that African agriculture is more likely to experience numerous rainbow evolutions, as we might term them,

African agriculture is more likely to experience numerous rainbow evolutions, rather than a green revolution of the type that we saw in South Asia.

— Jim Ryan

There is a need to cultivate and stimulate the evolution of African centers of agricultural research excellence to complement and strengthen national agricultural research systems.

– Jim Ryan

rather than a green revolution of the type that we saw in South Asia. This in turn implies that Africa is going to require a higher level of investment in research, development, and capacity building per unit of agricultural productivity gain than Asia did.

Africa's distinctive characteristics also have implications for capacity building. The panel's report discussed the issues related to capacity building under four strategic headings: institutions, scientific capacity, policies and markets, and science and technology options. I will focus on institutions and scientific capacity here.

To build impact-oriented research, knowledge, and development institutions, the panel believes there is a need for a paradigm shift from the linear research-extension-farmer model to what is termed a quadrangle approach, involving farmers, extension professionals, educators, and scientists working together in a participatory mode, increasingly aided and abetted by information and communications technology.

The panel dwelt on why the land grant university model in the United States has not worked very well outside of the United States. One of the factors seems to be that higher education is in one ministry and agriculture is in another, and that leads to all types of challenges.

The panel also believes institutions and mechanisms like the academies of sciences and national councils for science and technology must be encouraged to more effectively articulate and advocate science and technology strategies and policies, within the economic and political environments of their countries. There is a need to cultivate and stimulate the evolution of African centers of agricultural research excellence to complement and strengthen national agricultural research systems. These centers of excellence will increasingly become virtual centers. We are not necessarily talking here about new bricks and mortar—in most instances, one can build on current strengths both in universities and in national agricultural research institutions throughout Africa. This is consistent with the NEPAD approach as well. We are not saying anything dramatically new here, but rather reinforcing what seems to be an emerging consensus. There is a large unmet strategic research agenda that needs to be part of the programs of these centers of excellence in Africa.

The panel believes there also needs to be a substantial increase in investment in agricultural research as a share of agricultural gross domestic product. Today investment in agricultural research is around 0.7 percent of agricultural GDP. It needs to be at least double that.

There is also an immediate need to better integrate the programs, and possibly the institutions, of the international agricultural research centers that conduct activities focused on Africa. Those types of examinations are currently underway within the CGIAR system. There is also a need for a significant increase in core resources available to the international centers working within these African environments.

Next, how can we generate and retain the next generation of agricultural scientists? Currently about one-third of Africa's scientists are estimated to be in the African diaspora. Arresting a future brain drain of scientific capacity requires policies that create more personally and professionally awarding scientific opportunities, rewards, and recognition in Africa. The career path, particularly for agricultural scientists, should recognize and reward scientific excellence such that a good scientist might aspire to be more than he or she reckoned. In other countries, this works very successfully. The panel believes there should be a focus on retaining current and future graduates rather than drawing scientists from the diaspora back to Africa. There have been attempts to do that, but not very successfully.

There is a need to both broaden and deepen the political support for agricultural science. The scientists themselves have a responsibility here. The panel detected a degree of inferiority complex among African agricultural scientists, and that leads to a defeatist

Currently about one-third of Africa's scientists are estimated to be in the African diaspora.

– Jim Ryan

attitude about being advocates for science and for the implications of science.

The panel believes there is a need to closely examine current curricula in universities and to stress more holistic ecological and multidisciplinary systems approaches and information and communication technology, to better equip future graduates for the innovation, information, knowledge, and education quadrangle. If scientists are going to mobilize farmers' organizations and have a market-driven strategy of productivity enhancement and food security improvement, then the next generation of scientists must work with the demand side more effectively.

There is also a need to mobilize large and sustainable funding for higher education in science and technology, improving quality and minimizing dependence on external donor support, and to develop an appropriate balance of graduate training in African and foreign universities. The African centers of research excellence that arise in university environments could provide an increasing opportunity for that to happen.

Finally, it is extremely important to strengthen science education at all levels, starting at the primary and secondary school levels through to the tertiary levels.

Discussion

In her opening remarks, panel chair Angeline Kamba acknowledged the importance of science and technology in achieving food and nutrition security but noted that it is people who are responsible for using these tools effectively. How do we ensure that there is human capacity at every level that is appropriately equipped to address issues of food production, food availability, nutritional assurance, alleviation of poverty, and the improvement of livelihoods through agriculture? Kamba looked to the session to focus on several issues:

- education for giving people a solid foundation for understanding the principles underlying food and nutrition security issues, as well as for equipping people with knowledge and skills;
- planning and strategic alliances between researchers and policymakers to ensure effectiveness in building human capacity and ensuring that all the key players are included;
- institutional arrangements and coordination needed to maximize resources and find solutions that go beyond defined geographical boundaries; and
- effective methods for disseminating research findings to ensure their application. Although Africa has worked on building its human capacity for years, the chair noted that it must do better at both renewing and retaining that capacity.

Participants in the lively and spirited discussion noted from the very beginning that the issue of capacity building had come up time and time again in other sessions of the conference; this convinced them that it is a critical issue when addressing the assurance of food and nutrition security.

Some comments from participants concerned the question of whose capacity should be enhanced. Among those actors mentioned were individuals; households; communities, including farmers, traders, and consumers; and institutions, including both the private and public sectors, NGOs and community-based organizations (CBOs), donors, and researchers.

Owing to technical difficulties, the discussion in this session was not audio recorded. Certain elements of the discussion may inadvertently have been left out of this report.

Participants also suggested a number of specific areas in which capacity should be improved, including communication skills; knowledge and skills development; management; monitoring and evaluation; multidisciplinary, multisectoral, and participatory approaches; skills related to scaling up successful initiatives; agenda setting and prioritization; bridging the gap between research and policy; and linking policy analysis, formulation, and implementation. In addition, the urgency of training all Africans about nutrition was mentioned.

Several participants pointed out that improving capacity on a broad scale in Africa would be a massive task, ranging all the way from strengthening primary, secondary, and tertiary education to training farmers, researchers, policymakers, and other professionals involved in areas related to food and nutrition. Challenges to building capacity, such as HIV/AIDS and poverty, were identified, and it was stated that they must be taken into account as strategies for capacity building are developed. Some participants emphasized the importance of training and other capacity-building activities for women, who carry much of the burden of agricultural production in Africa, in addition to caring for their households.

Much discussion concerned the brain drain out of Africa—whereas some participants believed that the solution was to create new human capacity to replace the people who left, others thought it might be possible to create incentives that would not only retain well-trained and -educated Africans, but also attract people back from the diaspora.

A wide range of potential actions for building human capacity were identified, including fully utilizing existing capacity; training farmers and strengthening farmer organizations; providing and managing information; forging genuine partnerships, such as networks of excellence like the AERC or the collaborative M.Sc. program in agricultural and applied economics in Eastern, Central, and Southern Africa, to promote sustainability; increasing public investment in education and research; defining the roles of partners in capacity strengthening and creating awareness of those roles for accountability purposes; providing nutrition training to all; improving the incentive structure in retaining and attracting those from the diaspora; improving recognition of intellectual achievements; and reforming the structure and function of institutions as needed—particularly the government.

Excerpt 12: Strengthening Africa's Capacity to Design and Implement Strategies for Food and Nutrition Security

Suresh Babu, Valerie Rhoe, Andrew Temu, and Sheryl Hendriks

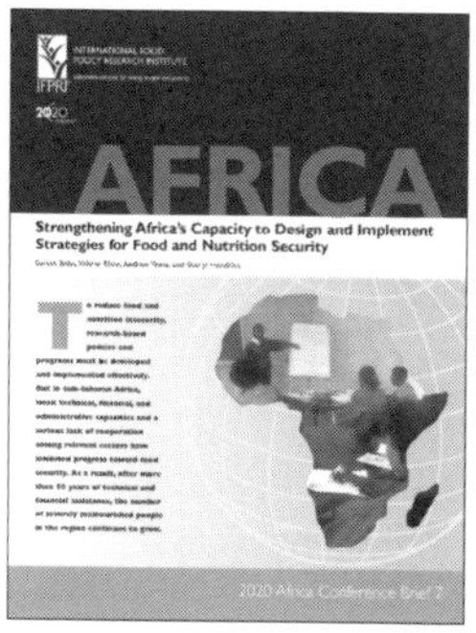

In Africa, where global and regional institutions play a key role in providing food and nutrition policy capacity, some safeguards are in place to prevent inappropriately designed programs from being implemented by global organizations. Yet foreign technical assistants continue to face challenges because they do not understand the culture, politics, governance, corruption, food habits, or market failures that exist in a region. Collaborating with national counterparts would enhance their understanding. Such collaboration should also create a sense of ownership among the local people and strengthen their ability to relate global food and nutrition goals to national strategies.

Within a country, most food and nutrition security actions are planned at the national level (or, in larger countries, at the provincial level). Government agencies, universities, and research institutions all contribute to policy design and implementation capacity. For policies and programs to be appropriately designed and adequately funded, donors, the government, and other institutions need to coordinate their activities. To strengthen cooperation, frequent national meetings of all potential donors, universities, research institutions, and policymakers should be held. These meetings should focus on the planning of current, medium-, and long-term activities to foster food and nutrition security. High-level participation is important for follow-up action. Emphasis should be on analyzing how past experience, research findings, foreign support, and technical outputs can all contribute to current and upcoming activities. Such coordination will help clarify the division of labor, leading to concentrated efforts, consistent policy promotion, and effective use of scarce resources. Donors and collaborating partners could also have access to a searchable database that consolidates the available information on projects and programs in a country. Close teamwork among foreign assistants, local experts, and development leaders would go a long way toward enabling African countries to address management weaknesses and accrue benefits from external support.

University training in Africa tends to focus on general education. This explains the preponderance of staff in policymaking organizations who have general training but limited expertise in the specifics of food and nutrition security. This significant skill gap should be addressed.

Short-term training in food and nutrition security policy is only a band-aid, however; the next generation of policymakers, policy advisors, and policy researchers requires training on food and nutrition security at the university level. Although institutional parameters (rules and regulations) and policymaking and program implementing organizations are important, enhanced human capacity through higher education is the strongest pillar for developing local organizations.

Although knowledge about the different dimensions of the food security issue is the foundation for a better understanding of how disciplines can interact fruitfully to solve the problem of food insecurity, those who acquire this knowledge will mostly be in specific localities. Africa needs the capacity for a continuous dialogue on food security across countries. Through such interactions, the experiences of specific geographical and economic areas can be communicated to the rest of Africa, helping to identify interrelated household food security problems across countries. Institutional and organizational arrangements that have proved successful in addressing food security challenges in one country should be communicated to other countries where they can be replicated.

This has been excerpted from 2020 Africa Conference Brief 7, published by IFPRI, Washington, DC, 2004.

Chapter 15 Improving Nutrition and Health

Chair: Kabba Joiner

Director General, West African Health Organization (WAHO), Burkina Faso

Moderator: Tola Atinmo

Professor of Nutrition at the College of Medicine, University of Ibadan, and President of the Federation of African Nutrition Societies (FANUS), Nigeria

Rapporteur: Todd Benson

Research Fellow, International Food Policy Research Institute, USA

Stuart Gillespie*

Senior Research Fellow, International Food Policy Research Institute (IFPRI), USA

HIV/AIDS is a long-wave global crisis whose impacts will be felt for decades to come. Nearly 30 million people in Sub-Saharan Africa—more than 70 percent of the global total—are infected with the virus. Whatever the impact of the planned rollout of antiretroviral (ARV) therapy, AIDS-related morbidity and mortality will continue to increase for years, and food and nutrition will remain critical priorities.

HIV/AIDS has a devastating effect on many aspects of development, including the ability of households and communities to secure adequate food. HIV/AIDS and food and nutrition insecurity may become increasingly entwined in a vicious circle—HIV/AIDS heightens *vulnerability* to food insecurity, which in turn may heighten *susceptibility* to HIV infection. Figure 1 is an attempt to map these interactions so that researchers and policymakers can better understand them and thus more effectively address them. More illustrative than comprehensive, the figure shows the waves of determinants of HIV infection, from macro to micro levels, and the subsequent waves of impacts, from micro to macro.

With time flowing from left to right, the top left quadrant shows the various factors that condition the *susceptibility* of individuals, households, and communities to the HIV virus. The bottom left quadrant shows some of the main types of *resistance*, the ability of an individual to proactively avoid infection by HIV.

Following HIV infection, the top right quadrant shows the various sources and levels of *vulnerability* to AIDS-related impacts. These impacts are not one-time events—they are processes, often hidden and slow-moving but very destructive. The bottom right quadrant shows

HIV/AIDS and food and nutrition insecurity may become increasingly entwined in a vicious circle—HIV/AIDS heightens vulnerability to food insecurity, which in turn may heighten susceptibility to HIV infection.

— Stuart Gillespie

* This presentation was largely drawn from a policy brief prepared jointly by Stuart Gillespie, Wilberforce Kisamba-Mugerwa, and Michael Loevinsohn, which has been subsequently published as "Assuring Food and Nutrition Security in the Time of AIDS," 2020 Africa Conference Brief 3, IFPRI, Washington, DC, 2004.

FIGURE 1—HIV/AIDS determinants, impacts, and responses

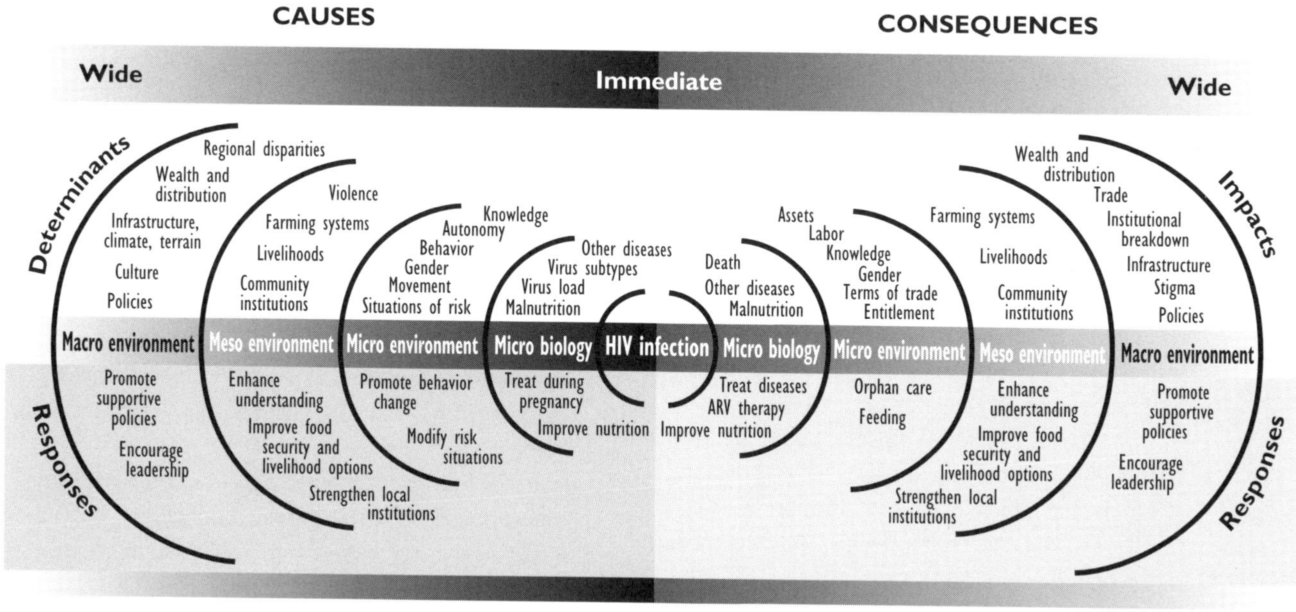

Source: M. Loevinsohn and S. Gillespie, "HIV/AIDS, Food Security, and Rural Livelihoods: Understanding and Responding," Food Consumption and Nutrition Division Discussion Paper 157 (Washington, DC: IFPRI, 2003).

resilience, which is to vulnerability as resistance is to susceptibility—it refers to the active responses that enable people to avoid the worst impacts of AIDS at different levels or to recover faster to a level accepted as normal.

The vicious circle kicks in when the waves of impact later become waves of determinants. Transactional sex may drive such a vicious circle. For example, a young woman whose poverty is deepened by a parent's illness or death from AIDS may be left with few options other than to sell her body in order to feed her siblings. In the process she drastically increases her own risk of becoming infected.

Food and nutrition security play a role in all three pillars of a comprehensive response to HIV/AIDS: prevention, care and treatment, and mitigation. Malnutrition hinders prevention efforts because it compromises immunity, and increases the risk of genital ulcers, sexually transmitted diseases, and mastitis. Food and nutrition insecurity complicate care because HIV raises energy requirements by 10 to 30 percent, and malnutrition hastens the onset and severity of opportunistic infections as well as the onset of AIDS and death. If a person being treated is malnourished, antiretrovirals may be less efficacious and the side effects may be worse, reducing compliance. Finally, mitigation efforts are hampered because malnutrition and associated ill health reduces resilience by compromising people's ability to work and their energy to innovate and cope.

A plethora of studies on the impacts of HIV/AIDS on food and nutrition security has emerged in recent years. Many researchers have used a sustainable livelihood approach to structure their investigations, and many have found that the effects of HIV/AIDS are significantly eroding human, social, financial, physical, and natural capital. It is, however, dangerous to generalize. The determinants and impacts of HIV/AIDS and the degree of resistance or resilience vary widely among geographical areas and livelihood systems.

This situation cautions against a blueprint response to HIV/AIDS–food security interactions. One size absolutely does *not* fit all, nor should everything necessarily have to change. What is needed is a tool to help policymakers and program managers navigate this new universe and figure out what needs to be done in the different situations they find themselves in.

One such adaptable tool is the HIV/AIDS lens. Essentially, the lens comprises the concepts already described, the generic map in Figure 1, and the current state of knowledge of the interactions between food and nutrition security and HIV/AIDS in any one situation. The lens is designed to support reflection on how a particular situation or particular policy may be

> *The effects of HIV/AIDS are significantly eroding human, social, financial, physical, and natural capital.*
>
> – Stuart Gillespie

increasing or reducing the risks people face, either of contracting HIV or of suffering severe consequences flowing from AIDS-linked illness and death. The lens thus helps clarify the options for response.

The lens is bifocal: it focuses on both the upstream factors of susceptibility and resistance and the downstream factors of vulnerability and resilience. It is flexible and adaptive—it may be used in different ways by a range of actors, not just policymakers. At the community level, the lens can reveal options for relevant policies and programs. It can be dynamic, evolving over time as knowledge of these interactions develops.

When the lens is used to review food- and nutrition-relevant policy, a situation analysis is first undertaken of HIV/AIDS and food and nutrition security—what is known about the nature and extent of their interactions, and what forms of institutional response currently exist? This analysis helps construct the lens. Second, key food- and nutrition-relevant policies and programs are reviewed in terms of their potential contribution—positive or negative—to HIV/AIDS prevention and mitigation. This review may be carried out in workshops, primarily by the researchers, program managers, or policymakers responsible for the programs and policies, with outside facilitation and the involvement of key stakeholders.

Looking through the lens, participants ask themselves the following questions:

- How might this policy or program be increasing people's susceptibility (or resistance) to HIV infection?
- How might this policy or program be increasing people's vulnerability (or resilience) to the impacts of AIDS?

The output of this review would be a list of policies and programs prioritized in terms of their potential positive or negative contribution to HIV/AIDS prevention and mitigation. In some cases, those responsible may feel compelled to alter the policy or program on the basis of the review alone, particularly where serious harm is thought likely and a remedy is obvious. Or, given the imperfect nature of the lens, they may conclude that evidence from the field is essential before taking action.

The next stage would seek the evidence for those policies and programs thought to have the greatest positive or negative effects. The methods used would be determined by the nature of the threat or opportunity but would in all cases include seeking the views of the social groups concerned.

This analysis may be followed by the modification of programs and policies, drawing from the results of the field assessments. Responses could range from changing nothing to changing everything (that is, stopping the existing program or initiating a new one). Particular aspects of programs and policies—the what, how, who, where—may need to change.

To maximize food and nutrition security, policies must derive from two overriding principles: community and household resistance and resilience must be augmented as far as possible, and safety nets must be in place for those who are unable to cope otherwise. Policymakers need to move from an individual-infected model to a community-affected one and to focus on strengthening community capacity. Similarly, in the approach toward care, there is a need to shift from a sequential continuum of care that moves from relief to rehabilitation to development, to a contiguum approach that recognizes that all of these elements are interrelated and that any one of them may be needed at any one time.

Another important issue is weighing the costs and benefits of short-term versus long-term responses. Where the capacities of households and communities are being eroded, often irreversibly, in ways that will reverberate across generations, how realistic is it to expect sustainable responses? Sustainability thus is something to strive for but not to be straitjacketed by.

While much can be learned from the proliferation of small-scale innovative responses, it is also crucial to look for ways of effectively and rapidly scaling up what works. Ultimately, scaling up—both organizationally and in terms of population coverage—is primarily a governmental responsibility.

One form of organizational scaling up consists of bringing HIV/AIDS considerations into the mainstream agenda of organizations across multiple sectors. Effective mainstreaming and broad collaboration can help the scale, breadth, and depth of response better match that of the pandemic.

The policy review described may open up policy options in a number of areas. Policies could seek to enable those affected by AIDS to make more efficient use of the land, labor, and other productive assets remaining to them. Programs could be designed, for instance, to increase access to labor-saving technologies such as lightweight plows and fuel-efficient stoves, particularly for poor women, and to reduce the labor intensity of cropping, soil conservation, and animal husbandry systems. Land and finance policies could help ensure land tenure, particularly for widows and orphans; improve the competitiveness and productivity of small-holder agriculture by increasing public investment in transport and communications infrastructure; and explore HIV-relevant microfinance options, savings clubs, or cash grants. Other policy approaches could help preserve and augment knowledge by developing HIV-aware and gender-proactive agricultural extension capacity, supporting "Farmer Life Schools" to ensure effective intra- and intergenerational knowledge transfer, and providing incentives for children to go to and stay in school. Finally, nutrition policies could provide incentives for improving diets, for strengthening the nutrition focus of health services (particularly in the context of ARV therapy and home-based care), and for ensuring nutritionally balanced food aid as a safety net for people who are acutely food insecure or at risk of becoming so, such as orphan-fostering households.

In all of these areas, it is vital that policies and programs recognize the diverse situations of rural people who do not all experience risks in the same way. What may be most helpful to a young, underemployed woman at great risk of contracting HIV may not be helpful to an AIDS widow struggling to keep her land and feed her children.

A tool like the HIV/AIDS lens, by mainstreaming HIV/AIDS into food- and nutrition-relevant policy, can help policymakers and practitioners across sectors build up evidence of what works, enhance their learning, and ultimately leave people better equipped to address the multiple threats of the pandemic.

Foreign-based food products are heavily advertised, and consumers choose them over indigenous foods.

— Amadou Kanouté

Amadou Kanouté
Regional Director, Office for Africa, Consumers International, Zimbabwe

Food insecurity has a dozen fathers: problems of geographic access or financial access; social factors; distribution inefficiencies; political and governance problems; civil wars and internal strife; imbalances in land distribution; natural disasters like droughts, floods, and landslides; unfavorable international trade rules and regulations such as protectionist tendencies, lack of access to markets, subsidies, overproduction, and price volatility; poor economic development policies such as failure to prioritize rural development and agriculture and misguided structural adjustment programs; high cost of agricultural production inputs; population pressure; and inadequate and inappropriate technologies.

Moreover, poor nutrition is a concern in both developed and developing economies. In developed countries, the problem is too much food and consequent obesity, and in developing countries, it is too little food and consequent malnutrition.

African consumers have important concerns related to the issues of food and nutrition insecurity. First, trade policies and practices are further compromising African food production and markets. Export subsidies in the North are distorting global markets and creating an unfair playing field for African farmers. Local production faces a lack of effective support, given the privatization of research and development, intellectual property rights regulations, constraints on subsidies and extension support to farmers, and the dismantling of strategic reserves. Protectionist food safety standards and other trade barriers are closing developed-country markets to African products. Food aid that is tied to certain policy conditions, not demand driven, not targeted, and not adapted to local consumption habits undermines local production capacity and markets. Vertical and horizontal integration and the concentration of food production and marketing in the hands of a few agribusinesses determines what types of seeds, chemicals, and technologies farmers will buy and what types of food consumers will buy and where they will buy them, thus reducing biodiversity, the variety of food products, and consumer choice. Food products are also priced inappropriately.

Second, agricultural policies and production models are not sustainable. To be sustainable, production models should be demand-led, site-specific, poverty-focused, cost-effective, and environmentally and institutionally sustainable.

We should put in place mechanisms for funding effective consumer representation in policy decisionmaking and standard setting.

– Amadou Kanouté

Third, models of consumption are exacerbating food insecurity. One manifestation of this is "The-bread-from-Dakar-is-better" syndrome. In addition, fast foods are growing in popularity. Foreign-based food products are heavily advertised, and consumers choose them over indigenous foods. Food aid is not culturally adapted. And dumping of food from world markets takes place in environments marked by poverty.

How can we address these consumer concerns? Consumers International is tackling poor nutrition at both the policy formulation level and the grassroots level. At the policy level, we are working with the Regional Codex Commission to set fair food standards in the Codex Alimentarius and lobbying for safety, labeling, traceability, and liability. We are involved in the campaign to fight sugar consumption and obesity with the World Health Organization. And we have worked to get a consumer protection clause included in the national PRSPs and in bilateral, regional (such as the Southern African Customs Union–United States of America Free Trade Agreement), and global trade agreements.

At the grassroots level we promote nutrition security by helping educate consumers and distributing information on, for instance, nutritional facts, informative labeling, street-vended food, and hygiene practices and by implementing pilot projects for access to water and sanitation by disadvantaged consumers. We support women's groups engaged in small-scale agricultural production schemes, like hydroponics nutritional gardens in Senegal.

Consumers International is also involved in fighting food insecurity at both policy and grassroots levels. At the level of policy dialogue, we research and advocate for sustainable and more appropriate agricultural models of production at national and global levels, as exemplified by NERICA. We lobby the main donor countries to break structures of food aid dependency. For example, Consumers International supported the Zambian government by lobbying the World Food Programme and the U.S. government and campaigning for respect from the major donor countries and institutions for the Zambian government's decision not to accept GM food aid but rather to support sustainable agricultural and rural development policies and approaches in the country.

We alert governments on the negative impacts of economic policies. In Malawi, for instance, trade in maize was liberalized and opened up to private traders, and there were plans to privatize the grain marketing board, ADMARC. During the period when ADMARC was restructured, it withdrew services from the rural areas. As a result, although maize farmers were selling their grain to private operators at market prices, when their stocks ran out they had to buy grain on the market at prevailing prices. This was creating a situation of food insecurity in the rural areas. ADMARC had previously played a key social function in the rural areas by buying grain from small-scale farmers at harvest and selling some of this stock back to farmers, at no profit, if farmers' stocks ran out. The Consumer Association of Malawi, in collaboration with other civil society organizations in Malawi, campaigned against the privatization of ADMARC, and the result was that the government decided to create a public limited company that would operate on a commercial basis but still ensure service and social delivery in the rural areas.

Finally, Consumers International lobbies and advocates for fairer trade rules at the global level, including protesting the developed countries' domestic agricultural supports and dumping practices, supporting nonrenewal of the so-called "peace clause," and promoting protections for small farmers.

At the grassroots level, we have started consumer buying clubs in Zimbabwe to spur competition and shorten the food chain for a fair and transparent marketplace. In addition, we offer consumer education.

What needs to be done for consumer concerns to be heard and addressed? First, it is important to facilitate and enhance policy dialogue on economic issues with civil society at both the national and the global levels for development of pro-poor policies. Second, we need to develop food safety standards that are more inclusive and more transparent and that are developed only with the aim of protecting consumer health, not for disguised protectionism. Third, we should put in place mechanisms for funding effective consumer representation in policy decisionmaking and standard setting. Fourth, we should implement the African Union Model Law on Safety in Biotechnology and the biosafety regulations as adopted at the latest meeting of the parties of the Cartagena Protocol. Fifth, we need to adopt a precautionary approach toward any new food technology until a reasonable level of safety and environmental sustainability is proven. Sixth, we should support and replicate wherever possible grassroots activities run by civil society organizations (CSOs) in food and nutrition to help promote the emergence of critical consumers and economic agents who have a say on policies formulated for them.

Robert Mwadime

Child Survival and Nutrition Advisor, Regional Center for Quality of Health Care, Republic of Uganda

Nutrition security refers to the ability of individuals (including unborn babies) to get access to the right mix of high-quality health care, care and support, and adequate food (in terms of quantity, mix of energy and nutrients, and timeliness) in order to live a healthy life to their full potential of development and with dignity. The three clusters of high-quality health care, care and support, and adequate food are essential for nutritional security. Loss of weight and failure to thrive are indications of failure in one or more of these clusters and therefore of nutrition insecurity.

In Africa, nutrition insecurity is almost universal among people with HIV/AIDS, although pregnant and lactating women and HIV-infected children who are orphans are most affected, as they have higher rates of chronic energy deficiency and micronutrient deficiencies. Nutritional insecurity among people with HIV/AIDS is due to many factors:

- HIV infection itself, which may alter metabolism or increase needs for energy and nutrients. The virus has a direct effect on key hormones needed for metabolism of nutrients, such as growth hormones, glucagons, insulin, and epinephrine. Higher levels of viral loads are associated with higher risk of decreased lean body mass, especially among children.
- Other underlying diseases, such as tuberculosis, pneumonia, diarrhea, and oral thrush.
- Inadequate macro- or micronutrient intake because of reduced food availability or oral disease (thrush); anorexia associated with illness but also due to depression and psychosocial effects; increased loss of nutrients due to diarrhea or malabsorption; the effect of the drugs commonly taken for HIV; or any combination of these.

Loss of weight, which diminishes the patient's functional capacity due to reduced body mass, is a strong predictor of survival and adversely affects quality of life.

Health sector interventions to address nutrition security can be grouped into those that aim to improve food security, care and support, and health care, and those that are basic level interventions. Research should guide the decision on which specific interventions to target as priorities. It will depend largely on the context, the stage of the disease, food availability, knowledge and attitude toward food, and sociocultural and stigma issues related to programming.

In implementing the interventions, it is important to understand the underlying context. The first step is to conduct formative research to identify what has been found to work in the context, what foods are eaten, and what the feeding patterns are; the nutritional status of different population groups; dietary intake levels; and demographic distribution of infection rates. Then it is useful to map the relationship between HIV/AIDS, food security, and nutrition. For example, who is food-insecure, where are they, and what are their characteristics? Next, there is a need to analyze the adequacy and effectiveness of existing systems (health, agricultural, education) and policies in providing high-quality services.

Other questions to ask are, What are the existing nutritional programs and their capacity to provide quality services? How much access does the general population, especially those with HIV infection, have to these programs? By whom, where, and under what criteria is antiretroviral therapy (ART) being used? What are the existing policies and guidelines that support food and nutrition initiatives, including prevention of mother-to-child transmission and infant feeding, ART policies, food and nutrition policies, and micronutrient policies? Who is involved in addressing the HIV/AIDS scourge in the localities (NGOs, AIDS support organizations [ASOs], donors, and governments), and is the government providing leadership? What are the local capacities to conceptualize and implement nutrition and HIV/AIDS interventions? Who holds any existing capacities? What are the priority areas of key stakeholders—what are they willing to invest in? This depends on what is politically, culturally, and technically appropriate. And what plans exist to integrate nutrition into HIV/AIDS management?

Nutrition security refers to the ability of individuals (including unborn babies) to get access to the right mix of high-quality health care, care and support, and adequate food in order to live a healthy life.

— Robert Mwadime

Implementation also requires creating and maintaining partnerships at all levels. We need to identify the key partners at the various levels and advocate to create buy-in and support of the process. It is important to use credible data and channels or people for the advocacy. There is a need to agree on the importance of and need to improve nutrition security as part of a comprehensive package of care for people living with HIV/AIDS. Clear roles among the partners must be defined, especially on leadership at the various levels (national, subnational, community, facility) and on resources. It is useful to encourage a spirit of complementarity. Partners should have same goal and undertake the activities they can do best rather than compete. Where possible, a technical working group should address issues of nutrition in HIV/AIDS.

It is crucial to have clear policies and guidelines or standards. Sometimes lack of policies or guidelines has been given as an excuse for not initiating programs on nutrition and HIV/AIDS. However, nutrition and HIV/AIDS guidelines should be harmonized with other policies and with activities of other sectors, should meet international standards, and should be credible among key stakeholders. The package of nutritional services to be provided needs to be defined. The package could include periodic growth and nutritional assessments, including dietary history; eating problems like chewing, swallowing, appetite, and intolerances and aversions; and supplementation. It could also include counseling on food and nutritional care for people living with HIV/AIDS and for children born to women infected with HIV. Key to this is demonstration for skill building and local initiatives to increase energy and micronutrient intake. Breast-feeding, a major source of "food" for young children, should always be viewed in relation to the child's nutrition and risk of mother-to-child transmission. If food is to be provided, policies and guidelines should define the purpose of food provision, the criteria for targeting services and distributing food—not everyone who is HIV-infected needs food—and which foods will be provided. Other nutritional services are food hygiene, sanitation, and use of public health services; prompt treatment of opportunistic infections and other illnesses and psychosocial care, whenever needed; and nutritional issues related to the use of ART.

Policies should clearly state the sources of funding and other resources for nutrition and HIV interventions and describe how their implementation will be monitored and evaluated.

It is not advisable to start separate nutrition activities, unless it is really necessary. Instead, they should be integrated with interventions operating at community, facility or program, and national levels. Access to high-quality health services is particularly important to ensure timely treatment of people living with HIV/AIDS and infants born to women infected with HIV. Examples of such services are oral rehydration solutions (ORSs) in the case of diarrhea, supplements, treatment of opportunistic infections and other infections like malaria, fever, and acute respiratory infections, diet advice and counseling, other primary health care like immunization and presumptive deworming each four to six months, vitamin A supplementation, hygiene, and sanitation. Links should be created between health units and community-based support systems, such as home-based care, community-based growth promotion and monitoring, community-based ASOs, and NGOs. This is essential in supporting families or family members with decisions on feeding, concerning, for instance, adhering to decisions on feeding infants less than six months old or diet modification for each individual such as in cases of oral thrush or nausea. It is important to integrate nutrition and food issues into treatment with ART to enhance its effectiveness and adherence. Nutrition should also be integrated into training guides and plans, into supervision checklists (update the supervisors on key issues in nutritional security for people with HIV/AIDS), and health management information systems (HMISs). Most HMISs do not cover nutrition and HIV/AIDS. They should be trained to administer ART, to carry out home-based care, and to provide palliative care on nutritional implications.

We also need to build the necessary capacities to address these new and evolving issues of nutrition and HIV/AIDS. Capacity is continuously needed at different levels. There should be a unit or department that is mandated to address nutrition in the management of HIV/AIDS, and the unit should be manned by persons who have skills and knowledge on the nutritional issues related to HIV/AIDS. In addition, service providers in the field and those joining the workforce need skills in nutrition and HIV, which they can acquire through either in-service or pre-service training. Curriculums need to be

It is essential to document promising practices in nutrition and HIV/AIDS at a programmatic level.

— Robert Mwadime

reviewed to include nutrition and HIV/AIDS, and this should be made practical by providing the necessary tools to facilitate learning and application.

The critical mass of staff at the national and grassroots levels should be trained. Where possible, mid-level staff should be trained through self-learning, on-site training, and use of job aids, wall charts, and fact sheets. A system of finding root causes of performance problems should be institutionalized, making sure that external support strengthens and does not undermine community initiatives and motivation. Model sites should be developed to handle problems, learn lessons, and provide training. Service providers need tools and materials to improve or assure their performance. Some of the tools include information, education, and communication materials like posters, brochures, and fact sheets for health workers; counseling tools like job aids, counseling cards, frequently asked questions (FAQs) sheets, and demonstration models; and learning and decisionmaking tools like protocols and guidelines, wall charts, and algorithms.

It is also important to evaluate the effectiveness of the strategies being suggested and to document and disseminate the lessons learned.

These actions raise several challenges. Service providers need to be able to make their messages clear and simple for HIV/AIDS-affected people and relevant to their context of limited financial and knowledge resources. Because many actors and many actions are involved, programs need to document and record the interventions they provide to people with HIV/AIDS. And it is essential to document promising practices in nutrition and HIV/AIDS at a programmatic level.

Ebrahim M. Samba

Regional Director, World Health Organization Regional Office for Africa, Republic of Congo

Malnutrition is one of the main and most frequent causes of morbidity and mortality among the poorest populations of the developing world. Food, health, and care are closely linked in determining the nutritional status of the populations. In most developing countries, malnutrition is a serious public health problem, owing to inadequate intake of protein, energy, and micronutrients, frequent infections, and disease. It affects 800 million people worldwide, killing, maiming, crippling, and blinding poor and vulnerable groups, and plays a major role in half of the 10.4 million annual child deaths. It is a cause and consequence of disease and disability in children. It is not only a medical problem, but also a social one, arising from and contributing to poverty. Malnutrition has economic ripple effects and compromises development. It is both a major cause and effect of poverty and underdevelopment.

The prevalence of iodine deficiency (goiter) is 10–40 percent, that of vitamin A deficiency among children under five is 25 percent, and that of iron deficiency anemia is 50 percent among children under five and 60 percent among pregnant women.

— Ebrahim M. Samba

In Africa, malnutrition is a serious public health problem. Children and women are the most affected groups. This situation is compounded by increasing chronic diseases due to overnutrition as well as by HIV/AIDS and emergency situations.

There is a high prevalence of low birth-weight, ranging from 11 to 52 percent. Protein energy malnutrition (PEM) is also severe. Among the children under five years old, the prevalence of stunting is 30–40 percent, the prevalence of wasting is 10 percent, and the prevalence of underweight is 30–40 percent. There are also serious micronutrient deficiencies. The prevalence of iodine deficiency (goiter) is 10–40 percent, that of vitamin A deficiency among children under five is 25 percent, and that of iron deficiency anemia is 50 percent among children under five and 60 percent among pregnant women. Other micronutrient deficiencies—beri-beri, pellagra, scurvy, rickets—occur mainly in emergency situations.

The burden of chronic diseases is rapidly increasing in Sub-Saharan Africa. For example, obesity, diabetes, cardiovascular diseases, and cancer contributed to 28 percent of morbidity and 35 percent of mortality in 1990.

The underlying causes of malnutrition are poverty; food insecurity; inadequate feeding habits and practices related to food quality, taboos, and food hygiene; infectious diseases and intestinal worms; HIV/AIDS; emergency situations; and vulnerability among particular groups such as orphans, disabled children, and aged people. Chronic diseases are related to overnutrition; increased intake of fats, sugar, and salt; lack of physical activity; rapid urbanization; and social and cultural beliefs.

The consequences of malnutrition are low birth-weight, growth retardation, brain damage, impact on the reproductive function and immune system, increases in morbidity and mortality, and impact on economic development.

In a normal situation, for prevention and control of nutritional problems, the following interventions must be formulated and implemented:

- nutrition assessment—suitable and sustainable interventions are designed after nutrition surveys are conducted to provide data for the planning;
- infant and young child feeding programs—exclusive breast-feeding during the first 6 months of age, pursuit of breastfeeding up to 24 months of age, and complementary feeding;
- management of severe malnutrition and micronutrient deficiency control—nutrition rehabilitation; medical and social care; supplementation of vitamin A, iron, and folate; promotion of consumption of iodized salt; diet diversification; and systematic deworming;
- nutritional surveillance system—continuous collection of data through existing services and activities;
- community empowerment, social mobilization, and advocacy;
- food security and food safety interventions;
- prevention and treatment of infectious and chronic diseases; and
- development of a national coordination and monitoring mechanism.

In the context of an emergency, nutritional interventions are as follows:

- rapid nutrition assessment;
- selective feeding programs—supplementary and therapeutic feeding programs, general food distribution, and mass feeding;
- prevention of micronutrient deficiencies—supplementation of vitamin A, iron, and folate; promotion of consumption of iodized salt; and systematic deworming of children;
- nutrition surveillance activities; and
- information, communication, and education.

At this stage, it is useful to start planning long-term interventions.

Finally, in a context of HIV/AIDS, nutrition interventions are as follows:

- prevention of mother-to-child transmission;
- nutritional care for infants, children, and adults;
- nutritional care for pregnant and lactating women;
- nutritional component in antiretroviral treatment;
- food-based approaches at individual, household, and community levels; and
- nutritional care for vulnerable children (orphans).

For a sustainable improvement of the nutritional situation in African countries, several steps need to be taken. These include developing and implementing national food and nutrition policies and plans of action; setting up integrated interventions for development through intersectoral collaboration with a suitable coordination mechanism; using a community-based approach with active community participation; training personnel for development and implementation of the interventions; and setting up a research program.

Flora Sibanda-Mulder

Senior Advisor, United Nations Children's Fund (UNICEF)–World Food Programme (WFP) Collaboration, Italy

Basic education is one of the most effective investments in improving economies and creating literate, self-reliant, and healthy societies. Yet more than 46 million children are out of school in Africa. They represent more than 40 percent of the world's out-of-school children. Girls are particularly at a disadvantage—more than 24 million of them are not in school. In April 2000, 164 countries participated in the World Education Forum in

In many African countries learning and school performance are compromised because of ill health, hunger, and undernutrition, which affect a significant proportion of school-age children.

— Flora Sibanda-Mulder

Dakar, Senegal, and adopted the Dakar Framework for Action to reaffirm their commitment to achieving education for all by the year 2015. But without a strong and concerted effort to reverse current trends, this goal will remain a dream for Africa.

The World Declaration on Education for All noted that poor health and nutrition are crucial underlying factors for low school enrollment, absenteeism, poor classroom performance, and early school dropout. In many African countries learning and school performance are compromised because of ill health, hunger, and undernutrition, which affect a significant proportion of school-age children.

In addition to the problems associated with malnutrition in school-age children, there is also evidence of negative consequences for children suffering from short-term hunger, common in children who are not fed before going to school. Children who are hungry are more likely to have difficulty concentrating and performing complex tasks, even if otherwise well nourished. Data from many studies on school breakfast programs suggest that omitting breakfast interferes with cognition and learning, an effect that is more pronounced in nutritionally at-risk children than in well-nourished children.

The WFP is the largest organizer of Food for Education (FFE) throughout the world. WFP provides food to schools in 70 countries, accounting for more than 15 million children in 2003. FFE includes a broad array of interventions designed to improve school enrollment, attendance, community-school linkages, and learning. Among possible FFE interventions are take-home rations targeted to girls, orphans, and other vulnerable children who attend school regularly, in-school meals or snacks to reduce short-term hunger along with associated cognitive impediments, and food-for-work targeted to teachers or parents engaged in activities to improve schooling outcomes. There is abundant evidence that such interventions can be effective in improving school enrollment, attendance, and children's active learning capacity.

Basic or primary school education is a prerequisite for nutrition and food security. Increases in literacy, numeracy, and education positively impact food security through increased productivity and employment enhancement, better resource management, higher incomes, smaller families, and improved household management. Educated individuals are more likely to access information and employ agricultural and environmental management techniques that contribute to increased production and greater food availability. Furthermore, individuals who receive a high-quality education are better able to earn a livelihood that provides the purchasing power to obtain nutritious food. Educated individuals are also more likely to practice safe food storage and preparation techniques and to practice basic principles of nutrition, health, and childcare. In the agricultural sector, studies show that four years of basic education significantly increase farm output. FFE aims at increasing enrollment and attendance and enabling children to complete basic education.

Children who are hungry are more likely to have difficulty concentrating and performing complex tasks, even if otherwise well nourished.

— Flora Sibanda-Mulder

FFE can have an impact on short-term household food security by improving access to food through an income transfer to families whose children attend school. FFE can be considered a direct transfer when girls, orphans, and vulnerable children receive take-home rations or an indirect transfer when children are fed at school. Income transfer is particularly important during the lean seasons just before harvests, when risk of food insecurity is particularly heightened.

Several strategies have been proven effective in successfully implementing food for education to improve nutrition and food security. From the outset of a project, planning discussions should identify anticipated benefits and develop an exit strategy that will maintain them, and such benefits, together with the strategy, should be monitored. An exit strategy should be developed in coordination with implementing partners, communities, and the relevant government authorities and should be based on six key components. These include setting of milestones for achievement; government commitment; community contributions; technical support; management and communication; and involvement of the private sector. For instance, WFP successfully phased out of Botswana and Namibia seven years ago, and the governments have continued their programs without WFP assistance.

UNICEF and WFP (through food for education) are giving priority to girls' education in order to reduce gender disparities in basic education by 2005. Needless to say, the promotion of girls' education is an important strategy for improving nutrition and food security because women play key roles in maintaining the three pillars of food security—food production, economic access to available food, and nutritional security. Millions of women work as farmers, farm workers, and natural resource managers. In doing so, they contribute to national agricultural output, maintenance of the environment, and family food security. Women account for 70 to 80 percent of household food production in Sub-Saharan Africa, 65 percent in Asia, and 45 percent in Latin America and the Caribbean.

Providing women with basic education would help improve nutrition and food security by increasing agricultural productivity and incomes, for better-educated farmers are more likely to adopt new technologies; ensuring that household members, particularly children, receive an adequate share of the food that is potentially available; and ensuring that food and other resources contribute to good nutrition.

The educational and nutritional value of an FFE program is thought to be enhanced if it provides a meal or snack early in the day and if it offers other school-based health and nutrition interventions in addition to food, such as multiple micronutrient supplementation and deworming. In consequence, WFP and UNICEF have been collaborating on an integrated package of health and nutrition interventions to accompany the FFE and improve the quality of education, nutrition, and health status of school children. Reduction of illness in this age group will also result in nutrition and food security. The integrated package includes support to basic education to improve the quality of education; food for education; deworming and micronutrient supplementation; provision of potable water and separate sanitary latrine facilities for boys and girls; health, nutrition, and hygiene education; HIV/AIDS awareness and prevention with life skills training; and malaria prevention. The effective implementation of these interventions requires a wider partnership with governments, NGOs, and communities and the participation of children themselves.

Collaboration with regional bodies such as NEPAD is critical to ensure governments' commitment and ownership and to promote sustainability. The NEPAD/Hunger Task Force Initiative aims at expanding school feeding programs to increase school enrollment while promoting increased local food production, marketing, and demand in rural food-insecure areas. NEPAD, in collaboration with the Hunger Task Force, WFP, UNICEF, and FAO, will guide the implementation of the initiative to link school feeding directly with agricultural development through the purchase of locally produced food, school gardens, and the incorporation of agriculture into school curricula. Interventions will also include support to small farmers to enable them to improve soil fertility, water management, and seed supply. Ten countries (Uganda, Mali, Senegal, Nigeria, Ghana, Malawi, Mozambique, Zambia, Kenya, and Ethiopia) have been selected for implementation.

Discussion

The chair of the session, Kabba Joiner, opened the session by highlighting the linkages between malnutrition and health insecurity and poverty. He sketched out a broad set of actions in the realm of health and nutrition that should be undertaken to foster development and poverty reduction, including promoting exclusive breast-feeding; instituting micronutrient supplementation and school feeding programs; assuring the food needs of at-risk individuals; and ensuring that all pregnant and lactating women are able to meet their nutritional requirements. He also noted the critical need for nutrition education—a need that will become increasingly important as poverty is reduced and increased incomes provide broader choices in food consumption. The chair cautioned that all of these efforts must be community-based to be

Owing to technical difficulties, the discussion in this session was not audio recorded. Certain elements of the discussion may inadvertently have been left out of this report.

Advocacy for nutrition was identified as a critical need throughout Africa.

sustainable. He concluded by noting that hunger and poverty are not immutable issues. Effective action to combat both scourges is possible and must be taken.

Much of the discussion centered on the need to heighten the visibility of nutrition issues and mainstream them into other development interventions. Participants noted the degree of attention paid to nutrition by the conference organizers, but expressed concern that the relatively small size of the audience for this health and nutrition session reflected the inability or unwillingness of African agriculturalists to consider how their work might promote nutrition security.

Advocacy for nutrition was identified as a critical need throughout Africa. It was noted that whether nutrition falls under health or agriculture is not important; what matters is that nutrition issues are addressed wherever they appear. Because nutrition interventions are critical to development and are very cost-effective, nutrition advocates were urged to not be shy.

Participants noted that how nutrition activities are carried out matters. There is a critical need for collaborative activity, particularly interagency collaboration, to address malnutrition. It was mentioned that the disorderly fragmentation of nutrition across sectors leads to problems of leadership, advocacy, and nutrition in broad policymaking. Since there are not many nutritionists in Africa, they need to make nutrition part of the activities of other sectors within a coordinated framework. This involves mainstreaming nutrition across all sectors. The need for cross-sectoral training in nutrition was emphasized, as human capacity remains an important constraint to nutrition security.

Participants recognized the important role of community participation in effectively addressing nutrition insecurity, mentioning that even illiterate people have knowledge that can be used to reduce malnutrition.

The discussion then shifted to other factors that affect health and nutrition, including population growth, water and sanitation, and agricultural research. Population growth issues were noted as having important nutritional corollaries. Pregnant women were described as the most susceptible of all adults to malnutrition, and child malnutrition and short child spacing were seen to play a role in this situation. Women need to be able to look after their own fertility if they are to assure their own nutritional security and that of those in their care. HIV/AIDS poses a particular problem of nutrition insecurity. The one exacerbates the other, with a vicious cycle of HIV infection and malnutrition resulting in hastened disease progression. Improved nutrition is fundamental to all four pillars of response to the HIV epidemic: prevention, care, treatment, and mitigation.

A participant also raised the point that good nutrition is impossible without good water and sanitation, which highlights the need for an integrated approach to the multiple determinants of nutrition security. Moreover, participants signaled the lack of attention in agricultural research for improved nutrition. It was mentioned that little had been said at the conference on this point. Breeders were urged to pay more attention to nutrition as they improve crops.

The moderator for the session, Tola Atinmo, summarized the discussion by listing four key issues: advocacy, intersectoral collaboration to address malnutrition, interagency collaboration, and capacity building. The chair closed the session by restating his earlier call for implementing a set of essential actions for health and nutrition continentwide and integrating such action at all levels, but particularly at the community level in a participatory mode. He noted that the tools are there to end malnutrition, and they have been there for decades. The chair emphasized the need to make use of what we know and put it into practice. Moreover, such effective nutrition interventions do not cost much. The chair concluded that we must always and at every opportunity engage in advocacy for the promotion of good nutrition.

Participants signaled the lack of attention in agricultural research for improved nutrition.

Excerpt 13: Improving Child Nutrition for Sustainable Poverty Reduction in Africa

Harold Alderman, Jere Behrman, and John Hoddinott

In Africa, as in other parts of the developing world, poor nutritional outcomes begin in utero. A number of maternal factors have been shown to be significant determinants of intrauterine growth retardation (IUGR), the characterization of newborns who do not attain their growth potential. Most important are the mother's height (reflecting her own nutritional status during childhood), her nutritional status prior to conception (as measured by her weight and micronutrient status), and her weight gain during pregnancy. Diarrheal disease, intestinal parasites, and respiratory infections may also lead to IUGR, and, where endemic, malaria is a major determinant as well.

A second vulnerable period is the first two years or so of life. Young children have high nutritional requirements, in part because they are growing so fast. Unfortunately, the diets commonly offered to young children in African countries to complement breast milk are of low quality—lacking variety and with low energy and nutrient density—and, as a result, multiple nutrient deficiencies are common. Young children are also very susceptible to infections because their immune systems fail to protect them adequately. Foods and liquids are often contaminated with bacteria and are thus key sources of infections. Infections both reduce appetite and increase metabolic demands. Furthermore, traditional African remedies for childhood infections, including withholding of foods and breast milk, are often suboptimal. Thus, infection and malnutrition reinforce each other.

A growing body of evidence indicates that growth lost in the early years is, at best, only partially regained during childhood and adolescence, particularly when children remain in poor environments. In Senegal, height at age three is strongly correlated with attained body size at adulthood. In Zimbabwe, children who were aged 12 to 24 months in the aftermath of the 1982–84 and 1994–95 droughts were, when assessed 6 to 18 years later, shorter than comparable peers not affected by these shocks. But the effects of malnutrition go beyond physical stature. Malnutrition, particularly severe malnutrition in early childhood, often leads to deficits in cognitive development. Malnourished children are found to score poorly on tests of cognitive function and have poorer psychomotor development and poorer fine motor skills. They tend to have lower activity levels, interact less with their environments, and fail to acquire skills at normal rates. Further, there is a growing body of evidence suggesting that undernutrition, particularly fetal undernutrition during critical periods, may result in permanent changes in body structure and metabolism that may lead to increased susceptibility to chronic noninfectious diseases later in life. Lastly, malnutrition may have long-term consequences due to the intergenerational transmission of poor nutrition and anthropometric status.

An additional contributing factor is micronutrient deficiency, particularly deficiencies in iodine, iron, and vitamin A. Approximately 42 percent of Africans of all ages are iodine deficient. Iodine deficiencies in utero and in the early years of life contribute significantly to increased risk of infant mortality and irreversible impairment of mental capacities. Vitamin A deficiencies contribute to increased infant and child mortality as well as increased prevalence of blindness. About 33 million African preschoolers—that is, one in three children—are deficient in vitamin A. Iron deficiencies lead to low birthweights as well as markedly affecting cognitive development. As with iodine deficiencies, the damage appears to be largely irreversible.

This has been excerpted from 2020 Africa Conference Brief 2, published by IFPRI, Washington, DC, 2004.

Chapter 16 Strengthening Governance

Chair: Bethuel A. Kiplagat
Executive Director, Africa Peace Forum, Kenya

Moderator: Charlotte McClain-Nhlapo
Commissioner, South African Human Rights Commission, South Africa

Rapporteur: Marc Cohen
Special Assistant to the Director General, International Food Policy Research Institute, USA

Tom Arnold

Chief Executive, Concern Worldwide, Ireland

The story of food in Africa over the past 30 to 40 years is by any standard depressing. It is particularly depressing when you compare it with the alternative story in Asia. The reasons these differences occurred are all very complex, but they can be reduced to a simple concept. Africa has been caught in a vicious circle over a number of years, where many things have interacted together to make the situation as it was. By contrast, Asia has created for itself a virtuous circle, where a number of things have gone correctly together.

The crucial elements of the vicious circle in Africa are conflict, governance, and in more recent decades HIV/AIDS. By contrast, the elements of the virtuous circle in Asia include stability, technology, infrastructure, and human capital.

The real task facing Africa is how to stop the downward spiral. If you can somehow cut that downward spiral and start on an upward trajectory, success will breed success.

Africa and African leaders are now realizing that unless substantial change happens, Africa is going to be completely marginalized from the world economy. To prevent that eventuality, substantial policy and political change must occur. The primary responsibility for that rests with African political leaders. I think those leaders, particularly through NEPAD, have begun to articulate a vision of how to go forward. With regard to NEPAD, however, there is a credibility issue. Fine words have been spoken and written down in the past couple of years. The rest of the world is watching: Are those fine words going to be delivered and put into action?

If African leaders have the primary responsibility, the outside world also clearly has responsibilities to help in this development crisis. This is where the significance of the MDGs comes into play. There is a compact here, and the responsibilities of the rich world involve commitments of financial resources and fairer trade arrangements. One of the Millennium Development Goals that is perhaps not as well known as others is Goal Number Eight, which talks about partnership. This means partnership at all levels, involving both government and nongovernmental actors. That framework is of crucial importance.

The MDGs can also help focus not just on what it is to be achieved, but on practical policies—the how-to's. If politics matter, in the shape of governments, so do policies. Policies can make a difference in whether you achieve the goals or not.

The crucial elements of the vicious circle in Africa are conflict, governance, and in more recent decades HIV/AIDS. By contrast, the elements of the virtuous circle in Asia include stability, technology, infrastructure, and human capital.

– Tom Arnold

There needs to be a sense of realism about the politics of agricultural subsidies in the rich countries.

– Tom Arnold

We have lessons to learn from policies that work and from policies that have failed. The Hunger Task Force, of which I am a member, is identifying what they call "entry points"—the short-term policy interventions they consider the most important. They acknowledge that other, longer-term actions must be taken, particularly dealing with education, the role of women, and other issues. But the Hunger Task Force is trying to say that there are priorities and sequences of policies that matter.

You can set policies and try to implement them, but ultimately this requires capacity. I believe strongly that at the moment there is an insufficient willingness to look at the capacity problems caused by the HIV/AIDS pandemic for the countries in this continent. The implications of this capacity issue must be examined much more systematically.

International NGOs, such as Concern, can have a foot both in the developing countries and obviously in their home base in the developed countries. But the role they can play, particularly in developing countries, clearly depends on the possibilities they have. The willingness of a government to enable and facilitate both its domestic civil society and its international NGOs is a crucial factor.

Assuming that that climate is reasonably healthful, what are the specific challenges that international NGOs face? One big challenge concerns how they create new forms of partnership with local NGOs and community-based groups. Moreover, if governments have responsibilities, international NGOs have responsibilities as well. They have to bring value. They have to bring innovation. They have to be catalysts of change and do things that otherwise would not happen. Concern, for example, has been working with other agents in a number of areas to find ways of combating chronic malnutrition.

Finally, I want to briefly touch on the role of NGOs in the North, particularly with regard to the question of agricultural subsidies. There is general agreement that agricultural subsidies are harmful to the developing countries. But the Hunger Task Force does not see the agricultural subsidy issue as an "entry point." In other words, in the short term, the agricultural subsidies, whether they stay or remain, are not going to be the crucial factor in the welfare of countries or of hungry people in poor countries. If they disappeared in the morning, it would not make a great deal of difference in the short term. The longer term is a different question.

There needs to be a sense of realism about the politics of agricultural subsidies in the rich countries, in both the European Union and the United States. You can do all the economic models you like about the impact of abolishing subsidies, but if the subsidies are not going to be abolished, it does not make a lot of difference. The alignment of the G-21 and the G-90 in Cancun was an important development. But the EU has reformed agricultural policy, and I do not see any appetite for further major reform. The US has at times talked about abolishing subsidies, but I see no evidence that the current or future administration will do so.

In practical terms, then, developing countries in Africa in particular need to be realistic about the time frame in which a change in the subsidy environment could occur and realize that dealing with their own food security needs is the crucial issue. Developing domestic and regional markets is essential. And in the longer term—in over a decade or so—they can begin to change the subsidy regime. In the meantime, the effects of those subsidies on poorer countries, and on the livelihoods of people in poorer countries, must be highlighted.

Overall, we may be at a moment where there is a possibility of real change. Political leadership is taking responsibility in Africa. If there is one symbol of hope at this conference, it is Norman Borlaug, who shows that if you try hard enough, change is possible.

Conference participants Graça Machel and Bethuel Kiplagat catch up in between sessions.

Meaza Ashenafi

Executive Director, Ethiopian Women Lawyers Association, Ethiopia

Within the broad issue of governance, I am going to focus on strengthening the judicial and legal mechanisms to enforce the right to food. I will highlight the international and national legal standards and consider if it is really possible to legally implement the right to food. I would also like to reiterate some of the concerns raised about the rights of women.

When we talk about legal standards, especially international legal standards, we usually refer to the Economic and Social Rights Convention that was adopted by the United Nations in 1966. This important convention talks about the right to food in Article 11. This convention has been elaborated by the committee established to monitor its implementation in General Comment Number 12 of the Economic and Social Rights Committee. In this general comment, food security is defined as availability of food and access to food in sufficient quantity and quality.

This convention talks about state obligation at three levels. The first level is *respect* for the right to food, which means, for example, not arbitrarily dispossessing farmers from their lands. The second level is *protection* for the right to food, which means protecting farmers from others who threaten their productive resources. And the third level is *fulfillment* of the right to food, which includes both facilitation and provision where necessary—for example, during emergencies and other humanitarian situations. This concept of facilitation is very important. It involves establishing sound policies and legislative frameworks, and holding governments accountable to the public for establishing good policies and laws.

There is also the issue of time frame in implementation. The General Comment Number 12 talks about progressive implementation. What do we mean by "progressive implementation"? It is always difficult, and sometimes controversial, to talk about implementation of economic and social rights, because they demand resources and require time. Nevertheless, General Comment Number 12 emphasizes that governments have to be held accountable and must adopt a time frame for implementation.

It also requires that governments be better able to deliver on food security because they are committed by international convention. And the General Comment highlights a hope for international cooperation.

In many of our national courts, it is not always possible to claim and demand the right to food and get a remedy.

— Meaza Ashenafi

This is a general framework and general standard. Justiciability in implementing this right becomes challenging. In many of our national courts, it is not always possible to claim and demand the right to food and get a remedy. For one thing, this is a new concept. The whole idea of implementing economic and social rights at the level of the court is only 10 years old. But some dynamic courts, like the Indian Supreme Court, are taking up these issues and creating awareness that this is a legal obligation. We all need to take up that example and agitate for the legal enforceability of the right to food.

I would like to highlight some of the challenges women face in accessing food security and nutrition security. Women as producers have critical roles in food security and agriculture in Africa, and this reality needs to be integrated systematically in whatever programs we plan. It has been noted that women represent 60 to 80 percent of producers in Africa. This includes production for household consumption as well as for sale. When it comes to nutrition, women eat last and least in most of our cultures, despite their nutritional needs as reproducers. The statistics related to maternal and child mortality are grim. Another challenge is violence against women, which really limits the potential of women. And the legal capacity of women to access land and to get titles or credit is another area of concern.

That being said, the importance of the participation of women is being recognized at the global and regional levels. For example, out of the eight Millennium Development Goals, four of the goals are focused on women. The goal of poverty reduction occurs within the framework of the feminization of poverty. Other goals are gender equality, reduced maternal mortality, and reduced infant mortality. So there is growing momentum supporting the idea that participation of women is critical for any program to be successful. Finally, the new African Union is also serious about the participation of women, for 50 percent of the commissioners in the new African Union are women.

When leadership changes, the legitimacy of the new group depends heavily on its capacity and political will to fight corruption.

— John Githongo

John Githongo

Permanent Secretary, Governance and Ethics, Government of the Republic of Kenya

As I speak on how to fight corruption in Africa, I shall draw on our own experience in Kenya and also the experience I gained across the African continent when I was at Transparency International for several years.

In Kenya we have condensed the fight against corruption into seven key areas for which we are implementing programs all at once. Our view is that we must do this to succeed in the fight against corruption, particularly in a context where corruption has become systemic. In many of our societies, petty corruption is not perceived as particularly wrong by ordinary people. They pay small bits of money, especially to junior civil servants, to facilitate transactions that are important in their lives, but they do not perceive that kind of corruption as being particularly wrong.

Moreover, in many of our societies, the political legitimacy of administrations has been undermined by corruption. When you conduct a poll of ordinary citizens, they will always list corruption in the ruling elite as one of the biggest problems. Therefore, when leadership changes, the legitimacy of the new group depends heavily on its capacity and political will to fight corruption.

The first and most important of the seven pillars in the fight against corruption, particularly where corruption has been systemic in the past, is leadership. It is often described as political will. This pillar recognizes the fact that in much of Africa, even though sometimes we do not say so directly, corruption starts at the top. It begins at the presidency and filters downward. Therefore, the will to fight corruption must start at the very top with the highest office in the land. The key anti-corruption institutions must be located as close as possible to the presidency.

The second pillar in the fight against corruption is the need for institutional change. In Kenya we are starting with the key governance institutions: the judiciary, the civil service, the legislature, and security services. Our priority has been to start with the judiciary. The judiciary guarantees the rule of law, which is absolutely essential to the fight against corruption and underpins all of the other issues we have been discussing at this conference. The judiciary sits at the apex of all the governance institutions. If the judiciary is corrupt, then you can forget about reforming any of the other institutions.

In terms of civil service reform, among the key institutions that affect food security across Africa are grain marketing and agricultural marketing boards as well as revenue collection agencies. If corruption affects the revenue collection agencies, particularly customs, then local farmers will have difficulties because goods are being dumped in the market, proper taxes are not being paid, and local farmers cannot compete on a level playing field.

The third pillar is legal reform that facilitates the institutional reforms that I have mentioned. In many African countries there is legislation creating anti-corruption agencies and legislation that facilitates the declaration of assets by public servants. But a range of these pieces of legislation is needed.

Where corruption has been systemic, land is often a key patronage resource and an instrument of corruption, especially by political leaders. Land tenure and security of land tenure can be affected by political decisions, so land is used to reward political favors and the like. When the security of land tenure is undermined, the poor are most affected, and this directly affects food security.

The fourth pillar is interaction with the private sector by an administration that is keen on fighting corruption. In Kenya the private sector is not very interested in attending conferences to discuss the fight against corruption. They much prefer a problem-solving approach, in which they bring problems to us and we solve them directly. They will come to us and say, "We have a problem at the port of Mombasa. There is a lot of corruption there. Can you please deal with it?" We have found this to be a very comfortable and useful relationship.

If the judiciary is corrupt, then you can forget about reforming any of the other institutions.

— John Githongo

We have also found it useful to work with the professions—the lawyers, the bankers, and the engineers, in particular. These professions—particularly the lawyers—are key to facilitating corruption. And, for example, clients' accounts across Africa are used in money laundering.

The fifth pillar is civil society and the media. The government must create an enabling environment for civil society and the media to fight corruption. The media in particular has an important role to play. Fifty percent of the war against corruption is perception, and the media is the number one mobilizer in this war.

The sixth pillar is the international community. In many of our countries, the interaction of our governments with the international community vis-á-vis governance has been reduced to conditionalities of the International Monetary Fund (IMF): You must pass this law to fight corruption; you must create this institution to fight corruption. It is important to move to a more interactive role. There are issues like mutual legal assistance, in which legal authorities in different jurisdictions cooperate to return assets.

The last pillar in our fight against corruption is dealing with past corruption in a systematic manner, especially when there is a transition of government. This task involves removing the worst abuses of past corruption from current institutions. For example, you can take all past land-related corruption and subject it to a land commission or a land tribunal. But if you do not remove the worst economic crimes of the past from the current institutions, they get bogged down there.

I want to mention two more issues. First, when a government embarks on the fight against corruption, corruption fights back. A new administration has a window of opportunity lasting no more than two years to completely disorient and break up corrupt networks.

Second, restitution is critical in the fight against corruption. Those who have been corrupt must be denied the enjoyment of what they have acquired corruptly. You must enact laws—money-laundering laws, asset forfeiture legislation—to take these assets out of the hands of those who have acquired them illegally. Otherwise, those resources are used to fight new administrations and to undermine democracy generally.

The challenge in decentralization is to answer: How do the poor and the powerless get their voices heard? How do their issues get into the policy debates?

— Yemi Michael Katerere

Yemi Michael Katerere

Assistant Director General, Center for International Forestry Research (CIFOR), Indonesia

What is the contribution of natural resources to the livelihood options that are available to people? People are trying to manage risk by spreading it. Forests are thus a critical resource for people's nutrition and livelihoods. Granted, there is increasing urbanization in Africa, but the majority of the population in Africa is still rural-based, and they are relying on forests, either directly or indirectly, for their livelihoods.

Forests contribute between 15 to 35 percent of household incomes in some countries. And 19 forest-rich countries in Africa derive at least 10 percent of their GDP from forests. At least 70 percent of the primary energy of rural and urban households is wood fuel. People need to cook their food. Where is that energy coming from? It is coming from the forest. So we must look at forests in terms of their contribution to the whole issue of nutrition.

If you ask rural people, "What is the value of a forest?" many will tell you it is land for agricultural expansion. There is a very complex interaction between agriculture, livestock, water, health, and the forests. Therefore, the forests are a key livelihood-supporting resource.

Where are we with forest governance? Many communities and households in Africa are already making decisions about how to manage forests and benefit from them, without central government involvement.

And many governments espouse the importance of decentralization. Many laws and policies granting some level of autonomy over forests to local authorities, communities, and other groups are already in place.

But this decentralization of responsibilities to local authorities raises some challenges. First is the issue of capacity for implementing decentralization. Often, the central government will declare, "We are now going to decentralize management of the forests to the district councils" or the communities. Sometimes the reason for this decentralization is political expediency: the government wants to be seen to be popular and to be decentralizing. Sometimes it is efficiency: they want to cut costs and avoid providing social services, so they decentralize and pass the costs on. Sometimes decentralization of forest management is demanded by local authorities because they also want to be seen to be driving the livelihood agenda and to be able to participate and to involve the local people. In any case, when there is not adequate capacity, what often happens is the decentralization of corruption. In the end, the people intended to benefit from decentralization of forest management actually become worse off.

The other challenge of forest governance and decentralization is the problem of multiple local authorities vying for influence in the same jurisdiction over the same forest resource. There is the central government agency, which is decentralized. There are the district authorities, who are elected. There are the party officials. Then there are the traditional authorities. And each one of these is vying to influence how these resources are allocated. In those circumstances, there is no accountability, and the result tends to be chaos. The communities get confused when conflicts arise, and conflicts invariably arise with forests, because forests have multiple uses and competing demands.

Decentralization is complicated by power and politics. Power and politics ultimately affect the ability of the poor and the powerless to develop appropriate livelihood strategies. Whereas the actions of the non-poor often are not taken into account in terms of demands on the resource, the poor and the powerless are seen as a problem in terms of forest degradation. And invariably, the poor and the powerless do not get to sit around the policy fire. So the challenge in decentralization is to answer: How do the poor and the powerless get their voices heard? How do their issues get into the policy debates?

The issues of equity, the issues of negotiation, the issues of real participation—not just being asked to participate in the project, but to really engage in a process through which people are able to demand their rights—all tend to be compromised.

So the world of governance is complex, uncertain, and very political. How do we deal with these issues of power and politics? I want to endorse the idea of a rights-based approach. The rights-based approach is underpinned by the concept of citizenship: not in the sense that you have a legal document that is given by the state, but in the sense that you are able to exercise your choice of with whom you want to associate, that you are empowered to demand your rights, and that you can operate in different platforms.

This does not mean that we have "win-win" solutions. There will always be winners, and there will always be losers. The important thing is for the losers to know why they lost and what they need to do in future negotiations.

We also need to invest in capacity building. The absence of capacity should not be an excuse for not decentralizing. In fact, we need to invest in capacity building just so we can devolve more decisionmaking to local authorities.

Rights over forests must be secure. If rights over forest resources can be withdrawn willy-nilly, then people respond by maximizing short-term gains. In other words, you have deforestation, because people know they are not going to be around for a long time, so they grab what they can and move on.

And we need to simplify the laws and regulations so that they are clear. In many countries agricultural laws give people incentives to go and cut forests, rewarding them with a certain amount of payment for every hectare of forest land cleared. At the same time, forestry laws say that it is illegal to clear-cut the forests. But it is not clear which law has precedent over the other. And it is not enough to simply clarify the relationship between the different laws, but we also need to be able to enforce these laws.

Finally, focusing on the issue of governance presents a risk. Fifteen years ago sustainable development was a radical concept. Today, sustainable development has lost its edge. I tried to count how many times the word "sustainable" or "sustainably" was used in the plenary session, and I lost count. We have to be careful that governance does not go the same way: that eventually "governance" means everything to everybody, and every time we meet we just talk about governance and governance and governance.

Farmers' organizations can also be a force for peace and stability.

— David King

David King

Secretary General, International Federation of Agricultural Producers, (IFAP), France

Discussions of governance usually get stuck on the topics of human rights and corruption. These issues are important for farmers, but we need to broaden this discussion to talk about participatory processes to build political will for achieving food security.

The International Federation of Agricultural Producers (IFAP) is made up of 100 national farmers' organizations globally. We are essentially a policy platform for farmers to get their voices into the international institutions. We feel very strongly that good governance should involve setting up consultative processes that ensure that development projects and programs reflect national priorities rather than the priorities of donors or personal interests. You do that by involving the farmers' organizations. Consultative processes also provide a sound basis for combining the energies of all actors and hence achieving a sustainable path for development.

I do not have to make the case here for people-centered development, but I would like to say that this approach should not be just an add-on. Mobilizing the strengths of civil society and involving them as partners in development efforts should be a cornerstone of implementing strategies for better governance for achieving nutrition and food security.

Unless development efforts are focused on people and their organizations, the poor will remain powerless politically and disadvantaged economically. So farmers' organizations have to participate. But they also have to be strong enough to participate in a meaningful way.

A lot of our members are called to participate in PRSP processes. But time and again two forms of bad participation arise. One is what I call "false participation." This occurs when you have well-educated government people and industry people in a meeting, and then the farmer comes along. He has no idea what the agenda is, and he is sitting there trying not to look too silly. That is false participation.

You have to build capacity in the farmers' organizations so the participation is meaningful. It is not very difficult. Every ministry that I know has policy and planning units. The minister should say to the director of each unit, "You meet with the farmers before our big consultation." Then the farmers can ask the basic questions that they would be too shy to ask in front of the minister, and that will help them understand what is going on. This is a duty of government if it is serious about participation.

Group structures like farmers' organizations and farmer cooperatives can be a force for social cohesion and empowerment and so contribute to political stability.

— David King

The second form of bad participation is called "window dressing participation." Some of our members are quite strong. They actually participate with governments and even agree on a negotiated program. Then what happens? The program goes up for approval, and when it comes back it does not look anything like the program they thought they had negotiated with government. This is window dressing. Government officials meet with the farmers because they think they should, but they do not pay any attention to what the farmers say. It is critical that we be strong enough to blow the whistle on this kind of bad governance.

We need strong farmers' organizations for several other reasons. They are valuable partners for governments because they reach down to the grassroots. Their job is to serve their members. The World Bank has often said to us, "How do you reach the poor? How do you get to these people?" And I say, "Well, if a farmer organization is working properly, they are its members. It should be finding out what their needs are and helping them."

Farmers' organizations can also be a force for peace and stability. A pure market system excludes the weak and inefficient, and the strong survive. That is how it is supposed to work. It is like natural selection—economic Darwinism. But this system has a very high social cost. In Africa, where 60 percent of the population is made up of young people, many of them unemployed, this is a totally unacceptable situation. Group structures like farmers' organizations and farmer cooperatives can be a force for social cohesion and empowerment and so contribute to political stability.

In regions of conflict, we have found dialogue between farmers' organizations much easier than dialogue between governments. IFAP has held meetings of Turkish and Greek farmers in the buffer zone of Cyprus, and they behaved like brothers to each other. IFAP has had meetings in Jerusalem with farmers from Israel and all the Arab countries—although we could not do it now—and it worked very well.

I also want to say something about governance as it applies to donors and international organizations. It is good governance to have donor cooperation. This requires more than just coordination of efforts. It requires donor coordination around programs developed by the African leaders themselves. It is not helpful when donors come into countries with their own programs and interfere with the efforts of local people. That is bad governance. All too often donors come in and give policy advice on market and trade reform to governments. You have 600 million people in Africa. Four hundred and fifty million are peasant farmers who do not know what a market is; they have never been to one. They are working with hand tools, have no money to buy fertilizer, and have no roads. Why do they want advice on market reform?

As a federation of farmers, we believe much more emphasis should be placed on the production of local crops from local resources to improve the nutrition of the local population. Only 10 percent of food is traded in the world, yet it gets 90 percent of the attention. We need to focus more on adding value to local resources.

To conclude, better governance is a necessary condition for achieving nutrition and food security goals in Africa. But this must include, in addition to human rights, setting out meaningful consultative processes that combine the strengths of governments, private sector, and civil society, particularly the farmers' organizations, in achieving food and nutrition security.

Norah Owaraga

Executive Secretary, Uganda Change Agent Association, Republic of Uganda

The premise of my presentation is that the government is not the giver of rights to the people. It is the people who are the source of the government's legitimacy. That is a liberal view, but as Africans we need to start moving closer to that.

The people at the grassroots in Africa do not believe that they are the source of the government's legitimacy. They are suffering from spiritual poverty, sustained by a psychological feeling of inferiority, that does not allow them to participate fully in the governance of Africa. And those in government and leadership in general in Africa do not believe that the source of their legitimacy is the people or that they are answerable to the people of Africa. By "leaders in general," I mean all of us: extension workers, members of parliament, NGO staff, anybody in a leadership position. We govern with an attitude of superiority that encourages us to believe that we are doing the people at the grassroots a favor.

How do we strengthen good governance at the grassroots level? We need to raise the consciousness of the people at the grassroots. They need to look inward to establish why they have a psychological feeling of inferiority, to grapple realistically with their problems, to attempt to find solutions to their problems, to develop a conscious awareness and physical awareness of their situation, and to analyze their situation and provide themselves with answers. This is the work of the Uganda Change Agent Association (UCAA).

At UCAA, we believe the foundation of all development is human development. Unfortunately, this sector is neglected in Africa. I am told that the rebuilding of Europe after World War II was successful because the human resources were there. When the Europeans were given development assistance, they had the human capacity to manage that assistance.

In Africa, it is different. The aid is given to us not to utilize the way we would like, but with the technical people who tell us how to utilize it. In Uganda, and in Africa in general, we need to focus on the grassroots first. People have complained that we do not have tractors, we do not have technologies, we do not have large infrastructure. But if we have that infrastructure and do not have a sophisticated human base, we are wasting our time.

Unfortunately, most of the development aid has gone to the roof, without looking at the foundation. We have invested a lot in ensuring social development, without realizing that social development can be sustained only if we have good political development and solid economic development. And those two pillars can be sustained only if the people are empowered.

At UCAA, we are running a capacity-building, change agent training program intended to provide the people at the grassroots with the knowledge and skills to be able to engage productively in their development work.

The government is not the giver of rights to the people. It is the people who are the source of the government's legitimacy.

— Norah Owaraga

When UCAA enters a community, we recognize that we are not the only ones there. We go directly to the community and find self-help groups. From those self-help groups, we find the leaders—who are mostly, of course, peasant farmers—and bring them to a training center, where we provide them with our change agent training. I will not go into the details of the change agent training. If you would like to know more, you can go to www.ucaa.or.ug.

The other way we get into the community is by partnering with other development organizations, including the government. We are collaborating with the government's Household Agriculture Support Program to provide training to farmers. They have realized that even if you provide modern equipment, if the farmers do not understand how to do basics like recordkeeping, that equipment will eventually be like the tractors that were described earlier.

The change agents we train are expected to go back to their communities and help the self-help groups to which they belong go through a process of consciousness raising as well. Then, if there are groups working in a similar field, they are expected to federate and form associations.

People mention farmers' associations as a possible solution. It is my conviction that the cooperatives in Uganda were not very successful because they tended to be top-down instead of bottom-up. The cooperatives' leaders would present balance sheets in English with complicated terminology, and the farmers did not understand what was happening. That is the source of corruption. It is difficult to prosecute because it is difficult for us to even detect the corruption.

To show the success of this methodology, I will give an example of one of our change agents. Paineto is a farmer now living in the Bukonzo area in the Rwenzori Mountains, the Mountains of the Moon. He is 39 years of age and married with five children. Before he took change agent training, he was a pauper living in Kasese Town. In a story typical of most Ugandan rural men and women, he did not have enough school fees to continue with his education and he stopped at Senior IV, higher level.

We trained him in 1991. After he received his training, he realized that it is better not to hang around the town and live in such deplorable conditions, but to go back to his rural area and start from there. He went back and began working on other farmers' land. Although he was very poor, he also began voluntarily working with 15 groups in his subcounty. He was covering a total of 300 men and women as a volunteer.

Among our biggest challenges in Africa are illiteracy and development "AIDS," which is aid-induced dependency thinking.

— Norah Owaraga

In 1994 he stimulated the formation of a Bukonzo East Branch of the Uganda Change Agent Association.

By 1997 he had accumulated enough savings and bought himself approximately 10 acres of land. He was able to build himself a three-room house up in the mountains. And he led the change agents of Bukonzo East in conceiving a plan to build an office building. There were 14 change agents, and each one bought a share. They also mobilized the groups with which they were working, and those groups bought shares. They completed their office building in 2001 without any external assistance. In 1991 he also convinced the local councils that change agent training was good for them and that they would benefit from the same process of consciousness raising. They contributed the money for training, and he then was among the facilitators. In 2001 we were very proud that he was among 12 Kenyans and a Tanzanian who were the first recipients of the East African Community Service Award.

Early this year Paineto came by the office. I said, "Paineto, I'm very busy." He said, "No, no, Norah. I don't want assistance from you. I want you to lend me one of the drivers so that I can go and buy myself a car." He purchased a station wagon for transporting his eggs, milk, and pineapples to the markets of Kasese Town. He is also assisting other farmers, of course, by hiring out his vehicle for them to transport their produce.

Paineto is now working with 23 well-organized groups who have shares amounting to 7 million Uganda shillings and savings amounting to 20 million Uganda shillings that they generated on their own.

I also want to read a quotation from one of our change agents who competed successfully in getting into the political system. Beatrice Ventice Ogony is now the woman representative, local council five, in Lira District. She says: "I had been looking at women councilors, but they would never come back to consult with the grassroots. When I realized that I had the knowledge of how to work with the grassroots people, I said, 'Let me try my luck.' Before training as a change agent, I looked at the LCV post as a no-go area. I thought that that was a post for very educated people, so how could a person like me with an advanced level certificate stand for that post? Change agent training helped me to attain self-confidence to reach out to the people, especially since they had taught us how to approach people. During the campaigns, I was just insisting on what I was coming to do. There were three of us, but I won."

Among our biggest challenges in Africa, and also for the change agent training program, are illiteracy and development "AIDS," which is aid-induced dependency thinking.

I am convinced that the only way we can assure food security in Africa is to stimulate processes of consciousness raising, not only at the grassroots level, but also for us as leaders.

Discussion

Session moderator, Charlotte McClain-Nhlapo, opened the discussion by reminding participants that good governance is a cornerstone of democracy. It entails a legal framework and elimination of inequalities. A human rights–based approach to dealing with food insecurity needs to be extended to all vulnerable people to ensure that nobody falls through the cracks.

Participants agreed that good governance needs to take place at all levels, and much of the discussion focused on the need for effective public participation to ensure government accountability. There was agreement that a vibrant civil society is crucial, that the current capacities of civil society organizations need to be realistically assessed, and that systematic approaches are needed to build the capacity of these organizations to be effective in consultative and participatory processes. A variety of actors needs to be brought in to ensure that all stakeholders are part of this social mobilization.

Participants expressed concern about the extent to which people in Africa, particularly rural people, know their rights, roles, and responsibilities in putting in place good governments and know what services to expect from governments. They called for educating people on their rights and building people's capacity to exercise their rights. It was noted that people get the kind of government they deserve, and if they want to change things, they will change them. It is up to the people to monitor the government, and they can do this through civil society organizations. Participants also discussed issues surrounding centralization of power and noted the long terms of many African leaders. Participants called for people to question governments because they put the governments into power. The need for accountability was stressed repeatedly.

Some discussion focused on the need for good governance within farmers' organizations and other civil society organizations, with some participants saying these organizations need to be more transparent, particularly in their financial management, and others pointing out that these organizations often reflect the society in which they operate. Farmers need greater capacity to hold organizations accountable. One participant pointed out that many African farmers are so poor they cannot even organize themselves to create farmers' organizations. Farmers' organizations need to be empowered so that they can become strong enough to lobby for good policies. Some participants remarked that in order to be effective, it is important for farmers' organizations to be independent of government.

Another hot topic was political will. Participants called for more attention to the problem of how to create political will to reduce hunger. Pressure from donors or from NGOs, farmers' organizations, lawyers' associations, and other civil society organizations can help build political will. A participant remarked that lobbying groups can sway governments more than consumers or farmers can, but corporate political will is different from public political will. Freedom of speech and freedom of press are critical in enabling the public to be better informed and in turn to communicate their concerns to policymakers. A participant noted that decentralization can improve local political will; in Thailand,

Concern was expressed that too much hope is being pinned on NEPAD as a way out of Africa's vicious cycle.

Charlotte McClain-Nhlapo moderates a lively discussion in the session on strengthening governance.

for example, malnutrition was reduced dramatically over 10 years through local ownership and community-based efforts for food security. With regard to sustaining political will, panelist John Githongo noted that political will is often high at the beginning of an administration when office holders have just been elected to power and want to fight corruption. After about 24 months, however, other priorities begin to take precedence. Therefore political will must be sustained in an active and aggressive way, and this effort is partly dependent on the integrity and accountability of the institutions that are created. Panelist Tom Arnold added that reports on how governments are working to achieve the Millennium Development Goals may be an important tool to help civil society actors demand accountability from their governments.

Anti-corruption measures were extensively discussed. Asked to what extent African countries were following the Kenyan example, Githongo responded that various elements of Kenya's strategy for anti-corruption can be found in different African countries. Since the late 1990s corruption has become a key part of the reform agenda of most African countries. A range of countries have implemented anti-corruption legislation, creating anti-corruption agencies. Eight countries require public servants to periodically declare their wealth, and these declarations are subject to scrutiny at various levels. Countries such as Angola, Congo, Kenya, Nigeria, and Zambia have put in place programs to try to recover assets that have been corruptly acquired and moved to different jurisdictions. African governments have been reasonably successful in making their development partners aware of the processes of fighting corruption.

Although prosecution is the most exciting approach to corruption, and new governments often wish to see big names associated with corruption taken to court, Githongo warned that prosecution is the bluntest instrument one can use against corruption. Because those who have been corrupt often have significant resources and better-paid lawyers than those of the government, they are able to keep the government in court for long periods of time. Githongo highlighted the importance of public awareness to change cultural attitudes toward corruption.

Another aspect of cultural change was noted by participants. In many countries where there has been a transition, particularly a violent one, corruption has often been seen as a way of getting at an unpopular regime, but the public's reluctance to expose corruption often extends past the transition period. This culture of keeping quiet needs to be addressed. NGOs, for instance, could provide support to people who would otherwise not come forward to expose these practices.

Another problem is the danger of relaxation once transition has happened. A participant expressed concern about whether activists, who once struggled for change, have become complacent and lost their values and understanding of the issues when they came into political power and occupied government offices. Another participant remarked that when many activists join government, it weakens civil society and sometimes media for a while. Once transition has taken place, it is important to nurture new leadership in these important sectors.

The potential for NEPAD to promote good governance in Africa was explored. Concern was expressed that too much hope is being pinned on NEPAD as a way out of Africa's vicious cycle and that many governments are treating NEPAD as something foreign being imposed on them. Concern was also expressed that NEPAD focuses too much on governments and not sufficiently on civil society organizations. Participants stressed the importance of including civil society in the NEPAD process, noting that if NEPAD is to be successful, a strong social movement needs to be built to ensure that the vision is implemented. The NEPAD peer review mechanism was mentioned, and participants were urged to familiarize themselves with it and to take it seriously.

Several people identified women's participation as a key factor in good governance. However, concern was expressed about "token" participation. There was agreement that when women and youth are brought into various sectors, they must be empowered so that they can have input in decisionmaking at all levels.

The central issue of land tenure and its relationship to politics and governance in Africa also received comment. Noting that insecurities around land often lead to exploitation and abuse of human rights, particularly of vulnerable groups, participants urged governments to create stable legislative frameworks in which people can secure their ownership or use of land and thereby pave the way for development. Moreover, given that politicians often use land as a political reward, bringing about the necessary changes has not only technical and legal dimensions, but also political ones.

The need to enforce legal frameworks was raised, particularly in the context of incorporating international agreements into domestic legislation. Until there is a culture of enacting laws that governments are committed to enforce, a participant explained, good governance cannot be realized. The lack of a vibrant civil society, strong media, and strong and independent judiciary hinders the implementation of international conventions and human rights charters at the national level. Another participant commented that in many cases, laws passed are actually not that good. Moreover, if laws have little political buy-in, they will be difficult to implement. It was also agreed that democratic systems, in which people are involved from the onset in developing legislation, are needed to facilitate political buy-in, rather than involving civil society only at the end.

Participants discussed the value of the voluntary guidelines on the right to food being developed by the intergovernmental working group resulting from the World Food Summit: five years later. The guidelines are little known in African countries, indicative of the limited trickle-down effects to Africa from global organizations such as the United Nations.

Issues surrounding conflict were highlighted during the discussion. Noting that 1.5 million people in Uganda are internally displaced and living in camps, one participant stated that an important task of governance is to protect people so they can stay in their homes and pursue their livelihood strategies, and not become displaced. Another pointed out that donor funds flowing into local communities can make local governments less accountable to the people they are serving. For instance, food aid can allow governments to avoid policy reform and to fail to promote agriculture in their own country or look for food security on their own. Participants asked why governments fail to protect their people, who is benefiting from the wars in Africa, and who is instigating these wars. Global proliferation of small arms was noted as a key factor in perpetuating conflict. Another participant added that conflict skims off the most vibrant section of society—the young people—and sends them off to war.

Other issues touched upon during the discussion included the need for an enabling environment, the role of parliamentarians in ensuring accountability, the institutionalization and perpetuation of colonial-era policies that make it difficult for rural communities and people to articulate their positions on issues of interest without ethnic considerations, and the need for African governments to continually engage and be frank with the international community and development partners on issues of governance.

The session also placed a great deal of emphasis on the rights-based approach to development as a way to foster empowerment of poor people, as well as on the importance of organizations that poor people can truly call their own.

Until there is a culture of enacting laws that governments are committed to enforce, good governance cannot be realized.

Excerpt 14: Implementing a Human Rights Approach to Food Security

Charlotte McClain-Nhlapo

The concept of the right to food is not new. The right to food has been formally recognized since the adoption of the United Nations Universal Declaration of Human Rights in 1948.

A commitment to the right to food was articulated in the International Code of Conduct on the Human Right to Adequate Food, initially proposed before the World Food Summit. The International Code of Conduct was pioneered by concerned nongovernmental organizations (NGOs). In essence, the proposal introduced a rights-based approach to food security. This concept has evolved to the point where states are developing voluntary guidelines for the progressive realization of the right to adequate food, including consideration of state obligations. To facilitate this process, an intergovernmental working group was established by FAO.

A further recommitment to the right to adequate food came in 1999 from the United Nations Committee on Economic, Social, and Cultural Rights, in the text of the International Covenant on Economic, Social, and Cultural Rights (hereafter, the International Covenant). An authoritative statement, General Comment 12, seeks to clarify the substance of the right to adequate food, stating that the right is realized "when every man, woman, and child, alone or in community with others, [has] physical and economic access at all times to adequate food or means for its procurement." This implies the "availability of food in a quantity and [of a] quality sufficient to satisfy the dietary needs of individuals, free from adverse substances, and acceptable within a given culture" and the "accessibility of such food in ways that are sustainable and that do not interfere with the enjoyment of other human rights."

The General Comment further identifies three types of obligations emanating from the International Covenant: like other economic and social rights, the right to adequate food confers an obligation on states to respect, protect, and fulfill that right. This means that states should not adopt measures that could ultimately prevent access to adequate food, that they should adopt measures to ensure that no individuals are deprived of their access to adequate food, and that they should proactively engage in activities to strengthen people's access to and use of resources, including means to ensure their livelihood and food security. This last obligation can be met through policies and programs—such as microcredit, incentives to the private sector to create jobs, and effective implementation of labor laws and agrarian reform—that create economic opportunities for those who are vulnerable and food insecure.

Whenever an individual or group is unable, for reasons beyond their control, to obtain adequate food through the means at their disposal, states have the obligation to fulfill that right directly. Importantly, this obligation also applies to persons who are victims of natural or other disasters.

It is worth noting that more than 40 countries already have the right to food entrenched in their constitutions, and FAO estimates that rights related to food are justiciable, or likely to be justiciable—meaning that courts can enforce the right—in a total of 54. Very few countries, however, have elaborated the constitutional provisions into domestic legislation as required by the International Covenant.

Good governance is essential in the realization of all human rights, including eliminating poverty and ensuring a satisfactory livelihood for all. The development of legislation is important, but it must be supported by implementation strategies.

This has been excerpted from 2020 Africa Conference Brief 13, published by IFPRI, Washington, DC, 2004.

Chapter 17 Plenary Panel Discussion on Implementing Action in Key Areas

Chair: Harris Mule
Executive Director, Top Investment and Management Services, and former Permanent Secretary in the Ministry of Finance and Planning, Kenya

During his keynote address, President Wade of Senegal underlined poor implementation of both policies and programs as a key constraint to agricultural development in Africa. Indeed, the African landscape, at the continental, subregional, national, and subnational levels, is replete with declarations, blueprints, programs, and projects that have never been implemented. The causes for these failures are many and varied, and they include lack of ownership, inadequate incentives, program and process design that do not adequately take into account implementation constraints, and inadequate capacities, both human and institutional.

This morning's plenary session and the ensuing parallel sessions have addressed the issues regarding implementation in depth. We need to answer the following questions, among others: Why is the implementation record in Africa so poor? What are the key challenges and constraints to implementation of agricultural policies and programs in Africa? What are the technical, institutional, and political solutions to the implementation constraints? And what is the way forward? What are the priority actions in terms of implementation feasibility?

The parallel sessions addressed some of these questions. They did so from different perspectives. Some of the parallel sessions put more emphasis on privatization and others on ownership; some focused on capacity and others on governance and other issues. The panel chairs will now present the outcomes of their deliberations.

Monty Jones
Executive Secretary, Forum for Agricultural Research in Africa (FARA), Ghana

In the session titled "Raising Agricultural Productivity," our group discussed increasing agricultural productivity in Africa by 2015 or 2020, and we looked at the actions that would allow us to do so. The group recognized that agricultural productivity has been declining in this region for the past two to three decades and that it is going to be a daunting task to reverse this trend during the period we are talking about. A number of participants, however, are optimistic that by taking the right actions and putting the right structure in place to get all of us to function as a team, we should be able to reverse this trend so that we come in line with other regions of the world.

The first action we identified is the development of dynamic and efficient output markets for Africa. We were very conscious of the fact that if we encourage the farmers to produce excess, they should be able to sell their goods in the market. We will need to create a system whereby the farmgate price is higher than the

We should inform farmers themselves about the products of research, not at the end but from the onset, so that the farmers themselves play a role in considering the problems, developing the protocol, and eventually implementing the protocol.

– Monty Jones

cost of production and serves as an incentive to the farmers. In developing output markets, we must also address product quality issues so that they can easily be sold in the market. These issues are related to product grading and improving product safety and quality.

The second action we discussed is the development of reliable and efficient input markets. We recognize that too often inputs—fertilizers, insecticides, and so on—do not get to the farm gate. And even when they get to the farm gate, they are often unaffordable for the majority of African farmers—the peasant farmers. We need to create an efficient and reliable input market system that will bring these inputs to the farm gate at lower transaction costs.

The third action we mentioned is the need to strengthen policy issues. We need to develop policies that will be favorable not just to the peasant farmers, but also to the researchers and all the major stakeholders, so that we can function efficiently and effectively. This will help to sustain agricultural development activities in the region. We also need reliable and consistent policies that favor exportation of our products and that address grading, health, and safety issues.

The fourth action we discussed is the development of appropriate technologies. We recognize that Africa is endowed with rich natural resources, but they are being degraded. This is reflected in water pollution, genetic erosion, deforestation, and soil degradation. Solving these problems is crucial for sustainable agricultural activities. To achieve this, we should inform farmers themselves about the products of research, not at the end but from the onset, so that the farmers themselves play a role in considering the problems, developing the protocol, and eventually implementing the protocol. It is important that farmers speak in their own voice and guide us in whatever technologies we develop. We should also consider the impact of new technologies on labor and farmers' capacity and work to build farmers' capacity as well.

On the development of appropriate technologies, we also talked about the potential for biotechnology. We acknowledged that the Green Revolution bypassed Africa and that we should not allow these new biotechnology tools to also bypass Africa. We are not just referring to GMOs. NERICA was developed from tissue culture. The TC banana was developed from a tissue culture process. These are modest biotechnology tools. But for problems that can be solved only through GMOs, we do not see why Africa should not adopt this important technology that will enable us to increase agricultural productivity.

We should also use modern technology to restore natural resources. We recognize that the issue of soil degradation is very important, and we have to reverse that trend. We should invest in soil fertility, exploring all possibilities, including both mineral and organic fertilizers, as well as agroforestry, conservation, tillage, and other practices. The central goal should be soil management rather than just fertilizer management.

It is important that farmers speak in their own voice and guide us in whatever technologies we develop.

— Monty Jones

There are lots of financial problems. We know that the resources are not enough to undertake meaningful research in our national programs, and we should explore ways of bringing in additional funding that will support all the stakeholders in agricultural research and development and eventually result in increased productivity. NEPAD has made an effort in this regard through the creation of the Comprehensive Africa Agricultural Development Programme, which emphasizes agriculture as the engine for economic growth in Africa. And NEPAD and other entities like FARA are putting together packages to bring in additional funding for agricultural activities in Africa.

We should also provide incentives to innovative farmers so they continue to play a leadership role in their communities. We should invest in irrigation systems—not the large-scale irrigation systems that exist in the West, but irrigation systems that suit the level of our farmers. They could be partial irrigation systems that offer very good water control and that farmers can relate to and manage.

We should also strengthen linkages between the IARCs and the NARSs, allowing for programmatic integration at the subregional and regional levels. Responsibilities should be assigned based on comparative advantage for the benefit of all the major stakeholders.

With regard to the international community, and donors in particular, we should request that they provide not only food aid but also fertilizer aid and that they reform international trade policies and relieve us of some of our debts.

Then we should strengthen local demand through school feeding programs, address farm energy constraints, and promote empowerment of women and youth. These two categories of people spend a lot of their time on the farm, so we should give them the opportunity to voice their views and to participate in the development of technologies that will enable them to function efficiently. We should promote farmers' organizations so that farmers can speak with a strong voice when they participate and come up to speed with researchers, extension workers, and other stakeholders.

Benno Ndulu
Research Manager, Development Economics Research Department, World Bank, USA

Two starting points were clear in our session, "Fostering Economic Growth and Improving Markets and Trade." One is that we should start caring about the returns that smallholders and African peasantry get for their efforts. The returns to their efforts, and the income they earn from their efforts, are fundamental ingredients in reducing food insecurity. Second, let's build on the progress made to date. We do not have to completely take down what exists in order to move forward.

That said, I will present the main points that emerged from our session. First I will cover fostering economic growth.

Economic growth is closely linked to poverty reduction and food security. In fact, undernutrition can be cut in half by 2020 if African countries maintain a growth rate of between 6 and 8 percent. And solid work has been done projecting that with about 3 percent per capita income growth, undernutrition can be halved by 2020.

But the link between growth and poverty reduction is closer if inequality is either low or falling. A country that is growing and at the same time reducing inequality will have a nearly sevenfold greater impact on poverty reduction than a country that is growing but increasing inequality. That is a big difference, so we need to pay attention to issues of inequality.

What should be done, then, to promote economic growth in Africa? First, good progress in some countries lays a solid foundation not only for learning from African cases themselves, but also for building upon positive macroeconomic policy actions and capitalizing on positive mindsets.

Second, we need to sustain growth and expand it to other countries.

Third, we need to address governance and conflict. Stability and an enabling environment are necessary for investment and growth. Here the panel emphasized the importance of a collective good reputation for Africa, which will matter for each individual African country as far as investment is concerned. And therein lies the importance of NEPAD.

A country that is growing and at the same time reducing inequality will have a nearly sevenfold greater impact on poverty reduction than a country that is growing but increasing inequality.

— Benno Ndulu

Other issues related to promoting economic growth are developing infrastructure, paying special attention to cost-effective methods and regional coordination; promoting agriculture because of its central role in growth and poverty reduction; diversifying incomes through nonfarm income sources; and promoting international cooperation, particularly through collective bargaining for improved assistance and reduction of subsidies for farmers in developed countries.

On the subject of improving markets, we identified key problems with agricultural markets in Africa, including high transaction costs, high transport costs, policy barriers to trade, incomplete information, and high risk, particularly related to weather.

Comparison of Asia and Africa has made it clear that we need to pay attention not only to the supply side, but also to the marketing side. In some cases success in expanding grain production caused price collapse and undermined the whole program. So markets must become an important lead for agricultural growth.

We identified several solutions. In order to get markets right, the panel focused on three I's. The first one is *incentives*—this involves getting prices right, which is necessary but not sufficient. The second "I" is *infrastructure*—roads to reduce transport costs, communication to improve market information, and regional coordination of infrastructure to improve grain movement across borders. The third "I" is *institutions*. This area has not been given adequate treatment to date, and this concern permeates the discussion concerning the definition of roles and the functionality of the state and the private sector. Institutions are important for grades and standards and market information—not just prices but also trade and weather. Farmer and trade organizations are needed. And institutions are needed to link farmers and processors and to provide for the flow of a variety of inputs and information.

Regional trade must be facilitated through information on prices, traders, and market flows. Exchanges are needed for buyers and sellers to find each other. Examples were given, particularly from the regional trade project dubbed Maize Without Borders in Eastern and Southern African countries.

Finally, appropriate marketing solutions depend on commodity types and levels of market interaction. We distinguished three main categories of market solutions. In the food grain trade, which is most important to the livelihoods of poor farmers, we particularly need to reduce transport costs, facilitate regional trade, and set standards. Spot markets work well, but commodity exchanges are likely in the future.

The next category, perishables, has high transaction costs in relation to risk. There is a need for more vertical coordination between farmers and buyers to ensure quality, quantity, and price. Important problems of contract enforcement need to be addressed. But there is potential for public-private partnerships to facilitate small-farmer participation in high-value sectors.

Finally, the third category is international trade. The main issues are market access, tariffs and quotas, which pose a serious problem, and the challenge of meeting high standards of food safety and food quality.

Overall, the panel concluded that we have a good foundation for moving forward, with hope for success.

Angeline Kamba

Member of UN/UNESCO World Commission on Culture and Development, Zimbabwe

Our session was titled "Building Human Capacity," and we noted that the issue of capacity building has come up time and time again as we talk about addressing food and nutrition security. One key area covered in our session concerns the actors or target groups who require capacity building. The first group is individuals, who may be targeted on the basis, for instance, of gender. As the backbone of agriculture, women may be selected for special training. We also identified households and communities as target groups. Communities could encompass groups like farmers, traders, or consumers. We also decided to target institutions, and that category could include private sector institutions, public sector institutions, NGOs, researchers, and donor organizations. Donors were emphasized because often they come into areas without much background information.

We went on to identify the areas of capacity development. We saw the need for capacity building in knowledge and skills development, in communications skills, and in scaling up successful initiatives. There are initiatives that have worked very well, and they require strengthening and support. Capacity building is also needed in management—many people work very well as in an operational capacity but falter when faced with management responsibilities. Monitoring and evaluation is another area that requires special attention, as do multidisciplinary and participatory approaches. Capacity building is also needed in agenda setting and prioritization and in bridging research and policy. It is not often that research results are fed into the policymaking framework, and the mechanisms are not always there for doing that. Often researchers and policymakers do not meet or listen to each other. Someone suggested that researchers need to exercise more initiative in approaching policymakers. We also saw the need to build capacity in linking policy analysis, formulation, and implementation.

Other areas for improvement are negotiation skills, science and technology, and nutrition. More education and training on nutrition matters are needed, and more can be done to supply consumers with nutrition information.

Whereas the formal presentations in our session dwelt largely on higher education and academic research, the discussion suggested that there should also be an emphasis on education at the primary and tertiary levels, so that you are building capacity at an early age.

We were under no illusion about the challenges and the problems. These challenges include the diversity of socioeconomic and physical complexities, disciplinary biases, and the enormous effort required to coordinate the various activities.

We also realized that we would have to build some mechanism into these measures to ensure sustainability. We do not want to find solutions that work for just a week or a month.

The retention of the built capacity is absolutely critical. We talked at length about the brain drain, and several ideas were voiced. As you build capacity, you should

The retention of the built capacity is absolutely critical . . . As you build capacity, you should put into place mechanisms for ensuring that you will retain the personnel you have developed and for replenishing them.

— Angeline Kamba

put into place mechanisms for ensuring that you will retain the personnel you have developed and for replenishing them, for renewal. With regard to the brain drain itself, some people thought, Let's forget about the people we have lost and build capacity afresh. Others thought we could create conditions that might attract them back.

We also need to build capacity to respond to the issue of HIV and AIDS. We need to make certain, for instance, that the planning of mechanization takes into account the fact that the workforce is not enjoying 100 percent health.

In addition, the poverty issue is enormous and must be treated as a challenge as we try to find strategies for capacity building.

Finally, we identified actions that should be taken. First, we should utilize existing capacity. We should put into place mechanisms for incentives, and we should focus on training farmers and building strong farmers' organizations. We should provide for information flow and information management. In addition, we need to build on the excellent research and other networks that have been established, taking care to strengthen and build on them rather than just starting new networks. We need to increase public investment in education. We must define the role of partners, create awareness of the roles of key players, and emphasize accountability, particularly for those in authority. We need more nutritional training and incentive structures for retention of trained people. We need to reform institutions, particularly within the government. And we should not just carry on year after year with whatever we inherited, but should continually look to see whether structures are working or whether they need to be reformed.

Kabba Joiner

Director General, West African Health Organization (WAHO), Burkina Faso

Our session, "Improving Nutrition and Health," was small in size, but very interactive. One of the issues we looked at is advocacy for nutrition. We feel very strongly that nutritionists shortchange themselves. They do not come out and say what they are capable of doing and how important they are in the scheme of things. Strong advocacy efforts are, therefore, needed at all levels to improve nutrition.

We looked at HIV/AIDS in terms of its effect on health. We also discussed the fundamental nutrition issues of care, prevention, treatment, and mitigation and the need to formulate policies and regulatory frameworks to help ensure that people suffering from HIV/AIDS are properly looked after. The discussion highlighted the seeming lack of urgency about the major threat the disease poses to food and nutrition.

Women's health, nutrition, and education are also central issues. When you educate the woman, you educate the nation. And women's nutrition raises the important issues of breast-feeding, supplementary feeding, and feeding of at-risk people, particularly children in difficult circumstances or HIV/AIDS-infected people.

Intersectoral collaboration was stressed. As one of us said, "You don't need to learn how to bark. You must use the dog." So to enhance nutrition we need to collaborate with other sectors. Health, agriculture, finance, trade, consumer associations, and education all need to work together to respond to issues of nutrition and health.

In most of our countries, strong leadership is needed for nutrition. The field of nutrition is an orphan—it does not know whether it belongs in health or in agriculture. We need to advocate for strong leadership that will be held accountable for good nutrition.

We also noticed that nutrition interventions are very small in terms of budgetary expenditures, but they have large impacts. And because the budget is small, people tend not to take it seriously or see it as a priority. With increased coverage for nutrition interventions, we can have a much greater impact from these small expenditures.

We also want to stress the essential actions for nutrition and health: breast-feeding up to the age of six months, supplementary feeding for children after six months, school feeding programs, feeding of at-risk people like children in difficult circumstances and people with HIV/AIDS, improvement of women's nutrition, reduction of maternal mortality, and reduction of micronutrient deficiencies like vitamin A deficiency, anemia, and iron deficiency.

Nutrition actions should be integrated at all levels, especially at the community level. We must listen to the community and have the community be part of our response.

Health, agriculture, finance, trade, consumer associations, and education all need to work together to respond to issues of nutrition and health.

— Kabba Joiner

Bethuel A. Kiplagat
Executive Director, Africa Peace Forum, Kenya

In the session "Strengthening Governance," our discussion focused first of all on identifying the stakeholders in the issue of governance. We assumed that governance is the management of resources, human, financial, or otherwise, for the well-being and the development of our people. Among the stakeholders that came out of our discussion are the African governments; our partners and donors abroad; and NGOs, both local and international. But the most important stakeholder for us consists of the farmers in the rural areas. All of these institutions need to practice good governance—the NGOs, civil society, and the corporate world as well. We are concerned with institutions and organizations that are involved in one way or another with ensuring food security for our people in this continent.

We believe that the rural people and the powerless need to be strengthened. This effort will be most effective if you strengthen them not just individually, but also collectively, if they have independence, and if their organizations and others are democratically organized. By strengthening them, you also make them better able to claim their rights. This can only occur, however, if there is rule of law and if the laws are enforced in our countries.

Rural folk must also genuinely participate in all the affairs of the nation, particularly in what touches them most. We do not want to see window dressing as so often happens—we say the farmers are here, the poor are here, but there is no genuine participation. Real participation will happen only if we strengthen them and build their capacity.

When outside organizations interact with farmers and rural people, the approach should be transparent and simple. Sometimes when we go out there with our complicated policies, they do not have the impact we are looking for.

We touched upon what happens when there is poor governance. One result, of course, is corruption. We were given a good example of an attempt at putting things right when corruption becomes endemic in a society and endangers the development of the country. The other result of poor governance is conflict.

Another element in empowering rural folk is to ensure that they have access and rights to land. There is no use talking of empowerment unless these people have secure access to and rights over land.

Let me end by quoting a statement once made by a politician: "Food without democracy is bitter. Democracy without food is empty."

Discussion

The importance of including communities and people at the grassroots level in efforts to assure food and nutrition security was a central element of the discussion. A participant noted that involving people at the grassroots in the design of programs helps assure that the agenda is not set by governments and donors alone. Building capacity and creating awareness at the grassroots will create motivation and facilitate development. Another participant drew attention to the lack of banks for grassroots people, noting that banks are designed for rich people, which is why poverty has remained a problem. In response to another participant who called for more attention to extension and mechanisms for delivering technologies to farmers, panelist Monty Jones reported that his session had discussed the need for participatory programs that would bring together all major stakeholders—not only the researchers, but also extension workers, nongovernmental organizations, and farmers—to consider problems and develop and implement protocols and programs.

Noting all of the talk about strengthening governance, a participant cautioned that experiences with decentralization should be reviewed to see whether they really brought decisionmaking closer to the people.

Standards and regulations were another area of discussion. While there was agreement that standards are necessary, a participant cautioned that they could become technical barriers to trade. In this context, it was noted that biotechnology holds potential but that it is important to put a regulatory framework in place to realize that potential.

Ghana's Minister of Agriculture Courage Quashigah takes the floor during discussion.

Jones said that to sell produce or develop export markets, African countries will need to maintain standards and put policies in place to ensure that standards are met. Panelist Benno Ndulu agreed that putting in place policies for standards is a good investment if Africa wants to open its doors to markets where quality requirements and preferences are stringent. He highlighted the example of fish exports from Lake Victoria, noting that three East African countries took action to open the market. The challenge of meeting standards is not insurmountable. Another participant noted if Africa is to move forward with food trade between countries, it is important to develop biosafety regulations within each country and across national boundaries. Unless those regulations are in place, African countries will not be able to attract investments or export to other countries concerned about biosafety, including other countries within the region.

In other areas of discussion, concern was expressed that little was said about natural resource management, but Jones reassured participants that issues of natural resource management were extensively discussed in the parallel session on "Raising Agricultural Productivity." In response to a participant's query about the boundaries to public investment, Jones noted that sources of additional funding to agriculture were also discussed in his session, and there was general agreement not only that investment from the public sector should be increased, but also that the private sector should be encouraged to also invest in agricultural research.

Finally, a participant disagreed with the comment that nutrition is an orphan, commenting that although nutrition security is a new concept, it is likely to catch up and become as well known as food security.

Experiences with decentralization should be reviewed to see whether they really brought decisionmaking closer to the people.

Excerpt 15: Linking Safety Nets, Social Protection, and Poverty Reduction: Directions for Africa

Michelle Adato, Akhter Ahmed, and Francie Lund

In Africa and elsewhere, safety nets were promoted in the 1980s as a response to the (presumably short-term) adverse effects of structural adjustment. Though some safety nets had a developmental component, safety nets are still largely associated with the idea of a short-term buffer. "Social protection" is a newer term that incorporates safety net programs but also includes a role for renewed state involvement, emphasizes a longer-term developmental approach, includes social assistance and social insurance, and is often advocated as a right rather than a reactive form of relief. Social protection policy addresses not only programs aimed at reducing the impact of shocks and coping with their aftermath, but also interventions designed to prevent shocks and destitution in the first place. Most societies have private interhousehold, intrafamily, and intrahousehold transfers that promote resilience to shocks, mitigating their negative effects. However, in countries or communities where people are universally poor, there is less to share, particularly in times of shocks that affect all or many in the society (such as drought, floods, AIDS, or widespread structural unemployment)—which is precisely when the need for help is most critical.

SAFETY NET PROGRAM OPTIONS

Cash Transfers and Conditional Transfers. These programs involve the direct transfer of cash to poor households. In recent years—primarily in Latin America but also elsewhere—"conditional transfers" have tied benefits (usually cash and nutrition supplements) to requirements such as children's high attendance rates at school, and mothers' attendance at health and nutrition workshops.

Free Food Distribution. In a pure relief program, food is distributed free, either as disaster relief or as an in-kind transfer to certain disadvantaged groups in the society.

Direct Feeding Programs. These distribute meals and nutritional supplements to people who are especially vulnerable to malnutrition, usually preschool children and women of child-bearing age from low-income households.

School-Based Food Programs. These distribute prepared food to children in school. Food-for-education programs distribute free food grain to low-income families if their children attend primary school.

Food Stamps. Distributed to eligible consumers, food stamps or coupons have a cash value when used for purchasing food in a commercial store, and the seller redeems the stamps from a bank or government office.

Price Subsidies. A general food price subsidy makes unlimited amounts of the subsidized foods available to all, such as in the case of the bread subsidy in Egypt.

Subsidized Agricultural Inputs. Agricultural inputs such as fertilizers are often subsidized to help poor farmers and increase crop productivity.

Public Works Programs. These kinds of programs transfer short-term wages or food, but if carefully designed they can also build needed assets such as schools, clinics, and water supply and irrigation networks; facilitate access to markets through the construction of roads and market stalls; and provide training and organizational capacity.

Social Health Insurance. In many African countries, social health insurance is a form of social protection. Social health insurance schemes are typically contributory, with participation by government, the beneficiaries themselves, and donor organizations or international agencies.

Microfinance. Microfinance can protect the poor during large shocks, helping them avoid drastic actions such as distress sales of land and draft animals that can permanently damage future earning potential.

This has been excerpted from 2020 Africa Conference Brief 12, published by IFPRI, Washington, DC, 2004

Part V | Strengthening Actors

Chapter 18 Roles and Responsibilities

Chair: Mildred Namwiinde Mpundu
Executive Director, Media and Communication, Step Out Media Communications and Business Development Consultancy Services, Zambia

The past few decades have not been successful agriculturally for the majority of African countries. Floods, droughts, food shortages, civil wars, disease, and, worse still, the HIV/AIDS pandemic have ravaged the continent, in the process hindering agricultural and other economic development.

Previous sessions have raised issues related to strengthening agricultural productivity and have brought forth suggestions on what African countries could do to support implementation of action for food and nutrition security on the continent. A number of questions have come up: How do we get over the hurdles of bad agricultural policies and financial constraints? How can we get access to appropriate and sustainable technologies, such as irrigation systems? How can Africa find her way onto global markets, and how can she make her products competitive as well as overcome import restrictions and high tariffs? How do we build the capacity of African farmers? How does Africa, now hit with the HIV/AIDS pandemic, get out of the double tragedy she is in?

The speakers for this session will highlight what various actors, within and outside Africa, can do to support implementation of action for food and nutrition security in Africa.

The solution lies in the restructuring of African economies and the transformation of agriculture.

— Augustin Fosu

Keynote Address: What African Countries Can Do to Support Implementation of Action for Food and Nutrition Security in Africa

Augustin Fosu
Senior Policy Adviser, United Nations Economic Commission for Africa, Ethiopia

I am delighted to provide this address on behalf of the Executive Secretary of the Economic Commission for Africa, Mr. K. Y. Amoako. The theme of this address is crucial and ought to engage the mind of every African, and indeed every Africanist, today. Why is it that, in spite of numerous efforts, strategies, and action plans, broad-based and sustainable growth has eluded the continent? And what can we do to reverse the trend and bring about growth? Many speakers before me have tried to answer this question, and the macro elements have been well examined. So I will paint the issue with a broad brush.

The solution lies in the restructuring of African economies and the transformation of agriculture. In most African countries, the key to achieving sustainable economic growth and to reducing the vulnerability of their economies to external shocks is to transform the structure of their economies. What do I mean by "structural transformation"? It is the process whereby a predominantly agrarian economy is transformed into a diversified, productive economy dominated by manufacturing and service sectors.

My emphasis here on export-led and industry-driven transformation is not an attempt to rehash the conventional argument of import substitution versus export promotion. Rather, it is an argument for creating an enabling environment for African economies to transform the static comparative advantages of agriculture into dynamic sources of competitiveness through targeted domestic investments in agribusiness industries.

Augustin Fosu, Akin Adesina, and Josué Dioné pause for a photo following the session.

The key is to strengthen the linkages between agriculture and industry to enhance value-added processing and exports. In Africa economic growth in the last decade has averaged only 2.1 percent per year—less than the population growth rate of 2.8 percent and considerably less than the 7 percent needed to cut in half the share of Africans in poverty by 2015.

More recently, in 2003, only four African countries registered growth rates above 7 percent. Forty-one countries exhibited positive growth rates that were below 7 percent. Eight countries experienced negative growth rates. This outcome suggests that most African countries are unlikely to achieve the internationally agreed-upon MDGs by 2015.

Economic growth alone would not sufficiently reduce poverty. The requisite growth would be in the context of macroeconomic policies that emphasize agricultural transformation, job creation, and productivity growth, and social policies that redress inequalities and discrimination.

This is the reality today. Economic growth has not been high, broad-based, or sustainable in Africa, because Africa has not succeeded in implementing the above program of transformation. But this reality need not be our destiny, and it is not. We need to reverse the trend. And we will, by restructuring our economies to begin to make progress in our efforts to achieve growth and reduce poverty. Fundamentally, food security and poverty reduction go hand-in-hand with sustained and broad-based economic growth.

Moreover, the spatial distribution of population and poverty in Africa indicates that the road to sustainable food and nutrition is broad-based economic growth built on agricultural transformation. Currently, three-quarters of all the poor work and live in rural areas, and more than 60 percent of them will continue to be rural in 2025. Furthermore, the incomes and livelihoods of the bulk of the African rural population depend primarily on agricultural enterprises in which 90 percent of the rural labor force is engaged directly or indirectly.

Urban poverty is also linked to rural poverty through strong backward and forward linkages between agriculture and the other productive and service sectors of the economies of most developing countries. Studies of some African countries, for instance, show that adding a dollar to farm incomes increased all incomes by two to three dollars. This multiplier effect is not paltry, by any means.

Widespread increases in income, and therefore broad-based agricultural growth, are crucial for achieving the full potential of this multiplier effect. Conversely, urban poverty and food insecurity feed on rural poverty through urban migration induced by acute poverty in the rural areas. For the majority of African households today, therefore, domestic food and agricultural production remains an overriding determinant of overall income, as well as the availability of and access to food.

Nevertheless, despite past efforts to remove the distortions and the incentive structures in the agricultural sector, the sector is not growing at the rate required for sustainable economic growth. Agricultural development needs to go beyond getting prices right and focus more on increasing productivity by removing the institutional and structural constraints responsible for poor performance—including getting markets right.

This task calls for increased investment in public research and infrastructure, better extension services, and increased access to credit to farmers. But agricultural conditions in Africa are not uniform, blunting the potential power of the Green Revolution that worked so well in Asia.

Therefore, we must develop region-specific technologies to increase yields and the likelihood of their adoption by local farmers. This is one of the cornerstones of an African "Green Revolution," on which we at the United Nations Economic Commission for Africa (ECA) are currently working, following the call last year by UN Secretary General Kofi Annan urging African countries to promote an African "Green Revolution."

We are convinced that this "Green Revolution" will succeed for the following reasons: First, it is specifically designed for the African context. Second, it takes into account new developments in technology, including biotechnology and information and communication technologies (ICTs). Third, it involves an extensive learning curve to ensure that we respect the past and not repeat it.

The key is to strengthen the linkages between agriculture and industry to enhance value-added processing and exports.

— Augustin Fosu

The ECA has already embarked on a strategic road map for promoting an African "Green Revolution" involving systematic identification and mobilization of the multiple stakeholders needed to trigger and sustain this revolution, ranging from the scientists who would deliver the designs and technologies on the ground, to the African governments or institutions that would make the supportive policies, to the international community, which must now focus more closely on Africa's potentials and challenges.

So research investment in Africa will focus on developing technologies appropriate to the conditions of different regions. Also, the prior relationship between researchers, extension services, and farmers will be promoted and sustained.

In yesterday's presentations, I learned that NERICA is generating a rice revolution. I also learned that we could actually increase the fertility and yields of our fields by the use of phosphorus rock that is abundant in Africa. But then I asked myself, How come this type of knowledge has not become public? Knowledge must be a public good, and ECA is well positioned to serve as the anchor of the effort to make knowledge a regional public good.

All of the efforts I mentioned will come to naught unless we also find the solution to the HIV/AIDS problem. As we pay more attention to agriculture as a springboard for broad-based growth, African countries must also actively respond to the HIV/AIDS epidemic in more creative ways. We must find ways to keep those infected by this virus alive longer, and we must prevent new infections. This imperative is now even more crucial in the face of another unfortunate African reality: HIV/AIDS has mostly affected the productive work force, especially those engaged in agriculture and related support services. The Commission on HIV/AIDS and Governance in Africa—which is chaired by ECA's executive secretary—is helping African governments cope with this disease and break the structural damage it has wrought. ECA has embraced this mandate and actively incorporated it into its work program.

In addition, the policies we advocate will promote sustainable growth only if we pay better attention to good, accountable governance across Africa. At ECA we have just concluded a landmark study of the state of governance in 28 African countries. We studied elements like institutional effectiveness, human rights, and proper governance, concentrating on institutional changes, the legitimacy of the democratic political system, and competitive electoral policies. We also looked at economic governance, with particular attention to a better macroeconomic environment, greater private sector support, and increasing space for the informal economy.

The complementarity of IFPRI's and ECA's respective roles cannot be overemphasized. As the Commission's mandate is concerned with all aspects of economic development of the African continent, that mandate would be empty without attention to food and nutritional security. The current conference clearly exemplifies that complementarity, as well as the cooperation between the two institutions.

Finally, let me emphasize the catalytic role of ECA as a primary pan-African institution. Together with all of you, we can achieve the above transformation.

Keynote Address: What Industrialized Countries Can Do to Promote Agricultural and Rural Development in Africa: Perspectives of a Development Organization

Bernd Eisenblätter
Managing Director, Deutsche Gesellschaft für Technische Zusamenarbeit, Germany

I would like to take this opportunity to explain why I believe that the contributions of countries from the North to Africa's agricultural and rural development are highly important, and perhaps even indispensable, for the future of the continent. And, as managing director of a development agency that is closely involved in implementing international cooperation, I would like to focus on real action that can make a difference to the lives of the African people.

The challenges we are facing are enormous. Agricultural development in Africa has faced an uphill struggle for the past 20 years. Sometimes this struggle has been lost, as the news about recurrent food shortages has shown. Yet if Africa can develop a comparative advantage in any sector, it is in agricultural products, raw commodities, and, more important, processed foods.

For most African countries wishing to integrate

into the global economy, increased agricultural trade is one, if not the only, option. This is true in spite of the fact that terms of trade for developing countries have deteriorated significantly. Today a given quantity of African primary agricultural commodities buys fewer manufactured goods from other parts of the world than it did some years ago. As a consequence, Africa's share of world trade has fallen from about 4 percent in 1980 to less than 2 percent today. There is no alternative, however, to agricultural export and agricultural development. African economies need to diversify their production and exports. They must defend existing market shares and capture new markets.

The worldwide trade liberalization of the past two decades has increased trade opportunities, but it has not yet enabled all countries to gain significant benefits from trade. Structural policies that could enhance economic efficiencies and strength and the competitiveness of the agricultural sector often failed, owing to a constant pattern of underinvestment from both public and private sources. Industrialized countries have contributed to distortions in agricultural trade, through a vast array of import restrictions, subsidies, escalating tariffs for processed goods, and nontariff trade barriers. Industrialized countries, therefore, must act as soon as possible to tear those barriers down.

Providing African countries fair trade opportunities in the global economy has moved to the top of the international agenda. I wholeheartedly support Minister Wieczorek-Zeul from Germany in her demand for more reforms of the Common Agricultural Policy of the European Union. But access to the European market is already given through the Everything But Arms Act, EBA. This offers developing countries real new opportunities.

Development agencies like to support those governments that actively look for increased exports to high-value markets in industrialized countries. As a contribution to this objective, Deutsche Gesellschaft für Technische Zusamenarbeit (GTZ), on behalf of the German government, is currently providing technical

If Africa can develop a comparative advantage in any sector, it is in agricultural products, raw commodities, and, more important, processed foods.

— Bernd Eisenblätter

If the African agricultural sector is not prepared for trade liberalization, the benefits of increased global trade will simply bypass Africa.

— Bernd Eisenblätter

assistance to a number of governments in strengthening their negotiation capacity in trade talks. We are also promoting consumer awareness in Europe for tropical products that are grown according to agreed social and ecological standards.

Fair trade offers significant potential for channeling additional income to producers through market-based mechanisms. We are looking forward to involving more African countries in these initiatives.

From the standpoint of an implementing agency, I would like to stress that we should not wait until the disputes of the World Trade Organization's Doha Round are resolved. The countries and trade blocs of the industrialized world can act unilaterally by removing trade barriers, once governments make the right priorities.

But we must also recognize the following: Even if agricultural trade distortions are phased out, African farmers may not automatically benefit. After many years of underinvestment and decline, African agrarian sectors and rural economies need to be rendered competitive. For example, exports need to comply with standards prevailing in the market. In some instances, even domestic markets need to be recaptured.

If the African agricultural sector is not prepared for trade liberalization, the benefits of increased global trade will simply bypass Africa. Other regions will capture market shares vacated by the OECD countries. The African market also needs trade liberalization. In this context, GTZ is supporting the efforts of the East African Community, as well as SADC.

What is the specific role of development agencies in strengthening African agriculture and rural economies? It is obvious that capacity development plays a decisive role. For GTZ, the term "capacity building" always means intervention in three ways: training people, strengthening the organizations they work in, and creating an enabling institutional environment.

Capacity building for African farmers, processors, and exporters, and for institutions that support them, is a precondition for competitiveness in markets. Other nations

Bernd Eisenblätter describes how industrialized countries can help promote development in Africa.

are well aware of this. As Brazilian President Luiz Inácio Lula da Silva remarked on his recent visit to India, "Nobody is going to buy from us just because there are 70 million poor people in India or 50 million poor in Brazil. They will buy from us when we are ready to compete, our products have the quality, and we dare to go out and sell."

Capacity development stresses the importance of local knowledge, institutional development, and social capital in the process of economic and social development. Going beyond technical assistance, it aims at strengthening national structures, supporting participatory processes of priority setting, and facilitating acquisition of knowledge. In our experience, capacity development addresses institutional failure and reduces the transaction costs of cooperation programs. Capacity development should include the whole society and involve the public sector, civil society, and the private sector.

All too often, development agencies have forgotten the private sector. Developing the private sector is vital for countries that face the tremendous challenge of building value chains from the level of smallholder farms to globalized markets. In countries like Ghana and Kenya, where we are developing new concepts for improving service delivery to private sector organizations, GTZ has helped to broker public-private partnership arrangements between farmer organizations, processors, food retailers, and local authorities, in order to provide for secure market outlets for farm products. For example, in the Wenchi tomato-processing project in Ghana, local farmers now benefit from high-quality processing and marketing facilities. This allows local production to compete against imports from Europe.

An enabling environment for more private sector investment in agriculture is a key success factor for poverty reduction in Africa.

— Bernd Eisenblätter

In the past two years, GTZ has renewed its emphasis on supporting agriculture and rural development in a number of countries, including Burkina Faso, Ghana, and Kenya. We follow a program-based approach that integrates support at national and local levels. Our programs provide new opportunities for cooperation with other development partners, the private sector, and civil society.

Because of our special emphasis on participatory approaches, we see our role as complementary to the efforts of national governments, civil society, the private sector, and the international donor community. Our agricultural support programs foster market orientation by strengthening the capacity of actors and institutions in the public and private sectors.

We are convinced that an enabling environment for more private sector investment in agriculture is a key success factor for poverty reduction in Africa. The private sector will not invest, however, unless there is more stable and reliable governance in the public sector.

Our programs address simultaneously constraints at various levels. At the project implementation level, we focus our strategy on strengthening groups and organizations of producers, processors, and other actors in the agricultural value chain. In this field, we can build on specific German experience.

At the level of supporting organizations and institutions, we focus on reform of service delivery systems to provide rural actors access to a broad range of services. We also support institutional arrangements for conflict resolution between agriculture and livestock households.

At the national level, we are engaged with our partners in reformulating agricultural policies and strategies and enhancing their compatibility with national strategy objectives, like the poverty reduction strategy paper. The current urban bias in public sector investment has to be carefully reversed.

Supporting the emergence and development of market-oriented agriculture is only one element of our strategy. Successful rural development also requires support for private sector development and the strengthening of local governance structures. For example, in South Africa we facilitated cooperation between local authorities and small-scale rural entrepreneurs in developing business clusters of the furniture industry.

A social protection strategy for rural areas is also urgently needed to reduce poverty and hunger. Such a strategy goes beyond the agricultural sector. In some parts of Africa, a large number of households do not have the resources to become successful agricultural producers. GTZ supports national food security strategies in Mozambique and Ethiopia. Since 1999, in Mozambique, provincial action plans have been developed in a participatory manner. Food security aspects have been progressively integrated into sector investment programs. A further integration into the national poverty reduction strategy is envisaged. Pertinent issues such as the national food aid policy, the consequences of HIV/AIDS for food security, and disaster preparedness will be addressed.

I want to stress that we should continue to press for fair trade opportunities for African countries in the world market, but African agriculture has to be rendered competitive by preparing the key actors for the rough storms of international markets. Yet promoting the agricultural sector alone is not the magic bullet for achieving the Millennium Development Goals of hunger reduction and poverty alleviation. Strategies for food security and general rural development should accompany agricultural development. We see our specific comparative advantage in capacity development in all these areas.

Finally, in addition to our bilateral support, we foster international agricultural research and in particular IFPRI and its 2020 Vision Initiative in its efforts to set the scientific basis for the development of the rural sector and agriculture.

Keynote Address: What Industrialized Countries Can Do to Support Implementation of Action for Food and Nutrition Security in Africa: Perspectives from USAID

Emmy B. Simmons
Assistant Administrator, United States Agency for International Development, Bureau of Economic Growth, Agriculture, and Trade, USA

Many of you know what the U.S. Agency for International Development (USAID) logo looks like: a handshake. In talking about what industrialized countries can do to support implementation of action for food and nutrition security in Africa, I wanted to avoid the obvious answer: bring money. The right answer is: a handshake. Industrialized countries such as the United States must work hand-in-hand with African countries to bring about the changes required to assure food and nutrition security for all Africans.

Industrialized countries such as the United States must work hand-in-hand with African countries to bring about the changes required to assure food and nutrition security for all Africans.

— Emmy B. Simmons

Market access, science and technology, and good governance are three fundamental areas where positive change is needed to achieve the greatest benefits in food and nutrition security. We both—Africa and the United States alike—need to make changes in our own systems in order to achieve that goal.

I believe firmly that the potential benefits of global trade liberalization for Africa—and for the rest of the world, including the United States—are enormous. A recent World Bank study showed that by 2015, gains to developing countries from trade liberalization in high-income countries would be US$31 billion. The additional gains from liberalization in developing countries, however, would be US$111 billion. That means that not only our partnership, but the partnership among your countries must be addressed. The global community, including Africa and the United States, needs to act together to reduce tariffs and subsidies that distort and hamper trade.

But the industrialized countries also need to open our markets to African producers. There has already been some impact in this area. Total agricultural exports from Sub-Saharan Africa grew from about US$13 billion in 1991 to US$21 billion in the year 2000. Somebody is earning more money.

Almost half of these total additional exports went to the European Union (EU), whereas only about 5 percent went to the United States. That indicates that we have some way to go in building trade relationships with Africa. Africa's largest agricultural exports in the year 2000, each exceeding US$2 billion, were fish, wood, and vegetables and fruits—not staple crops.

Vegetables and fruits and fish are probably the two biggest success stories. Vegetable-fruit exports to the EU were up 40 percent. And between 1990 and 2000 vegetable and fruit exports to the U.S. went up, from an

> *African countries find that market access is not enough. Market access needs to be accompanied by the ability to produce for a market.*
>
> – Emmy B. Simmons

admittedly low base, by almost 400 percent. Fish exports to the EU doubled and fish exports to the U.S. tripled in that period. Spices are another sector where African exports, though still relatively small, have seen huge growth rates.

Cotton is an important export crop for Africa. But it is not African cotton that has fueled the very large increase in textile and apparel imports to the U.S. that has come about in the past few years under the impetus of the African Growth and Opportunity Act. As we have learned through our AGOA experience, African countries find that market access is not enough. Market access needs to be accompanied by the ability to produce for a market.

Many people have said, "We just can't do it because of the industrialized countries' subsidies." But this is only part of the problem. There are a lot of barriers to increasing African participation in markets, and that is why USAID, and the U.S. government in general, have made trade capacity building our fastest-growing area of assistance. And when we talk about trade, we are talking not just about trade from Africa to the rest of the world, but about internal trade, regional trade, local trade, and domestic trade.

Groups such as COMESA have spent a lot of time focusing on reducing barriers to interregional trade and on improving the quality of products to meet consumer demand and understanding what consumers want. More and more, agricultural products are sold not just in local markets, but in supermarkets across the continent. It is one of the fastest-growing phenomena I have seen in economics. I think within a year or two there will be documentation of rapid growth in Asia and Africa, similar to the phenomenal growth that has already occurred in Latin America. Supermarkets, however, demand consistent and high-quality products. Farmers who are not used to meeting those consistency and quality standards need assistance to meet these market demands through improved infrastructure, including roads and market information.

But science and technology are also key to producing and delivering such high-quality products. High-value horticultural products rely on irrigation, pest management, and, for those of you who do not think energy is a constraint, cold storage.

The subsistence farmer working on a small plot of land, with a hoe and a strong back, for an uncertain crop yield, is not the future of farming in Africa. I believe the future is a more diversified farming sector, with high-quality products for both internal consumers and external consumers in Europe, the U.S., Asia, and the Middle East and with much more processing happening in Africa.

How do we get to this new vision? We at USAID, along with many other donor organizations, are focusing on accelerating the application of science and technology to production, processing, and sustainable natural resource management. The award of the World Food Prize to Monty Jones should give us all, and all of the kids now in college and high school around Africa, the desire to be part of this new science and technology revolution.

In the 1970s cassava mealy bug was inadvertently introduced to Africa from South America. The mealy bug devastated root and leaf yield. But scientists at the International Institute of Tropical Agriculture (IITA) in Nigeria and elsewhere in Africa worked in a cross-regional collaboration with colleagues in Latin America to find a biological control solution. They found a natural enemy, a parasitic wasp, and released it in cassava areas in Africa after careful study. Each dollar spent on the mealy bug control project has so far returned at least US$150 to African farmers. The overall benefit of controlling this one pest alone has been estimated at between US$9 and 20 billion. Surely this gain illustrates why we need to invest in science and technology.

Another success story from IITA and other NGOs is the control of cassava mosaic disease. It is also a success story for participatory evaluation by farmers in their own fields. The new cassava varieties developed since the 1980s have been quickly adopted across the region. In Uganda cassava production hit a record high of almost 5 million tons in 2001, up from a low of just

> *More and more, agricultural products are sold not just in local markets, but in supermarkets across the continent.*
>
> – Emmy B. Simmons

over 2 million tons in 1994. That is fast progress by any standard, and it is built on science and technology.

Biotech cotton, too, is a story worth repeating. A comprehensive review of the global experience with biotech cotton modified with the Bt gene shows that this variety increases yields, decreases costs, and yields environmental benefits by reducing the number of times that pesticides have to be sprayed on the crop. Secondary benefits noted in South Africa include an increased number of beneficial insects, because the use of broad-spectrum insecticides harmful to the nontarget insects is minimized. South African farmers, who have paid attention to their biosafety regulations, are already benefiting from Bt cotton, and trials of Bt cotton are underway in Burkina Faso.

Food quality is also an issue that can be addressed directly through science and technology. We have begun the transformation of indigenous foods to meet specific dietary needs—some through biotech, some through selection, and some just through careful crop development. Cutting-edge research being done by Africans and partners around the globe is drawing upon the latest developments in genetic and nutritional sciences to bring iron, vitamin A, and zinc to staple crops.

An example of importance to Africa, because it addresses the issue of vitamin A deficiency, is the orange flesh sweet potato. Research in South Africa showed that serum vitamin A levels rose substantially when school children had orange flesh sweet potatoes for lunch. Surely, this is good news, when 32 percent of the children under five in this continent are estimated to suffer from vitamin A deficiency. And even subclinical deficiency, which you cannot see, is associated with a 23 percent increase in preschooler mortality. This tells us that school feeding is not quite enough. We have to get the children before they get to school as well.

So are resources to agriculture at a turnaround? They peaked in 1988, peaked a little lower in 1991, and have been on a long downhill slide ever since (Figure 1). We are hoping that the figures for 2003 will show a slight up-tick. We have certainly seen a renewed interest and new commitment to building science, technology, and delivery systems in Africa among donors and our African partners. But if we do not get agriculture back on the development agenda, we are going to be discussing this issue for many, many years to come.

NEPAD has taken the lead with the CAADP. We hope, with the leadership that has been evident here over the past couple of days, to make it work. And I am hopeful that setting a target of 10 percent of national budgetary resources for agriculture by the African Union participants will be useful. It will not be useful if people play with the numbers and take a rural road or rural education and count it under agriculture. But if we stick to the 10 percent, I think we are in good shape.

FIGURE 1—OECD bilateral aid to agriculture, 1980–2002

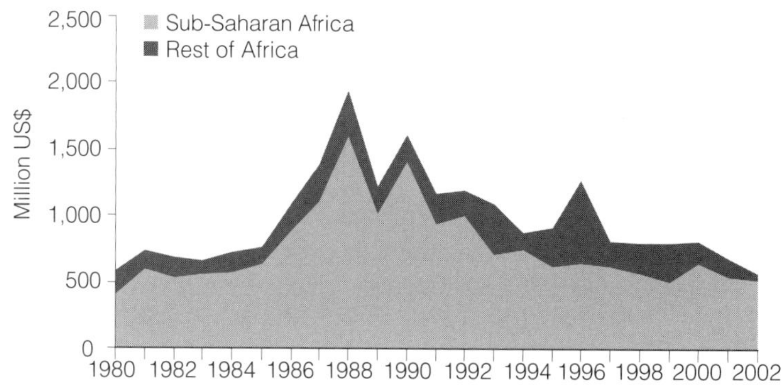

Source: OECD, *The DAC Journal Development Co-operation Report 2003* (Paris, 2004).

In line with this comprehensive commitment to change, our own policy in the U.S. is implementing a new program, the Millennium Challenge Account (MCA), which expands the amount of assistance that the U.S. is planning to provide to development around the world. This account will not be managed directly by USAID. Rather, it will supplement normal USAID programs and will incorporate a more competitive approach to programming.

The three areas of competitiveness are going to be ruling justly, investing in people, and economic freedom. These principles are beginning to have an effect on the overall aid program as well. They define the characteristics of countries that have made their own commitment to work in partnership with donors, including the U.S., to build a brighter future.

Trade liberalization is important, increased investment in agriculture is important, but neither of those are going to create economic growth without a commitment to good governance, or ruling justly. Good governance means, among other things, government effectiveness, reduced corruption, rule of law, better and smarter regulation, contract enforcement, protection of property rights, and civil liberties. Political rights must also be protected. Together with good governance, governments that invest in people and encourage economic freedom are, in our view, the best hope for Africa.

Countries selected for the MCA will be measured according to their commitment in these areas. It is our hope that working in partnership with those countries will provide more broad-based examples of agricultural growth, economic growth, and truly sustainable food and nutritional security.

Even with improved governance, we recognize that change does not happen overnight. Some countries in Africa are emerging from conflict. Others are struggling to put new governance systems in place, even as they are trying to cope with recent droughts or other disasters. In these countries, food aid continues to play an important temporary role, although it cannot be the basis for sustained food and nutrition security.

Most serious food and nutrition emergencies arise at the end of a chain of failed development processes across sectors, not just in agriculture. The basic cause is grounded in economic injustice and poor governance. Drought and poor harvests may push a country into famine, but we must not mistake the immediate cause of famine for the more fundamental ones.

We are working, for example, with the Government of Ethiopia, other donors, and NGO partners to build a new approach to food security in that country, with a productive safety net complementing more aggressive approaches to stimulating economic growth. That more productive safety net includes not only food aid, but also cash assistance, technical assistance, and a significant commitment of both human and financial resources from the Government of Ethiopia itself.

The central tenet of this collaborative approach is that economic, social, and governance strategies must be designed to build resilience at the national, district, and household levels if we are to have sustainable nutrition and food security. We must also improve the coordination of other programs and other sectors—health, education, and HIV/AIDS.

Working together, across sectors and in a consistent way, we can achieve a brighter future for Africa's families. We have made some progress, and we have to build on it.

FIGURE 1—HIV prevalence in adults in Sub-Saharan Africa, end 2001

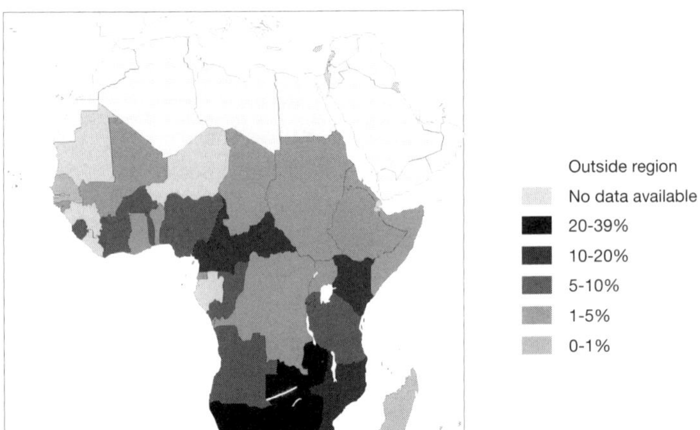

Source: UNAIDS, 2002.

We still do not know how much further the epidemic will spread, where it will peak, or what its impacts will be.

– Alan Whiteside

Keynote Address: Confronting AIDS and Hunger in Africa

Alan Whiteside

Director, Health Economics and HIV/AIDS Research Division, University of KwaZulu-Natal, South Africa

I am going to talk to you about the greatest health and development crisis facing Africa in modern times. HIV/AIDS is the elephant in the room. The bad news is that the situation is bad, and it is going to get worse. Unless there is significant and sustained action we could only be seeing the peak of impact by 2020. This is a sobering and perhaps, for some, an unbelievable thought. The good news is that we do have time to plan for what is happening.

Let me start with the scale (Figure 1). Black means bad, but where there is no black does not mean that there is no epidemic or that there is not going to be an epidemic. In parts of Africa we simply do not have the data. There has been some debate about the exact numbers. This is irrelevant. It is akin to asking how many angels can dance on the head of the pin. Many millions of Africans are infected. Many millions will die.

We have made rapid scientific advances in understanding the virus and how it works. We are moving toward developing treatments. But we still do not know how much further the epidemic will spread, where it will peak, or what its impacts will be.

Poorly nourished people are at greater risk of being infected, and poorly nourished people who are HIV-positive will fall ill faster.

— Alan Whiteside

Figure 2 shows the prevalence of HIV among women attending clinics across four southern African countries. In Swaziland nearly 40 percent of pregnant women are infected with this virus. In Botswana the figure is more than 35 percent. And the latest data from 2003 show an upturn in prevalence there. In my country, South Africa, prevalence among pregnant women is 25 percent—one in four women are infected. In my province, KwaZulu-Natal, HIV prevalence is 36 to 37 percent.

We can tell where we are on an epidemic curve and where we have been by measuring HIV prevalence (Figure 3). If we are at point A_1, that would tell us that we have seen an epidemic evolve. But we can change where we are going. This is the challenge of prevention. Uganda, for instance, has turned this curve around. In other countries the epidemic has not even taken off and there is evidence to suggest that this is because of their prevention efforts. We should not fail to recognize the importance of interventions. I think particularly of Senegal.

HIV does not matter on its own. It matters because after about eight years, people begin to experience periods of illness that increase in severity, frequency, and duration. In the absence of an effective, affordable, and deliverable treatment, they will die. If we are at point A_1 on the HIV curve, then we are going to be down at point B_1 on the AIDS curve (Figure 4). That curve is going to go up in the future. Those illnesses, those deaths, are still to come.

So the second challenge is care and treatment. And here adequate and appropriate nutrition is absolutely crucial. Antiretroviral drugs are only part of the solution; they are not a silver bullet. We must start with adequate, effective, appropriate nutrition.

The bad news is that if the HIV curve is going to lead to an AIDS curve, then the impact curve is even

FIGURE 2—HIV prevalence among women attending public antenatal clinics in four countries, 1990–2002

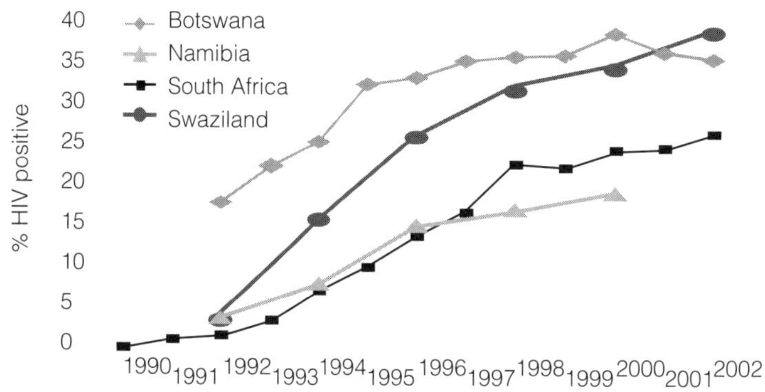

Source: Compiled by the Health Economics and HIV/AIDS Research Division of the University of KwaZulu-Natal from national data from Botswana, Swaziland, South Africa, and Namibia.

FIGURE 3—Epidemic curves, HIV

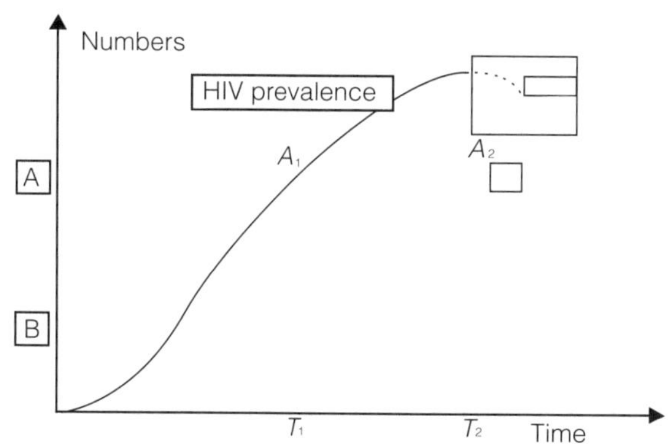

Source: Compiled by Alan Whiteside of the Health Economics and HIV/AIDS Research Division of the University of KwaZulu-Natal.

FIGURE 4—Epidemic curves, HIV and AIDS

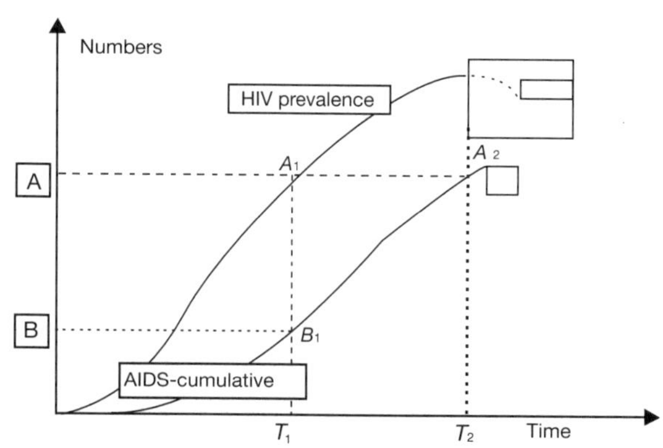

Source: Compiled by Alan Whiteside of the Health Economics and HIV/AIDS Research Division of the University of KwaZulu-Natal.

FIGURE 5—Epidemic curves, HIV, AIDS, and impact

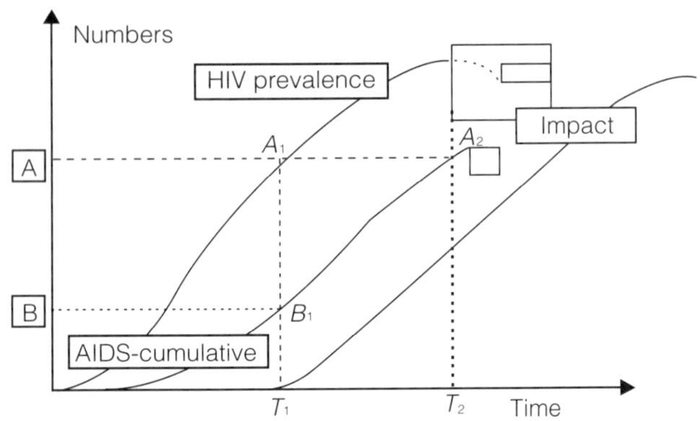

Source: Compiled by Alan Whiteside of the Health Economics and HIV/AIDS Research Division of the University of KwaZulu-Natal.

FIGURE 6—All orphans and orphans due to AIDS by HIV prevalence, Uganda, by year

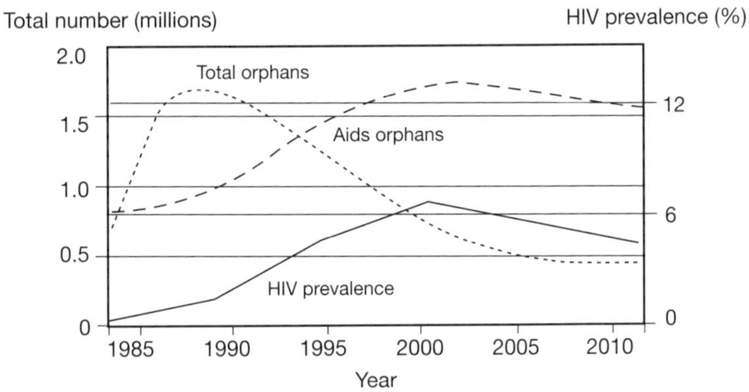

Source: UNICEF.

FIGURE 7—Estimated increase in women's death rates relative to the 1985 rates in South Africa

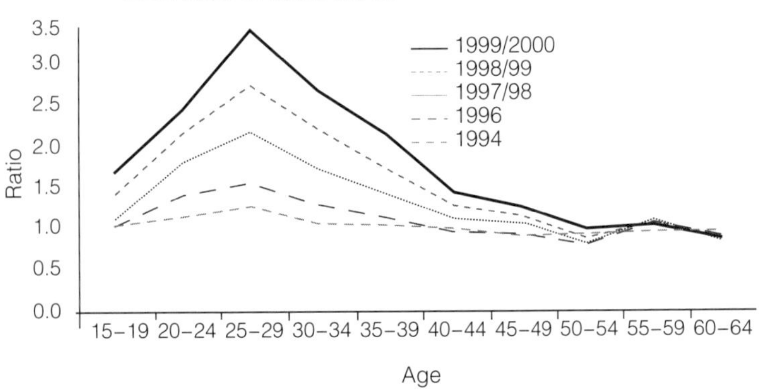

Source: R. Dorrington, D. Bourne, D. Bradshaw, R. Laubscher, I. M. Timmeaus, *The impact of HIV/AIDS on adult mortality in South Africa* (Johannesburg: Medical Research Council, 2001).

further ahead (Figure 5). But that is also the good news, because it gives us a chance to prepare for the future. We are going to see increased illnesses, loss of productive people, and rising numbers of orphans. The impacts will be many and varied, and they will make assuring food and nutrition security by 2020 very difficult, especially if we do not recognize and plan for this.

AIDS is a long-wave, complex catastrophe. Our third challenge is to understand and mitigate impact. Figure 6 illustrates what I mean by a long-wave epidemic. It shows that the total number of orphans peaks about 15 years after the prevalence peaks. That means that if HIV has peaked in Botswana or Swaziland or South Africa—and we do not know if it has—we would expect to see the peak of orphans in 2020.

Let me talk about impact. Already, we are seeing an increase in deaths. In South Africa a woman aged between 25 and 29 is three and a half times more likely to die in 2000 than she was in 1985 (Figure 7). Year after year, HIV prevalence has resulted in increased mortality.

Life expectancy is plummeting (Figure 8). In Botswana, according to the United Nations Population Division, which is quite conservative, it is estimated to be 37 years. This decline is reversing development gains. And note the contrast between the high-prevalence countries of Southern Africa and the other countries.

How does agriculture work when life expectancy is 37 years? How does agriculture work when the population pyramid in Botswana, instead of looking like the gray outline, starts to look like the black inner core (Figure 9)? What does this mean for agricultural production and nutritional needs? We do not know, but we do have a couple of pointers.

Figure 10 shows data taken from Boston University based on a study on a tea estate in Kenya—it shows the effect of HIV/AIDS on kilograms of tea plucked per day. The top line shows the productivity of people who died of non-AIDS illnesses, accidents, or other causes. The bottom line shows the productivity of people who died of AIDS. Productivity of HIV/AIDS-infected people in the commercial sector begins to fall two years before they die. We actually believe this is an underestimate, because we know that the people who plucked the tea were able to subcontract some of the work. These results are alarming.

More information is available from rural studies around Africa. Work in communal areas in Kenya showed that when a person's death was due to AIDS, a household's maize production declined by 67 percent. If the death had another cause, it declined by about 40 percent.

Table 1 shows the responses of rural households to being infected or affected by HIV/AIDS. Food security is hammered, income is affected, and labor has to be reallocated. Increased hours must be allocated to the care of orphans and of the sick.

The problem of AIDS is that it may push weaker households to the point where they cannot recover (Figure 11). And many households, communities, regions, and possibly even some countries fall into the category of "weak," as a result of drought, structural adjustment, poor government policy, overwhelming and unforgiven debt, and unfair trade policies that give a European cow three times as much subsidy as the per capita income of the average Ugandan.

Then there is the relationship between food and HIV (Figure 12). Poorly nourished people are at greater risk of being infected, and poorly nourished people who are HIV-positive will fall ill faster. Those people who are lucky enough to be offered antiretroviral therapy will, if they are poorly nourished, be less able to tolerate it and less able to benefit from it. The irony is that if you are HIV-positive, you need more calories and more micronutrients to fight the battle that is going on in your body.

There are things we can do. We have to improve nutrition and production by improving access to micronutrients, introducing labor-saving technologies, and offering appropriate training. We also have to provide inputs—agricultural and social transfers, not just in the short term, but for the next 5, 10, or 15 years—until 2020. We have to deal with the prevention, mitigation, and care and treatment of AIDS.

I have given you statistics, but let us remember the millions of ordinary people behind them. Here is the challenge for you: You are the experts. Armed with the information I have given you, what would you do?

FIGURE 8—Changes in life expectancy in selected African countries with high and low HIV prevalence, 1950–2005

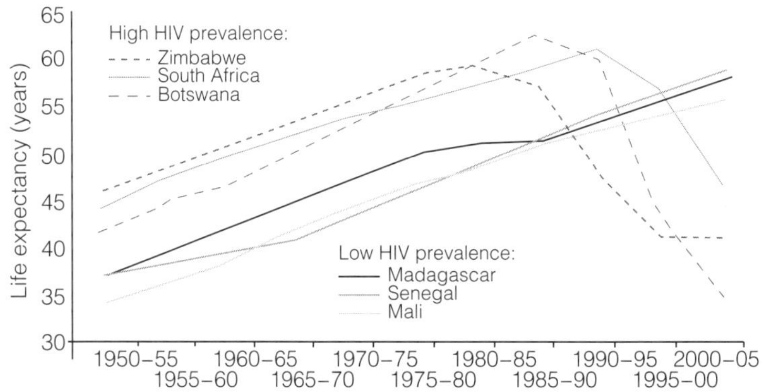

Source: UNAIDS, *Report on the global HIV/AIDS epidemic 2002* (Geneva: UNAIDS, 2002).

FIGURE 9—Projected population structure with and without the AIDS epidemic, Botswana, 2020

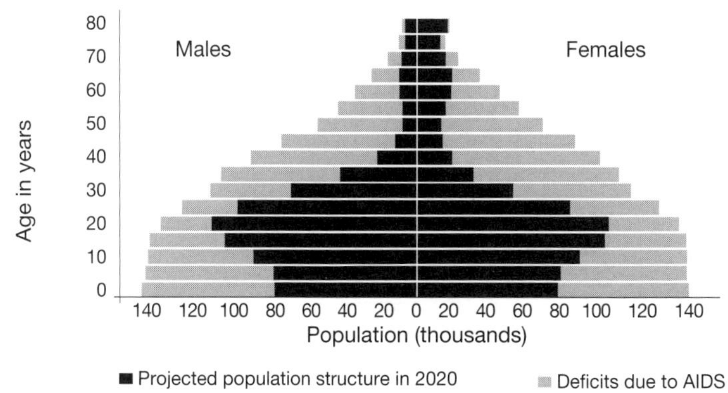

Source: U.S. Census Bureau.

FIGURE 10—Effect of HIV/AIDS on kilograms of tea plucked per day (adjusted)

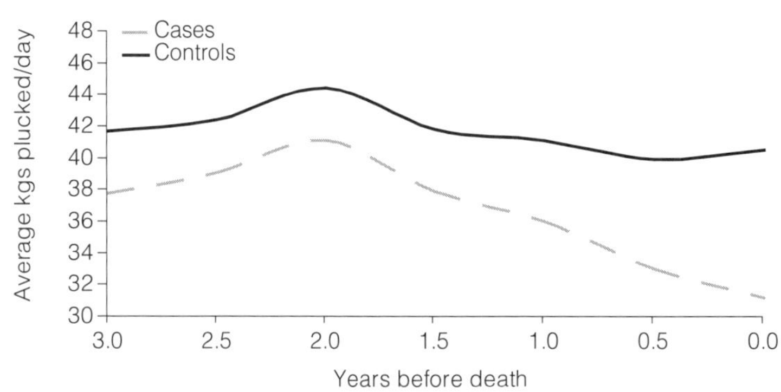

Source: M. P. Fox, J. L. Simon, M. Bii, K. M. Wasunna, W. B. MacLeod, G. Foglia, and S. Rosen, "The impact of HIV/AIDS on labor productivity in Kenya," paper presented at the meeting "Empirical evidence for the demographic and socio-economic impact of AIDS," Durban, South Africa, March 26-28, 2003.

TABLE 1—Rural household responses to being infected/affected by HIV/AIDS

Food Security	Income	Labor
Eat cheaper foods	Diversify income	Reallocate labor - e.g. children leave school
Reduce consumption	Migrate	Work extra hours
Call in social and familial obligations (send children to relatives)	Borrow (from informal sector/relatives)	Hire labor and draft animals
Eat wild foods	Sell assets (dissaving)	Decrease cultivated areas
Beg	Use savings or investments (dissaving)	Call in social and familial obligations (ask relatives to help)
	Beg	Diversify income

FIGURE 11—Effect of HIV on household security

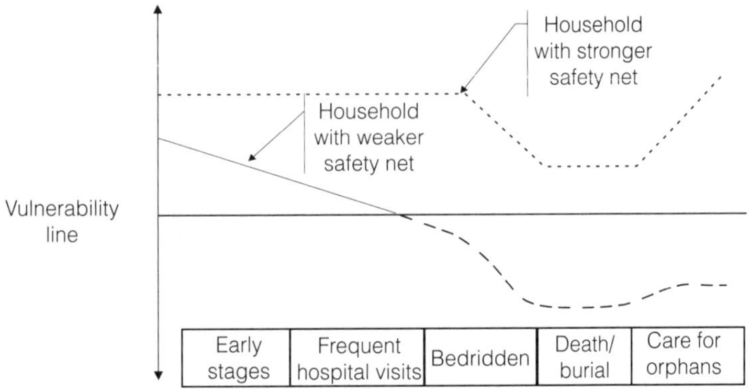

FIGURE 12—The relationship between good nutrition and HIV/AIDS

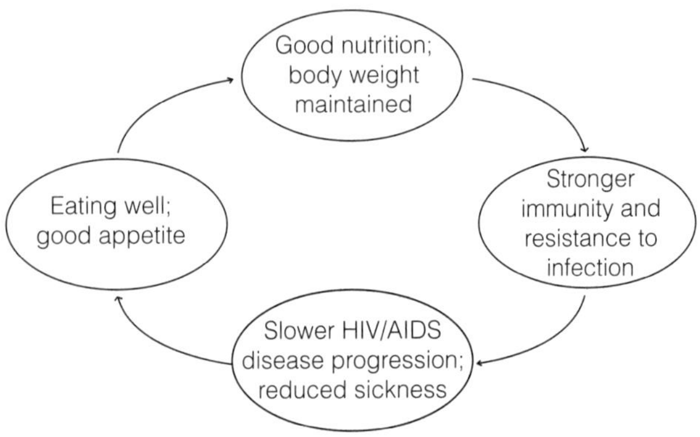

Keynote Address: Priorities for Action on Food and Nutrition Security in Africa: Perspectives from the African Union

Rosebud Kurwijila
Commissioner for Rural Economy and Agriculture, African Union, Ethiopia

Rosebud Kurwijila offers a perspective from the African Union.

The Commission of the African Union regards this conference as important and timely for two reasons. One is that we are addressing an issue that touches on the basic livelihood of all our people: their ability to access enough food, and of sufficient quality, at all times. This basic need has continued to elude every generation of Africa's leadership for over four decades now. We must act now, and act differently from the past. The second reason is that it comes at a time when our newly installed commission is in the process of translating the various decisions that have been made by our heads of state and government in the recent past into a concrete and actionable strategic development framework.

The inception of the African Union and the putting in place of its new commission signifies a departure from the past and a resolve by our heads of state and government to address more directly the socioeconomic development of the majority of our people. While the socioeconomic development of Africa requires us to address development issues from many fronts, including peace and security, I will confine myself to the issues of agriculture and food security. I will therefore share with you our current views, plans, and activities dedicated to Africa's agriculture and rural development.

The newly formed Commission of the African Union is in the process of rethinking forms of organization and seeking more effective mechanisms and strategies to address the critical challenges and emergencies facing the continent today. Since its inception the Commission has engaged in a process of consultations to view the information necessary for the development of viable plans and programs aimed at alleviating the continent's problems by integrating and optimizing the productivity of the continent's resources.

One of our roles as the Commission of the African Union is to draw the attention of member states and the international community to the urgent need to respond to the priorities and problems in Africa's agriculture and rural development. African countries have identified food security and poverty among the most urgent priorities requiring immediate action. In recognition of Africa's agricultural and rural development challenges, and in view of their inextricable linkage, the Maputo Summit approved an organizational structure for the Commission of the African Union that provides for a Department of Rural Economy and Agriculture. Agriculture has also been identified as one of the critical focal areas to be addressed within the framework of NEPAD, a program of the African Union whose objectives and implementation the Commission is mandated and committed to support.

The Commission of the African Union, through the Department of Rural Economy and Agriculture, appreciates the seriousness and urgency of Africa's troubles and seeks to inspire the necessary remedial action by promoting the policies, strategies, and actions that can kick-start growth, increase economic activity, and reduce poverty. Related to these objectives is the need to introduce measures that will encourage the integration and optimization of Africa's resources and contribute to the attainment of sustainable development.

Our challenge is to identify and address the key elements and factors that constrain Africa's agricultural productivity and rural development. The mission of the Department of Rural Economy and Agriculture is to work with member states, African institutions, civil society, and development partners to reverse the poor state of rural economies in order to improve the livelihoods of the African people by promoting increased agricultural productivity.

One core function of the department is the development and promotion of policy measures and strategies for the improvement of agricultural systems in order to attain food security, contribute to reducing poverty, expand the export market for agricultural products, and reduce the adverse effects of plant and animal diseases. The other core function of the department is the development and promotion of policies and strategies for the sustainable management of natural resources and protection of ecosystems.

To address its core functions, the Commission will focus on the following areas:

- contributing to food security through improving crop and animal resources, utilization, and management;
- improving access to markets and value adding, both local and international, for Africa's agricultural products;
- promoting cooperation in transboundary natural resource management and disease control;
- contributing to capacity building and strengthening of human capacity in agriculture, natural resources development, management, and research; and
- promoting access to agriculture information and communication.

To be able to execute its mandate in a focused and coordinated manner, the Commission will consolidate and strengthen the following regional offices and programs that deal with the different issues related to the identified core areas of interest to the African Union:

- the Inter-African Bureau for Animal Resources, IBAR, based in Nairobi, Kenya, which focuses on animal resources and the control of transboundary diseases;
- the Semi-Arid Food Grain Research and Development (SAFGRAD), based in Ouagadougou, Burkina Faso;
- the Inter-African Phytosanitary Council (IAPC), based in Yaoundé, Cameroon, which focuses on crop protection and pest control; and
- the Pan-African Tsetse and Trypanosomiasis Eradication Campaign (PATTEC), based at the Commission, which focuses on the eradication of the tsetse fly.

The activities of these regional offices and programs are supervised and coordinated by the Office of the Commissioner for Rural Economy and Agriculture.

The Commission of the African Union will operate within the framework of a four-year operational plan. The Department of Rural Economy and Agriculture is currently in the process of developing an integrated four-year plan of action for the period 2004 to 2007 that will take advantage of the synergy between the specific mandates of its regional offices and the harmonization with the Comprehensive Africa Agricultural Development Programme of NEPAD. This strategic framework will be presented to the African Union Summit in July 2004. The work of the Commission will be executed in collaboration with member states, scientific institutions, the regional economic communities, and our development partners.

Recognizing the urgent need for action to redress Africa's agricultural and rural development problems, our heads of state and government decided in Maputo in 2003 to hold a special summit on agriculture and water. The Second Extraordinary Summit was recently held in Sirte, Libya, on February 27, 2004.

The main objectives of the Second Extraordinary Summit were as follows:

- to focus the attention of Africa's political leadership on making concrete financial arrangements for investments, with particular regard to the agricultural sector;
- to mobilize political will and commitment for tapping, conservation, and management of Africa's water resources for agriculture;
- to make concrete arrangements for accelerated development, research, and marketing of strategic agricultural commodities;
- to agree on a political framework for shared water management for agricultural development and for the development of other horizontally linked sectors; and
- to agree on appropriate institutional arrangements for the agriculture and water sectors at the continental level.

After a series of discussions involving experts and ministers in the agriculture and water sectors and the Executive Council, the Extraordinary Summit in Sirte adopted decisions on concrete actions on policy issues, institutional arrangements, financing, and implementation and follow-up mechanisms.

Africa's agriculture and food production are constrained by many factors, including an unfavorable policy and institutional environment. In most countries agricultural production is dominated by smallholder farmers. Given the right incentives—such as access to land, financial and credit services, price stabilization mechanisms, institutional farmers' organizations, and market access within specific member countries—farmers can produce enough food to feed themselves and a surplus for export to other African countries.

But not all countries have the right soil, water, and weather conditions to produce all the food they need. Each country is endowed with different resources and agricultural production potentials. We need therefore to encourage countries to take stock of their comparative advantages and focus their efforts on a few strategic commodities. When countries manage to produce what they can produce best, with the maximum efficiency possible, intraregional trade should serve to even out imbalances and shortfalls in food production in one country or another. Based on this philosophy, our heads of state decided in Sirte that Africa should identify and support the development and production of strategic agricultural commodities and other key economic and industrial activities, in order to fully exploit the continent's special potentialities and the comparative advantages of member states, while reducing the expenditure and dependence on imports.

One other area where Africa needs to depart from the past is in the marginalization of livestock and fisheries in the context of food and nutrition security. In many instances, national, regional, and international agricultural development programs have focused exclusively on plant genetic resources. Food security is often narrowly defined in terms of meeting caloric needs. We need to recognize the synergy between crops and livestock in the livelihood of smallholder farmers and their complementarities in terms of environmental sustainability where appropriate husbandry practices are adopted.

Hence, the Sirte Declaration, for the first time, urges member states to put livestock and fisheries high on the development agenda. The decision on livestock requires African governments to promote the development of livestock production, including the improvement of natural pastures and distribution of veterinary products and genetic resources, with a view to improving food security.

The role of science and technology in agricultural development cannot be overemphasized. National agricultural research systems, including universities, are playing an important role, but they cannot be expected to deliver what is expected of them under conditions of gross underfunding and declining resources. This applies also to the regional and international research institutions and networks. Hence, the Sirte Declaration seeks to promote the idea of establishing centers of excellence for research and development, the functioning of which could be enhanced by more robust international partnerships within the UN system, as well as the CGIAR centers. Such centers of excellence should actively seek to bring the benefits of science and technology, including biotechnology or genetically modified organisms, to smallholder farmers on the African continent and mitigate any perceived or real adverse effects of the same.

Empowerment of farmers, especially women, will be important for the uptake of technologies that can enhance agricultural productivity on the continent.

— Rosebud Kurwijila

The Sirte Declaration is groundbreaking for many aspects of African agriculture. Most important of all is the linkage it seeks to establish between agriculture and water at the policy level. African agriculture cannot continue to be left to the vagaries of nature. We need to take deliberate measures to promote irrigation, especially small-scale irrigation and rainwater-harvesting technologies. It is only in Africa where less than 10 percent of farmland is irrigated. Yet most of the high-yield crop varieties—products of the "Green Revolution"—have high demands for water and other inputs such as fertilizers, the cost of which is often beyond the financial means of the majority of smallholder farmers.

The Sirte Declaration seeks, among other things, to encourage bilateral agreements on shared water resources and development of regional protocols by regional economic communities to guide integrated water resources management. The establishment of the African Water Facility under Water Vision 2025 is envisaged to facilitate articulation of water issues in agricultural and energy sector development.

In order for the proposed policies and strategies to be carried out, institutional arrangements at the farm, national, regional, and continental levels will be required. Empowerment of farmers, especially women, will be important for the uptake of technologies that can enhance agricultural productivity on the continent. Farmers' organizations will be important to enhance farmers' market access and participation in decisionmaking. Civil society needs to be facilitated and enjoined in enhancing farmers' rights and their position in decisionmaking. Farmers cannot continue to be on the receiving end of policy and research undertakings. They need to become active participants if uptake of technology is to take place at an accelerated rate.

At the continental level, the Sirte Declaration commits the African Union to incorporate the African

Ministerial Council on Environment, the Ministers Conference of Agriculture, and the Ministerial Conference on Water into the activities of the specialized technical committees of the African Union. Other mandates include institutionalization of plant and animal genetic resource banks at the national and regional level, provisions for registration of intellectual property rights, and the establishment of early warning systems at the national and regional levels with coordination at the continental level.

Other institutional issues that will require coordinated effort and support from our development partners include establishing an agricultural information and communication network on crop and livestock production, food security, and trading of agricultural commodities. African states must also work toward establishing an African common market for agricultural products, in line with the Lusaka Summit decision.

The long list of tasks that the African Union Commission and the African Union member states are being committed to fulfill has a similar long list of financial, human, and other resource requirements. The Sirte Declaration takes cognizance of this need and exhorts African governments, through the Commission, to work toward the expeditious establishment of an African investment bank, as well as an African agricultural development bank, and implementation of the declaration adopted in Maputo on the allocation of at least 10 percent of our national budgets to boost agricultural production.

Looking at the list of declarations that have been adopted in the past, some observers may be quick to conclude that the Sirte Declaration is just more wishful thinking, a dream by our heads of state that will never be fulfilled. But there is a difference now. We have great hope in the present-day generation of African leaders. The ideals of NEPAD, the newfound willingness of African statesmen to tackle Africa's development problems themselves, and the establishment of the Commission as an organ for implementing decisions by the African Union heads of state provide the impetus needed to turn Africa around.

The Commission of the African Union, in collaboration with NEPAD, has been tasked to work toward implementing the Maputo and Sirte decisions on agriculture and water, as well as all previous and future decisions on agriculture. Our success and failure will be judged on this basis.

We are encouraged by the fact that we are not alone in this onerous task of fulfilling the African dream for the future.

— Rosebud Kurwijila

The role of the Commission is largely one of coordination and mobilization of appropriate support and action. Every area of human endeavor on the African continent is in urgent need of attention, but in developing our plans and programs we shall focus on those areas of emphasis that we can do well with available resources.

We recognize, appreciate, and welcome the roles and activities of all the players working on issues of Africa's agriculture and development. One of the principal functions of the Commission is to assist our development partners in achieving their objectives. We are encouraged by the fact that we are not alone in this onerous task of fulfilling the African dream for the future.

I am aware that IFPRI and other CGIAR centers have been going through a period of deep reflection in recent years in order to make their agenda more relevant to the aspiration of smallholder farmers and to the alleviation of poverty, hunger, and malnutrition. Our biggest challenges are at the policy level. All human beings have the ability to harness our capacity to bring about the positive transformation of our societies if given the right policy environment. I am confident that IFPRI will put its mandate to good use and work in partnership with continental, regional, and national organizations and institutions to inform policymakers on what is required to create a conducive environment for the elimination of poverty, hunger, and malnutrition. I hope we can all do everything possible to achieve this objective by 2020, as the theme of this conference suggests.

Excerpt 16: Increasing Access to Infrastructure for Africa's Rural Poor

Maximo Torero and Shyamal Chowdhury

Inadequate and unreliable infrastructure services are a fact of life for the majority of rural communities in Africa. Many rural households do not have access to safe drinking water, electricity, good transportation, or modern communication services. For instance, in Burkina Faso, Uganda, and Zambia, walking is the principal means of transportation for 87 percent of rural residents. Ninety-five percent of rural households in Africa depend on traditional fuels, and very few African villages have a single telephone.

Ninety percent of Africa's land and 80 percent of its populated area lie more than 100 kilometers from the coast or from a navigable river. Although rural areas are generally characterized by poor access to infrastructure, it is the poor households within the rural areas that have the least access.

Development in the different rural infrastructure services in Africa in the 1980s and 1990s was sector specific, with little or no emphasis on cross-sectoral strategies. Despite sector specificity, the common strategy among sectors was to attract private capital and the users' contribution as the principal means of financing. Although the sector-specific strategy worked in some countries and communities, it largely failed to attract the necessary capital to build and maintain rural infrastructure. The policy of leaving the rural transport provision to the private sector was generally unsuccessful in Sub-Saharan Africa. In most cases, transportation markets remained uncompetitive and disproportionately dominated by transportation unions, associations, and formal and informal cartels.

The development of an efficient regional transportation infrastructure has remained elusive in most parts of Africa. This hinders regional and international trade and is a major barrier for landlocked countries. For example, importers in the Central African Republic and Chad pay CIF (cost, insurance, and freight) prices that are 1.3 to 1.8 times the cost of the products when they left the exporting countries. Similarly, CIF prices for coffee exported from the Central African Republic and Chad are, on arrival in Europe, 2.8 times the production cost.

Poor infrastructure services are partly to blame for disappointing domestic private investment and foreign direct investment in Africa. Although firms can make up for deficient infrastructure services by investing privately, such substitutions impose additional costs. Moreover, some types of infrastructure services—such as transport infrastructure—cannot be easily substituted.

Rural households in Sub-Saharan Africa pay much higher transportation costs than do households in developing countries in Asia. This is equally true for passenger fares and freight charges. For instance, a comparative study of rural transportation carried out in 1994–1995 found that Ghana and Zimbabwe's transportation charges were two to two and a half times more expensive than those in Thailand, Pakistan, and Sri Lanka. Similarly, in the 1986–1988 period, long-distance freight transport tariffs in francophone Africa were more than five times higher than tariffs in Pakistan.

Given the apparent failure of pure public provision in the 1970s and the failure of market provision in the 1980s and 1990s, it becomes necessary to search for institutional innovations that are appropriate for Sub-Saharan Africa. We suggest focusing on the following activities: evaluating existing institutional frameworks; learning from and replicating the positive impacts of market-led reforms; encouraging public intervention; forging public-private partnerships; and taking into account local demand for services.

This has been excerpted from forthcoming 2020 Africa Conference Brief 16, published by IFPRI, Washington, DC, 2005.

Chapter 19 Building Political Will and Changing Attitudes for Action

Chair: Moïse Mensah
Former Minister of Finance, Benin

Africa's ability to win the challenge of poverty reduction, with particular emphasis on food and nutrition security, depends on how effectively we can formulate and implement policies and programs that address a wide range of areas, such as agricultural research and production, trade, infrastructure, and human resources. Those policies inevitably will call for reforms that require changing attitudes, starting with the expression of a strong and convincing political will. Yet, when this forum was asked whether African leaders are prepared to demonstrate the required political will, the majority, by a vote, expressed strong doubt (see Box 5 for participant digital voting results). We must therefore look closely at the issue of building political will and changing attitudes for action.

Keynote Address: Fighting HIV/AIDS through Attitudinal Changes: Experiences from Uganda

H. E. Janet Museveni
First Lady of the Republic of Uganda

As you all know, the world has been in the struggle against HIV and AIDS for 20 years now. We are told that over 60 million people worldwide are infected with the disease, and millions have already died of it. Sub-Saharan Africa has been the worst-affected region on the globe, with a current total of about 30 million infected.

The overwhelming majority of those infected are young and able-bodied. They should be producing food; providing labor for industries; manning public institutions such as the civil service, banks, schools, and hospitals; and bringing up new generations of African leaders.

Here in Uganda AIDS has erased decades of progress. For example, the country's life expectancy fell from 56 years in 1986 to 42 years in 1999. The impact on the majority of households has been severe. AIDS has caused families to move from relative wealth to absolute poverty. In a developing country such as Uganda, whose economic backbone is agriculture, the effect of AIDS on rural household livelihoods has been disastrous.

Additional care, related expenses, the reduced ability of caregivers to work, and mounting medical and funeral expenses collectively push the affected households deeper into poverty. Falling food production, loss of family labor, and related factors translate into reduced household food security.

Of course, all the direct and indirect effects of HIV and AIDS ultimately translate into a macroeconomic impact. By impacting the labor force and the households and enterprises, HIV and AIDS have acted as a significant brake on economic growth and development here in Uganda. If we did not have HIV and AIDS in this country, I believe our development would be substantial.

The first AIDS cases in Uganda were identified in 1982. Nothing much was done, partly because the country was in political turmoil at the time. By the end of the 1980s, the disease had escalated to epidemic levels. And yet, in less than a decade, the country's HIV prevalence was brought down from a high of 30 percent in the 1980s to 19 percent in 1992, and it has since dropped to its current level of 6 percent.

To what should we attribute this dramatic drop in HIV and AIDS prevalence levels? In the context of an

> *With regard to prevention, and in the absence of any known cure, people's attitudes had to change.*
>
> — H. E. Janet Museveni

impoverished African nation just emerging from two decades of political turmoil, although it is still early to speak with certainty, some strategies stand out as key in turning around the runaway situation of HIV and AIDS.

The major one is today termed "social communication." In 1986, shortly after President Museveni came to government, he openly acknowledged HIV and AIDS as a national development problem. In 1990 the government realized that HIV and AIDS were best fought on many fronts since they are not just a health issue. Therefore, a multisector approach was adopted.

This approach emphasized the role of everyone in this struggle against HIV and AIDS. A special body, the Uganda AIDS Commission, was set up—not in the Ministry of Health, but in the Office of the President—to plan, oversee, coordinate, and monitor the national response to the epidemic in this broader national context. Using this strategy, the country decided to concentrate on four key interventions: prevention, care, support, and impact mitigation and strengthening of capacity. These interventions have benefited from the collective efforts of the various players at different levels.

With regard to prevention, and in the absence of any known cure, people's attitudes had to change. At the very beginning, attitudes had to be changed from superstition to scientific fact concerning how HIV was transmitted or contracted. Our people at first believed that the victims had been bewitched. It took many mass information and education campaigns, spearheaded by the highest office in the land and using all platforms, to equip the population with key messages on vulnerability to and prevention of HIV transmission.

Within the larger context, some subgroups require special messages and social communication. In some cultures, for example, widows are usually inherited by the male next-of-kin—a dangerous practice that spreads HIV and AIDS and wipes out entire families. This is a hard practice to break, because it involves the sensitive issues of property and children. In other cultures, circumcision must be carried out in seasonal ceremonial rituals that involve the use of sharp instruments, communally utilized—another sure way of transmitting HIV and AIDS to entire groups of adolescent males.

Attitudes also needed to be changed, and still need to change, regarding the way people treat the infected among them. Initial reactions to victims of AIDS were ruled by misinformation and fear, leading to stigmatization and sometimes condemnation of the infected, and even the affected, by the rest of society.

Messages have addressed the general public. And specific messages have been developed for the more

First Lady of Uganda Janet Museveni and Nobel Prize winner Wole Soyinka discuss how to change attitudes and behaviors.

vulnerable or high-risk groups within the population. As a result of this intensive and persistent information campaign, general awareness of HIV and AIDS in Uganda is now rated at 99.7 percent.

The next question is: Does awareness, or acquisition of mental knowledge, actually translate into behavior change? We believe that in our case it has.

Our strategy has been to mount an aggressive education, information, and communication campaign, using not only the electronic and print media such as radio, television, billboards, and print materials, but also devising other methods that have proved to be more effective in a basically rural and semiliterate population.

Starting with a head of state whose leadership against this enemy of the people has been resolute, passionate, charismatic, and consistent, and who has made it clear that fighting against AIDS is everyone's patriotic duty in this country, the campaign has been characterized by its ability to transform and become up close and personal in the different contexts. Each player at every level has taken the information and shaped it into a medium that is appropriate to the cultural context. While information is guided and monitored, the central coordinating body has allowed players at all levels to be innovative and imaginative as they bring the reality of the situation to their people.

An example of the success of this strategy is the behavior change that has taken place among our youth in Uganda. As a result of special interventions channeled to young people, youth between the ages of 14 to 25 years have contributed most to the country's declining infection trends. Independent studies and surveys by the Ministry of Health have established that the greatest

> *Our strategy has been to mount an aggressive education, information, and communication campaign.*
>
> — H.E. Janet Museveni

reduction in the number of new infections has been registered in this age group, because of behavior change brought about by effective social communication.

Studies have shown that adolescents in Uganda are now delaying sexual activity until they are older. Given that about 60 percent of Uganda's population is less than 20 years old, this change alone prevents thousands of new infections every year.

With messages of abstinence, cultures are slowly moving away from early sexual activity. Uganda has taken this very, very seriously. We have talked openly about abstinence from premarital sex and about teaching our youth messages of self-control. This was an idea that had been forgotten or eradicated altogether, and people were behaving more or less like the rest of the animals in the animal kingdom.

So we started asking questions like, What is the difference between us and the other animals, if we don't really practice self-control? What is so difficult about talking to our youth in our own families and households about them abstaining completely from sexual activity until they are married?—which was the African tradition in any case. So we revived these messages, and they have made an impact.

Traditionally, women are expected to be faithful to their partners in the context of marriage, but men are encouraged to have multiple partners, as a sign of wealth or strength. Now, by many accounts, this behavior in men is changing. This is partly attributed to the message of faithfulness to one's sexual partner here in Uganda. Even among men who were not really disciplined, the shock of seeing the deaths that were happening in our villages brought back the idea of spiritual discipline, of being faithful to their spouses. That has also made an impact. Grassroots communication has also brought about the empowerment of women, enabling them to be in a position to make informed choices.

The example of Uganda teaches us that it is possible to fight HIV and AIDS through behavior change, by presenting information to the people in a way they understand and, as much as possible, on a face-to-face basis. Of course, this approach takes serious commitment at the highest political level in order to be effective. It also takes involvement and participation by everybody, in an environment conducive to involvement by civil society. We have now in Uganda as many as 700 civil society organizations dealing with HIV and AIDS, many of them community-based organizations. Therefore, we can say that the success of Uganda in the struggle against HIV and AIDS really belongs to the people of Uganda. The President sounded an alarm, and everybody rose to the occasion.

As I conclude, I want to submit that what we have managed to do with regard to HIV and AIDS, we can also do in our struggle against poverty and lack of food security. When people are empowered with information and knowledge about how to think and innovate and find solutions from within, they can succeed at whatever goal they set for themselves.

In my work with orphans in the past decade and a half, I have interacted with many women in poverty-stricken rural areas in Uganda. Many of them head households and care for many children. Through training and a little economic empowerment, these women are being transformed. Through microfinance intervention, the women have acquired a culture of saving and have even been introduced to formal banking operations. If our governments in Africa would train such women—and they are everywhere in Africa—and make them the extension agents in their own villages, and facilitate them with bicycles and gum boots and other necessities, I assure you that every farmer in the country would be reached and served faithfully. Train the women, and the men, to help themselves in the areas of food production, food preservation, storage, and good nutrition, just as we have trained and entrusted them with the care of HIV and AIDS victims and orphans.

I appeal to you to let this be the century that ushers in the empowerment of the peoples of Africa, so that they can determine their own destiny and stop being the victims. Africa is the richest continent on the planet Earth. The populations of Africa, empowered with knowledge, are the ones who will find the key to unlock this wealth.

> *The example of Uganda teaches us that it is possible to fight HIV and AIDS through behavior change.*
>
> — H.E. Janet Museveni

Excerpt 17: Increasing the Effective Participation of Women in Food and Nutrition Security in Africa

Agnes R. Quisumbing, Ruth S. Meinzen-Dick, and Lisa C. Smith

Policy reform to eradicate gender discrimination aims to create a level playing field for women and men. Strengthening women's political voice is vital to any fundamental shift that increases women's effective participation. Women's human rights—political, civil, economic, social, and cultural—need to be respected, protected, and realized. The strengthening of democratic institutions via legislation, the rewriting of constitutions so that they explicitly disavow discrimination, and the reform and enforcement of an antidiscriminatory rule of law are important steps. In Uganda, for example, the national constitution encourages participation by requiring that at least one-third of officeholders in all elective positions be women. The new South African constitution explicitly guarantees freedom from discrimination on the basis of, among other things, race, gender, and disability. While such declarations do not automatically translate into changes on the ground, they provide an important signal of the government's commitment, to which women can appeal for stronger rights.

Eliminating gender discrimination in ownership of and access to economically productive assets is also critical. For example, the ability to inherit land, to join a credit and savings club, to join a water users group, to access extension advice, to start up a small enterprise, and to survive in the event of a family breakdown must be equal for women and for men. Customary laws in many countries treat women as minors, thereby restricting their rights to such assets and opportunities. In Lesotho and Swaziland, women are considered legal minors: they cannot own property, enter into contracts, or receive bank loans without a male relative. Rwanda's Matrimonial Regimes, Liberties, and Succession Act, in contrast, passed in 2000, allows women to own property.

Social protection programs that reduce risk and mitigate the impact of shocks are often biased toward males. Retirement benefits, for example, are usually lower for women. Family allowances give benefits to employed men with dependent wives but not to employed women with dependent children. An important exception is South Africa's noncontributory means-tested pension system for the elderly. Pensions received by women have been shown to improve the health and nutrition of children, especially girls, whereas pensions received by men do not show the same results.

Gender-based legal reform cannot be instituted without sensitivity to tradition. Customs do not change overnight, especially in countries with ancient cultures. Education and social marketing can play a role, but until majority values change, successful legal reform will have to build on positive traditional values. The Ethiopian constitution found a striking way of addressing the conflict between conservative customary laws and the progressive, egalitarian provisions of the 1960 Civil Code. First, after prolonged debate, it was decided that the constitution would revoke the abolition of personal laws (customary and religious). Disputants can participate in the decision regarding the application of laws concerning personal matters. If any party to a dispute does not wish to apply personal laws, she or he may opt for the application of the Civil Code provisions. Personal law arbitrators and courts, who formerly espoused the application of outdated customary law provisions, are rethinking their stand out of fear that women disputants may prefer to transfer the decision to the civil courts, thereby weakening the customary bodies.

This has been excerpted from 2020 Africa Conference Brief 4, published by IFPRI, Washington, DC, 2004.

Keynote Address: Changing Attitudes and Behaviors: The Role of Africa's Cultural Leaders

Wole Soyinka
Professor Emeritus, Obafemi Awolowo University, Nigeria; Director of Literary Arts, International Institute of Modern Letters, University of Nevada, USA; and Nobel Prize Laureate in Literature

I have a credential for addressing you today that even those who invited me here may not be aware of. At the age of four, I fought my best friend over food. It was pounded yam, a very special item of food that I sometimes describe as having a quasi-mystical status.

We made up, of course. My mother intervened. And I learned a lesson that has stayed with me all my life. I learned the lesson of extended families. I recognized finally that Osiki—that was his name—was actually a member of the extended family and that compared with him I was a privileged child, not that we were an affluent family. I realized that he actually relied for his daily sustenance on those meals that he used to share with me—with his over-large morsels, which is why we fought.

So we made up. But Osiki, unprivileged as he was compared with me, would consider his existence and my childhood to have been very privileged compared with that of millions of children today. He would swear to this ironic status of his even without watching contemporary footage of children from the hunger zones of the continent, their stomachs bloated in malnourishment, victims of perennial drought and of war displacements year after year, but also victims of the improvident attitude of African leadership. Today Osiki would stare unbelieving at the images of homesteads where the only evidence of abundance would be swarms of flies in competition for the least moisture on the eyes, lips, and nostrils of human beings sunk in lassitude. He would shudder at the attenuation of limbs of soon-to-be mortal statistics that continue to rebuke a continent of such diverse and abundant material resources. He would recoil at the portent of once-thriving farming villages whose productive routine has been drastically attenuated by HIV/AIDS, the surviving inhabitants being just wide-eyed, orphaned children, looking lost, uncertain of the source of their next meal.

Food is allied to culture in the most organic, interactive way, and one may be brought to the aid of, enhancement of, or celebration of the other.

– Wole Soyinka

Food is allied to culture in the most organic, interactive way, and one may be brought to the aid of, enhancement of, or celebration of the other. We observe this not only in the lyricism that food evokes in some societies, but in the shared weight of multiple creative arts that are dedicated to the planting season and harvesting, elaborate performance gatherings that also serve the purpose of cohering the community. Most of us, however, prefer such collaboration to the external dependency mode; such as once occurred in one of the critical periods of food shortage on the continent, when a helpless visage of this continent came to be stamped on global consciousness.

Now, I readily admit that I am not a fan of pop music, but at least I have kept my dislike for that frequent travesty of the musical art away from the actual creators—that is, until I heard the name of a certain Bob Geldof. The cause of my dislike was quite perverse. Bob Geldof was guilty of performing a duty that I considered mine, ours—the duty of the extended family that was the ethos of my upbringing and, I am certain, the upbringing of most of us here. Bob Geldof was the name that became identified, need I remind you, as the main initiator of a concert whose centerpiece was the famous "We Are the World." My dislike of Bob Geldof, in other words, had nothing to do with music, but with pride, racial pride. Who was this man, this foreigner, who took it upon himself to fill in a space of disregard, of indifference to the plight of a people by their own leaders?

There was, without question, also a sense of frustration, even envy. Only two years before that world music concert, I was editor of the African journal *Transition*, later to become *Ch'Indaba*. We warned of the crisis of drought and famine in parts of Ethiopia, based on firsthand reports. We tended to dramatize the beginnings of another round of famine-induced migrations of Ethiopian villagers while the Emperor, Haile Selassie, wined and dined foreign dignitaries in the splendor of his palace. To drive the point home, we published a facsimile of the menu of a typical banquet that took place in the imperial palace side by side with images of starving families and makeshift camps.

Two or three years later, under the so-called People's Revolutionary Regime of Mariam Mengistu, we were obliged to return to the same scenario of leadership planlessness, only this time, it had worsened beyond imagining. Once again, millions of humans were on the move, in flight from certain starvation. The lessons of the previous years in Tigre and other provinces had not been absorbed.

African humanity, it seemed, was always expendable to most leaders. Human skeletons, of both adults and children, denoted trails that were reminiscent of the routes of the trans-Saharan slave routes—journeys that many, incidentally, like to pretend never did take place. The continent was absorbing the bleak lesson that in the critical fulfillment of the primary mission of feeding its people, there was hardly any difference between neglect of the feudal kind and the myopia of revolutionary messianism.

What was singularly aggravating about the new famine in Ethiopia was that the increase in human suffering had been caused by an ill-digested notion of the productive strategies of collectivization. The ruling Dergue, stocked full of textbook notions about the transformation of means of production through centralism, commenced a policy of deliberate displacements, uprooted and dispersed entire peoples to artificial villages, but took no note of their traditions. Of course, some of these traditions have proved inadequate. But the inhuman revolutionary zeal of the Dergue only made matters worse.

The death toll mounted. The conscience of the world could stand it no longer. The pen may be mightier than the sword, but music proved far more efficacious than both. Revolutionary slogans made way for the lyrics of the pop musician reminding the affluent that indifference to material deficiency in one part of the world merely underlined the moral deficiency of the rest. I felt this rebuke personally and took a violent dislike to this man of conscience called Bob Geldof.

Many here will recall Chinua Achebe's *Arrow of God*, a work that offers itself so readily today as a parable of social responsibilities and the consequences of their betrayal. The conduct of a central character in that novel, Ezeulu, the priest and spiritual guardian of the deity Ulu in an Ibo community, is a cautionary tale for the contemporary leadership of this continent. Of Ezeulu's priestly duties, none was more crucial to the survival of the community than his role as the sign reader and transmitting medium for the planting season for the new yam—you know, that commodity over which I had fought my friend at four years of age.

If the harvest failed, and that meant if the seeds were not planted at the right moment—for instance,

African humanity, it seemed, was always expendable to most leaders.

— Wole Soyinka

before a seasonal change that burnt the seedlings in the earth—starvation was guaranteed for the ensuing year. The manner in which this authorization was provided goes to the very heart of an integrated community existence on many levels, and indeed, goes to the heart of what I described earlier as the quasi-mystical status of the yam, underlining the cyclic nature of Earth's renewal.

In Chinua Achebe's narrative, that signal is withheld by Ezeulu. The entire village waits on their priest, but he has a bone to pick with his people. He is smarting from a humiliation meted out to him by the colonial authority, in the person of a certain Captain Winterbottom, and additionally, from a political slight he has received from his own community. And so Ezeulu refuses to "see" the new moon whose appearance communicates to him the moment that he must eat the final symbolic tuber from the harvest of the previous year. He remains deaf to the pleas of the elders and turns a purely ritualistic procedure into a literal one. The welfare of the community is imperiled, but Ezeulu is unmoved. The priest, rather than make his world with his spiritual will and authority, was unmaking it, content to watch the community unravel at the seams.

Let me assert here the contemporary parallel that the conduct of Ezeulu evokes. It is a spiteful politics of some of our politicians who, because a constituency casts its votes for the opposition, proceed to impoverish that region, withholding public facilities, health, education, roads, water supply, including rudimentary bore holes, farming equipment, fertilizers, etc. Their language is, "You withheld your votes. Now go and eat your ballot."

Chinua Achebe, when he embarked on that work, may have been unaware that he was setting down a contemporary morality tale that is so applicable to the plight of the continent and to the leaders' betrayal of the natural expectations and confidence of their people. For one thing, when he wrote that novel, the notion of famine on the scale of the past two decades was unheard of on the continent, even in the Sahelian regions or in former colonies such as the Congo, where traditional food production systems had been subverted by the colonial policies that forced their subjects to substitute cash crops for food crops. I refer here to that

Let it never be forgotten that in the liturgies of worship, traditional songs, and rituals are lodged much knowledge concerning not merely the science of crops and food, but the pharmacology of healing.

— Wole Soyinka

period when thriving communities were turned into mere production appendages to King Leopold's commercial empire, a period of enforced quota systems when failure to attain was punished by the slicing of ears, slitting of nostrils, and amputation of limbs. In the colonial period, narrated in that work, the oil boom had not arrived to displace food as a primary preoccupation of peoples, resulting in once self-sustaining communities, now amalgamated into independent entities, finding themselves compelled to import even basic foods of which they were once, in some cases, exporters of surplus. When *Arrow of God* was written, neither the author nor anyone else had ever heard of a devastating affliction called HIV/AIDS.

Chinua Achebe's community of the deity Ulu is the paradigm of our continent, a continent awaiting the signal that would inaugurate a comprehensive planting that will sustain its people—that is, the annunciation of a creative, sustained, practical strategy attuned to the realities of uneven industrialization and new national entities, calling up a remedial response to the break-up of the organic productive systems of precolonial society, its demographic shifts, and the consequences of our brutal wars.

Could it be that IFPRI aspires to be the resurrected spirit of Ezeulu? But with the admonition that a community cannot wait on the voice of one individual alone, but must act collectively and methodically. IFPRI—well, not as euphonious a name as Ezeulu and hardly of totally indigenous origin, but as we say in my part of the world, if the man sees the poisonous snake, but it takes a woman to kill it, all that matters to the menaced homestead is that the snake is dead.

When *Arrow of God* was written in the early 1960s, the oil palm industry of southern Nigeria was still flourishing. The landscape of the northern part was adorned with groundnut pyramids, attaining such iconographic status that they were used on the national postage stamps. It is not mere nostalgia, therefore, but the necessity for our self-indictment, a bitter stock-taking, that wrung the following lines out of me, lines from the poem "Elegy for a Nation" in the collection *Samarkand and Other Markets I Have Known*:

> We grew filament eyes
> As heads of millet, as flakes of cotton responsive
> To brittle breezes, wraith-like in the haze of
> Harmattan
> Green of the cornfields of Oyo, ochre of groundnut
> pyramids
> Of Kano, indigo in the ancient dye-pots of Abeokuta
> We were the cattle nomads, silent threads through
> Forestries and cities, coastland and savannah
> Wafting Maiduguri to the sea, ocean mists to sand
> dunes
>
> Alas for lost idyll ...
> ... Ghosts are sole inheritors.
> Silos fake rotundity – these are kwashi-okor blights
> Upon the landscape, depleted at source. Even
> The harvest seeds were long devoured. Empty hands
> Scrape the millennial soil at planting.

Yes, "even the harvest seeds were long devoured," both figuratively, out of greed, by incontinent leadership, but sometimes also from necessity, as happened in Igboland during the civil war. This condition must be recognized as the continuing fate of many African zones of civil war today, where antipersonnel mines reduce the yield potential of land even further and finish off what HIV/AIDS has begun.

In *Samarkand* I was indeed invoking the nation that we once knew, but Nigeria was only one of many such travesties. At least there had been war in Nigeria, with attendant distortion of production processes. The ascendancy of a war industry that resulted in the abandonment of multiple economic devices—but agriculture most especially—was a phenomenon that simply transferred itself to the oil industry once oil was discovered.

Not even successive attempts at mobilization under slogans such as "Operation Feed Yourself," "Operation Feed the Nation," "Operation This and Whatever Else" have succeeded in the resuscitation of the farm as primary source for a people's food security. Often, the main target of such endeavors was youth—how to turn the sight of youth away from the glitzy attractions of urban living and challenge them with the vital contributions that can be extracted from that basic resource, land. Nigeria is only an illustration, and it is improving these days.

No one requires to be told that this anomaly has spread all over the continent, and even in nations, like

Ghana, that did not undergo the production distortion of civil war or an oil boom. I was sojourning in that nation when the markets dried up. The staple food, kenke, made from fermented corn, shrank until it virtually vanished into its wrapping of leaves, while the supermarkets' display cases held nothing but shelled coconuts. That was the paradox: There was no shortage of food in the land, but there was starvation. Food crops simply rotted away on the farms for lack of transportation thanks to the incontinent conduct, indifference, and neglect of the ruling military.

We cannot exactly return to that integrated phase of communal life, where the very process of cultivation, like other forms of life-preserving labor, was related to the overall cultural being of the community. But we can come reasonably close. We can reinvent the gods, exploiting their timeless functionalism.

I propose this dimension not merely because I am a compulsive mythologist, but because I would like to see when the new sign reader and interactive medium of our times—I'll call it "Ezeulu-IFPRI"—next sounds the gong for planting. But it is not merely experts who are summoned, but a fair representation of the small-scale, even subsistence, farmers, who remained faithful to their vocation, are closer to earth than most of us here, and are sometimes unconscious researchers into the science of food. It helps, of course, if we can link them, through familiar cultural symbols, to the world of modernity and constant technological innovations.

The two relevant deities here are, first, none other than that confessed favorite of mine, Ogun, in all his myriad transformations, the god of metallurgy and the patron deity of agriculture, a role he shares with another deity, Orisa-oko. Orisa-oko is the very spirit of leaves, the farm, and the moist elements, while Ogun is the technological impulse that transforms nature from the most rudimentary hoe and machete to the complex combine harvester, the churning mills, and transportation conveyances.

There are several models on whose scaffolding such basic, life-affirming strategies, the antithesis of hunger and starvation, can be mounted. I see no reason why a day cannot be dedicated to the culture of food renewal, its science and technology, every year, utilizing the seasonal festivals of Orisa-oko and Ogun, or their equivalents in other African cultures. Regionally or continentwide, it does not matter; the goal is to marry the cultural wealth and celebration of relevant mythologies to a forward focus on modernization through recall and celebration.

Let it never be forgotten that in the liturgies of worship, traditional songs, and rituals are lodged much knowledge concerning not merely the science of crops and food, but the pharmacology of healing. From the spirit of that past, new songs will emerge attuned to the present, abandoning the charity-propelled "We Are the World," that song of dependency, to the self-affirmation of "We Make Our World."

I envision, in short, a working festival that recovers the ethos of farming integration with life-sustaining processes, encounters that anticipate, not simply respond to, devastating vagaries of nature. Technical expositions, contests with awards that will stimulate inventiveness in the technology of food preservation and pest control, experimentation in the cultivation of new varieties, disease-resisting strains, high-yield varietals, promotion of organic fertilizers that do away with controversial chemicals—in short, an entire revolution in our approach to the food sciences that were developed for other climes, other soils, and other industrial cultures, instead giving primacy of place to our own authoritative voices, not simply the politicians', over the merits or demerits of genetically altered crops.

The past has much to teach, even if the present rides on the engines of the future. The trajectory of surplus and scarcity would be plotted in scientific caucuses that would be part of such a fiesta, with, of course, a gallery of negativities as correctives—those hideous scars on the African conscience that watched millions perish from neglect.

Culture and cultivation are deeply entrenched in traditional society. The younger generation, that is, the future, is the primary target—those who are more at home with Nintendo games than with a creative engagement with the soil that has nourished their ancestors from prehistory and sustains their very existence. If we can appeal to a youthful sense of imagination and excitement at the potential of this neglected field of resources, I believe that half the battle against hunger will be no battle at all, but a celebration of nature in transformation, stimulated by home-evolved ingenuities.

We must remember, however, that there is a condiment that must be swallowed with the food of charity: a chastening ingredient that is known as "pride."

— Wole Soyinka

Yes, culture and the arts can prove handmaidens of cultivation. We have a choice, however: either to create our own cultural incentives that motivate productivity and lead to self-reliance, or await the handouts from the charity of the world. We must remember, however, that there is a condiment that must be swallowed with the food of charity: a chastening ingredient that is known as "pride." The choice is therefore no choice at all.

We owe it to the future that those same fly-infested mouths of want that presently occupy the gallery of a failed past are filled with the self-empowerment that will launch a new chant from the Sahel to the Cape: "We Make Our World."

Keynote Address: Building Strong Partnerships to Improve Africa's Food Security and Rural Incomes

Peter McPherson
President, Michigan State University; Founding Co-Chair, Partnership to Cut Hunger in Africa, USA

I believe there will be progress in Africa in the years ahead. That may not be a revolutionary statement here, but outside these halls it is an assertion that many would challenge. Because many people are pessimistic, it is worth thinking about other parts of the world in times past where there has been deep pessimism about whether any progress was going to take place.

When President Kennedy and his Latin American colleagues announced the Alliance for Progress in 1961, Latin America was dramatically different from today. As late as the 1950s, in fact, Ecuador had the Indians legally tied to the land in a medieval serf connection. Today, Latin American countries like Brazil look very different. Not many people would have expected this progress in 1958 or 1959.

In Asia, it was accepted wisdom that Confucianism was going to be the hindrance to real progress. And somehow, this whole concept evolved so that Confucianism is now regarded as the bedrock of hard work and progress in Asia.

If we are unable to make progress in this continent in the next generation or so, it will be the historical exception. I see no reason to think it should be, though substantial progress will take decades, perhaps generations, as it has in some other places.

When we consider what should be done here, the experiences of the past couple of generations offer some lessons. These will no doubt need to be adapted, for every country and region is unique. But there are some common threads to sustained progress.

The foundation of the concept of development around the world has been that individuals will work very hard for their own progress. Everybody around the world wants their children to survive, they want a roof over their heads, they want their families to be successful, and to achieve these things, people will work very hard indeed.

When I was a Peace Corps volunteer in Peru in the early 1960s, I talked to an Indian who had come down from the Andes 10 years or so before and put together his grass-mat hut with a bunch of other squatters in the middle of the night. Here I was 10 years later, and he had a jerry-rigged but substantial brick home. I asked him, "How did you do this? This is really impressive." I vividly recall him standing up and tightening his belt.

So people will work very hard for their own success, and donors and political leaders often forget that that energy is the foundation, individually and collectively, of real change.

Another lesson is that it is hard for people to look beyond the immediate future if there is not some level of political stability and physical security. That goes beyond this discussion, but it is a critical lesson.

We also know that the right economic policies are very important for change. In early 1980 it was fairly clear that most of the Asian tigers were going to make progress. But what had just begun was economic policy change in China, and then it has come in recent years in India. And when you look where poor people have been most positively impacted over the past two decades it has been in the two biggest countries in the world, in large part because of some degree of stability and some key changes in economic policy.

Incidentally, the developed world and the donors certainly have key roles to play in promoting better economic policies. President Museveni talked about the importance of trade and the African Growth and Opportunity Act. I totally agree, and Europe, the United States, and Japan all need to play a role here.

The next lesson is one that we seem to have to relearn at least every generation. When a country is predominantly rural, you need to figure out how to have

If we are unable to make progress in this continent in the next generation or so, it will be the historical exception.

— Peter McPherson

rural income growth, or you are not likely to achieve growth in the country. Why do we have to re-learn that lesson? We now have a set of excellent studies done by people like John Mellor and others showing that when food production increases on a sustained basis, people eat some and sell some. With the sale there is a multiplier impact that can drive the whole economy.

Another lesson concerns the role of technology. An excellent case can be made that in the history of the world, many of the significant changes have come about as a result of technological improvement. We should not expect to make the progress needed here without major technology changes. For example, malaria vaccine is going to be really important to Africa. Of course, both creation and dissemination is important.

The next lesson is that training and education are key. Ted Schultz got the Nobel Prize in Economics years ago in connection with documenting the investment outcomes of training and education. Institutions where trained people often work are also important. Institutions are basically people in an organized fashion. Improvements in training, education, and institutions need to go together.

The next lesson is that infrastructure is essential. Most of us have seen what electricity has done for villages and communities. Information technology can jump generations of change. The World Bank is not playing the role it used to with physical infrastructure such as roads and donors, and there is no one else in a position to do the amount of work needed. Individual donors are not going to do it because of lack of resources and other reasons. The World Bank has to pick this up. The roads are not just to transport fertilizer. They are to open up the country, bring in doctors and teachers, and give people in the country a way to vote. When people are blocked off, you simply do not have a country in the modern sense.

All of those things I have just talked about are relatively long-term undertakings, and that is inconsistent with the way change works. Our political leaders want measurable outcomes so they can talk about them. We struggle in the donor community about how to convince people that this is a process lasting a generation or more. I am not as worried about finding specific solutions as I am about our political capacity as a donor community to stick to things over a long period of time.

There are some things I think we should avoid. We have to avoid massive resource transfers of goods and services. Walt Rostow's work in the 1950s and the 1960s argued that if you have large resources flow into a country, there will be a multiplier effect. In Europe with the Marshall Plan the trained people were already there, and there were some institutions. I do not know of any significant example where there has been sustained progress by putting a lot of resources into a developing country without other improvements such as training and policy change.

> *Political will is key, but there is nothing like an electorate to reinforce political will.*
>
> — Peter McPherson

The UN Millennium Development Goals are very important, and it is reasonable to ask the world to hold themselves accountable. But every now and then, that language has a Walt Rostow ring to it. I am for building the roads, but I am uncomfortable with subsidizing fertilizer. I would rather spend that money on the roads, on training people, etc.

As we look at the lessons, it seems to me that a historically important opportunity could be emerging in this continent. When I took over USAID in the early 1980s, there were almost no democratically elected leaders in this continent. Indeed, the world did not expect Africa to have democratically elected leaders. The Cold War was very much with us.

But in the past few years, there is a renewed assertiveness and a confidence on the part of African leaders in Uganda, Ghana, Mozambique, and Mali and a number of other countries. There are democratic processes. We have spoken often of generating the political will to get things done. Political will is key, but there is nothing like an electorate to reinforce political will. Chance occurs when for example, politicians have to go out and get votes from a rural population. Politicians respond to the majority of the voters if there is a true election process. Majorities sometimes do some silly things, and democracy is often messy, but in the end, with elections you address issues and problems that would not otherwise be considered.

There is new opportunity for a partnership between the donor community and individual countries and the people in those countries. I think more and more farmers will become organized and reflect their interests in the political process. A democracy where people in rural areas are genuinely part of the process will be a way for donors to understand what is needed, and incidentally get support for their appropriations back in their capitals. In the United States President Bush proposed to

Congress—and Congress agreed to—something called the Millennium Challenge Account. The idea is to help countries that can, among other things, hear from their people what they really need.

As you look back over a number of years, there is good reason to have hope for Africa. We have been pessimistic about so many places in times past and been proven wrong. And the pessimists will be proven wrong in Africa too.

Keynote Address: Assuring Food and Nutrition Security in Africa: Perspective of the African Development Bank

Theodore Nkodo
Vice President, Operations, North, East, and South, African Development Bank, Tunisia

In 1996 at the World Food Summit, world leaders agreed that it is morally unacceptable that in an era of material abundance, a large section of humanity should continue to lead a life of hunger and destitution. Since then, national governments and international development organizations, supported by the donor community, have taken various actions to address this challenge. Conferences, workshops, and seminars have also been organized in Africa, all aimed at finding ways to address the food security challenge in the continent.

What has been the outcome of all these interventions? What have we achieved on the ground? The stark reality is that almost a decade after the World Food Summit, food insecurity in Africa remains a major challenge for most countries. This is evidenced by the increasing incidence of poverty on the continent, with more than 300 million, or close to 50 percent of our population in Sub-Saharan Africa, believed to live in abject poverty. Another worrisome trend is that in recent years a larger proportion of Africans have moved from transitory, or seasonal food insecurity, to chronic, or year-to-year, food insecurity. With a little over a decade left for achieving the Millennium Development Goals, there is general agreement that if current trends continue, Africa will not be able to reduce by half the number of hungry people by the year 2015.

In light of these developments, permit me to share with you the perspectives of the African Development Bank (ADB) on the major challenge that African countries face in attaining food security and on what we believe needs to be done to address it.

A major factor behind the problem of food insecurity in Africa is the continuing low productivity of labor in agriculture. Despite the modest increase in agricultural output in Africa during the past decades, productivity is estimated to have remained virtually stagnant.

In addition, food insecurity has been engendered by a number of other factors, including the constraints of weather, postharvest losses, poor access to markets due to inadequate rural and marketing infrastructure, weak rural financial intermediation, and insufficient working capital for smallholder agriculture. Droughts and floods have also become common features of African agriculture.

On the institutional and policy fronts, high producer taxes and limited access to foreign markets, due largely to nontariff barriers, contribute to poor supply response and unstable and low household incomes. Efforts by African countries to add value to primary agricultural produce, such as cocoa, cotton, and coffee, by exporting them in a semiprocessed form, have also been constrained by food quality standards and trade barriers.

In addition, exogenous shocks such as the HIV pandemic and sociopolitical unrest and wars have led to serious erosion of African competitiveness in the agricultural sector. These factors all contribute to reducing the return to agriculture.

Thus, despite being the largest employer, African agriculture has not been profitable enough to raise household incomes above the poverty line. Transforming African agriculture into a profitable activity is therefore a necessary prerequisite to assuring food and nutrition security.

What should we do to help overcome these many challenges?

Our strategies and interventions in addressing food insecurity must continue to be multidimensional, and our programs multisectoral. They should aim simultaneously at the policy, institutional, infrastructure, and production aspects. In addition, we will need to work more closely to build synergy in our development efforts. This is essential in an increasingly globalized world market, where rural income will continue to depend on the extent to which domestic and international markets are integrated and complement each other.

I will briefly highlight some of the respective actions that need to be taken by African countries, the donor community, including the multilateral development banks, and the developed countries.

At the national level, African countries need to focus on the policy changes and the institutional arrangements that can turn the tide in favor of agriculture. First, this will require removing price controls and minimizing price distortions, as well as reducing taxes on agricultural produce. Such actions are required to render agriculture more attractive to both domestic and international private capital.

Second, African countries need to place more emphasis on marketing and rural infrastructure in order to engender strong linkages with agroindustry in order to add value to farm produce and enhance access to local and international markets.

Third, as land tenure arrangements continue to hamper not only the productivity of smallholder farmers, but also the effective entry into agribusiness by medium- and large-scale operators, African governments will need to address this important issue. Innovative land tenure policies that strike a balance between smallholder and commercial agriculture and also promote increased access of women to agricultural land should be adopted.

Fourth, the targets that African countries have set for agriculture in the context of their poverty reduction strategy papers tend to be too broad and too ambitious, and there is a need to revisit these strategies to set more realistic targets. The actions that governments should take in order to make agriculture a more profitable business for both domestic and international markets should also be clarified and clearly stated.

Fifth, governments need to put in place mechanisms through which they can effectively manage emergency food purchase funds or physical food stocks in a timely fashion for distribution to needy populations. In this regard, the accurate targeting of the poorest groups is essential to ensure minimum nutritional standards.

At the regional level, African countries should enhance their regional cooperation efforts to broaden market access and enhance their competitiveness in the globalized world market. It is generally agreed that the relatively fragmented and small markets of most African countries cannot be competitive. It is interesting to note in this regard that the SADC countries have demonstrated the large potential of size and scale economies at the regional level. Efficient and effective intracontinental trade will therefore be an important first step toward using African capacity to compete in world markets. The agricultural program of NEPAD could be used for this purpose.

Africa's agricultural development effort must necessarily be supported by the international donor community if it is to succeed. In this regard, donor countries should undertake the removal of agricultural and trade subsidies. It is now generally agreed that the bulk of the global distortion in agriculture derives mainly from the protectionist policies of the developed countries. Various forms of trade barriers—tariffs, quotas, phytosanitary restrictions—also constrain access of African produce to developed-country markets. These barriers should be removed to give African farmers a more level playing field to enable them to compete in the global markets.

The targets that African countries have set for agriculture in the context of their poverty reduction strategy papers tend to be too broad and too ambitious, and there is a need to revisit these strategies to set more realistic targets.

— Theodore Nkodo

In this connection, the initial results from AGOA confirm that, given a fair chance, African produce can compete on the world market. In 2001, following the first full year of the AGOA program, Sub-Saharan African producers exported additional goods worth US$8 billion to the United States, representing a 62 percent increase over the previous year. As a result of the AGOA initiative, the United States now trades more with Africa than with the nations of Eastern Europe.

What is ADB doing? In line with its vision of poverty reduction, ADB gives high priority to agriculture and rural development. Among the multilateral development banks, ADB has allocated the highest proportion of its concessional resources to agriculture and rural development. Since the 1996 World Food Summit, ADB has allocated more than US$3 billion to rural development programs, which is about 28 percent of the total commitment of the African Development Fund during this period.

Our assistance to the sector aims at improving food security and reducing poverty by increasing the productivity of farmers. ADB adopts participatory approaches, in both the design and implementation of its projects and programs, to ensure that its interventions are sustained in the long run. Indeed, in our rural development program, we foster a community-based and community-driven approach. As part of this process, we continue to support the decentralization of decision-making processes to enable rural communities to have a real say in matters that affect their livelihoods.

This approach has stimulated rural communities to set up their own development initiatives. One of the

In 2001, following the first full year of the AGOA program, Sub-Saharan African producers exported additional goods worth US$8 billion to the United States, representing a 62 percent increase over the previous year.

— Theodore Nkodo

most successful results has been the creation and establishment of local development investment funds. These funds finance community-based programs, such as the construction of roads, health centers, and schools, as well as the maintenance of infrastructure in rural areas.

We consider smallholders the dominant private sector group in the rural economy. Thus, in line with our strategy to enhance the rural economies of Africa, we complement our intervention in agriculture with investment in rural infrastructure such as roads, market centers, storage facilities, rural water supply, and rural electrification. The aim is to improve market access for farmers and to engender effective participation of the local private sector in food production.

In addition to its direct support to agriculture and rural development, ADB finances investment to create labor-intensive, nonfarm rural employment opportunities, especially off-season income-generating activities targeted at the rural poor. It further provides assistance to governments to build their capacity in establishing and maintaining early warning systems for food crops and more broadly based agricultural market information systems to assist in effective decisionmaking.

ADB also supports pilot programs aimed at removing specific obstacles to the attainment of food security. For instance, the Special Programme for Food Security, sponsored by the FAO and jointly financed by the ADB and other donors, is being implemented in several African countries. ADB is monitoring its progress closely to learn the lessons that could be usefully replicated in other countries. Similarly, ADB is providing support for the adoption of new farming technologies and innovations, such as the introduction of a New Rice for Africa, NERICA, which is initially being disseminated in seven West African countries.

We believe that our future efforts should continue in three important areas: managing water for agriculture, building adequate institutional capacity, and scaling up financial support to agriculture.

ADB believes that water management is one of the most important strategic entry points for achieving the goal of food security in Africa. To this end, it has joined hands with the FAO, the International Fund for Agricultural Development (IFAD), the International Water Management Institute, the World Bank, and the NEPAD Secretariat in a collaborative program to invest in agricultural water management in Sub-Saharan Africa. We are seeking to reverse the recent trend of declining investment in agricultural water development by drawing lessons from the past and identifying innovative approaches for the future.

With respect to building institutional capacity, which holds the key to ensuring the sustainability of food security in the long run, ADB assistance is tailored not only to government institutions, but also to the needs of local community organizations, including farmers' organizations.

Finally, we all agree on the need to scale up investment in African agriculture. The current levels of support are simply too small to tackle the many challenges that we face in raising agricultural productivity and ensuring food security. In promoting the allocation of more resources to the sector, it is essential to expand the supply of microfinance to meet the financing needs of poor and small-scale producers. In addition, an increasing share of the resources being released for debt relief under the Heavily Indebted Poor Countries (HIPC) Initiative should be channeled to this sector.

By adopting the Millennium Development Goals, the international community has pledged to halve hunger and malnutrition in developing countries by 2015. Since the time of the pledge, some progress has been made toward this goal, but surely a lot remains to be accomplished in Africa, more than in any other region faced with the real risk of not achieving this important goal of improving food security.

The task before us, while daunting, is not beyond the collective capacity of African countries and their development partners. The challenge is to work closely and in a concerted manner to bring synergy to our individual efforts. We call on all to redouble their efforts to meet the challenge of assuring food and nutrition security. In this endeavor, you will find a committed partner in the African Development Bank.

Part VI | Facilitating Partnerships

Chapter 20 Parliamentarians and Business Leaders: A Discussion

Co-Chair: Edith Nawakwi
Member of Parliament, National Assembly of Zambia, Zambia

Co-Chair: Alhaji Bamanga Tukur
Executive President, African Business Roundtable, and Chairman, New Partnership for Africa's Development (NEPAD) Business Group, Nigeria

Rapporteur: Nienke Beintema
Program Head, IFPRI/ISNAR Agricultural Science and Technology Indicators (ASTI) Initiative, International Food Policy Research Institute (IFPRI), USA

Co-chair Alhaji Bamanga Tukur began by stating that achieving the goals of the conference calls for public-private partnerships in producing, processing, and distributing agricultural commodities. There is an emerging consensus on what the challenges are, as well as on the solutions for assuring food and nutrition security. What is now required is a road map that identifies the implementation steps that must be taken by various stakeholders, with clear and measurable performance indicators for each of them. It should be owned by the stakeholders so they will execute it and fulfill their responsibilities. The road map must be enshrined in an enforceable document, such as a memorandum of understanding.

All actors in the food value chain, from production to consumption, should be involved in assuring food and nutrition security. Each partner must be given adequate authority to execute the responsibilities assigned to it. Tukur pointed out the need to differentiate between the man and the meal. Sometimes the efforts of the private sector are undermined by public sector policies, not deliberately but because they are not working together. Successful partnerships, Tukur added, require not only good policies from the public sector and good intentions from the private sector, but also the infusion of input from each party to the other.

Co-chair Edith Nawakwi prefaced her remarks by saying that food and nutrition insecurity are often due not to a lack of political will, but to a lack of strategies. The task of this session is to develop a general strategy and then to identify roles for business and the various branches of government. She offered the example of her country, Zambia, where 85 percent of people are extremely poor. How can Zambia emerge from the vicious cycle of hunger and poverty? The answer, Nawakwi explained, lies in a concerted effort and partnership by all stakeholders, with clear roles to ensure transparency and accountability.

The business sector sometimes finds the government too overbearing but, in Nawakwi's view, the role of the public sector needs to be more clearly defined. Parliamentarians alone cannot deliver. The government has three arms—the legislature, the judiciary, and the executive—so parliamentarians' roles must be defined within that context. In some countries, constituents see parliamentarians as providers of everything from the maternity ward to the undertaker. How can legislators strengthen their roles so that they can take appropriate action?

Successful partnerships require not only good policies from the public sector and good intentions from the private sector, but also the infusion of input from each party to the other.

Nawakwi pointed to ignorance as part of a vicious cycle of poverty, hunger, and disease. Moreover, many African countries seesaw between food surpluses one season and food deficits the next. Africans must find a solution to this trap.

It is critical to build on positive developments and to promote indigenous and appropriate strategies. To systematically come out of the food crisis requires sequenced interventions that emphasize recovery and the initiation of sustainable development. The capacity for resource mobilization must be improved. Stakeholders must also work to promote natural resource conservation and strengthen support systems for AIDS-affected households. AIDS and other health issues often affect poor communities the most. What is the role of a corporation in addressing these problems and in educating its workers?

Nawakwi higlighted the need to devise pro-poor governance and decisionmaking frameworks. There is no democracy where there is poverty and food insecurity, she argued, noting that in some countries a tin of beans is enough to buy a vote. What is the role of legislators? How can parliaments be effective in inducing change and looking after the people they represent?

The discussion that followed centered to a large extent on the appropriate role of each actor, how to engage the business community and parliaments more effectively in actions related to food and nutrition security, and how to strengthen partnerships. Participants also shared their perspectives on the causes of food insecurity in Africa and offered options and strategies for tackling them.

There was broad agreement that all actors need to be involved in actions to address food and nutrition security in Africa, but their roles vary. A participant commented that the public sector has two roles—to protect consumers and to undertake unprofitable activities. Activities such as production, processing, and distribution are done more effectively by the private sector. The public sector should thus step back from these activities. It should also step back from distributing emergency aid; the participant noted that distributing emergency aid through the private sector will help strengthen the small and weak, but necessary, distribution networks in rural areas. The public sector can, however, assist with developing a banking sector, training more business managers, developing an enabling and stable environment, and building infrastructure.

Another participant pointed out that the business community often feels that they are left out in the cold since they are not involved in the policy decisionmaking process. Marketing strategies that address food and security are often developed by the government only. Yet government decisions on import and export restrictions, intervention in the market with strategic grain reserves, and other issues have a huge impact on the market. To make progress, the participant continued, governments need to sit down on an equal footing with business leaders to discuss the overall strategy for food security and marketing. The government must engage with the banking community and international traders to strengthen marketing changes so that short-term surpluses and deficits can be eliminated.

Alhaji Bamanga Tukur and Edith Nawakwi exchange notes on their session, which brought together parliamentarians and business leaders.

Another participant, a businessman, offered thoughts on how food security can be assured through agribusiness. Businesses want to provide nutritious, appealing, and affordable food. The business sector plays a different role in urban food security than it does in rural food security. In urban areas, the role of the business sector is to serve the consumer market—that is, to produce and make food available following the tastes and preferences of the urban population. In rural areas, the business sector provides a secure market for farmers by acquiring raw materials and integrating the rural community into national economic activities so that they can gain income to be able to afford nutritious food. To perform these roles, however, the business sector needs specific national targets for food and nutrition, incentives to become engaged in these activities, institutions that set rules and enforce compliance, and infrastructure to get into rural areas. The same participant noted that

Parliamentarians alone cannot deliver. The government has three arms—the legislature, the judiciary, and the executive—so parliamentarians' roles must be defined within that context.

in Nigeria, the government has been able to meet key national goals for food and nutrition through agribusiness by legislating that all flour is to be enriched with vitamin A—such legislation automatically provided business with an incentive and infrastructure, and now everyone has value-added flour or bread that contains vitamin A.

Similarly, participants called for parliamentarians to be more involved in decisionmaking processes. Concern was expressed that parliamentarians, who are representatives of the people, are not consulted by or involved in discussions with donor agencies. Another participant seconded this concern, noting that negotiations with regard to NEPAD or the African Union are conducted through the executive branch and are often not fed back to the legislative branch. Parliamentarians should be empowered to have a say in decisionmaking on matters such as NEPAD and the African Union. The participant added that it is impossible to take the politics out of NEPAD, but that it should not be a matter of party politics.

The opposition is not seen as an alternative that can make a positive contribution, this participant continued. Similarly, concern was expressed that the private sector is afraid to associate with the opposition. The participant reiterated that parliamentarians should be provided with the necessary information based on the best knowledge from all partners in order to make their decisions.

Another participant called for more structured exchanges between business people, members of parliament, and political decisionmakers in order to address questions such as why committees on agriculture continue to be unable to convince their counterparts from finance and planning that more needs to be done in the agricultural sector and what are the interests of big business in relation to exports and small-scale farming. Finally, it was recommended that parliamentarians monitor how their decisions have been implemented.

Continuing the discussion on the need to engage various actors in decisionmaking, the comment was made that although mistrust is traditional between the public and the private sector, mechanisms for broad partnership have led to successful dialogue. A participant pointed to an example of a consultative forum in Zambia that brings together actors from all sides—executive, legislative, farmers, NGOs, agribusiness, and donors—providing opportunities for dialogue and the building of trust, leading to public-private partnerships.

Another key aspect of the discussion revolved around solutions to Africa's food security problem. One participant observed that whereas Europe and the Western world have a business culture in which food security is defined on the basis of physical and economic access, Africa has a production-consumption culture that is divorced from market realities. This participant suggested that the guiding principle should be production for the market so that all people can achieve economic access to food and that this principle should be embedded in the policy framework of each country. A participant suggested that parliamentarians and business leaders should push partners from the European Union and United States to open their markets. Another observed, however, that Africa's production is not based on the market; in other words, Africa is not producing those commodities for which there would be market opportunities. Africa needs to stop complaining about the big powers and focus on production.

The need for Africa to have strategic grain reserves was noted, but these reserves should operate within market conditions, a participant commented. Governments are giving bad signals when they penalize farmers for overproduction, because when there is a crisis later, it costs much more to solve a food shortage. Overall, governments need to reconsider when they need to be involved in markets and when they do not.

Issues of individual and political will were also discussed. Wondering whether food and nutrition security is really unachievable, a participant remarked that attaining food security requires commitment by both political leaders and individuals. Another participant linked the issue of political will with NEPAD. Many people had reservations about NEPAD, this participant commented, but these reservations are declining. There have been many bodies like this before in Africa, but it is said that the difference is that NEPAD has political will and commitment. If so, this commitment will be manifested in a few areas, such as following through on international agreements. For instance, the heads of state committed themselves to increasing the budget share to agriculture to 10 percent—how many will indeed do so? For NEPAD to succeed, politics should not take over. Instead, technocrats should take over to implement the strategy.

The role of ignorance in contributing to malnutrition and hunger was noted. A participant pointed to the need for nutrition education, particularly to inform people about the best way to utilize available foods, such as fruits, which do not often make it to the table. African countries, the participant continued, need to put into place proper policies on nutrition, including emphasizing nutrition in health policies.

Many of the issues raised highlighted the need for more information. A participant suggested that the African Union write down needed information—perhaps by creating a magazine in English and French—and present a road map of what farmers should do. The participant used the analogy of a stage play, noting that all the stakeholders are mere actors, and information can let them know how the act is to be played. The participant observed that people in the private sector often keep knowledge about technologies, market locations, and so on to themselves. Similarly, many African governments use the knowledge of economists, but they do not use the knowledge of those who have business and marketing experience. In addition, there are too few managers.

In summing up the discussions, the co-chairs highlighted several key points: the need for dialogue; the need for the private sector to recognize the legislative branch, including those in the opposition, as one; the need to improve interactions between the executive branch of government and the parliament so that it is not "us" versus "them"; the need to reexamine the top-down approach to development; and the need to make farming profitable. They also mentioned the importance of mobilizing young people; of building mutual trust and defining a common agenda; of educating and training and thereby building knowledge and power; of recognizing the power of interest of individuals, without which there will be no commitment or collaboration; of talking and continuing to talk; and of sticking to problems until they are solved.

Although mistrust is traditional between the public and the private sector, mechanisms for broad partnership have led to successful dialogue.

Chapter 21 National Policymakers and Development Partners: A Discussion

Co-Chair: Helder Monteiro Muteia
Minister of Agriculture, Mozambique

Co-Chair: Judy O'Connor
Country Director, Tanzania and Uganda, World Bank, Tanzania

Co-Chair: Amalia Garcia-Tharn
Food Aid/Food Security Policy, Development Directorate-General, European Commission, Belgium

Rapporteur: Andrew Temu
Visiting Research Fellow, International Food Policy Research Institute (IFPRI), USA

Co-chair Amalia Garcia-Tharn raised a number of issues that require attention in the effort to achieve food and nutrition security. Human capacity is key for development in Africa. Institution building is also a key task, but a difficult one. Although donors usually come in with their models and technical assistance experiences, institution building must be nationally owned. The only way to do it, she said, is to have the government in the driver's seat to decide on a sector framework for putting institutions in place.

Creating political will is another challenge. Donors can help to create political will through conditionalities, Garcia-Tharn noted. Donors, such as the European Community, are putting emphasis on respect for human rights, democracy building, conflict prevention, conflict resolution, and good governance. They do that through policy dialogue and political dialogue. She noted, however, that corruption has been a long-standing problem, not only for recipients but also for donors, who are finally beginning to speak aloud about it. Corruption around land tenure, for instance, is of concern. Donors are also encouraging more accountability and transparency, not only with regard to democratic processes, but also in financial matters. For example, will governments actually allocate 10 percent of their budgets to agriculture as they promised last year in Maputo?

Another key issue raised by Garcia-Tharn was the strengthening of local capacities, especially among farmers and women. Much is done through local and international NGOs, but can other ways be found? One way of strengthening local actors is by untying aid—that is, giving resources to recipient countries to decide how to meet their own needs in the most appropriate way.

Finally, trade has an important role to play in Africa, but much needs to be done before Africans can enter global markets. Moreover, there is a lot of potential to be tapped within the continent. She acknowledged that donors often have a difficult time moving food surpluses to food-deficit regions because of a lack of infrastructure and barriers to trade.

Next, co-chair Judy O'Connor spoke about the role of development partners, in particular her organization, the World Bank. She stated that the World Bank and other development partners are trying to harmonize their approaches to countries to reduce costs and be more effective. She admitted that the World Bank has not always been good at listening and learning, but the bank's mission statement says that in addition to fighting poverty with passion and professionalism, it is to listen and learn. The role of culture and indigenous institutions now has much more resonance among

Will governments actually allocate 10 percent of their budgets to agriculture as they promised last year in Maputo?

management and staff at the World Bank as they try to be more effective partners in development.

Picking up on key themes coming out of the conference deliberations, O'Connor noted that if the capacity of government is relatively weak in many African countries, then development partners who are involved in designing government programs and giving policy advice should find ways to limit the demands on government. She noted that it is not for governments to do what the private sector or others could do, and do it a little better or even a little worse, but rather to do things that nobody else can do. She also warned that when donors try to promote reform, they often underestimate how difficult it is to do so without undercutting domestic accountabilities. Hence, they bypass aid recipients' internal systems and accountability relationships, thereby weakening existing institutions instead of strengthening them. In addition, O'Connor said, donors may be missing opportunities to forge partnerships outside of government.

In his introductory remarks, co-chair Helder Monteiro Muteia stressed the importance of getting all actors and partners to talk the same language. Mozambique, he pointed out, has about 40 main donor agencies, 50 international NGOs, and 60 national NGOs working in agriculture. If each one decides alone what the priorities are, when to undertake them, and how much money to spend on them, then it becomes a very difficult situation to manage. It is important to hold appropriate forums to bring these groups together to set priorities and responsibilities and thereby work more effectively together instead of at cross-purposes. There must be space for discretion and for creativity. At the same time, actors need to allow specific localities to follow approaches most appropriate to their own cultural, social, and economic reality. What works in Tanzania or Uganda, he said, may not work in Mozambique. Muteia remarked that he has seen cases where the government, NGOs, and donors talk and work in different directions, and the result is malnutrition. When everyone has the opportunity to bring ideas to the same forum, to set priorities, and to target specific objectives, Muteia concluded, the results can be very good.

The frank discussion in this session raised a number of major issues concerning how Africans can mobilize resources to fund their own development, the need to strengthen collaboration and common ground within Africa itself, ways of interacting with donors and their conditionalities, the challenge of bringing diverse players together, the role of safety nets versus development investments, and mechanisms for strengthening capacity and disseminating technology.

When everyone has the opportunity to bring ideas to the same forum, to set priorities, and to target specific objectives, the results can be very good.

There was extensive discussion on how African governments can mobilize local resources for funding development initiatives. There were pleas for Africa to contribute more of its own resources to development rather than relying so heavily on outside donors. This approach may call for changing methods of mobilizing development funds and designing new ones. A participant suggested that NEPAD should first ask each African country to contribute a certain amount based on its population before it asks non-African nations for funding; those nations that do provide funding could then be viewed as equity shareholders. A participant gave an example from Tunisia of self-reliance in funding development. In Tunisia, he said, people willingly give once a year to the National Solidarity Fund. This fund disburses money to build roads, schools, health services, and other facilities that have helped to promote development and self-sufficiency. Various mechanisms for co-financing were explored. Participants suggested that governments should adequately co-finance investments

Amalia Garcia-Tharn of the European Commission shares her views.

There were pleas for Africa to contribute more of its own resources to development rather than relying so heavily on outside donors.

and honor commitments; engage donors to adhere to their commitments and honor disbursement schedules; explore models for institutionalizing common agricultural sector funds across African countries; and avoid heavy, unsustainable debt.

The need to finance, and in fact to articulate, safety nets differently from development initiatives emerged during the discussion. One of the participants wondered why development activities are viewed as investments, whereas safety nets are seen as transfers or consumption goods. Why do we not see feeding malnourished mothers and children as investments and apply the same economic analysis to nutrition and prevention programs for vulnerable groups that we do to judge whether to build a bridge or a dam? It was pointed out that the two are different: safety nets are an important mechanism to protect or safeguard vulnerable groups in times of crisis whereas development investments aim at longer-term growth. It was observed that Africa can pay for agricultural development by eliminating waste and by reducing conflict, which imposes enormous costs in terms of labor, land, and money.

Issues of commitment to achieving food and nutrition security were raised. A participant said that African leaders are sincerely committed to food and nutrition security, but the technocrats and policymakers often fail to develop the strategies that will achieve the presidents' visions.

There was a related discussion about the role of external donors in African policymaking. One participant said that creating political will in Africa will depend on external pressure and conditionalities set by aid donors because currently Africa has "reluctant democracy." Another responded that African governments know the problems of their own people and pointed to Asia's success with homegrown economic policies. Participants observed that past experiences with conditionalities have instilled fear, weariness, and anxiety on the part of African government officials when they interact with donors on development grants and loans. Concern was expressed that this "collaboration backlash" is working against harmonious future collaboration. African countries should initiate dialogues with their development partners in which they can air views on modes of assistance, challenge areas of assistance they consider non-optimal, and express concern about the effects of aid. The conveners of such dialogues, it was thought, ought to be individual governments rather than donor agencies.

The challenge of bringing diverse players together to talk the same language and work together was a key theme running throughout the discussion. Several participants questioned donors' willingness to listen. Others noted the existence of multiple donors within a single country, often with varied strategic commitments. They called for donors to coordinate so they have a common stand on objectives, priorities, and strategies in each country, and even common baskets of funds for each country. The challenges of accommodating multiple stakeholders on the domestic frontier while acknowledging their vested interests was also noted. Farmers, youth, and women, in particular, must get involved in policymaking. Farmers, it was said, have for too long been recipients of, and not contributors to, policy. Consultations between farmers and the public and private sectors are important, and it is crucial for farmers' organizations to be created and strengthened to give them a voice in policy discussions.

The issue of nutrition was also highlighted. One participant said that improving nutrition does not necessarily require new or better technology, opening of markets, or new policies. It requires delivering to people the knowledge, services, and resources to help them use practices and processes that are already well known. Because malnutrition is largely an invisible problem, the participant acknowledged that it is difficult to build the capacity and create the needed partnerships across the food, health, and nutrition sectors. When heads of state promise 10 percent of the budget to agriculture, what does that mean for health and nutrition? The participant asked whether interministerial secretariats on nutrition might help address the multisector challenge of nutrition.

The introduction of technological advancements, particularly biotechnology, was another item of discussion. Views were very mixed on current dissemination modalities, and participants called for clear and commonly agreed upon methods of dissemination. Related to this, a participant pointed out that Africa has built up national research capacity, but the research needs to be better linked to the people who can use it for policymaking. Links should be strengthened between research and extension and between the research centers of the CGIAR and the national agricultural research systems.

The co-chairs then responded to some of the comments made. Garcia-Tharn said that when donors really call for respect for human rights, democracy, transparency, and accountability, change will occur. She commended participants for recognizing that African problems require African solutions and pointed out that NEPAD's peer review mechanism is intended as a means of applying pressure within the continent. She agreed with the need to look a bit more carefully at how best to empower farmers' organizations and asserted the need for more gender analysis and for donors to work harder on gender issues. Garcia-Tharn also pointed out that funds follow the priorities that have been set, but agriculture and food security are not well represented in the poverty reduction strategy papers. Moreover, many times funds are available but not spent because of lack of capacity or inadequate methods of delivering aid. Finally, in pursuing nutrition security, it is difficult to know how to prioritize and sequence programs and projects for best results.

O'Connor said she was glad to see the sense of impatience expressed by many of the participants. She remarked that financial assistance from outside is available to scale up programs that are working, so the task is to identify and analyze those programs. Responding to a comment about unequal power between central governments and communities, she noted there are a number of examples across Africa where community-based development is working. Communities themselves can do a lot to promote their own development and food and nutrition security. They can set up their own programs without waiting for central or local governments to step in. On the issue of conditionality, she expressed doubt that donor-set conditions really work, in contrast with the view offered by Garcia-Tharn. Instead, said O'Connor, persuasion may be more effective in generating long-term buy-in for certain strategies or policies.

Past experiences with conditionalities have instilled fear, weariness, and anxiety on the part of African government officials when they interact with donors on development grants and loans.

Finally, Muteia noted that several themes were repeated throughout the discussion: common objectives, participation, consultation, political will, national solidarity, and self-development. He emphasized that Africans themselves must lead their own development effort to achieve food security.

Chapter 22 Nongovernmental Organizations, Farmers' Organizations, and Media: A Discussion

Co-Chair: Ayo Abifarin
Director, Food Security Program, Africa Region, World Vision, Ghana

Co-Chair: Mercy Karanja
Chief Executive, Kenya Federation of Agricultural Producers, Kenya

Co-Chair: Ibiba don Pedro
New Age Newspaper, Nigeria, and Winner, 2003 CNN African Journalist Award, Nigeria

Rapporteur: Marc Cohen
Special Assistant to the Director General, International Food Policy Research Institute (IFPRI), USA

Co-chair Ayo Abifarin, speaking from the perspective of NGOs, began by reviewing different definitions of food security. In 1986 the World Bank defined food security as when everybody has access at all times to enough food for an active and healthy life. In 1992 USAID defined it as when all people at all times have both physical and economic access to sufficient food to meet their dietary needs for a productive and healthy life. At World Vision, food security is considered to have four components: food availability, food access, food use, and asset creation. Food use includes the element of nutrition.

Abifarin reminded the participants that this session focuses on how the three players—NGOs, farmers, and the media—can work together to address issues of food and nutrition security. He asserted that NGOs, farmers, and the media are presently not well linked. Although NGOs may sometimes collaborate with farmers, they often design projects without consulting farmers, and they rarely work with the media, aside from perhaps asking them to come to a ceremony at the end of a project. He made several suggestions for promoting better collaboration. First, all three groups should meet, perhaps on a national or regional basis, to discuss the constraints to food and nutrition security and how to address them together. It is important that they know the basic concepts of food and nutrition security. Second, they should all work together in designing projects. Third, they should pursue joint advocacy for policy change and food and nutrition security on a long-term basis. Fourth, they could pursue joint contact with donors, which might prove to be more cost-effective and more attractive than individual efforts. And finally, in designing projects together, the groups can discuss anticipated impacts together to help ensure that each actor is satisfied with the proposed goals and the outcomes.

Co-chair Mercy Karanja, representing farmers' interests, described some ways that have been used to bring African farmers into the fight against hunger, poverty, and environmental degradation. An effort to involve farmers and their organizations in the World Food Summit: five years later resulted in a lengthy consultation process among farmers' organizations across Africa, and even beyond, which contributed to a successful forum at the summit. The forum enabled farmers to see themselves for the first time as having a role to play in overcoming hunger in Africa and gave them a common vision of themselves. Farmers have

Although NGOs may sometimes collaborate with farmers, they often design projects without consulting farmers, and they rarely work with the media.

subsequently worked to get involved in the possibilities for participation in policymaking that NEPAD has created. Although it was difficult at first, given the weakness of farmers' organizations in Africa and the mainly intergovernmental character of NEPAD, farmers have mobilized around this institution during the past two years. They have agreed on the need for food sovereignty for their countries, for recognition of and political participation of the people who are producing the food, and for examination of the negative effects of globalization on African agriculture. Farmers are seeking ways to become involved in food security efforts with other development partners and stakeholders.

Karanja also emphasized the need to build capacity in farmers' organizations and strengthen their institutions for continuity and sustainability. It is also important to strengthen interactions between the various actors. For a long time, NGOs in Africa spoke "on behalf of" farmers. Now, NGOs should help farmers build their own institutions so that these institutions are accountable to the people they serve. Farmers need to hold NGOs accountable as well. European farmers are one of that society's most formidable lobbying forces, Karanja noted, and African farmers should seek that kind of voice. In addition, the media need to report on good things that are happening, not just the bad news. The information revolution needs to reach the rural areas. Karanja concluded by stating that farmers need to be empowered to be effective partners in the struggle to achieve food and nutrition security.

Speaking from the perspective of the media and as CNN African Journalist of the Year, an award she received for her work in rural areas, Ibiba don Pedro began by noting that rural communities often expect the media to work miracles in bringing about change. The media, she explained, traditionally provide society with information with which to govern itself and run its affairs, as well as serving as a tool for education and entertainment. The media are under great pressure from all sides to provide access for all voices, address power imbalances, and provide a "public square" in which policy issues get debated. But there is only a limited amount of space in the media, whether print or broadcast. Moreover, media companies are run for profit and not for charity, and they are confronted with the reality that bad news, celebrities, and the views of the powerful sell newspapers and advertising. Stark images of hunger push coverage of complex, longer-term issues such as agriculture, food, and nutrition out of the limited reporting space that is available. However, there are

Farmers are seeking ways to become involved in food security efforts with other development partners and stakeholders.

ways out of this. Based on her experiences, don Pedro suggested that farmers' groups and NGOs develop effective news management strategies by doing research, getting photos, explaining ideas in simple language, and, most important, actively seeking out media attention and building linkages with journalists who are interested in their particular issues.

Discussion was then opened to the floor. Much of the lively discussion focused on farmers and farmers' organizations. It began with one of the participants predicting that farmers' organizations would be as important in the 21st century as trade unions and the suffrage movements were in the 19th and 20th centuries, and therefore anything that the other groups can do to secure the power, influence, and impact of farmers' organizations is an important step forward. There was general agreement that strengthening farmers' organizations was one of the most important tasks. Since African governments come and go, it was argued that farmers are the ones who must solve their own problems. Another participant brought up several issues: it is important to understand why farmers' organizations collapse and to do better at identifying the factors motivating the formation of farmers' organizations in order to help make them sustainable; the leaders of farmers' organizations should not take over all decisionmaking power from the members; and training is needed to help farmers' organizations become viable and sustainable. Commenting that the link between research and extension is very important, another participant wondered whether farmers' organizations could employ extension agents themselves, to ensure that they provide services relevant to farmers' actual needs. Moreover, is the current trend toward setting the agricultural research agenda from the bottom up a realistic idea? It was observed that research that has been done is often not used by NGOs, which points to the need for better coordination between NGOs and research institutions. The need for a grassroots bank for farmers was also identified.

The media are under great pressure from all sides to provide access for all voices, address power imbalances, and provide a "public square" in which policy issues get debated.

On several occasions the need for farmers to speak for themselves was stressed. Another representative from a farmers' organization expressed appreciation that farmers are included in discussions but asked that consideration be given to the modality of their participation. Programs or institutions that wish to have farmers involved in discussions often pick a representative themselves instead of letting the farmers' organizations nominate representatives who actually answer to them. It was suggested that NGOs could help build confidence in farmers to speak by teaching them advocacy skills. There is an urgent need to help women farmers be heard. Observing that agricultural experts have the upper hand in ministries of agriculture, a participant pointed out that the ministries generally receive funds from donors, who seldom provide funding directly to farmers.

Participants discussed coordination among the NGOs themselves. Concern was expressed that most international NGOs implement their projects directly, but for the projects to be sustained the international NGOs need to work with local NGOs, who are engaged in communities for the long term and better know the situation on the ground. NGOs were urged to stop confusing farmers with a variety of messages and lack of coordination. They were also encouraged to pay greater attention to the impact of HIV/AIDS, malaria, and tuberculosis on food security.

The role of the media was energetically discussed. One participant said that the media can play two important roles in achieving food and nutrition security and other development goals. First, they can promote external investment and communication by persuading policymakers of the strategic and fundamental importance of agriculture. Second, they can enhance inward communication by facilitating the sharing of information between and among farmers, farmers' organizations, traders, food processors, and others involved in the food chain. Several participants noted that there are in fact two kinds of media: private media and official media. Private media often do not take on development issues because they do not sell. Official media generally report on what the government is saying. It was also pointed out that the ethical foundation of each sector—NGOs, farmers' organizations, and the media—should be considered. Another participant said that the media are not an amorphous mass, but tens of thousands of individuals, so the task is to identify the individuals who are serious about covering these issues and form relationships with them.

Another participant said that development issues demand a real communication strategy in which precise messages are defined and appropriate tools are used. Daily newspapers in urban centers do not have the same target as radio in rural communities, but a well-developed media strategy can help NGOs and farmers' organizations advance food and nutrition security. A participant shared an experience from Uganda: although a farmers' radio program, which was broadcast in about 23 languages on Radio Uganda, died out with the liberalization of the airwaves, new FM stations, many of them regional, have again opened a window of opportunity for farmers and others to call into radio stations and exchange views.

Another participant raised three issues: First, how can farmers sustain funding for the radio airwaves? Second, more money is needed to develop farmers' institutions, because farmers are the ones who vote and can put pressure on politicians. Third, the media can be used to generate knowledge and share information about food and nutrition or to help raise funds.

The issue of political will was raised when a participant said that NGOs, farmers' organizations, and the media are all important in building political commitment and mobilizing society. More discussion is needed on how to actually build that commitment in both developing and developed countries. A participant faulted the conference for not devoting enough attention to the question of how

Since all actors together are wiser than any single actor, working together and complementing each other can move agriculture forward in Africa.

to foster political will; presidents alone cannot do it. Another speaker encouraged the assembled group to identify a common agenda so that NGOs, farmers' organizations, and the media can work together to help create political will. Local governments have an important role to play and can be truly representative of rural people. Another participant observed that if national and local budgets reflect political commitment, then agriculture is very low on the list. How can agriculture become a higher priority? A representative of an international NGO noted that besides providing money to poor farmers in Africa, the NGO is mobilizing and educating individual donors, churches, universities, and others in the developed countries and trying to encourage people in the developed countries to lobby their governments to provide more assistance to equitable and sustainable development in the developing world.

E-conferences were identified as an important information medium.

A participant recommended involving institutions of higher learning in the discussion because they are actually producing the knowledge and technologies pertinent to overcoming food and nutrition insecurity, but the results of their work must be made accessible to poor farmers.

There was spirited discussion over coordinating and unifying efforts among the three actors. Some participants noted that since all actors together are wiser than any single actor, working together and complementing each other can move agriculture forward in Africa. The process around developing Zambia's Poverty Reduction Strategy Paper, for example, engaged a very broad range of stakeholders. Another participant described the formation of the Forum of African Civil Society following the World Summit on Sustainable Development. It seeks to forge consensus among African civil society organizations on sustainable development issues.

Farmers should speak for themselves, NGOs should help them to build their capacity, and the media should make sure policymakers know about food and nutrition security issues.

One of the participants noted that while the three sectors are important for improving people's livelihoods, they need to understand each other if they are to work together in an intelligent way and succeed. Moreover, why should NGOs speak for farmers? Farmers should speak for themselves, NGOs should help them to build their capacity, and the media should make sure policymakers know about food and nutrition security issues.

Chapter 23 Plenary Panel Discussion on How Actors from All Levels Can Work Together to Achieve Food and Nutrition Security

Chair: Charlotte McClain-Nhlapo
Commissioner, South African Human Rights Commission, South Africa

Edith Nawakwi
Member of Parliament, National Assembly of Zambia, Zambia

In the session with "Parliamentarians and Business Leaders," which I co-chaired, participants agreed that Africa is perpetually hit by hunger, malnutrition, and disease, and that these conditions arise because Africa is poor. Whichever way you look at it, we come back to the vicious circle of poverty, as expounded by Malthus, the population theorist.

We looked at what the role of each player can be. For instance, are parliaments effective at legislating clear and implementable rules? It was concluded that most parliaments are modeled on previous colonial systems and that these systems are designed to take corrective, not proactive, measures. So parliaments must be reformed if Africa is going to move forward. We noted the need to build mutual trust in order to consolidate our ideas so that we can move forward together.

Parliaments must be reformed if Africa is going to move forward.

— Edith Nawakwi

Alhaji Bamanga Tukur
Executive President, African Business Roundtable and Chairman, New Partnership for Africa's Development (NEPAD) Business Group, Nigeria

We agreed in our session on "Parliamentarians and Business Leaders" that these groups have to work together. For business to become engaged, appropriate legislative and regulatory forums need to be in place. There should be a clear road map indicating the areas of shared responsibility, where we are, where we want to go, and how we want to get there.

This road map should be measurable. Each stakeholder should execute what is actually assigned to him or her. It should be inscribed in an enforceable document, such as a memorandum of understanding or a charter. It is necessary to ensure that information is available and leadership is present, so that people take responsibility and things do not fall through the cracks. Trust and confidence building are also required, in order to make sure it all coheres into one actionable process.

For agriculture to benefit, farmers are the ones to deliver, but there is a need to examine the value chain from production to processing, marketing, and consumption. It is important to differentiate between the menu and the meal: you can have a beautiful menu, but what matters is what comes to the table. So actors must pursue action that delivers on promises.

Conference participants have heard many good ideas, but are they being implemented? Implementation is key. Session participants believe that if all engage in a joint effort and distinguish between the menu and the meal, we will all get there.

Owing to scheduling issues, the presenters in this session were asked to keep their remarks extremely brief. Ayo Abifarin, Mercy Karanja, and Ibiba don Pedro, as co-chairs of the session on "Nongovernmental Organizations, Farmers' Organizations, and Media," agreed that Ms. Karanja would deliver remarks on behalf of that session.

For business to become engaged, appropriate legislative and regulatory forums need to be in place.

— Alhaji Bamanga Tukur

Helder Monteiro Muteia

Minister of Agriculture, Mozambique

In our group of "National Policymakers and Development Partners," participants came up with a number of findings.

First, bringing together diverse players to talk the same language can present a challenge. It is important for all partners to have the same vision and to be able to orient their energy in the same direction. There are a lot of partners in each country, and sometimes each one has its own agenda and its own priorities. In that situation it is difficult to achieve sound results. The session participants felt that it is important to have all the partners—the government, the NGOs, the donors, the private sector, the farmers' organizations—talking about the same priorities. At every forum to discuss those priorities, it is important to pick several of them and orient the partners' energy toward those priorities.

In my country, Mozambique, we achieved this goal through a program called "PROAG," which is a forum involving all the public actors, the donors, the NGOs, and the private sector. They discuss priorities and plan annually what they are going to do. They have one basket where they put the money. They have said, "All donors who want to help us develop agriculture, put money in this basket. We are going to implement these activities." By agreeing on activities and priorities, they achieve better results.

Past conditionalities related to development assistance and the debt from past assistance hinder collaboration and should be resolved.

— Helder Monteiro Muteia

The participants in the session discussed other points as well. There is a need for human capacity building and mechanisms for co-financing strategies. It is important to articulate the roles of safety nets versus development. Donors and governments need to acknowledge and discuss problems and suggest solutions. Mechanisms are needed for ironing out controversial advocacy on the part of donors and controversial uptake of technological advancements on the part of governments, as in the debate over biotechnology. Donors and governments should work out strategies to popularize and advance ownership of international agreements. Countries should take a "national solidarity fund" approach toward funding investments. Collaboration within Africa needs to be strengthened first. Finally, past conditionalities related to development assistance and the debt from past assistance hinder collaboration and should be resolved.

While there was agreement that governments should be in the driver's seat, participants in the session noted that was often more the theory than the practice.

— Judy O'Connor

Judy O'Connor

Country Director, Tanzania and Uganda, World Bank, Tanzania

One of the concerns of the "National Policymakers and Development Partners" session was the ability of donors to listen to clients, including governments, private sector representatives, and community activists. All have something tangible to add to the development challenges and the development solutions. While there was agreement that governments should be in the driver's seat, participants in the session noted that was often more the theory than the practice.

Then the group talked about the three "I's"—but not exactly the same three "I's" that have already been discussed at the conference. The first "I" is *impatience*, in the sense of "Let's stop talking and act." The next "I" is *implementation*. This concerns scaling up what is working, scaling back what is not working, learning from mistakes, and moving on. In relation to that, it concerns finding finance for what is working and scaling it up. And the third "I" is *institutions*. Here there is concern about whether African leaders, with help from development partners, can achieve the Millennium Development Goals. Is the capacity there to use funds effectively?

Donors have to live up to their commitments.

— Amalia Garcia-Tharn

Amalia Garcia-Tharn

Food Aid/Food Security Policy, Development Directorate-General, European Commission, Belgium

I have four key points to convey, which may not only reflect the discussion of the session for "National Policymakers and Development Partners," but also the rest of the conference as everything is coming together at the end of the meeting.

First, we discussed partnership, noting that partnership can be achieved only when there is a nationally owned strategy. The poverty reduction strategy papers that many countries have developed are one instrument, but these should be nationally owned strategies that spell out common objectives for all of us—donors, governments, civil society. They should help actors to agree on priorities, on policy frameworks, and on sector approaches.

Participants also emphasized the phrase "nationally owned." What is a nationally owned strategy? Not only governments, but also civil society should own the strategy. How can civil society participation be strengthened? Three groups in particular have been mentioned several times at the conference: youth, especially when they represent such a large share of the population on this continent; women; and farmers. Actors have to find mechanisms for improving the participation of these groups.

My second point concerns strengthening actors by strengthening human capacity, not only on the individual level, but also at the institutional level. This is a key task, and a difficult one. The development institutions must promote participation. One way of doing this is by decentralization. Farmers and other groups in civil society need to have an opportunity to help design and develop policies. Development institutions need to come to the groups and seek their participation, and they need to make long-term commitments.

Third, we asked, "Who is failing?" All of us are failing. Donors have to listen better, but they also have to make ownership and partnership concepts into realities. The European Union is very proud of its partnership with the African, Caribbean, and Pacific countries. The Cotonou agreement has really made a difference. But the agreement includes civil society participation, and both Europe and Africa need improvements in this area.

Donors are also failing because they are not coordinating themselves. The European Union has the three "C's"—not the three "I's." They are *coherence*, *complementarity*, and *coordination*. It is a challenge to live up to these three "C's" in the European Union, not to mention with others.

Finally, donors have to live up to their commitments. They made commitments not only to Africans in last year's Maputo Declaration, but also to donors at Monterrey. Those commitments have to be met.

Mercy Karanja

Chief Executive, Kenya Federation of Agricultural Producers

Participants in the session on "Nongovernmental Organizations, Farmers' Organizations, and the Media" agreed that these three groups are complementary actors and that they can collaborate on analyzing issues and even designing projects. Working together, these three actors are key in enforcing political commitment to all the actions conference participants have heard about. Besides doing their own day-to-day activities, they can check whether the other partners are doing their bit, especially in partnership with farmers, to achieve food and nutritional security.

Farmers need a strong, independent, and democratic organization that enables them to speak with their own voices as they interact with media and NGOs. The roles are very clear. The farmers need to speak for

We agreed that the three groups should work closely among themselves to understand the farmers, the NGOs, and the media.

— Mercy Karanja

themselves. NGOs and the media are facilitating agents. Participants also agreed that it is important to be conscious of having female and male voices within all three actors and that farmer-driven research and extension are needed.

Since farmers are consistently present and do not leave the area like NGOs, they are important political constituencies. Others can use that to strengthen farmers and create a strong lobby group.

Information and communication technologies should be used to empower farmers and NGOs. NGOs have a critical role in building the capacities of farmers and helping them strengthen themselves. In addition, NGOs and farmers' organizations need targeted media strategies to attract the kind of media who are interested in the issues related to food insecurity. Media are also crucial for effective advocacy, assisting NGOs and farmers. Independent agricultural media and press freedom should be strengthened to advance food and nutrition security.

Better coordination of NGOs' development and advocacy activities is needed. The international NGOs should also work more closely with the local NGOs, because they are the ones who are in close contact with the people. And the groups need contacts, so that they can better understand and work with each other. If the right hand does not understand what the left hand is doing, partnerships are not as effective as they should be.

We agreed that the three groups should work closely among themselves to understand the farmers, the NGOs, and the media. Then, by making sure everybody else does their best in this big assignment, they can be a formidable force for ensuring that Africans actually achieve a hunger-free continent.

Discussion

The chair of the session, Charlotte McClain-Nhlapo, noted that ideas about how to achieve food and nutrition security were beginning to come forward. These ideas point to the need to look at concerted efforts; the need to speak the same language and share the same vision; the need to invite all the players to the table, including youth, women, and farmers; and the need to get all players to operationalize the same priorities. Donors need to listen. Many participants stressed that strategies need to be organic, nationally owned, and nationally driven. In approaching the closing of the conference, McClain-Nhlapo described a sense of a common thread weaving through the three days that says Africa can achieve food security by 2020.

Much of the discussion from the floor focused on the role of Africans themselves in relation to external assistance. It began with a participant who urged others not to leave the conference thinking that Africa is poor. Africa has abundant resources, but African politicians have not managed these resources well. Africans should not leave the running of their countries to a few individuals, he said.

Another participant shared an evocative experience from Ethiopia. Some Chinese contractors in charge of building a ring road around Addis Ababa looked at the Ethiopian laborers working on the road and asked, "Do these people have another country? Are they from Ethiopia? They are not working on this road as if it is their country." We do not have another Africa, said the participant. If there is anything that has been learned from this conference, it is that pride and self-determination must be the primary attitudinal changes that Africans must bring to the effort to make food and nutrition security a reality.

Plenary speaker Jeffrey Sachs's call for donors to invest much more in Africa motivated a participant to ask: Is Sachs optimistic that this money will come from the donors, and are there examples of countries that have been developed by donors?* Or must the local people build up their own pride and somehow generate surpluses to advance their own development? The answer, responded Sachs, is both: success will require all of Africa's ample will, leadership, and intelligence, and it will also require help from outside. No country, he asserted, has developed on its own. Europe got the Marshall Plan, and in 2004 Iraq is getting US$21 billion of development aid from the United States. Many of Iraq's debts were cancelled, as Germany's debts were cancelled in the mid-20th century. It is fine to appeal to pride, he said, but to say that therefore it is not right to ask the richest countries in the world to help is not correct. All countries in the world depend upon each other, and everyone must do what they can. Without leadership in Africa, it will be impossible, said Sachs, but to condemn Africans who lack the means to stay alive by telling them that their struggle is due only to their lack of pride or willpower is intolerable.

Participants pointed to the need to confirm political will and commitment from African leaders. The big disparity between political commitment and financial commitment was noted; quite often governments pledge to support farmers and agriculture and reduce malnutrition, but the reality on the ground is different. Where is the financial commitment to support the political will? Another participant stated that whereas it is relatively easy for city dwellers to make their voices heard by government, it is more difficult for people in rural areas. One way to start empowering farmers and other rural people could be to form associations and cooperatives, driven by demand, not started by governments.

Whereas Africans need to do a lot of work themselves and whereas African leaders are questioned about their sincerity and commitment, a participant noted that the sincerity and commitment of Africa's development partners must be similarly questioned. Africans cannot make their own short-term plans, a participant said, when people outside of Africa are making plans for what will happen in the continent in the next 20 years. External and internal actors must plan together so that their thinking is united. More important than aid from donors, said another discussant, is a commitment by the developed countries to level the playing field for African farmers. It was also pointed out that despite the general lamentation about developed-country agricultural subsidies, no concrete strategy has been advanced for addressing them. Who will help the world's farmers, the majority of whom cannot speak for themselves?

The issue of nutrition was also raised by a participant who expressed concern that nutrition had received too little attention over the three days of the conference. Increased food production is an important component of food and nutrition security, she said, but good nutrition requires food, health, and care, and all three components must be addressed to achieve food and nutrition security by 2020. Disease, lack of education, and low agricultural production are all problems in Africa. The framework for nutrition would bring all of these sectors—agriculture, health, nutrition, and education—together.

A farmer from Uganda highlighted an issue from the parallel session on NGOs, farmers' organizations, and the media, pointing out that NGOs have made an important contribution in empowering farmers to fight the effects of HIV/AIDS, which are decimating them. In Uganda, said the participant, President Museveni talks directly about HIV/AIDS, and as a consequence the country is experiencing success stories.

Other issues mentioned during the discussion included the need for a major initiative to combat malaria; the need to revisit the public expenditure ceilings on agriculture; and the need to give more attention to the management of food reserves at various levels, particularly the national level, so that every drought does not lead to food and nutrition insecurity.

* Because of scheduling issues, Jeffrey Sachs's keynote address, which immediately follows this chapter, was delivered before the session described in this chapter.

Chapter 24 Actions Needed for Reaching the Millennium Development Goals in Africa with a Focus on Overcoming Hunger

Jeffrey D. Sachs
Director, The UN Millennium Project; and Director, The Earth Institute at Columbia University, USA

Africa could achieve the Millennium Development Goals, but not on the current trajectory. The current path means a disaster in Africa: a virtually unabated AIDS pandemic, a resurgence of malaria, a resurgence of tuberculosis, environmental degradation, deforestation, impoverishment, and continuing rapid population growth. These are not the goals that Africa hopes to achieve, and unfortunately we are no closer to a positive trajectory today than we were 3 years ago, 5 years ago, or 10 years ago.

I am not here to deliver a pessimistic message. In fact, those of you who know me know that I am almost always optimistic. The optimistic view is that, with 11 years to go to meet the 2015 targets, every one of the goals could still be met in Africa. But we would have to change what we are doing and how we perceive the situation.

I am not an agriculture specialist, but as a macroeconomist, I can tell you that Africa is too poor to save enough right now to address its critical challenges. Those challenges remain unaddressed in much of Africa, not due to lack of will but due to lack of means.

Africa has the lowest saving rate in the world because it is the poorest place in the world. When people are struggling to survive, they do not have a surplus to save for the future. Africa's governments also lack that surplus to save for the future. I am a bit tired of the world lecturing to Africa to do better when many governments in Africa are doing everything they can merely to stay alive right now.

What happens when you are living at subsistence, as three-fourths of this continent is, and when there is no surplus? You find a lack of infrastructure, environmental degradation, and uncontrolled diseases. As a result, Africa is not only the poorest part of the world, but many parts of the continent are actually going backwards.

The rich world has convinced itself that this is because Africa is badly governed. This is wrong. Africa has some good governments and some bad governments, like all other parts of the world. But even well-governed African countries are slipping backward because the challenges of impoverishment are too great right now and because the rate of population growth is outpacing what the economy and environment can provide. This is itself a reflection of extreme poverty, because impoverished people in rural areas have large families since children will later act as their parents' social security and means of staying alive.

So the story is not simply one of people suffering because they do not behave themselves. This is a human tragedy that has remained unaddressed in the world, and especially in the rich countries, which have preferred to lecture African countries rather than actually work with them to solve these problems.

There is a way out of the poverty trap, and that is why the Millennium Development Goals can be met. Specific, proven interventions can be done in every area of Africa's needs.

I am a bit tired of the world lecturing to Africa to do better when many governments in Africa are doing everything they can merely to stay alive right now.

— Jeffrey D. Sachs

At the rate that security spending by the United States in Africa is rising, security spending will probably overtake development assistance.

— Jeffrey D. Sachs

If African farmers had soil nutrients, through chemical fertilizers or agroforestry, they would be able to triple their crop yields. If they had the means to harvest water, they could substantially raise their crop yields and decrease their vulnerability to climatic shocks. If there were roads to take goods from farms to cities and fertilizer from cities to farms, life could improve.

If there were clinics stocked with proper medicines, we would not have more than 10,000 Africans dying every day—needlessly and tragically—from AIDS, tuberculosis, and malaria. They are dying every day because the antimalarial drugs no longer work and donors have not yet seen fit to help finance ones that would work; because the directly observed therapy short course for tuberculosis, which is incredibly effective, is too expensive for African governments to expand; and because despite 23 years of the AIDS pandemic, the rich countries have gotten serious about action only recently. As a result, 10,000 people will die needlessly of these three diseases.

For the past four years I have been looking at the costs of actually making these investments required in health. This is an extraordinarily painful thing to do, because while the costs are beyond the means of the impoverished countries of Africa, they are such a tiny fraction of the means of the rich countries that what we are seeing amounts to the neglectful loss of life for almost nothing. When I chaired the Commission on Macroeconomics and Health for the World Health Organization, we found that just US$25 billion from the rich world to the poor world could save 8 million lives a year. The United States alone is spending US$450 billion on the military this year, US$150 billion in Iraq in the last two years, but only about US$3 billion a year on all of Africa. The Millennium Development Goals in Africa will be determined by our will, pure and simple, and in my opinion it is a pretty straightforward proposition. It starts in agriculture, because that is where about 80 percent of Africa's impoverished people live. We need to make investments in basic infrastructure: roads, soil nutrients, water, clinics, schools. Nothing ingenious about it.

We need to make investments in Africa's urban centers, so they can be the bases of manufacturing and service production. We also need ports; Uganda needs a decent road from Kampala to Mombasa instead of the current one which is inadequate and is suffocating this country's economy. Having such a high price for connection to world markets can be fatal for business.

The UN Millennium Project, an advisory project for Secretary General Kofi Annan, estimates that the necessary interventions for meetings the MDGs would require an additional US$50–75 billion per year in donor assistance, with which countries could address the scourges of disease, the more than 100 million children who are not regularly at school, and the crises of agriculture that are holding crop productivity in Sub-Saharan Africa to perhaps one-third of what it could be. This amount is roughly 0.3 percent of rich world gross national product (GNP) right now, because the rich world income is around US$25 trillion a year. The United States is giving less than US$15 billion in development assistance and spending US$450 billion on the military this year—this cannot help Africa develop, and it is not making Americans safe. At the rate that security spending by the United States in Africa is rising, security spending will probably overtake development assistance—as if new security programs in West Africa and East Africa could make this continent stable in the midst of such poverty, disease, rapid population growth, environmental degradation, and unhappiness.

There are a lot of geniuses in this room. They know how to triple crop productivity. The world's political leadership needs to hear it. We do not have to wring our hands at the suffering. We can make practical, step-by-step investments to overcome these challenges. But we need the resources to do it. These resources represent just about the greatest bargain in history, only 30 cents out of every hundred dollars of income in additional official development assistance, in exchange for a more peaceful and prosperous world.

Part VII | Moving Forward

Chapter 25 Closing Remarks

Chair: Rajul Pandya-Lorch
Head, 2020 Vision Initiative, International Food Policy Research Institute (IFPRI), USA

Joachim von Braun
Director General, International Food Policy Research Institute (IFPRI), USA

Uganda is a very fertile land, and I am told there is a saying about this: If you throw some seeds in this country, they grow. You, the participants of this conference, have thrown a lot of seed. I am sure they will grow, not only in Uganda, but beyond, elsewhere in Africa and outside of Africa. But a lot of seed multiplication and cultivation still has to happen after this conference.

It would not be in the spirit of this conference if I were to present a synthesis. You can do your own synthesis, each and every one of you. The spirit of this conference is respect for and recognition of the diversity of the audience—the multiple stakeholder groups—and for the diversity of Africa and the different conditions under which Africa must address its food and nutrition insecurity problems. So I am not going to give you a synthesis but rather a few remarks about what I think we from IFPRI take home, what we from IFPRI, as a research organization, feel strongly about toward the end of this conference. I have five points.

First, there are different pathways to economic and social development. What is needed is to optimize these pathways within Africa, country by country, subregion by subregion. We from IFPRI will work closely with a number of countries, but especially also with the African Union and NEPAD, to map out such strategic concepts for pathways. We plan to locate more senior staff in Africa to work on strategic issues and governance issues, including in the NEPAD Secretariat, with whom we have a memorandum of understanding.

Second, we have not been sufficiently clear at this conference on the how-to of strengthening actors and the whole field of capacity strengthening. Capacity strengthening needs to happen at the community level and at the public administration level, but also in research and in education systems. We need to be more specific, and that needs to be a follow-up activity of this conference. We from IFPRI will take one specific step, together with our colleagues in the CGIAR, and locate a division, the International Service for National Agricultural Research division, in Addis Ababa. That will be our contribution to strengthening national and regional agriculture research systems worldwide, but especially in Africa.

Third, investment in markets has been talked about a lot. We from IFPRI are strengthening our research on markets. But we also understand that markets do not work if the state does not work, and the state does not work if markets do not work. So the research on markets will have to be linked to governance failures and state failures and not be narrowly focused on so-called market failures. The expanded research on markets and governance in Africa will be part of IFPRI's contribution to this area.

Fourth, direct attacks on poverty are needed, parallel to the strategic development orientation. Africa and the rest of the world need to get ready to address, for instance, the escalating HIV/AIDS-orphan problem. The curve of numbers of orphans will only peak by 2020. The social safety net policies to address that problem through the education system and through the social security system, need to come into place now. We know very well from elsewhere that such systems can be badly designed or they can be efficiently designed. That is a research agenda for us at IFPRI, and action for broad social safety nets must be initiated.

Fifth, I believe the setting of goals, such as the Millennium Development Goals like cutting hunger in half by 2015, or the even more ambitious goal to achieve food security by 2020, require that we provide road maps—milestones for reaching the goal. Road maps are needed for government leaders, and for all actors in the room, combined with monitoring devices so that we know what is missing and when we are on track or off track. So we from IFPRI will provide conceptual information and assistance in research, to work toward providing road maps to reach the goals. We will focus not just on the final goalpost, but on lots of intermediate goalposts, to facilitate reaching the final goal, which is not just cutting hunger in half, but ending hunger.

On the first day of this conference, at least two of the heads of state explicitly stated that they are not particularly fond of these goals. They want to know what we can do today, tomorrow, and the day after tomorrow rather than being confronted with such a goal. I respect that expression of dismay by President Obasanjo and President Museveni. But I must also say that these goals—all agreed to by heads of state in the year 2000—have been established to haunt policymakers and to help civil society, the public, parliamentarians, and the media confront policymakers with the goals to which they have subscribed. And we have subscribed to them.

For us at IFPRI, as facilitators of this conference, this has been a marvelous and rewarding opportunity to help convene this gathering. The conference has been on implementation, on strengthening actors, and on forging new partnerships. The participants have worked hard in plenary and breakout sessions and have come up with creative concepts and ideas related to strengthening markets, addressing key governance issues, and reforming institutions at the local level and at the central government level. They have come up with a general conclusion that the science systems in Africa need to be strengthened and that there are technologies to move small farmers forward with the existing knowledge base. Action is possible.

The conference has also emphasized the key role of international trade and the responsibilities of the rich countries to open access to their markets and to cut back quickly and drastically on their market- and price-distorting subsidies. Meeting this goal requires action not only of an international institute like ours, but also of others in this audience. We must work not only on Africa, but also on the framework conditions of the global trade, investment, and aid system in general. The system that allocates aid resources to Africa needs to move forward with investments at the appropriate scale to cut hunger fast and to invest in infrastructure, agriculture, health, and education.

Dr. J. J. Otim of the Conference Advisory Committee and Minister Kisamba-Mugerwa will now table a concluding statement on the way forward from this conference. This document is not a declaration, but a document that outlines what steps the community here believes are necessary to move us forward on a road map to achieve the 2020 goals and vision.

President Museveni, I would like to call upon you and your staff to carefully review the document, and perhaps also call on your two colleagues, the presidents from Nigeria and Senegal, who gave us their wisdom at the beginning of the conference, to move this document forward to other all-Africa forums, such as the July head of state meeting in Addis Ababa. All of us have clearly expressed the need to move forward and have laid out concrete action in that document.

With these remarks, Mr. President, I would like to take the opportunity to thank you and the Government of Uganda, as well as your ministers and the national organizing committee. I am especially grateful for their tremendous support and their fabulous collaboration with IFPRI.

John Joseph Otim

Senior Presidential Adviser to the President of the Republic of Uganda; President, Uganda Agricultural Council; and Chair, Conference Advisory Committee

Over the past three days, insightful presentations have been made and thought-provoking discussions have taken place. Arising out of these deliberations, we have made a synthesis on the way forward.

This conference has provided an opportunity to lay the foundation for partnerships, for networking, and for collaboration. In essence, the consensus has been that

Conference Advisory Committee Chair J.J. Otim reflects upon the concluding remarks.

Food and nutrition security for Africa can, and must, be achieved, because it is a human rights issue, as well as a moral and socioeconomic imperative.

— John Joseph Otim

food and nutrition security for Africa can, and must, be achieved, because it is a human rights issue, as well as a moral and socioeconomic imperative. How can this be achieved will be contained in the "Way Forward" document.

A son of the continent of Africa has been honored with the World Food Prize. Monty Jones developed the new rice variety known as NERICA, which is now spreading throughout the continent. This gives us hope that Africans are now prepared to take charge of their destiny, only calling on the international community for backup.

I would like to end by thanking the distinguished delegates for their valuable time and for a job well done. I also want to thank the national organizing committee, under the leadership of the Ministry of Agriculture, for their excellent work. And I would like to thank the chairpersons who ably steered all the sessions with dedication and sharpness of mind. And to all of you participants, I want to thank you sincerely. This has been a groundbreaking pan-African conference. Let us not stop here, but move on to greater heights, translating what we have deliberated on here into action on assuring food and nutrition security on this continent.

Rajul Pandya-Lorch, head of the 2020 Vision Initiative at IFPRI, listens intently to the closing presentations.

Wilberforce Kisamba-Mugerwa

Minister of Agriculture, Animal Industry, and Fisheries, Republic of Uganda

This has been a very successful conference. It was successful in terms of turnout, for all stakeholders and the regions of Africa were well represented.

The main conclusions of this conference appear in the draft "Way Forward" document.[1] These are the following:

First, food and nutrition security for Africa can and must be achieved because it is a human rights issue as well as a moral and socioeconomic imperative.

Second, food and nutrition security in Africa is receiving renewed attention and commitment, and it is increasingly recognized that with "business as usual," the goal will not be achieved.

Third, the 2020 Africa Conference is part of a long-term consultative process on real action toward food and nutrition security in Africa. The steps forward must focus on implementing action.

Fourth, the highest-priority actions are raising agricultural productivity for sustained economic growth through improved markets, better infrastructure, and greater trade competitiveness; building institutional and human capacity; improving nutrition and health, with due attention to HIV/AIDS; and strengthening governance. All of these require added resources, but the benefits of food and nutrition security outweigh the resource needs.

Fifth, strengthening actors calls for acknowledging and respecting their diversity, creating windows of opportunity for them to exercise their influence, enhancing their capacity to influence and implement actions, and empowering them by linking information to analysis.

Sixth, the rights of all who have a stake in achieving food security, especially food-insecure people themselves, must be respected, protected, facilitated, and fulfilled. Without mechanisms for generating

[1] For the full text of the "Way Forward" document, see page 252 of this document.

improved incentives for good governance and accountability of all actors, no sustainable progress can be expected.

Seventh, facilitating partnerships calls for clear contracts based on mutually agreed-upon, monitorable targets that are legally enforced.

Finally, sound decisionmaking and implementation of needed action is constrained by lack of capacity and by governance and institutional weaknesses.

All of these constraints must be addressed simultaneously. Implementation must focus on strong government capacity, strong farmers' organizations, strong incentives for the business sector to engage in agriculture and the food industry, strong consumers' associations and media, and strong, healthy systems serving the needs of the poor.

H. E. Yoweri Museveni

President of the Republic of Uganda

You may be curious about my altruism in spending so much time with you. This is not really altruism; it is purely self-interest. In my language we say that when somebody invites you to have a meal with him, it is because he expects you to do something in return. When I listened to the sort of people who were here, I was of the conviction that if we harmonize our positions, in terms of both perception and the way forward, we can influence decisions more easily. So it is out of self-interest that I am cultivating you.

It is now 47 years since the first Black African country, Ghana, gained independence in 1957. In that time, not a single Black African country has transitioned from Third World to First World. Something is wrong.

I am not so sure the problem is lack of implementation. I am more inclined to believe that it is lack of direction. The Europeans spent many years wandering from theory to theory after 1500. With the Bullionist theory, people believed that you should go to South America and rob gold and silver, and then you would be rich. And some of the European countries did exactly that. Then there was a group of thinkers especially in France called Physiocrats, who believed that agriculture should be emphasized.

Now, there was this gentleman, Adam Smith, who came along and seemed to introduce rationality into Europeans' thinking about the age-old human questions: How do you produce wealth, and how do you distribute it? Then another European, Karl Marx, came along and said, "All evil starts with private property. You must therefore abolish private property and build a communist society." You saw how much confusion that caused. Karl Marx wrote his booklet in 1848, and his ideas were finally buried in 1990. That makes 140 years of confusion in one-half of Europe.

I am not so sure the problem is lack of implementation. I am more inclined to believe that it is lack of direction.

— H. E. Yoweri Museveni

From my perspective in the thick of events for the past 40 years, I believe the problem is not implementation, but the way forward. In NEPAD, we have tried to address this. When President Wade introduced NEPAD, the original document talked about developing infrastructure on a supranational basis, rather than a national basis, but it left out trade. So I put up my hand in that conference and told President Wade, "You have left out something else. This is trade access." And it is now one of the NEPAD points.

It is not a question of trade or infrastructure; both are needed. Someone said that choosing between them is comparable to having to choose between your left leg and your right leg. It would be a difficult choice. And I wonder whether trade is more comparable to the brain, which is a unique organ that controls all other organs. I am still thinking about this, and I have not come to a conclusion.

In my opinion, when we emphasize trade, the rest will easily follow. Of course, you cannot trade without infrastructure. You cannot trade without research, increased productivity, and so on. Conversely, you can have infrastructure and research products, but if you do not use these for trade, you will not sustainably develop.

Black Africa also has big strategic problems. For instance, with 53 states in Africa, there is excessive political balkanization. One consequence is that we cannot negotiate credibly. Nobody listens to us, because we are not able to intimidate anybody. When you are able to tell somebody, "If you don't do this, I will not do that," that is negotiation. Begging and supplications are not negotiation. This is a strategic bottleneck that impacts food security.

This balkanization also means that each country in Africa is a small market unto itself. Large markets like the United States offer large opportunities, but in Africa the units are too small. They do not give you enough room for growth.

We have already lost 47 years since independence; let us not lose another 47 years.

It is now my pleasure to declare this wonderful conference closed. Thank you very much.

A Way Forward from the 2020 Africa Conference*

IN BRIEF

- Food and nutrition security for Africa must be achieved because it is a human right as well as a moral and socioeconomic imperative.
- Food and nutrition security in Africa is receiving renewed attention and commitment, and it is increasingly recognized that the goal can only be achieved with a positive change of attitude, increased investments, and prudent management of resources.
- The 2020 Africa Conference is part of a longer-term consultative process on real action toward food and nutrition security in Africa. The steps forward must focus on implementing action and on developing a process of learning and change. Specific "road maps" of change must be developed at regional and country levels, building on existing strategies where appropriate, and facilitated by an organic process. Thus, this statement is not another declaration or another investment plan.
- The highest-priority actions are (1) raising agricultural productivity; (2) fostering pro-poor economic growth through improved access to markets, better infrastructure, and greater trade competitiveness; (3) building institutional and human capacity; (4) improving nutrition and health with due attention to HIV/AIDS; and (5) strengthening governance. All of these require added resources, but the benefits of food and nutrition security outweigh the resource needs.
- Strengthening actors calls for acknowledging and respecting their diversity, creating windows of opportunity for them to exercise their influence, enhancing their capacity to influence and implement action, and empowering them with information and analysis.
- The rights of all who have a stake in achieving food security, especially food-insecure people themselves, must be respected, protected, facilitated, and fulfilled. Without mechanisms for generating improved incentives for good governance and accountability of all actors, no sustainable progress can be expected.
- Sharing responsibilities through sound partnerships to achieve food and nutrition security is needed and is promising. African governments, private sector, farmers' organizations, civil society organizations, and traditional institutions must commit to measurable good governance, pro-poor development policies, and the scaling up of best practices. Rich countries for their part must commit themselves to providing access to their markets, expanded knowledge and technology transfer, and greater financial assistance. Facilitating partnerships calls for mutually agreed upon clear contracts and achievable targets that are enforced and monitored.

* This document is available in French and Portuguese at http://www.ifpri.org/2020AfricaConference/pubs.asp.

- Sound decisionmaking and implementation of needed action is possible with capacity, good governance, and strengthened institutions. Implementation must focus on strong government capacity, farmers' organizations, incentives for the business sector to engage in agriculture and the food industry, consumers' associations, media, and health systems serving the needs of the poor. As part of good governance, the remaining conflicts on the continent of Africa must be speedily brought to an end if we are to achieve food and nutrition security.

BACKGROUND

1. With new political initiatives gaining momentum, there is renewed attention and commitment to Africa's food and nutrition security. The 2020 Africa Conference took place between two seminal events on the continent: the February 2004 African Union Summit on Agriculture and Water and the July 2004 African Union Summit, which will focus attention on cutting hunger by half. By bringing together key traditional and new actors and stakeholders from across the continent, the 2020 Africa Conference offered a unique opportunity to focus on prioritizing actions, strengthening actors, and facilitating partnerships and thereby address implementation constraints.
2. The 2020 Africa Conference is part of a longer-term consultative process on real action toward food and nutrition security in Africa. It brought the various actors together to strengthen implementation. The way forward from the conference must focus on implementing action and on developing a process of change and action, not just on another declaration.

PRIORITIZING ACTIONS

1. **The goals:** The goals are already clearly defined and require no debate. These goals are (a) assuring food security (reliable access to food in sufficient quantity and quality for a healthy and productive life for all individuals); and (b) assuring nutrition security (where secure access to food is coupled with a sanitary environment, adequate health services, and knowledgeable care to foster good nutritional status through the life cycle and across generations). But the political priority assigned to these goals is deficient, particularly in a world that has doubled per capita incomes in the past 20 years while experiencing growing populations. The actions being taken to reach these goals are incoherent in many countries and are poorly understood by many actors.
2. **The timelines:** Implementing action for achieving food and nutrition security should serve three timelines:
    - Hunger must be halved by 2015 (the Millennium Development Goal, meaning that the proportion of calorie-deficient people is reduced by half by 2015 in each country).
    - The goal must remain ending hunger, not just cutting hunger by half. By 2020 at least, no one should be calorie deficient in Africa.
    - Nutrition security should be achieved step by step. This should include overcoming preventable micronutrient deficiencies of iron, vitamin A, and iodine by 2015. Public health investments and direct nutrition interventions to reduce maternal and child malnutrition (e.g., low birthweight) must be scaled up urgently.
3. **Focusing on people and their problems:** Actions toward food and nutrition security should be prioritized according to their potential for delivering fast and sustainable impact. It makes sense to address worst things first, such as famine and severe hunger related to significant calorie deficiencies. Addressing food and nutrition security directly and indirectly requires recognizing people's problems, situation, and context. Most food- and nutrition-insecure people are in rural areas, and many of their constraints relate to agriculture. Poor African governments must be supported to make the most strategic investments in rural areas and rural communities.
4. **Strategizing and linking goals to means:** The people-focused agenda needs to link the goals to a set of means in an appropriate context. And that context must be addressed when formulating sound "road maps". The agenda must be shaped with input from poor people, who require greater voice and influence. Strategies must build on these basics. Adjusted to context and country, these are the five priority areas of action:

a. Strengthen governance and public accountability and end conflicts. If these basics are not met, little can be done for sustainable food and nutrition security.

b. Foster macroeconomic growth and stability facilitated by free access to domestic, inter-regional, and international markets and trade; a more cohesive and louder African voice in the World Trade Organization (WTO); better investments in the assets of the poor; more effective management of vulnerability to shocks, including through household, national, and regional food storage; and greater investments in infrastructure to lower transportation and communication costs and encourage rural-urban and intraregional linkages.

c. Invest in raising agricultural productivity, especially among small farms, thereby addressing the food availability and income poverty aspects of food and nutrition security within the larger context of policies for agricultural and rural development. The sustainability of agricultural productivity requires strong attention to environment and natural resources, especially soils, watersheds, and biodiversity. Invest in processing for more value addition and quality assurance in the supply chain of agricultural products.

d. Invest in pro-poor public health policies and actions, in particular the prevention, control, and management of HIV/AIDS, malaria, and tuberculosis, to foster food and nutrition security and raise labor productivity.

e. Invest in building human capacity by addressing the education needs of women, girls, and boys; upgrading the professional skills of farmers and other rural producers; and meeting the need for higher education to produce better-educated and more-informed actors and stakeholders who can implement actions for nutritional improvement.

5. **Aligning the scale of investments in food and nutrition security with the expected returns:** The search for marginal improvements in food and nutrition security at the lowest cost must be replaced by a focus on the political change and investment needs for getting the job done. Searching for cures to symptoms of food and nutrition insecurity that cost a dollar or two per affected person is unrealistic. For example, preventable low birthweight costs national economies hundreds of dollars per child in lost lifetime earnings. It is important to recognize those levels of potential gains, as they are the proper yardsticks for massive scaling up of public and private investments to address food and nutrition security.

6. **Establishing and strengthening social safety nets:** Effective social safety nets must also be added to help those who would be bypassed or otherwise negatively affected by growth-oriented approaches and also to help households marshal productive assets toward growth. No uniform approach is advocated, but different types of safety nets will be called for in different settings. The success of their implementation will rest, by and large, with governments and nongovernmental organizations (NGOs).

7. **Appreciating Africa's diversity:** Africa's diverse geographical, ecological, social, and economic contexts and institutional strengths offer both challenges and opportunities. Prioritizing actions for food and nutrition security must build on this diversity, which can facilitate learning from within Africa. Different subregional speeds in achieving food and nutrition security for all will contribute to the process of prioritizing actions.

STRENGTHENING ACTORS

1. **Recognizing and respecting the different actors and their comparative strengths:** Many traditional and new actors are influencing food and nutrition security today, including national and local government policymakers, policy advisers, parliamentarians, business leaders, civil society leaders, farmers and farmers' organizations, regional and subregional institutions, international donor agencies, media, and the research community. They often talk different business languages, so improving communication between them is a key priority. Each of these actors requires strengthening but to different degrees in different ways in different countries, and especially in rural areas.

2. **Equipping the actors with influence:** Any strategy for food and nutrition security requires an assessment of the strength of key actors at the outset. A country that has weak business organizations, local governments, community organizations, or farmers' organizations, for instance, needs to invest up front in strengthening this set of actors through appropriate organizational formation, rather than forging ahead just on the basis of a strong central government. Effective prioritization of actions is often done by fruitful, sometimes conflicting, interactions between actors who have access to information and the capacity to articulate. Actors involved in food and nutrition security need to gain more influence.
3. **Facilitating the human rights–based approach:** Strengthening the rights of food-insecure people is an element of improving food and nutrition security. With the judiciary watching over and enforcing the rights of the poor and food insecure, a new set of actors is beginning to come to the table. Civil society and parliamentarians in particular are encouraged to articulate and facilitate rights-based approaches for enhancing food and nutrition security. National institutions are encouraged to monitor the rights of the food insecure.
4. **Building capacity in food and nutrition policymaking and policy assessment for all actors:** This requires accelerated investments in upgrading university education, training for the main groups of actors, and strengthening actors on the job to identify solutions to food and nutrition insecurity.
5. **Empowering actors with information and analysis:** Information is the key to power in addressing food and nutrition security. Information relevant to food and nutrition security needs to be accessible to civil society and the media, not only to government. Information must include analyses (and appropriately simplified communication of related results) on causes and effects of food and nutrition insecurity and likely outcomes of policy changes and public investments. Continuous education in food and nutrition security should be part of the empowerment process. As farmers' organizations are strengthened and empowered, due consideration should be given to those organizations that serve women farmers.
6. **Mainstreaming gender:** In view of women's roles in African rural development and agriculture and as agents for food and nutrition security, mainstreaming gender through women's empowerment and capacity strengthening must be given priority in the implementation of action. African women must not be deprived of opportunities to exhibit their entrepreneurial talent.
7. **Mobilizing advanced science and relevant technologies to address the food and nutrition problems in Africa:** Hunger and the underlying problems in agriculture, health, and politics must be addressed comprehensively. This is a matter not of conducting studies, but of building, strengthening, and linking Africa's science and technology systems with food and nutrition programs.

FACILITATING PARTNERSHIPS

1. **Developing partnerships:** Partnerships to improve food and nutrition security must be developed to accelerate the mobilization of resources and promote their efficient use. Partnerships that foster synergies between the public interest (such as investment in roads), institutional innovation (such as improved rural banking serving traders and farmers), and civil society (supporting/creating cultures of human rights and mobilizing for public action toward the health conditions that reduce malnutrition) must be supported as priority. But such partnerships must be based on clear targets and contracts and need to have legal bases. Governments have a responsibility to create enabling environments for partnerships and the legal security around them.
2. **Improving coordination among new partners:** A number of new actors have come into play who need to better coordinate their work in partnership to create the synergy needed for success. These actors include leaders from the public sector (central and local government), the private sector, civil society, cultural and religious institutions, as well as lawmakers and others. Currently, partnerships between the public sector and the other players are weak, leading to slow progress.

3. **Moving forward together:** Food and nutrition security is cross-sectoral and involves national and international as well as public and private actors. It therefore requires that teams of actors leap forward together rather than separately. This need applies, for instance, to cooperation between government ministries and between business and civil society organizations working together to address food and nutrition insecurity (such as micronutrient deficiencies). New partnerships are also needed, such as with cultural and religious leaders, to support the food and nutrition security agenda as a societal task. Ending hunger is not just a matter of investment and technology.
4. **Improving the interaction between parliament and the private sector:** In the young democracies in Africa, the interaction between parliament and the business sector is not well developed. The public sector cannot get things done alone. Therefore, for sound lawmaking, the interaction between parliaments and civil society, including business, is essential for effective actions for food and nutrition security.

ADDRESSING IMPLEMENTATION CONSTRAINTS

1. **Implementation test of strategies:** No food and nutrition security strategy, whether at a continental, subregional, national, or local level, is viable if it does not include a well-developed and well-articulated implementation framework.
2. **The responsibility and accountability** of the key food and nutrition security policy actors need to be clearly communicated and understood. Holding governments accountable, facilitating vigorous competition, assuring transparency in and building the capacity of civil society organizations, exposing the research community to national or international peer review for quality testing, and monitoring the quality of actions taken are key ingredients in enhancing the responsibility and accountability of strengthened actors. The implementation of this step, based on sound and transparent indicators, is an important task for the African Union/New Partnership for Africa's Development (AU/NEPAD).
3. **Governance in the food and agricultural sector** needs to be addressed at the macro as well as sectoral levels. This requires national governments to adopt and implement policies that encourage transparency and efficiency of food- and agriculture-related public organizations as well as of public and private operators serving agriculture and food and nutrition security. The adequacy of food and agriculture policies should be assessed and refined as necessary and integrated into the peer-review system proposed under NEPAD.
4. **African countries that lead can help others:** Countries showing good progress in achieving food and nutrition security in Africa can function as subregional leaders by sharing the knowledge and approaches that contribute to their success. A structured effort by NEPAD and the African Union or regional bodies to identify and support such lead countries would be an attractive and sustainable self-help approach. Moreover, it would be complementary to and should be supported by external aid. Focusing on outcomes in terms of sharp reductions in and achieved low levels of food and nutrition insecurity is advocated.
5. **Mobilizing international support:** There are four key areas where mobilization of large-scale investments and political support require continent-wide and international efforts in order to yield success:
   - coping with the HIV/AIDS crisis;
   - managing drought- and other crisis-related food security shocks;
   - investing in building and maintaining regional infrastructure; and
   - coping with transboundary issues such as livestock and crop diseases and pests, trade, labor migration, and management of regional common resources.

   An international compact between Africa (and its countries) and the donor community is called for, perhaps under the AU/NEPAD framework. It would consist of the following: (a) Africa acts to address these basic problems with existing means (including the goal set in Maputo in 2003 of allocating 10 percent of national budgets for agriculture); and (b) the international community "underwrites" insurance against natural calamities through food and other aid, provides support for a massive scaling up of action to overcome HIV/AIDS infections, and supports agriculture and large-scale infrastructure investment based on well-designed investment and finance planning.

6. **Setting priorities for implementation and sequencing:** First, scale up agricultural growth in the smallholder sector to help reduce poverty and food insecurity. Second, scale up investment in local, national, and regional infrastructure, including roads and provision of safe water and proper sanitation. Third, design policy change to bring down domestic and interregional barriers to trade for food and agricultural products within Africa, and to open up OECD markets for African products, especially high-value products. Fourth, scale up nutrition- and food security-related investments in combined health and education programs, reaching the food and nutrition insecure through schools, health centers, hospitals, and communities, and support social safety nets. Each of these must be implemented by different groups of actors, which can change from country to country. The best means of implementation can be determined only in a country context. But best practices can and must be shared across Africa. The leaders of the African Union and of regional and subregional organizations play an important role in this context.
7. **Investing in agriculture:** The agricultural investment needed, both public and private, is highly diverse based on agro-ecology. There are, however, at least three common top priorities: (a) investing in improved seeds and livestock that fit the agro-ecology; (b) investing in the development and utilization of water for productive purposes and rural health; and (c) investing in a continent-wide effort to achieve sustained soil fertility.
8. **Monitoring implementation:** A small and transparent set of criteria for evaluating the quality of actions implemented to achieve food and nutrition security should be followed in country peer reviews. These evaluations must monitor progress or lack thereof in achieving food and nutrition security, based on clearly understood indicators, such as those monitored by the Food and Agriculture Organization of the United Nations and the World Health Organization. National human rights institutions should be encouraged to monitor the achievement of food and nutrition security.

In summary, the two goals of food and nutrition security in Africa are intimately related and should be jointly pursued. Food security is certainly achievable for all African citizens by 2020. The more complex goal of nutrition security for all may not be completely achievable by 2020, but it must move higher on the agenda, and central aspects of the nutrition security goal, such as overcoming micronutrient deficiencies ("hidden hunger") and reducing child malnutrition, must and can be addressed by 2020. The road map for the way forward toward ending hunger in Africa is clearly drawn. If the actors are strengthened and walk forward together in new partnerships, then the goal can be reached in this generation.

Appendix 1 Conference Program

Thursday, April 1

0900–1030 **PLENARY SESSION: WELCOME AND OPENING REMARKS**

Call to Order

Conference Director: **Rajul Pandya-Lorch,** *Head of the 2020 Vision Initiative, International Food Policy Research Institute (IFPRI)*

Welcome and Opening Remarks

Chair: **Isher Judge Ahluwalia,** *Chair of the Board of Trustees, International Food Policy Research Institute (IFPRI)*
Speakers:
John Joseph Otim, *Senior Presidential Advisor to H.E. President Museveni of the Republic of Uganda; President, Uganda Agricultural Council; and Chair, Conference Advisory Committee, Republic of Uganda*
Joachim von Braun, *Director General, International Food Policy Research Institute (IFPRI)*
Wilberforce Kisamba-Mugerwa, *Minister of Agriculture, Animal Industry, and Fisheries, Republic of Uganda*
H.E. Yoweri Museveni, *President, Republic of Uganda*
H.E. Maître Abdoulaye Wade, *President of the Republic of Senegal*
H.E. Olusegun Obasanjo, *President of the Federal Republic of Nigeria*

1030–1100 COFFEE AND TEA BREAK

1100–1140 **PLENARY SESSION: TAKING STOCK**

Chair: **Mamadou Kone,** *Minister of Scientific Research, Côte d'Ivoire*

"Africa's Food and Nutrition Security Situation—Where Are We and How Did We Get Here?"

Keynote: **Isatou Jallow,** *Executive Director, National Nutrition Agency (NaNA), The Gambia*

"Looking Ahead: Long-Term Prospects for Africa's Food and Nutrition Security"

Keynote: **Mark Rosegrant,** *Director of the Environment and Production Technology Division, International Food Policy Research Institute (IFPRI)*

1140–1250 **PLENARY SESSION**

Panel Discussion: "Why Has Africa Not Yet Achieved Food and Nutrition Security?"

Chair: **Richard Mkandawire,** *Agricultural Advisor, New Partnership for Africa's Development (NEPAD) Secretariat, South Africa*
Panelists:
Josué Dioné, *Director, Food Security and Sustainable Development Division, UN Economic Commission for Africa, Ethiopia*
Rosebud Kurwijila, *Commissioner for Rural Economy and Agriculture, African Union, Ethiopia*
Robbie Mupawose, *Chairman, Barclays Bank of Zimbabwe, Zimbabwe*
Mandivamba Rukuni, *Program Director, W.K. Kellogg Foundation, South Africa*

1250–1300 **Digital Opinion Poll of Participants**

1300–1400 LUNCH

1400–1600 **PARALLEL SESSIONS: REGIONAL FORUMS**

Priorities for Action: Perspectives from the Regions

Southern Africa

Chair: **Bongiwe Njobe,** *Director General, National Department of Agriculture, South Africa*
Moderator: **Tobias Takavarasha,** *Chief Executive Officer, Food, Agriculture, and Natural Resource Policy Analysis Network (FANRPAN), Zimbabwe*
Rapporteur: **Andrew Temu,** *Visiting Research Fellow, International Food Policy Research Institute (IFPRI)*
Panelists:
Johann Frederick Kirsten, *Professor and Head, Department of Agricultural Economics, Extension and Rural Development, University of Pretoria, South Africa*
Ajay Vashee, *President, Southern African Confederation of Agricultural Unions (SACAU), Zambia*

West Africa

Chair: **Mamadou Kone,** *Minister of Scientific Research, Côte d'Ivoire*
Moderator: **Achi Atsain,** *President, West African Economic Association (WAEA); President, Network of Ivorian Intellectuals for Peace, Democracy and Governance; and former Minister of Employment, Civil Service, and Social Welfare, Côte d'Ivoire*
Rapporteur: **Tidiane Ngaido,** *Research Fellow, International Food Policy Research Institute (IFPRI)*
Panelists:
Rosanna Agble, *Chief Nutrition Officer, Ghana Health Service, Ghana*
Michel Benoît-Cattin, *Associate Director for Economics and Social Sciences, Scientific Direction, French Agricultural Research Center for International Development (CIRAD), France*
Uzo Mokwunye, *Director, The United Nations University, Institute for Natural Resources in Africa, Ghana*
Kanayo Nwanze, *Director General, WARDA-The Africa Rice Center, Côte d'Ivoire*

East and Central Africa

Chair: **Newai Gebre-ab,** *Chief Economic Advisor to the Prime Minister, Ethiopia and Director of Ethiopian Development Research Institute (EDRI), Ethiopia*
Moderator: **Isaac Minde,** *Coordinator, Eastern and Central Africa Programme for Agricultural Policy Analysis (ECAPAPA), Republic of Uganda*
Rapporteur: **Steven Were Omamo,** *Research Fellow and Regional Network Coordinator, International Food Policy Research Institute (IFPRI)*
Panelists:
Asha-Rose Migiro, *Member of Parliament and Minister of Community Development, Women, and Children, Tanzania*
Kankonde Mukadi, *Professor, Protestant University of the Congo, Democratic Republic of Congo*

Northern Africa

Chair and Moderator: **Mohand Laenser,** *Minister of Agriculture and Rural Development, Morocco*
Rapporteur: **Martine Padilla,** *Scientific Administrator, International Center for Advanced Mediterranean Agronomic Institute/Mediterranean Agronomic Institute (CIHEAM/IAMM), France*
Panelists:
Mohammed El Mourid, *Regional Coordinator for North Africa Regional Program, International Center for Agricultural Research in the Dry Areas (ICARDA), Tunisia*
Mustapha Guellouz, *Director General, President of the Board of the Enterprise, Livestock and Pasture Office, Tunisia*
El-Sayed Zaki, *former Minister of Finance and Economic Planning, Sudan*

1600–1630 COFFEE AND TEA BREAK

1630–1730 **PLENARY SESSION**
Panel Discussion: "Priorities for Action: Perspectives from the Regions"

Chair: **Per Pinstrup-Andersen,** *Chair of Science Council, CGIAR; H.E. Babcock Professor of Food and Nutrition Policy, Cornell University; and 2001 World Food Prize Laureate*
Panelists: Chairs of Parallel Sessions
Bongiwe Njobe, *Director General, National Department of Agriculture, South Africa*
Mamadou Kone, *Minister of Scientific Research, Côte d'Ivoire*
Newai Gebre-ab, *Chief Economic Advisor to the Prime Minister, Ethiopia and Director of Ethiopian Development Research Institute (EDRI), Ethiopia*
Mohand Laenser, *Minister of Agriculture and Rural Development, Morocco*

1730–1740 **Digital Opinion Poll of Participants**

1740–1850 **PLENARY SESSION**
Chair: **Godfrey K. Binaisa,** *former President of the Republic of Uganda*

"Mitigating, Preventing, and Ending Conflicts in Africa"
Keynote: **Graça Machel,** *President of the Foundation for Community Development, Mozambique; former Expert of the Secretary General of the United Nations on the Impact of Armed Conflict on Children; and former Minister of Education, Mozambique*

"Will Food Security in Africa Be Achieved by Sustained, Increased, and More Effective Aid?"
Keynote: **Poul Nielson,** *European Union Commissioner for Development Cooperation and Humanitarian Aid, Belgium*

"Achieving Sustainable Agricultural Growth in Africa: Lessons from Experience"
Keynote: **Norman Borlaug,** *President, Sasakawa Africa Association, and Nobel Peace Prize Laureate, Mexico*

1850–1855 **ANNOUNCEMENT OF THE WORLD FOOD PRIZE 2004 LAUREATE**
Presenters: **Norman Borlaug** and **Robert Havener,** *Members of the Council for Advisors of the World Food Prize Foundation*

1855–1910 **YOUTH WRITING CONTEST AWARD CEREMONY**
Presenter: **Omukama (King) of Tooro Rukirabasaija Oyo Nyimba Kabambaiguru Rukidi IV,** *Republic of Uganda*

1910 **Welcome Reception**

Friday, April 2

0900–1000 **PLENARY SESSION: IMPLEMENTING ACTION**
Chair: **Courage Quashigah,** *Minister of Food and Agriculture, Ghana*

"Strategies for Improving Food and Nutrition Security in Africa"
Keynote: **Victoria Sekitoleko,** *Subregional Representative, Food and Agriculture Organization of the United Nations (FAO) Subregional Office for Southern and East Africa, Zimbabwe*

"Technological Options for Africa's Small-Scale Farmers"
Keynote: **Gordon Conway,** *President, The Rockefeller Foundation, U.S.A.*

"Implementing Action to Reduce Hunger: Learning from Mali's Experiences"
Keynote: **Oumar Ibrahima Touré,** *Delegate Minister for Food Security, Mali*

1000–1100 **PLENARY SESSION**
Panel Discussion: "Improving Implementation: What Can Lessons from Successes and Failures Teach Us?"

Chair: **Hamid Narjisse,** *Director, Institut National de la Recherche Agronomique (INRA), Morocco*
Panelists:
Peter Hazell, *Director of the Development Strategy and Governance Division, International Food Policy Research Institute (IFPRI)*
Wilberforce Kisamba-Mugerwa, *Minister of Agriculture, Animal Industry, and Fisheries, Uganda*
Hezron Nyangito, *Principal Policy Analyst, Kenya Institute for Public Policy Research and Analysis (KIPPRA)*
Hans-Joachim Preuss, *Secretary General, Deutsche Welthungerhilfe, Germany*

1100–1110 **Digital Opinion Poll of Participants**

1110–1140 COFFEE AND TEA BREAK

1140–1510 **PARALLEL SESSIONS: ACTION FORUMS**
Implementing Action in Key Areas

Raising Agricultural Productivity
Chair and Moderator: **Monty Jones,** *Executive Secretary, Forum for Agricultural Research in Africa (FARA), Ghana*
Rapporteur: **John Pender,** *Senior Research Fellow, International Food Policy Research Institute (IFPRI)*
Panelists:
Glyvyns Chinkhuntha, *Executive Director, Freedom Gardens, Malawi*
Seyfu Ketema, *Executive Secretary, Association for Strengthening Agricultural Research in Eastern and Central Africa (ASARECA), Republic of Uganda*
Pedro Sanchez, *Director of Tropical Agriculture, The Earth Institute at Columbia University; Co-chair, Millennium Project Hunger Task Force; and 2002 World Food Prize Laureate, U.S.A.*
Carlos Seré, *Director General, International Livestock Research Institute (ILRI), Kenya*
Eugene R. Terry, *Implementing Director, African Agricultural Technology Foundation, Kenya*
Florence Wambugu, *Executive Director, A Harvest Biotech Foundation International, Kenya*

Fostering Economic Growth and Improving Markets and Trade
Chair: **Benno Ndulu,** *Research Manager, Development Economics Research Department, World Bank, U.S.A.*
Moderator: **Akinwumi Adesina,** *Associate Director, Food Security, Rockefeller Foundation, Kenya*
Rapporteur: **Nicholas Minot,** *Research Fellow, International Food Policy Research Institute (IFPRI)*

Panelists:
Eleni Gabre-Madhin, *Senior Economist, Africa Region, World Bank, U.S.A.*
Hans Jöhr, *Corporate Head of Agriculture, Nestec Ltd., Switzerland*
Eusebius J. Mukhwana, *Director, Sustainable Agriculture Centre for Research Extension and Development in Africa (SACRED), Kenya*
Stephen Njukia and Bernard Kagira, *Regional Agricultural Trade Expansion Support (RATES) Program, Kenya*

Building Human Capacity

Chair: **Angeline Kamba,** *Member of UN/UNESCO World Commission on Culture and Development, Zimbabwe*
Moderator: **Soumana Sako,** *Executive Secretary, African Capacity Building Foundation, Zimbabwe*
Rapporteur: **Willis Oluoch-Kosura,** *Program Coordinator, Collaborative Masters Program in Agricultural and Applied Economics, Kenya*
Panelists:
Kwadwo Asenso-Okyere, *Vice Chancellor, University of Ghana, Ghana*
Suresh Babu, *Senior Research Fellow/Senior Advisor, Training, International Food Policy Research Institute (IFPRI)*
Carl Greenidge, *Director, Technical Center for Agricultural and Rural Cooperation (CTA), The Netherlands*
William M. Lyakurwa, *Executive Director, African Economic Research Consortium, Kenya*
Jim Ryan, *Visiting Fellow, Economics Division, Research School of Pacific and Asian Studies, Australian National University, Australia*

Improving Nutrition and Health

Chair: **Kabba Joiner,** *Director General, West African Health Organization (WAHO), Burkina Faso*
Moderator: **Tola Atinmo,** *Professor of Nutrition at the College of Medicine, University of Ibadan, and President of the Federation of African Nutrition Societies (FANUS), Nigeria*
Rapporteur: **Todd Benson,** *Research Fellow, International Food Policy Research Institute (IFPRI)*
Panelists:
Stuart Gillespie, *Senior Research Fellow, International Food Policy Research Institute (IFPRI)*
Amadou Kanouté, *Regional Director, Office for Africa, Consumers International, Zimbabwe*
Robert Mwadime, *Child Survival and Nutrition Advisor, Regional Center for Quality of Health Care, Republic of Uganda*
Ebrahim M. Samba, *Regional Director, World Health Organization Regional Office for Africa (WHO/AFRO), Republic of Congo*
Flora Sibanda-Mulder, *Senior Advisor, United Nations Children's Fund (UNICEF)-World Food Programme (WFP) Collaboration, Italy*

Strengthening Governance

Chair: **Bethuel A. Kiplagat,** *Executive Director, Africa Peace Forum, Kenya*
Moderator: **Charlotte McClain,** *Commissioner, South African Human Rights Commission, South Africa*
Rapporteur: **Marc Cohen,** *Special Assistant to the Director General, International Food Policy Research Institute (IFPRI)*
Panelists:
Tom Arnold, *Chief Executive, Concern Worldwide, Ireland*
Meaza Ashenafi, *Executive Director, Ethiopian Women Lawyers Association, Ethiopia*
John Githongo, *Permanent Secretary, Governance and Ethics, Government of the Republic of Kenya, Kenya*
Yemi Michael Katerere, *Assistant Director General, Center for International Forestry Research (CIFOR), Indonesia*
David King, *Secretary General, International Federation of Agricultural Producers (IFAP), France*
Norah Owaraga, *Executive Secretary, Uganda Change Agent Association, Uganda*

1510–1540 COFFEE AND TEA BREAK

1540–1700 **PLENARY SESSION**
Panel Discussion: "Implementing Action in Key Areas"

Chair: **Harris Mule,** *Executive Director, Top Investment and Management Services, and former Permanent Secretary in the Ministry of Finance and Planning, Kenya*
Panelists: Chairs of Parallel Sessions
Monty Jones, *Executive Secretary, Forum for Agricultural Research in Africa (FARA), Ghana*
Benno Ndulu, *Research Manager, Development Economics Research Department, World Bank, U.S.A.*
Angeline Kamba, *Member of UN/UNESCO World Commission on Culture and Development, Zimbabwe*
Kabba Joiner, *Director General, WAHO, Burkina Faso*
Bethuel A. Kiplagat, *Executive Director, Africa Peace Forum, Kenya*

1700–1710 **Digital Opinion Poll of Participants**

1710–1840 **PLENARY SESSION**
Chair: **Mildred Namwiinde Mpundu,** *Executive Director, Media and Communication, Step Out Media Communications and Business Development Consultancy Services; and outgoing Assistant Features Editor, Times Printpak, Zambia*

"What African Countries Can Do to Support Implementation of Action for Food and Nutrition Security in Africa"
Keynote: **Augustin Fosu,** *Senior Policy Advisor, United Nations Economic Commission for Africa, Ethiopia*

"What Industrialized Countries Can Do to Promote Agricultural and Rural Development in Africa: Perspectives of a Development Organization"
Keynote: **Bernd Eisenblätter,** *Managing Director, Deutsche Gesellschaft für Technische Zusamenarbeit (GTZ), GmbH, Germany*

"What Industrialized Countries Can Do to Support Implementation of Action for Food and Nutrition Security in Africa: Perspectives from USAID"
Keynote: **Emmy B. Simmons,** *Assistant Administrator, United States Agency for International Development (USAID), Bureau of Economic Growth, Agriculture, and Trade, U.S.A.*

"Confronting AIDS and Hunger in Africa"
Keynote: **Alan Whiteside,** *Director, Health Economics and HIV/AIDS Research Division (HEARD), University of KwaZulu-Natal, South Africa*

"Priorities for Action on Food and Nutrition Security in Africa: Perspectives from the African Union"
Keynote: **Rosebud Kurwijila,** *Commissioner for Rural Economy and Agriculture, African Union, Ethiopia*

Saturday, April 3

0900–1030 **PLENARY SESSION: BUILDING POLITICAL WILL AND CHANGING ATTITUDES FOR ACTION**
Chair: **Moïse Mensah,** *former Minister of Finance, Benin*

"Fighting HIV/AIDS through Attitudinal Changes: Experiences from Uganda"
Keynote: **H.E. Mrs. Janet Museveni,** *First Lady of the Republic of Uganda*

"Changing Attitudes and Behaviors: The Role of Africa's Cultural Leaders"
Keynote: **Wole Soyinka,** *Professor Emeritus, Obafemi Awolowo University, Nigeria; Director of Literary Arts, International Institute of Modern Letters, University of Nevada; and Nobel Prize Laureate in Literature*

"Building Strong Partnerships to Improve Africa's Food Security and Rural Incomes"
Keynote: **Peter McPherson,** *President, Michigan State University, and Founding Co-Chair, Partnership to Cut Hunger in Africa, U.S.A.*

"Assuring Food and Nutrition Security in Africa: Perspective of the African Development Bank"
Keynote: **Theodore Nkodo,** *Vice President, Operations, North, East and South, African Development Bank, Tunisia*

1030–1100 COFFEE AND TEA BREAK

1100–1300 **PARALLEL SESSIONS: STAKEHOLDER FORUMS**
Strengthening Actors and Facilitating Partnerships

Parliamentarians and Business Leaders
Co-Chair: **Edith Nawakwi,** *Member of Parliament, National Assembly of Zambia, Zambia*
Co-Chair: **Alhaji Bamanga Tukur,** *Executive President, African Business Roundtable, and Chairman, New Partnership for Africa's Development (NEPAD) Business Group, Nigeria*
Rapporteur: **Nienke Beintema,** *Program Head, IFPRI/ISNAR Agricultural Science and Technology Indicators (ASTI) Initiative, International Food Policy Research Institute (IFPRI)*

National Policymakers and Development Partners
Co-Chair: **Helder Monteiro Muteia,** *Minister of Agriculture, Mozambique*
Co-Chair: **Judy O'Connor,** *Country Director, Tanzania and Uganda, The World Bank, Tanzania*
Co-Chair: **Amalia Garcia-Tharn,** *Food Aid/Food Security Policy, Development Directorate-General, European Commission, Belgium*
Rapporteur: **Andrew Temu,** *Visiting Research Fellow, International Food Policy Research Institute (IFPRI)*

Nongovernmental Organizations, Farmers Organizations, and Media

Co-Chair: **Ayo Abifarin,** *Director, Food Security Program, Africa Region, World Vision, Ghana*
Co-Chair: **Mercy Karanja,** *Chief Executive, Kenya Federation of Agricultural Producers, Kenya*
Co-Chair: **Ibiba don Pedro,** *New Age Newspaper, Nigeria, and Winner, 2003 CNN African Journalist Award, Nigeria*
Rapporteur: **Marc Cohen,** *Special Assistant to the Director General, International Food Policy Research Institute (IFPRI)*

1300–1400 LUNCH

1400–1415 **PLENARY SESSION**

Chair: **Charlotte McClain,** *Commissioner, South African Human Rights Commission, South Africa*

"Actions Needed for Reaching the Millennium Development Goals in Africa with a Focus on Overcoming Hunger"

Keynote: **Jeffrey Sachs,** *Director, Millennium Project; Director, The Earth Institute at Columbia University; and Professor, Columbia University, U.S.A.*

1415–1530 **PLENARY SESSION**

Panel Discussion: "How Actors from All Levels Can Work Together to Achieve Food and Nutrition Security"

Chair: **Charlotte McClain,** *Commissioner, South African Human Rights Commission, South Africa*
Panelists: Chairs of Parallel Sessions
Edith Nawakwi, *Member of Parliament, National Assembly of Zambia, Zambia*
Alhaji Bamanga Tukur, *Executive President, African Business Roundtable and Chairman, New Partnership for Africa's Development (NEPAD) Business Group, Nigeria*
Helder Monteiro Muteia, *Minister of Agriculture, Mozambique*
Judy O'Connor, *Country Director, Tanzania and Uganda, The World Bank, Tanzania*
Amalia Garcia-Tharn, *Food Aid/Food Security Policy, Development Directorate-General, European Commission, Belgium*
Ayo Abifarin, *Director, Food Security Program, Africa Region, World Vision, Ghana*
Mercy Karanja, *Chief Executive, Kenya Federation of Agricultural Producers, Kenya*
Ibiba don Pedro, *Guardian Newspaper, Nigeria and Winner, 2003 CNN African Journalist Award, Nigeria*

1530–1540 **Digital Opinion Poll of Participants**

1540–1630 **PLENARY SESSION: MOVING FORWARD AND CLOSING REMARKS**

Chair: **Rajul Pandya-Lorch,** *Head of the 2020 Vision Initiative, International Food Policy Research Institute (IFPRI)*
Speakers:
Joachim von Braun, *Director General, International Food Policy Research Institute (IFPRI)*
John Joseph Otim, *Senior Presidential Advisor to H.E. President Museveni of the Republic of Uganda; President, Uganda Agricultural Council; and Chair, Conference Advisory Committee*
Wilberforce Kisamba-Mugerwa, *Minister of Agriculture, Animal Industry, and Fisheries, Republic of Uganda*
H.E. Yoweri Museveni, *President, Republic of Uganda*

Appendix 2 Conference Participants

NAME	POSITION	ORGANIZATION	CITY/COUNTRY
Dr. Millie Abaru	Social Economics Advisor	Regional Land Management Unit (RELMA)	Nairobi, KENYA
Dr. Ayo Abifarin	Director, Food Security Program, Africa Region	World Vision International	Accra, GHANA
Dr. Richard Oginga Abila	Assistant Director	Kenya Marine and Fisheries Research Institute	Kisumu, KENYA
Ms. Consolata Acayo	Principal Information Scientist	Ministry of Agriculture, Animal Industry and Fisheries (MAAIF)	Entebbe, UGANDA
H.E. Koenraad Adam	Ambassador	Royal Belgian Embassy	Kampala, UGANDA
Dr. Akinwumi Adesina	Associate Director, Food Security	Rockefeller Foundation	Nairobi, KENYA
Mr. Vijay Adolkar	Research Scientist	International Centre of Insect Physiology and Ecology (ICIPE)	Nairobi, KENYA
Mrs. Rosanna Agble	Chief Nutrition Officer	Ghana Health Service	Accra, GHANA
Ms. Caroline Aguti		Association for Strengthening Agricultural Research in Eastern and Central Africa (ASARECA)	Entebbe, UGANDA
Dr. Isher Judge Ahluwalia	Chairperson, IFPRI Board of Trustees	International Food Policy Research Institute (IFPRI)	Bethesda, MD, USA
Dr. Jiro Aikawa	Representative	Sasakawa Global 2000 Tanzania	Dar es Salaam, TANZANIA
H.E. Grace Akello	Minister of State, Northern Uganda Rehabilitation	Office of the Prime Minister	Kampala, UGANDA
Dr. Isaac Akinyele	Professor and President, Nutrition Society of Nigeria	University of Ibadan	Ibadan, NIGERIA
Mr. Afework Aklilu		African Development Bank	Tunis, TUNISIA
Ms. Abenaa Akuamao-Boateng	Regional Nutrition Officer–Ashanti	Ghana Health Service	Kumasi, GHANA
Mr. Zerihun Alemayehu	Promotion Department Head	Ministry of Agriculture and Rural Development	Addis Ababa, ETHIOPIA
Mr. Joel Milton Aliro-Omara	Commissioner	Uganda Human Rights Commission	Kampala, UGANDA
Mr. Boma Simeon Anga	Chairman	Nigerian Presidential Committee on Cassava Market Development and Export	Lagos, NIGERIA
Mr. Tom Arnold	CEO	Concern Worldwide	Dublin, IRELAND
Mr. Abdoulaye Arona Ka	Secretaire General	Union Nationale Des 3 (Paysan, Pêcheur, Pasteur)	Dakar, SENEGAL
Dr. Kwadwo Asenso-Okyere	Professor/Vice Chancellor	University of Ghana	Legon, GHANA
Ms. Meaza Ashenafi	Executive Director	Ethiopian Women Lawyers Association	Addis Ababa, ETHIOPIA
Dr. Samuel Asuming-Brempong	Head, Department of Agricultural Economics and Agribusiness	University of Ghana	Legon, GHANA
Dr. Tola Atinmo	Professor of Nutrition and President of African Unions of Nutritional Sciences	University of Ibadan	Ibadan, NIGERIA
Dr. Achi Atsain	Professor/Senior Research Fellow	Ivorian Center for Economic and Social Research (CIRES)	Abidjan, CÔTE D'IVOIRE
Dr. Gezahegn Ayele	Senior Scientist/Department Head	Ethiopian Agricultural Research Organization (EARO)	Addis Ababa, ETHIOPIA
Mr. Samuel Ayodele	Special Assistant to the President	African Business Roundtable	Abuja, NIGERIA
Dr. Suresh Babu	Senior Research Fellow and Senior Training Advisor	International Food Policy Research Institute (IFPRI)	Washington, DC, USA
Dr. Ousmane Badiane	Senior Research Advisor	International Food Policy Research Institute (IFPRI)	Washington, DC, USA
Ms. Evelyn Banda	Senior Communications Specialist	International Food Policy Research Institute (IFPRI)	Washington, DC, USA
Ms. Laeticia Basemerar	Programme Manager	Save the Children in Uganda (SCIU)	Kampala, UGANDA
Rev. David Beckmann	President	Bread for the World	Washington, DC, USA
Ms. Nienke Beintema	Coordinator, Agricultural Science and Technology Indicators (ASTI) Initiative	International Food Policy Research Institute (IFPRI)	Washington, DC, USA
Dr. Azene Bekele-Tesemma	Capacity Building Advisor	Regional Land Management Unit (RELMA)	Nairobi, KENYA
Dr. Mateete Bekunda	Professor and Dean	Makerere University–Kampala	Kampala, UGANDA
Dr. Samuel Benin	Research Fellow	International Food Policy Research Institute (IFPRI)	Kampala, UGANDA
Dr. Michel Benoit-Cattin	Associate Director for Economics of Social Sciences	Centre de coopération internationale en recherche agronomique pour le développement (CIRAD)	Montpellier, FRANCE
Dr. Todd Benson	Research Fellow	International Food Policy Research Institute (IFPRI)	Washington, DC, USA
Dr. Tareke Berhe	Country Director	Sasakawa Global 2000 Programs in Africa	Conakry, GUINEA
Mr. John Bichemano	Consumer Journalist	Uganda Consumers Protection Association	Kampala, UGANDA
Mr. Jack Bigirwa	National Chairman	National Union of Coffee Agribusiness and Farm Enterprises (NUCAFE)	Kampala, UGANDA
Hon. Godfrey Binaisa	Former President of the Republic of Uganda	The Republic of Uganda	UGANDA

This list contains participants registered by IFPRI. Other participants were registered by the host, the Government of Uganda.

NAME	POSITION	ORGANIZATION	CITY/COUNTRY
Ms. Nakalema Binaisa	Assistant/Farmer		Kampala, UGANDA
Mr. Deusdedit Blkwasizehi	Member of Parliament	Parliament of Uganda	Kampala, UGANDA
Dr. Norman Borlaug	President	Sasakawa Africa Association	Mexico, MEXICO
Mr. Abdramane Bouare	Secretary General	Assemblée Permanente des Chambres d'Agriculture du Mali (APCAM)	Bamako, MALI
Mr. Ndalegh Jairus Boyoma	Librarian		Kampala, UGANDA
Mr. Sumiter Broca		Food and Agriculture Organization of the United Nations (FAO)	Rome, ITALY
Mr. Apuuli Bwango	Commissioner for Meteorology	Department of Meteorology	Kampala, UGANDA
Dr. Madan Mohan Lal Chadha	Director	AVRDC-The World Vegetable Center	Arusha, TANZANIA
Mr. Jordan Chamberlin	Research Analyst	International Food Policy Research Institute (IFPRI)	Washington, DC, USA
Ms. Doreen Chanje	Consultant, Food Security and Nutrition	Foodsec Consulting	Blantyre, MALAWI
Mr. Peter Chase	Special Negotiator for Agricultural Biotechnology	U.S. Department of State	Washington, DC, USA
Prof. Chunming Chen	Professor	Chinese Center for Disease Control and Prevention	Beijing, CHINA
Mr. Augustin Charles Chikuni	Programme Officer	The Royal Norwegian Embassy, Malawi	Lilongwe, MALAWI
Dr. Glyvyns Chinkhuntha	Executive Director	Freedom Gardens	Lilongwe, MALAWI
Mr. Georges Codjia	Food and Nutrition Officer	Food and Agriculture Organization of the United Nations (FAO)-SAFR	Harare, ZIMBABWE
Dr. Marc Cohen	Special Assistant to the Director General	International Food Policy Research Institute (IFPRI)	Washington, DC, USA
Dr. Gordon Conway	President	Rockefeller Foundation	New York, NY, USA
Mr. Peter Helmut Conze	Director General	Deutsche Gesellschaft für Technische Zusammenarbeit (GTZ)	Eschborn, GERMANY
Dr. Rodney Cooke	Head, Technical Advisory Division (PT)	International Fund for Agricultural Development (IFAD)	Rome, ITALY
Ms. Bernadette Cordero	Senior Administrative Coordinator	International Food Policy Research Institute (IFPRI)	Washington, DC, USA
Mr. Paul Crawford	Team Leader, Economic Growth	U.S. Agency for International Development (USAID)/Uganda	Kampala, UGANDA
Ms. Djhoanna Cruz	Program Assistant	International Food Policy Research Institute (IFPRI)	Washington, DC, USA
Mr. Søren Damgaard-Larsen	Water and Soil Fertility Advisor	Regional Land Management Unit (RELMA)	Nairobi, KENYA
Dr. William Dollente Dar	Director General	International Crops Research Institute for the Semi-Arid Tropics (ICRISAT)	Hyderabad, INDIA
Mr. Gabriel Labão Dava	Director	Canadian International Development Agency Program Support Unit in Mozambique (CIDA-PSU)	Maputo, MOZAMBIQUE
Mr. Ken Noah Davies	Representative/Country Director	UN World Food Programme	Kampala, UGANDA
Ms. Corrine De Gracia	Program Analyst	International Food Policy Research Institute (IFPRI)	Washington, DC, USA
Dr. Jochen de Haas	Head, Rural Development and Global Food Security Division	Federal Ministry of Economic Co-operation and Development (BMZ)	Bonn, GERMANY
Dr. Christopher Delgado	Director, ILRI-IFPRI Joint Program on Livestock Market Opportunities	International Food Policy Research Institute (IFPRI)	Washington, DC, USA
Mr. Niama Nango Dembélé	Assistant Professor of International Development/PASIDMA Project Coordinator	Michigan State University	Bamako, MALI
Dr. Glenn Denning	Hunger Task Force Associate	World Agroforestry Centre (ICRAF) and Hunger Task Force	Nairobi, KENYA
Mr. Alain Derevier	Senior Advisor for Research	Ministry of Foreign Affairs, France	Paris, FRANCE
Ms. Birte Asja Detjen	Journalist	Deutsche Welthungerhilfe (German Agro Action)	Koeln, GERMANY
Mr. Aliou Dia	Parliamentarian	Forces Paysannes	Dakar, SENEGAL
Dr. Abdoulaye Diallo	Secretary General	Mano River Union	Freetown, SIERRA LEONE
Dr. Mamadou Diomande	Inspector General	Ministère de la Recherche Scientifique	Abidjan, CÔTE D'IVOIRE
Dr. Josué Dioné	Chief, Food Security and Sustainable Development	United Nations Economic Commission for Africa (UNECA)	Addis Ababa, ETHIOPIA
Mr. Moussa Diop	Journalist	Sud Quotidien	Dakar, SENEGAL
Amb. Thomas Djurhuus	Agricultural Ambassador	Royal Danish Embassy	Kampala, UGANDA
Ms. Ibiba Don Pedro		New Age	Lagos, NIGERIA
Mr. Elie Dote		African Development Bank	Tunis, TUNISIA
Dr. Christopher Dowswell	Special Assistant to Sasakawa Africa Association President	Sasakawa Global 2000	Mexico, MEXICO
Ms. Lisa Dreier	Program Manager	The Columbia Earth Institute	Palisades, NY, USA
Mr. James Dunn	Senior Agricultural Specialist	U.S. Agency for International Development (USAID)/Uganda	Kampala, UGANDA
Mr. Ricardo Dunn	Information Officer	Integrated Regional Information Network	Johannesburg, SOUTH AFRICA
Mr. Milton Egesa	Executive Director	Uganda Wetlands and Resource Conservation Association	Kampala, UGANDA
Dr. Bernd Eisenblätter	Managing Director	Deutsche Gesellschaft für Technische Zusammenarbeit (GTZ), GmbH	Eschborn, GERMANY
Mr. El Sheik Mohamed El Mak	Director General of Resources Sector	Ministry of Finance and National Economy (MOFNE)	Khartoum, SUDAN
Dr. Mohammed El Mourid	Regional Coordinator for North Africa Regional Program (NARP)	International Center for Agricultural Research in the Dry Areas (ICARDA)	Tunis, TUNISIA
Mr. Brahim El Youssi	Advisor to Minister of Agriculture and Rural Development	Ministry of Agriculture and Rural Development	Rabat, MOROCCO
Dr. Lire Ersado	Economist	World Bank	Washington, DC, USA

NAME	POSITION	ORGANIZATION	CITY/COUNTRY
Hon. Dr. Peter Esele	Member of Parliament	Parliament of Uganda	Kampala, UGANDA
Ms. Angeles Estrada	Logistics Coordinator– Sustainable Developments	International Institute for Sustainable Development (IISD)	New York, NY, USA
Mr. Shenggen Fan	Senior Research Fellow	International Food Policy Research Institute (IFPRI)	Washington, DC, USA
Dr. William Fiebig	Technical Advisor	Save the Children Federation, Inc.	Washington, DC, USA
Dr. Michael Foster	Country Director–Uganda	Sasakawa Africa Association	Kampala, UGANDA
Dr. Augustin Fosu	Senior Policy Advisor/Chief Economist	UN Economic Commission for Africa	Addis Ababa, ETHIOPIA
Mr. Martin Fowler	Advisor	Ministry of Agriculture, Animal Industry, and Fisheries (MAAIF)	Kampala, UGANDA
Mr. Tim Fowler	Country Director	Concern Worldwide	Kampala, UGANDA
Ms. Heidi Fritschel	Consultant		Arlington, VA, USA
Dr. Eleni Gabre-Madhin		World Bank	Washington, DC, USA
Ms. Lullit Paulos Gabre-Michael	Journalist/Media Consultant/Researcher		Addis Ababa, ETHIOPIA
Ms. Amalia Garcia-Tharn	Food Aid/Food Security	European Commission	Brussels, BELGIUM
Dr. Dennis Philip Garrity	Director General	World Agroforestry Centre (ICRAF)	Nairobi, KENYA
Mrs. Lis Garval	Counselor	Royal Danish Embassy	Kampala, UGANDA
Ms. Luisa Gaskell	Travel Coordinator	International Food Policy Research Institute (IFPRI)	Washington, DC, USA
Hon. Newaye Christos Gebre-Ab	Economic Advisor	Office of the Prime Minister	Addis Ababa, ETHIOPIA
Mr. Mulugeta Debebe Gemechu	General Manager	Oromo Self Help Organization (OSHO)	Addis Ababa, ETHIOPIA
Mr. Helder Gemo	National Director for Rural Extension	Ministry of Agriculture and Rural Development	Maputo, MOZAMBIQUE
Hon. Ato Yonas Gidey	Member of Parliament	House of Peoples' Representatives/Ethiopian Parliament	Addis Ababa, ETHIOPIA
Dr. Stuart Gillespie	Senior Research Fellow	International Food Policy Research Institute (IFPRI)	Washington, DC, USA
Mr. John Githongo	Permanent Secretary	Republic of Kenya	Nairobi, KENYA
Dr. Julia Gitobu	Regional Director, Awlae	Winrock International	Nairobi, KENYA
Mr. Michael Go	Administrative Coordinator, Publications Services	International Food Policy Research Institute (IFPRI)	Washington, DC, USA
Dr. Clifford Gold	Scientist	International Institute of Tropical Agriculture (IITA)	Kampala, UGANDA
Ms. Laurie Goldberg	Head, Policy Seminars Program	International Food Policy Research Institute (IFPRI)	Washington, DC, USA
Mr. Carl Barrington Greenidge	Director	Technical Center for Agricultural and Rural Cooperation (CTA)	Wageningen, NETHERLANDS
Dr. Michel Griffon	Special Advisor, Office of the DGO	Centre de coopération internationale en recherche agronomique pour le développement (CIRAD)	Paris, FRANCE
Mr. Mustapha Guellouz	Director General–President of the Board of the Enterprise	Office de l'Élevage et des Paturages (O.E.P.)	Tunis, TUNISIA
Mrs. Nafissatou Konare Guindo	Technical Advisor	Government of Mali	Bamako, MALI
Mr. Philippe Guiton	Regional Relief Director–Africa	World Vision	Nairobi, KENYA
Dr. Ashok Gulati	Division Director, Markets, Trade, and Institutions Division	International Food Policy Research Institute (IFPRI)	Washington, DC, USA
Ms. Maria Gutierrez		International Institute for Sustainable Development (IISD)	New York, NY, USA
Dr. Wayne Haag	Regional OPM-SEED Coordinator	Sasakawa Global 2000	Maputo, MOZAMBIQUE
Dr. Steve Haggblade	Consultant	International Food Policy Research Institute (IFPRI)	Lusaka, ZAMBIA
Mr. Mohammed Haidara	Coordinateur	Afrique Verte Mali	Bamako, MALI
Mr. Abdul-Rahman Harruna Attah	Managing Editor	Accra Daily Mail	Accra, GHANA
Mr. Robert Havener	President Emeritus	Winrock International	Sacramento, CA, USA
Dr. Peter Hazell	Division Director, Development Strategy and Governance Division	International Food Policy Research Institute (IFPRI)	Washington, DC, USA
Dr. Simon Heck	Research Scientist	WorldFish Center	Cairo, EGYPT
Mr. Patrick Heffer	Executive Secretary	International Fertilizer Industry Association (IFA)	Paris, FRANCE
Mr. Andrew Hepelwa	Secretary General	MVIWATA (National Network of Farmers Groups)	Dar es Salaam, TANZANIA
Mr. Glenford Hlongwane		Department of Agriculture, South Africa	Pretoria, SOUTH AFRICA
Mr. Manfred Hochwald	Director of Programmes and Projects	Deutsche Welthungerhilfe (German Agro Action)	Bonn, GERMANY
Ms. Janet Hodur	Communications Specialist	International Food Policy Research Institute (IFPRI)	Washington, DC, USA
Dr. Julie A. Howard	Executive Director	Partnership to Cut Hunger and Poverty in Africa	Washington, DC, USA
Dr. Gary Howe	Director, Eastern and Southern Africa Division	International Fund for Agricultural Development (IFAD)	Rome, ITALY
Mr. Patrick Hudak	Foreign Affairs Officer	U.S. Department of State	Washington, DC, USA
Mr. Charles Hurly	Senior Export Manager	Omnia Fertilizer Ltd.	Gauteng, SOUTH AFRICA
Ambassador Sigurd Illing	Head of Delegation	European Union	Kampala, UGANDA
Mr. Michio Ito	Administrative Officer	Sasakawa Africa Association	Tokyo, JAPAN
Rwoth Opar Edward Jalcebo	Tribal Leader	Kingdom of Alur, Nebbi District	UGANDA
Ms. Isatou Jallow	Executive Director	National Nutrition Agency (NANA)	Banjul, THE GAMBIA
Dr. Bashir Jama	Regional Coordinator of Eastern and Central Africa, ICRAF, and Hunger Task Force Member	World Agroforestry Centre (ICRAF) and Hunger Task Force	Nairobi, KENYA
Mr. Ousman Jammeh	Permanent Secretary	Ministry of Agriculture	Banjul, THE GAMBIA

NAME	POSITION	ORGANIZATION	CITY/COUNTRY
Dr. Mohamed Jaouad	Agroeconomist and Senior Advisor to the Minister, Agricultural Policies	Ministry of Agriculture and Rural Development	Rabat, MOROCCO
Mr. Hans Joehr	Corporate Head of Agriculture	Nestle Ltd.	Vevey, SWITZERLAND
Dr. Kabba Joiner	Director General	West African Health Organization (WAHO)	Bobo-Dioulasso, BURKINA FASO
Dr. Monty Patrick Jones	Executive Secretary	FARA (Forum for Agricultural Research in Africa)	Accra, GHANA
Mr. Emmanuel Ruguuza Kabishanga	Country Liaison Manager	New Horizons Women's Education Centre	Kampala, UGANDA
Ms. Charity Kabutha	Gender Consultant		Nairobi, KENYA
Mr. Billie Okae Kadameri	African News Producer/Journalist	Radio France International	Paris, FRANCE
Ms. Dorothy Kaggwa	Senior Programme Officer	Environment Alert	Kampala, UGANDA
Mr. Bernard Kagira	Trade Advisor	Common Market for Eastern and Southern Africa (COMESA), Regional Agricultural Trade Expansion Support (RATES) Program	Nairobi, KENYA
Mr. Fred Kalibwani	Africa Coordinator	International Federation of Organic Agriculture Movements (IFOAM)	Bonn, GERMANY
Dr. Thomson Kalinda	Lecturer and Head of Department	University of Zambia	Lusaka, ZAMBIA
Dr. Henrietta Kalinda-Chilumbu	Monitoring and Evaluation Coordinator	Agriculture Support Programme (ASP)	Lusaka, ZAMBIA
Ms. Angeline Kamba	Chair of the IRRI Board of Trustees	International Rice Research Institute (IRRI)	Harare, ZIMBABWE
Dr. David Kamukama		Agricultural Policy Network of Uganda (APONU)	Kampala, UGANDA
Mr. Amadou Kanouté	Regional Director	Consumers International, Africa Office	Harare, ZIMBABWE
Ms. Mercy Karanja	Chief Executive	Kenya National Farmers Union	Nairobi, KENYA
Mr. Leonard Nduati Kariuki	Chairman	Kenya National Federation of Agricultural Producers	Nairobi, KENYA
Mr. Matia Kasaija	Under Secretary	Ministry of Agriculture, Animal Industry and Fisheries	Kampala, UGANDA
Dr. Eve Kasirye Alemu	Chairperson	Association of Uganda Professional Women in Agriculture and Environment	Kampala, UGANDA
Mr. Yemi Michael Katerere	Assistant Director General	Center for International Forestry Research	Bogor Barat, INDONESIA
Ms. Maître Françoise Kaudjhis-Offoumou	Avocate à la Cour and Barreau de Côte d'Ivoire	Présidente Fondatrice de AID-Afrique (Association internationale pour la démocratie)	Abidjan, CÔTE D'IVOIRE
Mr. Bruce Kaunda	Reporter	Zambia Daily Mail	Ndola, ZAMBIA
Mr. Batson Kayaayo	Program Coordinator/Administrator	Sasakawa Global 2000 Programs in Africa	Kampala, UGANDA
Mr. Tom Kelly	Regional Humanitarian Advisor	UK Department for International Development	Pretoria, SOUTH AFRICA
Dr. Christoph Kessler	Division Chief	KfW	Frankfurt, GERMANY
Dr. Seyfu Ketema	Executive Secretary	Association for Strengthening Agricultural Research in Eastern and Central Africa (ASARECA)	Entebbe, UGANDA
Dr. Stanley Khaila	Director	Center for Agricultural Research and Development (CARD)	Lilongwe, MALAWI
Prof. Fathi Mohamed Khalifa Abbas	Deputy Director General	Arab Organization for Agricultural Development (AOAD)	Khartoum, SUDAN
Hon. Dr. Israel Kibrige-Sebunya	Minister of State for Agriculture	Government of the Republic of Uganda	Entebbe, UGANDA
Mrs. Olive Kigongo	President	Uganda National Chambers of Commerce and Industry (UNCCI)	Kampala, UGANDA
Dr. Irene Kiiza	Nutrition Specialist	World Vision Uganda	Kampala, UGANDA
Dr. Joyce Kikafunda	Head, Department of Food Science and Technology	Makerere University	Kampala, UGANDA
Mr. David King	Secretary General	International Federation of Agricultural Producers (IFAP)	Paris, FRANCE
Ambassador Bethuel Kiplagat	Executive Director	Africa Peace Forum	Nairobi, KENYA
Mr. Philip Macharia Kiriro	President	Eastern Africa Farmers Federation	Nairobi, KENYA
Dr. Roger Kirkby	Africa Coordinator	International Center for Tropical Agriculture (CIAT)	Kampala, UGANDA
Ms. Ingrid Kirsten	Researcher Agriculture	New Partnership for Africa's Development (NEPAD) Secretariat	Midrand, SOUTH AFRICA
Dr. Johann Frederick Kirsten	Professor and Head, Department of Agricultural Economics, Extension, and Rural Development	University of Pretoria	Pretoria, SOUTH AFRICA
Hon. Wilberforce Kisamba-Mugerwa	Minister of Agriculture, Animal Industry, and Fisheries	Ministry of Agriculture, Animal Industry, and Fisheries	Entebbe, UGANDA
Dr. Aichi Kitalyi	Animal Husbandry Advisor	Regional Land Management Unit (RELMA)	Nairobi, KENYA
Mr. Samuel Mubiru Kizito	Chairman	Uganda Beef Producers' Association	Kampala, UGANDA
Dr. Saidou Koala	Regional Representative	International Crops Research Institute for the Semi-Arid Tropics (ICRISAT)	Niamey, NIGER
H.E. Mamadou Kone	Minister of Scientific Research	Ministry of Scientific Research	Abidjan, CÔTE D'IVOIRE
Ms. Metta Kongira	Representative	National Youth Association for Food Security (NaYAFS)	Banjul, THE GAMBIA
Dr. Bernard Kouassi	Sécrétaire Executif	Fondation SADAOC	Ouagadougou, BURKINA FASO
Ms. Malgorzata "Mak" Kowalska	Intern	International Food Policy Research Institute (IFPRI)	Washington, DC, USA
Dr. Stephan Krall	Project Manager, BEAF	Deutsche Gesellschaft für Technische Zusammenarbeit, GmbH	Eschborn, GERMANY
Ms. Jenna Kryszczun	Program Analyst	International Food Policy Research Institute (IFPRI)	Washington, DC, USA
Dr. Rosebud Kurwijila	Commissioner	African Union	Addis Ababa, ETHIOPIA
Dr. Freddie Kwesiga	Principal Scientist; ICRAF Regional Coordinator for SADC and Southern Africa Programme	World Agroforestry Centre (ICRAF)	Harare, ZIMBABWE
Mohand Laenser	Minister of Agriculture and Rural Development	Ministry of Agriculture and Rural Development	Rabat, MOROCCO

NAME	POSITION	ORGANIZATION	CITY/COUNTRY
Mr. Jean-Charles Le Vallee	Food Security Guide	Development Gateway	Gatineau, CANADA
Ms. Vickie Lee	Graphics Specialist	International Food Policy Research Institute (IFPRI)	Washington, DC, USA
Ms. Maria Lovelace-Johnson		Food and Drug Board	Accra, GHANA
Mr. Patrick Lubega	Research Enumerator	International Food Policy Research Institute (IFPRI)–Kampala	Kampala, UGANDA
Mr. Patrick Luganda	Senior Features Writer	The New Vision	Kampala, UGANDA
Mr. A. Mutumba Lule	Journalist	The East Africa	UGANDA
Dr. William Lyakurwa	Executive Director	African Economic Research Consortium	Nairobi, KENYA
Ms. Susan Mabonga	Journalist	Biosafety News–Picasso Productions	Nairobi, KENYA
Mrs. Graça Machel	President	Foundation for Community Development (FDC)	MOZAMBIQUE
Mr. Toshiro Mado	Program Officer	Sasakawa Africa Association	Addis Ababa, ETHIOPIA
Mr. Octavian Mageni		Ministry of Community Development, Gender and Children	Dar es Salaam, TANZANIA
Mr. John Gordon Magnay	Chief Executive Officer	Uganda Grain Traders Ltd.	Kampala, UGANDA
Mr. Chebet Maikut	President	Uganda National Farmers' Federation (UNFFE)	Kampala, UGANDA
Ms. Cathy Majtenyi	Journalist	Voice of America	Nairobi, KENYA
Mr. Eben Mabibi Makonese	Managing Director	Chemplex Corporation Ltd	Harare, ZIMBABWE
Mrs. Kaddy Manneh-Suso	Acting Director General	Economic Community of West African States (ECOWAS) Gender Development Centre	Dakar, SENEGAL
Sra. Margarita Marino de Botero			Santafe de Bogota, COLOMBIA
Mr. Sadibou Marone	Journalist	Le Soleil	Dakar, SENEGAL
Mr. Peter Robert Masebu	Journalist	PANAPRESS SA	Dakar, SENEGAL
Dr. Oswald Mashindano	Senior Research Fellow	Economic and Social Research Foundation (ESRF)	Dar es Salaam, TANZANIA
Mr. Patrick Matsiko	Journalist	Monitor	UGANDA
Dr. Charles Mataya	Policy Economist	International Fertilizer Development Center (IFDC)–Malawi	Lilongwe, MALAWI
Dr. Peter Matlon	Director, Africa Regional Program	Rockefeller Foundation	Nairobi, KENYA
Ms. Janet Maughan	Deputy Director, Global Inclusion	Rockefeller Foundation	New York, NY, USA
Mr. Vincent Paul Mayanja	Correspondent	Agence France Presse (AFP)	Kampala, UGANDA
Ms. Jennifer Mayer		U.S. Agency for International Development (USAID)	UGANDA
Ms. Susan Mbaya	Regional Programme Officer	Consumers International	Harare, ZIMBABWE
Mr. Paul Hyacinthe Mben	Journalist	L'Indépendent	Bamako, MALI
Mr. Masiphula Mpazima Mbongwa	Deputy Director-General	Department of Agriculture, South Africa	Pretoria, SOUTH AFRICA
Ms. Charlotte McClain-Nhlapo	Commissioner	South African Human Rights Commission	Gauteng, SOUTH AFRICA
Mr. Robert S. McNamara			Washington, DC, USA
Mr. Peter McPherson	President	Michigan State University	East Lansing, USA
Ms. Leila Mead	Digital Editor–Sustainable Developments	International Institute for Sustainable Development (IISD)	New York, NY, USA
Ms. Helina Megersa	Editor in Chief	The Daily Monitor PLC	Addis Ababa, ETHIOPIA
Dr. Soukou Emmanuel Mel Eg	Deputy Director of Food	Ministry of Animal Production and Fisheries	Abidjan, CÔTE D'IVOIRE
Dr. Moïse Mensah	Consultant		Cotonou, BENIN
Dr. Douglas Merrey	Director for Africa	International Water Management Institute (IWMI)	Pretoria, SOUTH AFRICA
Mr. Deodatus Mfugale	News Editor	The Guardian Newspaper	Dar es Salaam, TANZANIA
Dr. Asha-Rose Migiro	Member of Parliament and Minister	Ministry of Community Development, Gender and Children	Dar es Salaam, TANZANIA
Dr. Isaac Joseph Minde	Coordinator	Association for Strengthening Agricultural Research in Eastern and Central Africa (ASARECA)/ Eastern and Central Africa Programme for Agricultural Policy Analysis (ECAPAPA)	Entebbe, UGANDA
Ms. Marilyn Minderhoud-Jones	Communications Coordinator	Information on Low External Input and Sustainable Agriculture (ILEIA)	NETHERLANDS
Mr. Nicholas Minot	Research Fellow	International Food Policy Research Institute (IFPRI)	Washington, DC, USA
Mr. Masaaki Miyamoto	General Manager	Sasakawa Africa Association	Tokyo, JAPAN
Mr. Crispin Mkandawire	President	Farmers Union of Malawi	Lilongwe, MALAWI
Prof. Richard M. Mkandawire	Agricultural Advisor	New Partnership for Africa's Development (NEPAD) Secretariat	Halfway House, SOUTH AFRICA
Mr. Uday Mohan	Senior Communications Specialist	International Food Policy Research Institute (IFPRI)	Washington, DC, USA
Dr. Uzo Mokwunye	Director	United Nations University (UNU/INRA)	Accra, GHANA
Dr. Hussein Mongi	Director of Research and Development	Alpha Seed Company Limited	Moshi, TANZANIA
Ms. Vickie Moore	Director, Uganda Office	U.S. Agency for International Development (USAID)	Kampala, UGANDA
Ms. Mildred Namwiinde Mpundu	Assistant Features Director	Times Printpak Limited	Lusaka, ZAMBIA
Mr. Edwin Mtei	Board Member/Former Chairman	Tanzania Coffee Growers Association (TCGA)	Arusha, TANZANIA
Mrs. Bathabile Mtsweni	Estate Agent		Johannesburg, SOUTH AFRICA
Ms. Nelisiwe Mbali Mtsweni	Student		Johannesburg, SOUTH AFRICA
Ven. Rev. Christopher Charles Muchenga Madeesi	Executive Director	Uganda Wholistic Development Programme AGOA (UWDP)	UGANDA
Mrs. Mary Consolate Muduuli	Deputy Secretary to the Treasury	Ministry of Finance, Planning and Economic Development (MFPED)	Kampala, UGANDA
Mr. Samuel Mugarura	Research Assistant	International Food Policy Research Institute (IFPRI)–Kampala	Kampala, UGANDA
Dr. Martin Mugenzi	Head of Economics Department	National University of Rwanda	Butare, RWANDA
Ms. Christine Muhindo		SPA/ Mass Mobilization	Kampala, UGANDA
Dr. Kankonde Mukadi	Professor	Université Protestante au Congo	Kinshasa, DEMOCRATIC REPUBLIC OF CONGO

NAME	POSITION	ORGANIZATION	CITY/COUNTRY
Dr. Adrian Mukhebi	Executive Director	Kenya Agricultural Commodity Exchange (KACE)	Nairobi, KENYA
Dr. Eusebius J. Mukhwana	Director	SACRED (Sustainable Agriculture Centre for Research and Development in Africa)	Bungoma, KENYA
Ms. Joyce Mulama	Correspondent	Inter Press Service (IPS)	Nairobi, KENYA
Mr. Harris Mule	Executive Director	Top Investment Management Services, Ltd.	Nairobi, KENYA
Ms. Mildred Mulenga	Journalist	Pan African News Agency (PANA)	Johannesburg, SOUTH AFRICA
Mr. Elliud Muli	Research Scholar	International Centre of Insect Physiology and Ecology (ICIPE)	Nairobi, KENYA
Dr. Robbie Mupawose	Chairman	Barclays Bank Zimbabwe	Harare, ZIMBABWE
Mr. Aggrey Musamba	Second Vice President	Zambia National Farmers' Union	Lusaka, ZAMBIA
Prof. Richard Musangi	Chairman of the Board of Trustees of the Africa Rice Center (WARDA)	Villa Maria Enterprises Ltd.	Nakuru, KENYA
H.E. Mrs. Janet Museveni	First Lady	Republic of Uganda	Kampala, UGANDA
H.E. Yoweri Museveni	President	Government of the Republic of Uganda	Kampala, UGANDA
Mr. David Mushabe	Research Assistant	International Food Policy Research Institute (IFPRI) - Kampala	Kampala, UGANDA
Mr. Kabodo Mutalibi			UGANDA
Dr. Gladys Mutangadura	Food Security and Sustainable Development Officer	United Nations Economic Commission for Africa (UNECA)	Lusaka, ZAMBIA
H.E. Helder Monteiro Muteia	Minister of Agriculture	Ministry of Agriculture	Maputo, MOZAMBIQUE
Mr. Patrick Mutsiko	Assistant News Editor	The Monitor	Kampala, UGANDA
Mr. Abbey Mutumba-Lule	Bureau Chief/Editor	The East African and Daily Nation	Kampala, UGANDA
Dr. Gertrude Muwanga	Lecturer	Makerere University Institute of Economics	Kampala, UGANDA
Mr. Murinda Muzirakugomwa	Executive Member	Forum of African Civil Society for Sustainable Development (FACS)	Pretoria, SOUTH AFRICA
Dr. Robert Mwadime	Child Survival and Nutrition Advisor	Regional Center for Quality of Health Care	Kampala, UGANDA
Dr. Anthony Mwanaumo	Coordinator	Agricultural Consultative Forum (ACF)	Lusaka, ZAMBIA
Dr. Wilfred Mwangi	Regional Economist	International Maize and Wheat Improvement Center (CIMMYT)	Nairobi, KENYA
Mr. Michael Mwaniki	Journalist	Nation Media Group	Nairobi, KENYA
Mr. Raphael Mwenenguwe	Freelance/Correspondent	Baird Publications (Australia) and Mail and Guardian (South Africa)	Lilongwe, MALAWI
Ms. Rosetti Nabbumba-Nayenga	Policy Analyst	Ministry of Finance, Planning and Economic Development	Kampala, UGANDA
Ms. Pamela Nahamya	Senior Research Assistant	International Food Policy Research Institute (IFPRI) - Kampala	Kampala, UGANDA
Dr. Silim Nahdy	Executive Director	National Agricultural Advisory Services (NAADS)	Kampala, UGANDA
Ms. Stella Nambuya	Chairperson	Federation of Uganda Women Business Organizations Industry and Agriculture	Kampala, UGANDA
Hon. Visolela Rosalinda Namises	Member of Parliament	Parliament of Namibia-National Assembly	Windhoek, NAMIBIA
Mrs. Specioza Kiwanuka Namiwebe	Programme Coordinator	Vredeseilanden Coopibo Uganda	Kampala, UGANDA
Mr. Magameso Namungala	Chief News Editor, Radio Uganda	Department of Information, Office of the President	Kampala, UGANDA
Ms. Edith Namutabi	Foreign Service Officer	Ministry of Foreign Affairs	Kampala, UGANDA
Dr. Hamid Narjisse	Director General/Professor	Institut National de la Recherche Agronomique (INRA)	Rabat, MOROCCO
Dr. Luis A. Navarro	Senior Program Specialist	International Development Research Centre (IDRC)	Nairobi, KENYA
Ms. Edith Nawakwi	Member of Parliament	National Assembly of Zambia	Lusaka, ZAMBIA
Ms. Oumy Khaïry Ndiaye	Head	Technical Centre for Agricultural and Rural Cooperation (CTA)	Wageningen, NETHERLANDS
Dr. Benno Ndulu	Research Manager	World Bank	Washington, DC, USA
Mr. Radek Nedved	Manager	The Czech Daily Lidove Noviny	Prague, CZECH REPUBLIC
Mr. Mesfin Negash	Senior Editor	Media and Communications Center (MCC)	Addis Ababa, ETHIOPIA
Mr. Tidiane Ngaido	Research Fellow	International Food Policy Research Institute (IFPRI)	Washington, DC, USA
Dr. Peter Ngategize	National Coordinator	Ministry of Finance, Planning and Economic Development	Kampala, UGANDA
Dr. Antoine Kabwit Nguz	Laboratory of Food Technology and Engineering	Faculty of Agricultural and Applied Biological Sciences	Gent, BELGIUM
Dr. Oumar Niangado	Foundation Delegate	Syngenta Foundation for Sustainable Agriculture	Bamako, MALI
Dr. Victoriano Nicolau	Member of Parliament and Coordinator Economic Subcommittee	Parliament of Angola	ANGOLA
Mr. Martin Nissen	Head of Division	German Federal Ministry of Consumer Protection, Food and Agriculture	Berlin, GERMANY
Mrs. Bongiwe Njobe	Director General	Department of Agriculture	Pretoria, SOUTH AFRICA
Mr. George Njoroge		Regional Land Management Unit (RELMA)	Nairobi, KENYA
Mr. Stephen Kiuri Njukia	Commodity Specialist	Common Market for Eastern and Southern Africa (COMESA), Regional Agricultural Trade Expansion Support (RATES) Program	Nairobi, KENYA
Mr. Theodore Nkodo	Vice President	African Development Bank	Tunis, TUNISIA
Dr. Ephraim Nkonya	Research Fellow	International Food Policy Research Institute (IFPRI)	Washington, DC, USA
Dr. Johnson Nkuuhe	Member of Parliament	Parliament of Uganda	Kampala, UGANDA
Mr. Remy Noe	First Counsellor, Head of Section	European Union	Kampala, UGANDA
Ms. Irene Novotny	Programme Officer	Austrian Embassy	Kampala, UGANDA
Mr. Eridadi Ntanda	Director	Uganda Commercial Farmers Association	Kampala, UGANDA
Ms. Prisna Nuengsigkapian	Writer/Editor-Sustainable Developments	International Institute for Sustainable Development (IISD)	New York, NY, USA
Dr. Kanayo Nwanze	Director General	WARDA-The Africa Rice Center	Abidjan, CÔTE D'IVOIRE

NAME	POSITION	ORGANIZATION	CITY/COUNTRY
Hon. Chidi Nwogo	Deputy Chairman	National Assembly–House of Representatives for Nigeria	Abuja, NIGERIA
Dr. Hezron Omare Nyangito	Principal Policy Analyst	Kenya Institute for Public Policy Research and Analysis (KIPPRA)	Nairobi, KENYA
Dr. Zerubabel Nyiira	Executive Secretary	Uganda National Council for Science and Technology	Kampala, UGANDA
Mr. Kenneth Nyombi	Research Assistant	International Food Policy Research Institute (IFPRI) - Kampala	Kampala, UGANDA
Mr. Timothy Nzioka	Chief Executive Officer	Kenya Gatsby Trust	Nairobi, KENYA
H.E. Olusegun Obasanjo	President	Federal Republic of Nigeria	Abuja, NIGERIA
Capt. Oyet Obiya		Agricultural Council of Uganda	Kampala, UGANDA
Mr. David Obong	Permanent Secretary	Ministry of Agriculture, Animal Industry, and Fisheries	Entebbe, UGANDA
Ms. Judy O'Connor	Country Director–Tanzania and Uganda Office	World Bank	Dar es Salaam, TANZANIA
Dr. Stella Odebode	Lecturer	University of Ibadan	Ibadan, NIGERIA
Mr. Edwyn Odhiambo Odeny	Team Leader	Kenya Youth Foundation	Nairobi, KENYA
Dr. Dick Odur	Chair	Uganda Local Government Finance Commission	Kampala, UGANDA
Dr. Willy Odwongo	Executive Director	Plan for Modernization of Agriculture (PMA)	Kampala, UGANDA
Chief Audu Ogbeh	Adviser to H.E. Obasanjo on Food and Agriculture	The Presidency	Abuja, NIGERIA
Hon. Prof. Morris Ogenga-Latigo	Member of Parliament	Parliament of Uganda	Kampala, UGANDA
Mr. Kenneth Ojoro	Chairman	Kibanda Farmers Forum	Masinoi, UGANDA
Mr. Basilio Okello	Senior Program Manager	World Vision International	Kampala, UGANDA
Ms. Josephine Okot	Chairperson	Uganda Seed Trade Association	Kampala, UGANDA
Dr. Justin Okullu-Mura		Department of Information	UGANDA
Dr. J.J. Oloya	Rural Development Specialist	World Bank	UGANDA
Dr. Willis Oluoch-Kosura	Professor	University of Nairobi/International Food Policy Research Institute (IFPRI)/International Development Research Centre (IDRC)	Nairobi, KENYA
Mr. John Olweny	Programme Officer	Royal Danish Embassy	Kampala, UGANDA
Dr. Steven Were Omamo	Research Fellow and 2020 Regional Network Coordinator	International Food Policy Research Institute (IFPRI)–Kampala	Kampala, UGANDA
Mr. Paul Osborn	CEO/Chair	Mediateurs/Agricultural Media Professionals	Uithoorn, NETHERLANDS
Dr. John Joseph Otim	Senior Presidential Advisor on Agriculture and Veterinary Services to H.E. President Museveni, and President, Uganda Agricultural Council	Office of the President of Uganda and Agricultural Council of Uganda	Kampala, UGANDA
Dr. Peter Otimodoch	Executive Director	Uganda Seed Producers and Producers Association	Kampala, UGANDA
Dr. Bakari Vasseri Ouayogode	Co-Manager	African AgriBusiness Inc. (AABI)	Abidjan, CÔTE D'IVOIRE
Ms. Norah Owaraga	Executive Secretary	Uganda Change Agent Association	Kampala, UGANDA
Mr. Ramsey Owot	President	Uganda Honey Beekeepers' Association	Kampala, UGANDA
Sr. Veronica Oyela	Chairperson	Forum for Kalongo Parish Women Association	Kampala, UGANDA
Dr. Luke Oyugi	Senior Lecturer	Jomo Kenyatta University of Agriculture and Technology	Nairobi, KENYA
Dr. Martine Padilla	Administrateur Scientifique	CIHEAM/IAMM	Montpellier, FRANCE
Dr. Cheryl Palm	Senior Research Scientist	The Earth Institute at Columbia University	Palisades, NY, USA
Ms. Rajul Pandya-Lorch	Head, 2020 Vision Initiative	International Food Policy Research Institute (IFPRI)	Washington, DC, USA
Dr. Louis Augusto Pelembe	Assistant Professor	Eduardo Mondlane University	Maputo, MOZAMBIQUE
Dr. John Pender	Research Fellow	International Food Policy Research Institute (IFPRI)	Washington, DC, USA
Ms. Michele Pietrowski	Communications Specialist	International Food Policy Research Institute (IFPRI)	Washington, DC, USA
Mr. Klaus Pilgram	RD Adviser	Deutsche Gesellschaft für Technische Zusammenarbeit (GTZ)–Sector Network Rural Development (SNRD)	Hatfield, SOUTH AFRICA
Dr. Per Pinstrup-Andersen	H.E. Babcock Professor of Food and Nutrition Policy	Cornell University	Ithaca, NY, USA
Dr. Hans-Joachim Preuss	Secretary General	Deutsche Welthungerhilfe	Bonn, GERMANY
Mr. Detlev Puetz		International Food Policy Research Institute (IFPRI)	Washington, DC, USA
Dr. Diana Putman	Director	U.S. Agency for International Development (USAID)-REDSO/ESA	Nairobi, KENYA
Hon. Maj. Courage Quashigah	Minister of Food and Agriculture	Ministry of Food and Agriculture	Accra, GHANA
Dr. Marco Quinones	Africa Director	Sasakawa Africa Association	Addis Ababa, ETHIOPIA
Mr. Ajmal Qureshi	Resident Representative	Food and Agriculture Organization of the United Nations (FAO)	Kampala, UGANDA
Ms. Maria-Waltraud Rabitsch	Consultant	Austrian Development Agency (ADA)	Vienna, AUSTRIA
Mr. Haja Rajaonarivo	Managing Director	Nestle Foods Kenya Ltd.	Nairobi, KENYA
Ms. Valerie Rhoe	Research Analyst	International Food Policy Research Institute (IFPRI)	Washington, DC, USA
Mr. Juergen Richter	Senior Project Manager	InWEnt Capacity Building International	Feldafing, GERMANY
Mr. Malcolm Ridout	Food Security and Livelihoods Advisor	Department for International Development (DFID)	London, UNITED KINGDOM
Ms. Gabriella Roesch	Student	Western Washington University	Bellingham, WA, USA
Dr. Mark Rosegrant	Division Director, Environment and Production Technology Division	International Food Policy Research Institute (IFPRI)	Washington, DC, USA
Mr. Michael Rubinstein	Head of Media Relations	International Food Policy Research Institute (IFPRI)	Washington, DC, USA
Dr. Lovemore Rugube		University of Zimbabwe	Harare, ZIMBABWE
H.M. Rukirabasaija Oyo Nyimba Kabambaiguru Rukidi IV	Omukama (King) of Tooro		UGANDA

NAME	POSITION	ORGANIZATION	CITY/COUNTRY
Dr. Mandivamba Rukuni	Program Director	W.K. Kellogg Foundation	Pretoria, SOUTH AFRICA
Mr. Sudhir Ruparelia	Chairman	Ruparelia Group of Companies	Kampala, UGANDA
Mr. Charles Rusoke		Regional Land Management Unit (RELMA)	Nairobi, KENYA
Ms. Cathy Rutivi	Program Coordinator	Food, Agriculture and Natural Resources Policy Analysis Network (FANRPAN)	Harare, ZIMBABWE
Dr. James (Jim) Garett Ryan	Study Director	Inter-Academy Panel	Aranda, AUSTRALIA
Mr. Jeff Sachs	Director	The Earth Institute at Columbia University	New York, NY, USA
Dr. Aristide Sagbohan	Regional Adviser for Nutrition (RA/NUT)	WHO Regional Office for Africa (AFRO)	Brazzaville, CONGO
Dr. Frederick Sai	Presidential Advisor-Reproductive Health and HIV/AIDS	Ghana Aids Commission	Accra, GHANA
Dr. Soumana Sako	Executive Secretary	African Capacity Building Foundation	Harare, ZIMBABWE
Dr. Ebrahim Samba	Regional Director	World Health Organization/Africa (WHO/AFRO)	Brazzaville, REPUBLIC OF CONGO
Dr. Pedro Sanchez	Director of Tropical Agriculture	The Earth Institute at Columbia University	Palisades, NY, USA
Ms. Hon. Nora Schimming-Chase	Vice President-African Group	National Assembly	Windhoek, NAMIBIA
Dr. Ebbe Schiøler	Consultant	International Food Policy Research Institute (IFPRI)	Roskilde, DENMARK
Ms. Lisa Schipper	Team Leader-Sustainable Developments	International Institute for Sustainable Development (IISD)	New York, NY, USA
Dr. Hans Schoeneberger	Senior Advisor	Deutsche Gesellschaft für Technische Zusammenarbeit (GTZ) (German Agency for Technical Cooperation)	Bonn, GERMANY
Hon. Ms. Victoria Sebagereka	Chairperson of the Women's Committee in Agriculture	Parliament of Uganda	Kampala, UGANDA
Hon. Richard Sebuliba-Mutumba	Legislator	Parliament of Uganda	Kampala, UGANDA
Mr. Sechele Teleka Sechele	Editor	Dikgang Publishing Co. Trading as Mmegi Newspaper	Gaborone, BOTSWANA
Mr. Omar Seck	Conseiller Technique en Agriculture Elévage et Pêche	Présidence de la République du Senegal	Dakar, SENEGAL
Prof. M'Hamed Sedrati	Member of Targa-aide/Consultant	TARGA-a.i.d.e-Association Interdisciplinaire pour le Développement et l'Environnement	Rabat, MOROCCO
Dr. Samuel Sefa-Dedeh	Program Director/Professor	Ghana Private-Public Partnership Food Industry Development Program	Accra, GHANA
Ms. Amanda Segovia	Administrative Coordinator	International Food Policy Research Institute (IFPRI)	Washington, DC, USA
Hon. Muhammed Seid	Chairperson	Parliament of Ethiopia	Addis Ababa, ETHIOPIA
Ms. Victoria Sekitoleko	Subregional Representative	Food and Agriculture Organization of the United Nations (FAO)-SAFR	Harare, ZIMBABWE
Mr. Inspector Seleke		Foundation for Community Development (FDC)	MOZAMBIQUE
Mr. Samuel Semanda	Assistant Commissioner/Head of Policy Analysis Unit	Ministry of Agriculture, Animal Industry and Fisheries	Kampala, UGANDA
Dr. Carlos Seré	Director General	International Livestock Research Institute (ILRI)	Nairobi, KENYA
Dr. Paco Sereme	Executive Secretary	CORAF/WECARD	Dakar, SENEGAL
Mr. Patrick Seruyange	Rural Development Officer	European Union	Kampala, UGANDA
Mr. Don Sexton	Desk Officer	Department Cooperation Ireland, Department of Foreign Affairs	Dublin, IRELAND
Ms. Flora Sibanda-Mulder	UNICEF-WFP Coordinator	WFP (World Food Programme)	Rome, ITALY
Mr. Muzwakhe Alfred Sigudhla	Executive President	Southern African Development Community (SADC) Youth Movement	Pretoria, SOUTH AFRICA
Dr. Said Nahdy Silim	Regional Representative	International Crops Research Institute for the Semi-Arid Tropics (ICRISAT)	Nairobi, KENYA
Dr. Emmy B. Simmons	Assistant Administrator	U.S. Agency for International Development (USAID)	Washington, DC, USA
Dr. Woldeyesus Sinebo	Postdoctorate Research Fellow	United Nations University/Institute of Advanced Studies	Tokyo, JAPAN
Dr. Rachel Slater	Research Fellow	Overseas Development Institute	London, UNITED KINGDOM
Hon. Ibrahim Sorie	Member of Parliament/Minority Whip of the House	Parliament of Sierra Leone	Freetown, SIERRA LEONE
Mr. George Soule	Associate Director of Communications	Rockefeller Foundation	New York, NY, USA
Prof. Wole Soyinka	Professor Emeritus	Obafemi Awolowo University	Ibadan, NIGERIA
Dr. Dunstan Spencer	Managing Director	Dunstan Spencer and Associates	Freetown, SIERRA LEONE
Dr. Pancras John Mukasa Ssebuwufu	Vice Chancellor and Professor	Makerere University	Kampala, UGANDA
Ms. Therese St. Peter	Head, Programme and Policy Development	Syngenta Foundation for Sustainable Agriculture	Basel, SWITZERLAND
H.E. Habib Sy	Minister of Agriculture	Ministry of Agriculture	Dakar, SENEGAL
Dr. Tobias Takavarasha	Chief Executive Officer	Food, Agriculture, and Natural Resource Policy Analysis Network (FANRPRAN)	Harare, ZIMBABWE
Dr. Thomas Fofung Tata	President	Forum of African Civil Society for Sustainable Development (FACS)	Geneva, CÔTE D'IVOIRE
Mr. Alex Tatwangire	Research Assistant	International Food Policy Research Institute (IFPRI)-Kampala	Kampala, UGANDA
Mr. Michael Taylor	Senior Fellow and Director	Resources for the Future	Washington, DC, USA
Dr. Bino Teme	Director General	Institute of Rural Economy (IER)	Bamako, MALI
Dr. Andrew Temu	Research Fellow	International Food Policy Research Institute (IFPRI)	Washington, DC, USA
Dr. Eugene Terry	Implementing Director	African Agricultural Technology Foundation (AATF)	Nairobi, KENYA
H.E. Jean Bernard Thiant	Ambassador	French Embassy	Kampala, UGANDA
Mr. Benjamin Thompson	Journalist/Chairman	Africa Science and Agriculture Journalists Network (ASAJ)	Dar es Salaam, TANZANIA

NAME	POSITION	ORGANIZATION	CITY/COUNTRY
Ms. Susanna Thorp	Director	WRENmedia	Suffolk, UNITED KINGDOM
Mrs. Ntatoleng Mampho Thulo	Managing Director	Rural Self-Help Development Association	Maseru, LESOTHO
Mr. Simon Thuo	Regional Coordinator	Global Water Partnership–Eastern Africa	Entebbe, UGANDA
Mr. Roger Thurow	Africa Correspondent	Wall Street Journal	Zurich, SWITZERLAND
Mr. Lucas Daniel Tivane	Research Officer	University of Reading	Reading, UNITED KINGDOM
Dr. Eric Tollens	Professor	Katholieke Universitet, Leuven	Leuven, BELGIUM
Mr. Muima Tonda			UGANDA
Mr. Maximo Torero	Research Fellow	International Food Policy Research Institute (IFPRI)	Washington, DC, USA
Minister Oumar Ibrahima Touré	Delegate Minister for Food Security	Ministry of Agriculture, Livestock and Fisheries	Bamako, MALI
Mr. Bamanga Mohammed Tukur	Executive President, ABR, and Chairperson of the New Partnership for Africa's Development (NEPAD) Business Group	African Business Round Table (ABR)	Abuja, NIGERIA
Mr. Godber Tumushabe		Advocates Coalition for Development and Environment	Kampala, UGANDA
Ms. Rhoda Tumusiime		Ministry of Agriculture, Animal Industry and Fisheries	UGANDA
Mr. Nathan Twinamasiko	Executive Director	Dairy Development Authority	Kampala, UGANDA
Dr. Jose Antonio Valencia Villarreal	Malawi County Director	Sasakawa Africa Association	Lilongwe, MALAWI
Mr. Ajay Vashee	President	Southern African Confederation of Agricultural Unions (SACAU)	Ndola, ZAMBIA
Mr. Thomas Rolf Veser	Journalist	Press Agency Seegrund	Kreuzlingen, SWITZERLAND
Prof. Nicholas Vink	Professor of Agricultural Economics	University of Stellenbosch	Stellenbosch, SOUTH AFRICA
Mrs. Barbara von Braun		International Food Policy Research Institute (IFPRI)	Washington, DC, USA
Dr. Joachim von Braun	Director General	International Food Policy Research Institute (IFPRI)	Washington, DC, USA
Dr. Klaus von Grebmer	Division Director, Communications Division	International Food Policy Research Institute (IFPRI)	Washington, DC, USA
H.E. Maître Abdoulaye Wade	Président	Présidence de la République du Senegal	Dakar, SENEGAL
Prof. Judith Wangalwa Wakhungu	Executive Director	African Centre for Technology Studies	Nairobi, KENYA
Mr. Michael Wales	Principal Adviser to the Director	Food and Agriculture Organization of the United Nations (FAO)	Rome, ITALY
Ms. Rhona Walusimbi	Senior Research Assistant	International Food Policy Research Institute (IFPRI)	Kampala, UGANDA
Dr. Florence Wambugu	Chief Executive Officer	A Harvest Biotech Foundation International	Nairobi, KENYA
Ms. Mamadou Abdoul Aziz Wane	Journaliste/Redacteur en Chef	Le Messager (journal quotidien)	Dakar, SENEGAL
Ms. Ursula Wangwe	Principal Nutritionist	Ministry of Health	Kampala, UGANDA
Dr. Joseph Wanjama	Director of Agriculture and Livestock Production	Ministry of Agriculture and Rural Development	Nairobi, KENYA
Mr. Ongeri John Wanyancha		Twiga Bulletin	Dar es Salaam, TANZANIA
Mr. Henry Wasswa		German Press Agency (DPA)	Kampala, UGANDA
Dr. Patrick Webb	Chief, Nutrition Service	U.N. World Food Programme	Rome, ITALY
Dr. Alan Whiteside	Professor and Director, Health Economics and HIV/AIDS Research Division	University of KwaZulu-Natal	Durban, SOUTH AFRICA
Mr. Lars Wiersholm	Consultant	UN Millennium Task Force on Hunger	Dilling, NORWAY
Mr. Christopher Williams	Director	The Rural Action Committee of Mpumalanga Province (TRAC-MP)	Nelspruit, SOUTH AFRICA
Mr. David Kirkham Wilson	Interactive Products Manager	Conference Communications	Johannesburg, SOUTH AFRICA
Mr. Klaus Winkel	Senior Advisor	Danish International Development Agency (DANIDA), Ministry of Foreign Affairs	Copenhagen, DENMARK
Hon. Oliver Wonekha	Member of Parliament	Parliament of Uganda	Kampala, UGANDA
Mr. Stanley Wood	Senior Scientist	International Food Policy Research Institute (IFPRI)	Washington, DC, USA
Mr. Tadesse Kuma Worako	Associate Research Fellow and Member of Parliament	Ethiopian Development Research Institute	Addis Ababa, ETHIOPIA
Mr. Tim Wright	Senior Specialist	World Vision Canada	Mississauga, CANADA
Dr. Yonas Yemshaw	Scientific Program Officer	African Academy of Sciences (AAS)	Nairobi, KENYA
Dr. El Sayed Zaki	Former Minister of Finance and Economic Planning	Global Investment Services	Khartoum, SUDAN
Mr. Carlos Zandamela	Technical Adviser/SG2000 Project Coordinator	Ministry of Agriculture and Rural Development	Maputo, MOZAMBIQUE

Appendix 3 Conference Materials

The following materials were prepared in conjunction with the 2020 Africa Conference.

DISCUSSION PAPERS

- **Africa's Food and Nutrition Security Situation: Where Are We and How Did We Get Here?** by Todd Benson, 2020 Discussion Paper 37.
- **Development Strategies and Food and Nutrition Security in Africa: An Assessment**, by Franz Heidhues, Achi Atsain, Hezron Nyangito, Martine Padilla, Gérard Ghersi, and Jean-Charles LeVallée, 2020 Discussion Paper 38.
- **Looking Ahead: Long-Term Prospects for Africa's Food and Nutrition Security**, by Mark W. Rosegrant, Sarah A. Cline, Weibo Li, Timothy Sulser, and Rowena A. Valmonte-Santos, forthcoming 2020 Discussion Paper.
- **Government Spending and the Poor in Africa**, by Shenggen Fan and Connie Chan-Kang, draft discussion paper prepared for the conference.

CONFERENCE BRIEFS

- **Assessing Africa's Food and Nutrition Security Situation**, by Todd Benson, 2020 Africa Conference Brief 1.
- **Improving Child Nutrition for Sustainable Poverty Reduction in Africa**, by Harold Alderman, Jere Behrman, and John Hoddinott, 2020 Africa Conference Brief 2.
- **Assuring Food and Nutrition Security in the Time of AIDS**, by Stuart Gillespie, Wilberforce Kisamba-Mugerwa, and Michael Loevinsohn, 2020 Africa Conference Brief 3.
- **Increasing the Effective Participation of Women in Food and Nutrition Security in Africa**, by Agnes R. Quisumbing, Ruth S. Meinzen Dick, and Lisa C. Smith, 2020 Africa Conference Brief 4.
- **Trading Up: How International Trade and Efficient Domestic Markets Can Contribute to African Development**, by David Orden, Hans Löfgren, and Eleni Gabre-Madhin, 2020 Africa Conference Brief 5.
- **Exploring Market Opportunities for African Smallholders**, by Xinshen Diao and Peter Hazell, 2020 Africa Conference Brief 6.
- **Strengthening Africa's Capacity to Design and Implement Strategies for Food and Nutrition Security**, by Suresh Babu, Valerie Rhoe, Andrew Temu, and Sheryl Hendriks, 2020 Africa Conference Brief 7.
- **Investing in Sub-Saharan African Agricultural Research: Recent Trends**, by Nienke Beintema and Gert-Jan Stads, 2020 Africa Conference Brief 8.
- **Strengthening Agricultural Research in Africa**, by Monty Jones, 2020 Africa Conference Brief 9.
- **Breaking the Links between Conflict and Hunger in Africa**, by Ellen Messer and Marc Cohen, 2020 Africa Conference Brief 10.
- **Making Information and Communication Technologies Work for Food Security in Africa**, by Romeo Bertolini, 2020 Africa Conference Brief 11.

- **Linking Safety Nets, Social Protection, and Poverty Reduction: Directions for Africa**, by Michelle Adato, Akhter Ahmed, and Francie Lund, 2020 Africa Conference Brief 12.
- **Implementing a Human Rights Approach to Food Security**, by Charlotte McClain-Nhlapo, 2020 Africa Conference Brief 13.
- **Assessing Development Strategies and Africa's Food and Nutrition Security**, by Franz Heidhues, Achi Atsain, Hezron Nyangito, Martine Padilla, Gérard Ghersi, and Jean-Charles LeVallée, forthcoming 2020 Africa Conference Brief 14.
- **Reforming Land Rights in Africa**, by Tidiane Ngaido, forthcoming 2020 Africa Conference Brief 15.
- **Increasing Access to Infrastructure for Africa's Rural Poor**, by Maximo Torero and Shyamal Chowdhury, forthcoming 2020 Africa Conference Brief 16.

OTHER MATERIALS

- **A Way Forward from the 2020 Africa Conference**, 2020 Africa Conference Advisory Committee (available in English, French, and Portuguese).
- **Building on Successes in African Agriculture**, edited by Steven Haggblade, 2020 Focus 12 (set of 10 briefs).
- **A Full Food Basket for Africa by 2020/Un Plein Panier d'Aliments pour l'Afrique d'ici 2020**, compilation of selected entries from the 2020 Africa Conference youth writing contest (in English and French).
- **BibliogrAfrica: An Experts' Selection of Readings on African Food Security**, a CD-ROM selection by invited experts of the most important literature on African food and nutrition security of the last five decades.
- **Recent Country Briefs and Datasets on Sub-Saharan Africa**, a CD-ROM of recent material from the Agricultural Science and Technology Indicators (ASTI).
- **Key Areas for Actions in Africa Now**, a collection of maps, by Jordan Chamberlin and Stanley Wood, draft prepared for conference.
- **Ready for Action in Africa?** Special Issue of IFPRI's newsletter, *IFPRI Forum*, May 2004.

Appendix 4 Conference Advisory Committee

Chair: **Dr. John Joseph Otim**, Senior Presidential Advisor to H. E. President Museveni of the Republic of Uganda, and President, Uganda Agricultural Council

Dr. Ayo Abifarin, Director, Food Security Program, World Vision International (Ghana)

Dr. Akin Adesina, Associate Director, Food Security, Rockefeller Foundation (Kenya)

Dr. Mohamed Ait-Kadi, President of the General Council of Agricultural Development, Ministry of Agriculture, Rural Development, and Forestry (Morocco)

Hon. Grace Akello, Parliamentarian and Minister of State for Entandikwa (Uganda)

Prof. Achi Atsain, Professor of Economics and Econometrics at the University of Abidjan, Côte d'Ivoire and Senior Research Fellow, Ivorian Center for Economic and Social Research (CIRES) (Ivory Coast)

Dr. Åke Barklund, Former Director, Regional Land Management Unit (RELMA) (Kenya)

Dr. Glyvyns Chinkhuntha, Executive Director, Freedom Gardens (Malawi)

Dr. Josué Dioné, Director, Sustainable Development Division, UN Economic Commission for Africa (UNECA) (Ethiopia)

Dr. Baba Dioum, Coordinator General, Conference of West & Central African Ministers of Agriculture (Senegal)

Ato Newai Gebre-ab, Chief Economic Advisor to the Prime Minister and Director, Ethiopian Development Research Institute (Ethiopia)

Dr. Jochen de Haas, Head, Rural Development & Global Food Security Division, Federal Ministry of Economic Co-operation and Development (BMZ) (Germany)

Ambassador Sigurd Illing, Head of Delegation of the European Union (Uganda)

Ms. Isatou Jallow, Executive Director, National Nutrition Agency (NaNA) (The Gambia)

Dr. Monty Jones, Executive Secretary, Forum for Agricultural Research in Africa (FARA) (Ghana)

Dr. Seyfu Ketema, Executive Secretary, Association for Strengthening Agricultural Research in Eastern and Central Africa (ASARECA) (Uganda)

Hon. Wilberforce Kisamba-Mugerwa, Minister of Agriculture, Animal Industry, and Fisheries (Uganda)

Dr. Stephan Krall, Senior Advisor/Coordinator, Advisory Service for Development-Oriented Agricultural Research (BEAF), Deutsche Gesellschaft für Technische Zusammenarbeit (GTZ) (Germany)

Ms. Charlotte V. McClain, Commissioner of Economic and Social Rights, South African Human Rights Commission (South Africa)

Dr. Isaac Minde, Coordinator, Eastern and Central Africa Programme for Agricultural Policy Analysis (ECAPAPA) (Uganda)

Dr. Uzo Mokwunye, Director, Institute for Natural Resources in Africa, The United Nations University (Ghana)

Dr. John Mugabe, Executive Director, Commission for Science and Technology, New Partnership for Africa's Development (NEPAD) (South Africa)

Mr. Harris Mule, Executive Director, Top Investment & Management Services, Limited (TIMS) (Kenya)

Mr. James Mulwana, Managing Director, Nice House of Plastics; Chairman of the Board, Standard Chartered Bank, Uganda; and Chairman, Advisory Committee, Uganda Manufacturers Association (Uganda)

Dr. Claude Nankam, Agriculture Program Manager, World Vision International (USA)

Mrs. Bongiwe Njobe, Director General, Department of Agriculture (South Africa)

Dr. Kanayo F. Nwanze, Director General, The Africa Rice Center (WARDA) (based in Ivory Coast)

Prof. Ruth Oniang'o, Member of Parliament and Professor of Food Science and Nutrition, Jomo Kenyatta University of Agriculture and Technology (Kenya)

Dr. Hans-Joachim Preuss, Secretary General, Deutsche Welthungerhilfe (Germany)

Dr. Diana Putman, Director, Food Security Office, United States Agency for International Development (Kenya)

Dr. Marco Quinones, Regional Director for Africa, Sasakawa Africa Association (Ethiopia)

Mr. Jürgen Richter, Senior Project Manager, Rural Policy and Strategy, International Agricultural Research, InWEnt (Germany)

Dr. Mandivamba Rukuni, Director, Africa Program Office, W.K. Kellogg Foundation (South Africa)

Mr. Omar Seck, Technical Counselor in Agriculture, Livestock, and Fisheries, Presidency of the Republic (Senegal)

Mrs. Victoria Sekitoleko, Representative, Subregional Office for Southern and East Africa, the Food and Agriculture Organization of the United Nations (FAO), (based in Zimbabwe)

Dr. Mohamed F. Sessay, Programme Officer, United Nations Environmental Programme (UNEP) (Kenya)

Dr. Tobias Takavarasha, Agriculture Advisor, New Partnership for Africa's Development (NEPAD) (based in South Africa)

Dr. Joachim von Braun (ex-officio), Director General, International Food Policy Research Institute (IFPRI) (based in USA)

Ms. Rajul Pandya-Lorch (secretary), Head, 2020 Vision Initiative, IFPRI (based in USA)

Appendix 5 2020 Advisory Council

H.E.Yoweri K. Museveni (Chairman)
President, Republic of Uganda

H.E. Olusegun Obasanjo
President, Federal Republic of Nigeria

H.E. Abdoulaye Wade
President, Republic of Senegal

Mr. Sartaj Aziz
Former Finance Minister and Foreign Minister, Government of Pakistan

Mr. Lennart Båge
President, International Fund for Agricultural Development (IFAD), Italy

Rev. David Beckmann
President, Bread for the World, USA

Ms. Catherine Bertini
Chair, United Nations Standing Committee on Nutrition, USA

Dr. Keith A. Bezanson
Former Director, Institute of Development Studies, University of Sussex, UK

Dr. Norman E. Borlaug
Nobel Laureate and Distinguished Professor of International Agriculture, Texas A&M University, USA

Mr. Lester Brown
President, Earth Policy Institute, USA

Dr. Margaret Catley-Carlson
Chairperson, Global Water Partnership

Prof. Chen Chunming
Senior Advisor and President, Chinese Academy of Preventive Medicine, China

Dr. Gordon R. Conway
President, The Rockefeller Foundation, USA

Dr. Bernd Eisenblätter
Managing Director, Deutsche Gesellschaft für Technische Zusammenarbeit (GTZ), Germany

Dr. Leonard Good
CEO & Chairman, Global Environment Facility, USA

Dr. Michel Griffon
Scientific Director, Centre de Coopération Internationale en Recherche Agronomique pour le Développement (CIRAD), France

Mr. Robert D. Havener
President Emeritus, Winrock International, USA

Dr. Dean R. Hirsch
President and CEO, World Vision International, USA

Mr. Johan Holmberg
Former Ambassador to Mozambique, Sweden

Mr. Ian Johnson
Chairman, CGIAR, and Vice President, Environmentally and Socially Sustainable Development, The World Bank, USA

H.E. Speciosa Wandira Kazibwe
Former Vice President, Republic of Uganda

Dr. Mark Malloch Brown
Administrator, UNDP, USA

Sra. Margarita Marino de Botero
Corporacion El Colegio Verde, Colombia

Dr. Alexander F. McCalla
Professor Emeritus, University of California-Davis, USA

Mr. Robert S. McNamara
Former President, The World Bank, USA

Mr. Peter McPherson
President, Michigan State University, USA

Dr. Moïse Mensah
Former Minister of Finance, Government of Benin

Hon. Dame Billie A. Miller
Minister of Foreign Affairs and Foreign Trade, Barbados

Mr. James Morris
Executive Director, World Food Programme, Italy

Mr. Harris Mutio Mule
Executive Director, Top Investment and Management Services (TIMS), Limited, Kenya

Dr. Maureen O'Neil
President, International Development Research Centre (IDRC), Canada

Dr. Per Pinstrup-Andersen
H.E. Babcock Professor of Food and Nutrition Policy, Cornell University, USA

Mrs. Mary Robinson
Director, Ethical Globalization Initiative, USA

Dr. Jeffrey Sachs
Director, The Earth Institute at Columbia University, USA

Dr. Pedro Sanchez
Director of Tropical Agriculture, The Earth Institute at Columbia University, USA

Mrs.Victoria Sekitoleko
Subregional Representative, Food and Agriculture Organization of the United Nations (FAO), Zimbabwe

Prof. Amartya Sen
Nobel Laureate and Master of Trinity College, United Kingdom

Dr. Ismail Serageldin
Director, Library of Alexandria, Egypt

Dr. Ammar Siamwalla
Former President, Thailand Development Research Institute Foundation, Thailand

Dr. M. S. Swaminathan
Chairman, M. S. Swaminathan Research Foundation, India

Mr. M. Syeduzzaman
Former Minister of Finance, Bangladesh

Mr. Paul Thibault
President, Canadian International Development Agency (CIDA), Canada

Dr. Bamanga Mohammed Tukur
Executive President, African Business Roundtable and Chairperson of the NEPAD Business Group, Nigeria

Prof. Joachim von Braun (Ex-Officio)
Director General, IFPRI, USA

T.H. Youssef Wally
Deputy Prime Minister and Minister of Agriculture and Land Reclamation, Egypt

Mr. Jack Wilkinson
President, International Federation of Agricultural Producers (IFAP), France

Dr. Vo-Tong Xuan
Rector, Angiang University, Vietnam

Dr. Muhammad Yunus
Founder, Grameen Bank, Bangladesh